CHINA'S RISE IN THE GLOBAL SOUTH

CHINA'S RISE IN THE GLOBAL SOUTH

THE MIDDLE EAST, AFRICA, AND BEIJING'S ALTERNATIVE WORLD ORDER

DAWN C. MURPHY

STANFORD UNIVERSITY PRESS
STANFORD, CALIFORNIA

Stanford University Press
Stanford, California

The views expressed in this book are those of the author and do not necessarily reflect the official policy or position of the Air Force, the Department of Defense, or the U.S. Government.

Printed in the United States of America on acid-free, archival-quality paper

ISBN 9781503368150
First paperback printing 2024

The Library of Congress has cataloged the hardcover edition as follows:

Names: Murphy, Dawn C., author.
Title: China's rise in the Global South : the Middle East, Africa, and Beijing's alternative world order / Dawn C. Murphy.
Description: Stanford, California : Stanford University Press, 2022. | Includes bibliographical references and index.
Identifiers: LCCN 2021020156 (print) | LCCN 2021020157 (ebook) | ISBN 9781503630093 (cloth) | ISBN 9781503630604 (ebook)
Subjects: LCSH: Middle East—Foreign relations—China. | China—Foreign relations—Middle East. | Africa—Foreign relations—China. | China—Foreign relations—Africa. | China—Foreign relations—21st century.
Classification: LCC DS63.2.C5 M865 2022 (print) | LCC DS63.2.C5 (ebook) | DDC 327.51056—dc23
LC record available at https://lccn.loc.gov/2021020156
LC ebook record available at https://lccn.loc.gov/2021020157

Cover design: Kevin Barrett Kane

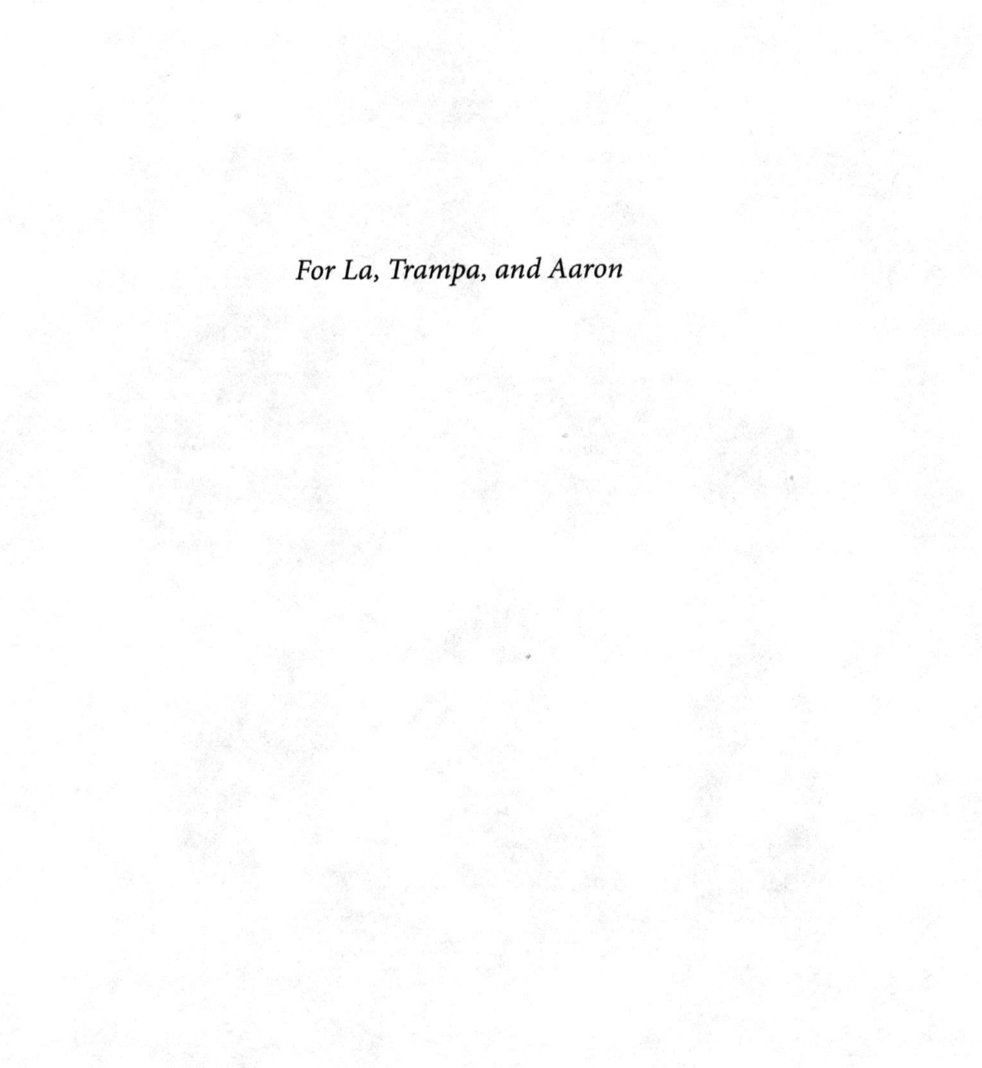

For La, Trampa, and Aaron

CONTENTS

FIGURES AND TABLES

Figures

Tables

ACKNOWLEDGMENTS

I thank the George Washington University Sigur Center for Asian Studies, Princeton University, and the US Department of Defense Minerva program for their generous support of field research for this project. Also, sincere thanks to all of the many individuals I interviewed for this book. I appreciate your time and insights.

Over the years, many scholars have provided valuable feedback for this book. Thank you to David Shambaugh, David Shinn, Bob Sutter, Susan Sell, and Jim Lebovic for your patience in providing feedback on this work in its earliest stages. Xiaoyu Pu, Sun Yun, Jon Alterman, Andrew Scobell, David Sorenson, and Stephen Burgess were all incredibly generous with their time in helping me to shape this work as it evolved. Although they may not know it, fellow alumni of the Princeton (Columbia)-Harvard China and the World postdoctoral fellowship program and the National Committee on United States–China Relations Public Intellectuals Program have inspired much of my work and served as an incredible professional network for improving my scholarship and public outreach. There are too many of you to name, but I have cherished all the time we have spent together. Finally, a special thank you to Tom Christensen for constructive feedback over the years about this project and literally helping me survive the process of pursuing a career in academia. Words are not enough to express how thankful I am to have worked with all of you over the years.

CHINA'S RISE IN THE GLOBAL SOUTH

CHAPTER 1

INTRODUCTION

The world today is in the midst of a potential great power transition between the United States and the People's Republic of China (PRC).[1] That trend makes China's rise one of the most critical economic, political, and military phenomena of the twenty-first century. Over the past several years, the United States started to prioritize great power competition with China as the top threat to US national security.[2] Increasingly, the United States characterizes China as a revisionist and rival across all functional domains. China also recognizes that strategic competition with the United States is rising.[3] In a time of escalating tensions between the United States and China over issues such as economic policies, the East and South China Seas, cyber-espionage, the Belt and Road Initiative, the origins of and response to COVID-19, and China's influence outside its borders, it is essential to better understand China's global rise.

In an era of great power competition, how do we understand China's behavior? Due to insights from international relations theory regarding the potential for war resulting from great power transitions and the increasingly adversarial relationship between the United States and China, an understanding of China's rise is urgently required. Since China launched economic reform and opening in 1978, its overall power has dramatically increased. As its capabilities grow, what type of rising power is it becoming: a rising competitive power or a cooperative member of international society? Is its behavior converging with international norms or diverging? Is China building an alternative world order? If yes, what are the characteristics of that new order?

How does China portray and differentiate itself as a great power? How is it building spheres of influence? This book answers these questions through an in-depth analysis of the understudied topic of China's relations with the Middle East and sub-Saharan Africa in the post–Cold War era.

This book argues that although China does not seek to change the international distribution of territory in the Middle East and sub-Saharan Africa, as its power grows, it increasingly builds spheres of influence in these regions and challenges the rules of the international system by constructing an alternative international order to facilitate interactions.[4] Although China does not yet seek to replace the existing international order, if the current liberal order unravels or excludes China, this alternative order could serve as the foundation of China's economic, political, and military relations with the Middle East and sub-Saharan Africa as well as much of the developing world.[5]

Why Study China's Rise in the Middle East and Sub-Saharan Africa?

For this study, the region of the Middle East includes the following twenty countries (in alphabetical order): Algeria, Bahrain, Egypt, Iran, Iraq, Israel, Jordan, Kuwait, Lebanon, Libya, Morocco, Oman, Palestine, Qatar, Saudi Arabia, Syria, Tunisia, Turkey, the United Arab Emirates, and Yemen.[6] Similar to the definition that many governments around the world use, this book includes Egypt and the African Maghreb countries of Algeria, Libya, Morocco, and Tunisia in the Middle East region and categorizes all other African countries as part of sub-Saharan Africa.[7]

There are many reasons to examine China's rise in these regions. This book strives to fill gaps in both the theoretical and empirical literature regarding China's global rise to enrich understanding of its behavior to date and provide insights into possible future behavior and the type of alternative international order it is building.

From a theoretical standpoint, scholars of international relations and Chinese foreign policy produce diverse and contradictory insights into the degree to which a rising China will cooperate or compete with the United States in the international system. They also disagree about how much China's behavior converges with or diverges from international norms. Chapter 2 explores those concepts and debates.

Also, much of the literature analyzing China as a rising power tends to examine its behavior toward the United States or in the Asia Pacific region. Understanding China's rise in this limited way is no longer adequate because its rise is now global, not regional. Since 2000, China has emerged as a great power and a global actor with interests and ability to exert influence around the world.[8] As a result, the need to examine China's behavior outside Asia is increasingly urgent. This book strives to contribute to the existing theoretical literature by tying an understanding of China's relations with the Middle East and sub-Saharan Africa into the broader scholarly debate about China's global rise in this century.

This book also contributes to the empirical literature on China's rise. Despite striking developments in China's relations with the Middle East and sub-Saharan Africa over the past twenty-five years and the importance of understanding the meaning of these interactions as part of China's overall rise, analysis of China's post–Cold War relations with these regions is limited.

China–Middle East relations scholarship is still relatively sparse, although it has been growing.[9] Work by Burton, Bianchi, Ehteshami, Horesh, Fulton, Dorsey, Alterman, Scobell, Nader, and Olimat provides significant empirical insights into the current characteristics of China's relations with specific countries in the Middle East, but they do not tend to speak to broader regional themes or theoretical questions about China's role or rise in the region. They also do not compare China's behavior in the Middle East to other regions.

China-Africa relations are also an expanding area of scholarly inquiry.[10] Although more is written on China's relations with sub-Saharan Africa in the post–Cold War era than on its relations with the Middle East, especially during the mid-2000s, the China–sub-Saharan Africa literature is still limited. Many authors such as Alden and colleagues, Lahtinen, Dollar, Hanuaer, Morris, Xing, Farah, Shinn, and Eisenman examine China in Africa as a region across functional areas. That said, they do not tend to address explicitly theoretical questions from broader international relations literature about China's rise and do not compare sub-Saharan Africa to other regions.

Comprehensive, theory-driven comparison of China's rising behavior in the Middle East versus sub-Saharan Africa in the post–Cold War era is virtually nonexistent. A few recent books do include analysis of China's behavior across regions, including the Middle East and sub-Saharan Africa.[11] That said, those books analyze China's behavior globally, but do not spend extensive time considering China's role in the Middle East and sub-Saharan Africa specifically. This book provides a much more detailed comparison of China's behavior in these two regions. It strives to close these empirical gaps in existing scholarship and tie an understanding of China's relations with the Middle East and sub-Saharan Africa into the broader scholarly debate about China's rise in the twenty-first century.

Another reason for analyzing China's relations with the Middle East and sub-Saharan Africa is that it provides an opportunity to compare and contrast China's behavior toward two regions. Comparing these two regions teases out similarities and differences in China's behavior. The Middle East and sub-Saharan Africa are both resource-rich regions that have been arenas of past great power competition, specifically between the PRC and the United States, as well as the PRC and the Soviet Union. In light of China's growing resource needs, especially for oil, natural gas, and industrial minerals, its interactions with both of these regions will likely increase over time. Due to their resource endowments, both regions are potential future areas of conflict between China and the United States, as well as other great powers in an era of global resource scarcity.

This approach also provides an opportunity to examine China's behavior toward a region where the United States has vital national interests, the Middle East, and a region where the United States does not, sub-Saharan Africa. US vital national interests in the Middle East include the continued flow of energy resources;[12] fighting global terrorism, including the Islamic State of Iraq and Syria (ISIS);[13] preventing Iran from acquiring nuclear weapons; and supporting Israel. In sub-Saharan Africa, US interests are more limited. They include energy security, preventing the spread of terrorism (due to failed states and the rise of groups such as ISIS, al-Qaeda, Al-Shabab, and Boko Haram), and public health concerns such as the spread of Ebola and COVID-19.[14] Increasingly, US government policy documents also emphasize emerging great power competition between the United States and China in Africa as a policy priority.[15]

Understanding China's behavior in the Middle East and sub-Saharan Africa is also essential because it may further irritate United States–China relations and sour US public opinion of China. For example, US media harshly criticize China's engagement in both regions. The media, the US government, and nongovernmental organizations often accuse China of neocolonial behavior, supporting states of concern (e.g., Iran, Sudan, Syria, or Zimbabwe), standing in the way of peace in Syria through United Nations

Security Council vetoes, and human rights violations in these regions. Especially in an era of increasing tensions between the United States and China, a comprehensive examination of China's behavior toward these regions is needed to ensure that alarmist media reports or scholarly analysis do not dominate the US domestic political discourse about China's relations with these regions.

This book also contributes to an understanding of China's relations with the developing world more broadly. The Middle East and sub-Saharan Africa contain many of the world's developing countries. Academic analysis of China's contemporary relations with the developing world is limited.[16] Examining China's relations with the Middle East and sub-Saharan Africa provides broad insights into China's behavior as a rising power toward the developing world as a whole.

Finally, examining China's relations with the Middle East and sub-Saharan Africa serves as an illuminating case study for understanding its Belt and Road Initiative, a strategic initiative building on decades of its interactions with these regions that aims to facilitate its growth as a Eurasian power across all domains: economic, political, military, and foreign aid.

China's Role in the Middle East and Africa

China is not a newcomer to the Middle East and sub-Saharan Africa. Although its contact with these regions spans hundreds of years, including the ancient Silk Road routes that began over two thousand years ago, the vast majority of interactions have occurred over the past seventy. This book's emphasis is China's post-Cold War relations with these regions (1991 to the present), but the very long history of China's interactions with these regions in many ways shapes today's relations. China's Silk Road overland trade routes with the Middle East date back to the Han dynasty in the second century BC. There are also Chinese claims that China's interactions with Africa date back to that time. During the early Ming dynasty (AD thirteenth to fourteen century), Chinese Admiral Zheng He led many expeditions to both Africa and the Middle East. As a Muslim, he reportedly performed the hajj on one trip. China's current BRI is an explicit attempt to leverage those historical connections with these regions as well as Central Asia, South Asia, and Europe.

In the Mao era, China supported anticolonial movements and national liberation groups in these regions, provided foreign aid, and sought recognition of the PRC in the United Nations. During the 1980s and 1990s, China's attention focused inward on economic development and outward to seek sources of foreign direct investment and aid from the developed world for its domestic economy. As a result, China's interactions with the Middle East and sub-Saharan Africa became more circumscribed.

After 2000, China reengaged the Middle East and sub-Saharan Africa, and its relations with these regions expanded to include a vast array of political, economic, foreign aid, and military interactions. Some of the most prominent developments include China's:

- Rapidly growing trade with, investment in, and overseas development assistance (ODA) to many countries in these regions
- Proactive establishment of two regional organizations outside its territorial perimeter: the Forum on China-Africa Cooperation (FOCAC) in 2000 and the China-Arab States Cooperation Forum (CASCF) in 2004
- Appointment of three special envoys: the China-Middle East issues special envoy (2002), the China Africa issues special envoy (2007), and the China Syria issues envoy (2016)
- Announcement of China's Silk Road Economic Belt and Twenty-First Century Maritime Silk Road (2013) later consolidated into the Belt and Road Initiative (BRI) (2015)
- Contributions of peacekeeping forces to United Nations peacekeeping operations (UNPKO) missions in the Middle East and sub-Saharan Africa
- Deployment of Chinese navy ships to the waters off Somalia to participate in antipiracy operations (2008)
- Building a Chinese naval base in Djibouti (2017)

In light of these increased contemporary interactions, how should one interpret China's rise in the Middle East and sub-Saharan Africa? What do China's relations with these regions illuminate about its global foreign policy behavior, ambitions, and approach to the international order?

The Approach

To understand China as a rising power, the main questions driving this book are: What are China's interests in the Middle East and sub-Saharan Africa? Is China cooperating or competing with the United States in these regions? Is China's behavior converging with or diverging from liberal international norms? Is China building an alternative international order in these regions? If yes, what are the characteristics of that order? How does China portray and differentiate itself as a great power in these regions? How is it building spheres of influence? Ultimately, what does China's behavior in the Middle East and sub-Saharan Africa indicate about its rise globally? Based on extensive fieldwork in China, Washington, DC, the Middle East (Egypt, Kuwait, Oman, Qatar, Saudi Arabia, and the United Arab Emirates), sub-Saharan Africa (South Africa) and Europe (Belgium, France, the Netherlands, and the United Kingdom) and over two hundred interviews, in this book, I analyze China's interests in and foreign policy approach toward the Middle East and sub-Saharan Africa over time to answer those questions.

Empirically, this book is distinctive because it methodically evaluates a wide range of foreign policy tools over time and across functional areas. As opposed to solely examining China's bilateral relations with countries in the region, I analyze China's approach toward these regions as a whole. This book is purposely broader in scope than previous studies to provide a deeper understanding of China's rise. It covers over thirty years of China's interactions with these regions in a comparative perspective across a range of functional areas—political, economic, foreign aid, and military relations—and is up-to-date with critical developments after the Arab awakening, the rebalance to Asia, increasing tensions between the United States and China, and the COVID-19 pandemic. This book is also unique because it analyzes understudied foreign policy tools in the region (e.g., China's cooperation forums, special envoys, free trade agreements) and uses China's behavior in these regions to understand BRI.

The book evaluates China's post–Cold War (1991–2019) interests and behavior in the Middle East and sub-Saharan Africa. Over the past thirty years, China established similar bilateral and multilateral foreign policy mechanisms for interacting with these two regions that allow for a detailed comparison of similarities and differences in China's approach to the regions. This analysis selected post–Cold War foreign policy tools based on the availability of data that allow a side-by-side comparison of China's approach toward the regions and specific countries within the regions. They include cooperation forums, special envoys, state support for Chinese companies, foreign aid, free trade agreements, special economic zones, agricultural technology demonstration centers, UN Security Council voting, strategic partnerships, UN peacekeeping operations, conventional arms sales, antipiracy activities, the base in Djibouti, and BRI.[17] Many of these foreign policy tools have never been examined in a comparative perspective across these regions. This analytical approach across foreign policy tools over time facilitates understanding when, why, and how China competes or cooperates with the United States and other Western countries and when, why, and how China's behavior converges with or diverges from international norms.

Of course, there are drawbacks to this macrolevel approach. It glosses over many nuanced aspects of China's interactions with specific countries. China's behavior in global organizations in these regions, such as the World Bank, the International Monetary Fund, and the World Trade Organization, is underanalyzed. Also, since this study primarily examines state-to-state interactions, it neglects often problematic substate relations and concerns of nonstate actors such as nongovernmental organizations (NGOs). That said, there are also immense benefits to a broad macrolevel study. Examining a wide range of foreign policy behaviors over time and across countries and regions helps to avoid the analytical trap of selecting on the dependent variable (e.g., only examining China's competitive foreign policy behavior and excluding cooperative behavior from the analysis). This analysis provides the opportunity to identify significant changes and consistencies in China's behavior over time.[18] At its core, it seeks to identify long-term patterns in China's activities to better comprehend its behavior in these regions and globally. Ideally, it will provide insights into possible future trajectories of China's approach to these regions and China's overall relation to the international order.

The Argument

So what are China's interests in these regions? Is China cooperating or competing with the United States in the Middle East and sub-Saharan Africa? Is its behavior converging with or diverging from liberal international norms? Why does China's level of cooperation with the United States and adherence to liberal norms vary across functional areas and regions? Is China building an alternative world order? If so, what are the characteristics of that order? Is it meant to complement or replace the existing order?

This book argues that although China does not seek to change the international distribution of territory in the Middle East and sub-Saharan Africa, as its power grows, it increasingly competes with the United States and the West, challenges the rules of the liberal international system, and builds spheres of influence in these regions. China is constructing an alternative international order to interact with these regions. If the current international system unravels due to actions by China or the United States, this alternative order will serve as the foundation of China's economic, political, and military relations with the Middle East and sub-Saharan Africa, as well as much of the rest of the developing world. In an era of emerging great power competition, it is both theoretically and practically essential to understand the specific features of that order and how China competes. This book explores the characteristics of that competition and emerging order.

This book advocates for a new approach to understanding China as a rising power toward these regions. As will be demonstrated in later chapters, China's behavior toward the Middle East and sub-Saharan Africa varies dramatically over time, across functional areas, and between regions. In light of its actual conduct, it is not particularly useful to categorize it as merely a revisionist or status quo power. Instead, to understand China's behavior requires examining its behavior across specific functional areas. Rather than describing China's behavior as revisionist or status quo supporting, this book uses the concepts of competitive versus cooperative with the United States and norm convergent versus divergent from the liberal international order. It examines China's behavior across specific foreign policy tools. Chapter 2 elaborates on how the book uses those concepts.

This book attributes changes in China's behavior toward the Middle East and sub-Saharan Africa over time and differences across functional areas and regions to China's interests. China's domestic economic and political systems and threat perception in the international environment shape those interests. In many ways, its foreign policy behavior is a reflection of its domestic systems and resulting interests on the international stage.[19] As a result, this book argues that the best way to interpret China's behavior toward the Middle East and sub-Saharan Africa is to understand deeply its interests and external threat perceptions over time.

During the post–Cold War era, the degree of China's competition and norm-divergent behavior has varied widely across functional areas. This book argues that as China's power grows, it is increasingly competing with the United States economically and politically in the Middle East and sub-Saharan Africa. It is often exhibiting behavior divergent from liberal international norms in the functional areas of politics (e.g., humanitarian intervention, democracy promotion, and human rights), economics (e.g., free markets and the role of the state in the economy), and foreign aid (e.g., aid conditionality).

In contrast, it is cooperating with the United States and demonstrating behavior converging with liberal international norms in the military realm by participating in UN peacekeeping operations, multilateral antipiracy activities, and limiting conventional arms sales to countries in these regions. Its perception of the external threats from the United States amplifies its competitive and norm-divergent behavior. Cooperative and norm-convergent behavior is more likely when it perceives that external threats are relatively low.

In the post–Cold War era, China's domestic political and economic interests have driven differences in its behavior toward the Middle East and sub-Saharan Africa between functional areas and over time. China's domestic state-led capitalist economic system and nationalist, Leninist political system shape its interests. Those interests are acquiring resources and markets to fuel China's domestic growth; fostering international support in an era of emerging multipolarity; ensuring its domestic stability; advocating for developing country causes based on its own experience as a developing country; safeguarding its citizens and businesses abroad; and protecting its territorial integrity and sovereignty from the United States. Perceived external threats have amplified China's competitive and norm-divergent behavior in the Middle East and sub-Saharan Africa in recent years. Since the beginning of the Arab awakening, China has demonstrated escalating sensitivity over foreign interference in the domestic politics of states. It also increasingly perceives that the United States is challenging and attempting to contain China in the Pacific through the Obama era rebalance to Asia and supporting US allies in the East China Sea and the South China Sea. Chapter 3 examines China's interests and threat perceptions in the post–Cold War era.

In the functional areas of economics and politics directly related to its vital interests, China is establishing institutions outside the liberal international order (e.g., cooperation forums, BRI) and advocating for changes to some norms of the current order. In contrast with its competitive and norm-divergent political, economic, and foreign aid activities, China's military behavior in the post–Cold War Era is primarily cooperative and norm convergent with the liberal order.

The Structure of the Book

Chapter 2 introduces the analytical approach of the book, and chapter 3 explores China's contemporary interests. Next, two in-depth paired cases studies of foreign policy tools illuminate China's interests and behavior in the post–Cold War era. Chapter 4 examines China's cooperation forums with these regions: the Forum on China-Africa Cooperation established in 2000 and the China-Arab States Cooperation Forum established in 2004. The chapter also compares the these two forums to the Shanghai Cooperation Organization. Chapter 5 then compares and contrasts special envoys established by China to address regional issues: the China–Middle East special issues envoy (2002), the China-Africa special issues envoy (2007), and the China Syria special issues envoy (2016).

Next, three functional chapters—economic, political, and military—examine China's contemporary relations with these regions from 1991 to the present. The economic relations chapter (chapter 6) focuses on trade, contract services, foreign direct investment, aid, free trade agreement negotiations, special economic zones, and agricultural technology demonstration centers. The chapter on political relations (chapter 7) examines China's UN Security Council voting and strategic partnerships. The military relations chapter (chapter 8) analyzes United Nations peacekeeping operations, antipiracy operations, conventional arms sales, military exchanges, and China's naval base in Djibouti.

Finally, chapter 9 analyzes China's Belt and Road Initiative. The chapter defines what BRI is and how it relates to China's interactions with the Middle East and sub-Saharan Africa. BRI spans every functional area of China's international interaction with the Middle East and sub-Saharan Africa. The chapter explores how BRI interacts with the economic, political, and military foreign policy tools examined in chapters 4 to 8. Each chapter of the book categorizes China's foreign policy behavior as competitive versus cooperative with the United States and norm divergent versus norm convergent with the liberal order.

The concluding chapter (chapter 10) analyzes these findings over time, across functional areas and between regions to provide insights into China's rising power behavior in the Middle East, sub-Saharan Africa, and globally.

CHAPTER 2

THE ANALYTICAL APPROACH

What are China's interests in the Middle East and sub-Saharan Africa? Is China cooperating or competing with the United States in these regions? Is its behavior converging with or diverging from liberal international norms? Is China building an alternative international order in these regions? If yes, what are the characteristics of that order? How does China portray and differentiate itself as a great power in these regions? How is it building spheres of influence? Ultimately, what does China's behavior in the Middle East and sub-Saharan Africa indicate about its rise globally?

By answering these questions, this book seeks to contribute to theoretical and empirical assessments of China's rise in the Middle East and sub-Saharan Africa, the rest of the developing world, and globally. This chapter introduces the analytical approach used to accomplish that purpose. First, it explores conventional wisdom about China as a rising power and explains how this book contributes to those debates. Next, it discusses concepts used throughout the work. Finally, it describes how the book evaluates China's interests, perception of threat, and behavior to draw broader conclusions about China as a rising power in these regions.

What Is the Conventional Wisdom about China as a Rising Power?

One primary goal of this book is to explain when and why China cooperates or competes with the United States in the Middle East and sub-Saharan Africa and when and why its behavior converges with or diverges from liberal international norms in those regions. From a theoretical and empirical standpoint, scholars of international relations and Chinese foreign policy produce diverse and contradictory insights into the degree to which a rising China will cooperate with the United States, the most powerful state in the international system. They also disagree about how much China's behavior converges or will converge with international norms. For example, both offensive realism theory and international relations scholar Robert Gilpin assert that a rising power like China will likely compete with the United States in the Middle East and sub-Saharan Africa. Gilpin's theory predicts that China will strive to make changes to the norms of the international system to better accommodate its interests. Various strands of liberalism and constructivism portray a rising China learning to cooperate with the United States and Western states more broadly and adopting international norms through its interactions in the international system. Some constructivist and liberal scholarship argues that the United States and the West are socializing China into the liberal international political and economic order. The next section briefly discusses the insights of the literature about China's potential behavior as a rising power.

Competition and Divergence?

Two significant sets of literature within international relations scholarship offer theories emphasizing the potential competitive and norm-divergent tendencies of rising powers: offensive realism and Gilpin's writings regarding systemic change. Both of these theories draw from realism, which tends to assume that the natural state of the international system is one of conflict and focuses on the material power of states. The theoretical arguments of the following authors reflect those metalevel assumptions.

As exemplified by the work of John Mearsheimer, offensive realism assumes that great powers seek to maximize their share of world power and that their ultimate aim is to become the global hegemon or at least a regional hegemon.[1] Rising states do not tend to cooperate with the existing hegemon. In Mearsheimer's view of the world, all rising great powers seek to maximize power to ensure their survival. States derive their interests from the structural factors of anarchy and distribution of power in the international system.[2] In this quest for maximum power, great powers seek to prevent rival powers from dominating wealth-generating areas of the world.[3] According to Mearsheimer's theory, if China's power continues to grow, it is destined to become a challenger of the United States due to system-level material structural factors beyond either state's control.[4] Mearsheimer's China is a competitive great power that will seek to prevent the United States from dominating wealth-generating areas of the world that possess critical raw materials, such as the Middle East and sub-Saharan Africa.[5]

Robert Gilpin is another scholar who predicts a high likelihood that a rising power will become a competitive and norm-divergent rising power in the Middle East and sub-Saharan Africa.[6] He claims that "those actors who benefit most from a change in the social system and who gain power to effect such a change will seek to alter the system in ways that favor their interests."[7] His observations regarding the behavior of rising states are more nuanced than Mearsheimer's assertion that all great powers seek to maximize power, establish regional hegemony, and prevent others from becoming regional hegemons. Gilpin argues that the objectives of states are to pursue the conquest of territory to advance economic, security, and other interests; increase influence over the behavior of other states; and exercise influence over the world economy.[8] He asserts that a dissatisfied rising state will attempt to change the "rules governing the international system, the division of spheres of influence," and "the international distribution of territory."

Although his approach considers state-level variables more than Mearsheimer's offensive realism does, Gilpin's work ultimately is also a system-level analysis that assumes consistent behavior of rising powers due to structural factors. That said, only competitive rising great powers populate Mearsheimer's world, but Gilpin's world contains two types of rising powers: satisfied and dissatisfied. His satisfied states are cooperative and the dissatisfied states competitive. Dissatisfied states seek to change the international system in various ways, including the distribution of territory, the division of spheres of influence, and the rules governing the system.

Gilpin published his work before China's contemporary rise began, so he does not explicitly write about China as a rising power. That said, his theoretical assertions imply that if China is dissatisfied with the distribution of power, rules of the international system, or the hierarchy of prestige, it will become a competitive and norm-divergent rising power as its capability increases. In the Middle East and sub-Saharan Africa, Gilpin's theory would suggest that if China is a dissatisfied power, as its relative capability increases, it will seek to balance against the hegemonic United States or other great powers, establish spheres of influence, and strive to alter the norms and rules of international society within these regions in its favor. For example, one could interpret China's cooperative relations with Russia in the Middle East as a way to balance against the United States to prevent it from maintaining hegemony in the region. One could also see China's Belt and Road Initiative as balancing behavior striving toward that same goal. Both of these research agendas—offensive realism and Gilpin's work—understand that a rising power's interests is key to interpreting its behavior and the long-term probability of conflict with an existing hegemon.

Many international relations and Chinese foreign policy scholars portray China as the dissatisfied and competitive rising power these theories predict. Most authors who explicitly characterize China's contemporary behavior as competitive and norm divergent are examining China-US relations and China's behavior in its neighborhood, Asia. Some prominent examples include Allison, Pillsbury, Friedberg, and Jacques.[9] Other authors observe that China and other rising powers are routing around the West and building an alternative international system.[10] For example, Barma, Ratner, and Weber argue that a new order is forming in the developing world led by rising powers China, India, and Russia. In this new order, wealth and power are derived from natural resources and industrial production. The order they observe has a neo-Westphalian normative basis stressing state sovereignty, noninterference in the domestic politics of states, and economic, social, and cultural autonomy. Another author, Gat, observes that China and Russia may be forming an authoritarian capitalist order.

Cooperation and Convergence?

In contrast with particular strands of realist international relations theory emphasizing the importance of structural factors in determining state behavior and the competitive qualities of rising powers toward existing great powers and the rules of the international system, other international relations theories focus on the potential for rising powers to cooperate and integrate into the international normative order. These theories provide explanations for changing state interests and approaches to international society. In general, the philosophical underpinnings of liberalism, including economic liberalism, political liberalism, and neoliberal institutionalism, influence authors who highlight China's cooperative behavior and integration into the international order. As opposed to realism's focus on the conflictual nature of the international system, liberalism tends to see opportunities for cooperation among states. This cooperation is possible through various mechanisms (e.g., institutions in neoliberal institutionalism, economic integration in economic liberalism, and shared values in political liberalism).

Many authors inspired by the philosophical underpinnings of liberalism provide insights into the potential behavior of China as a rising power. They include John Ikenberry's arguments about China's apparent satisfaction with the current international order, scholars who emphasize the socialization of China into international institutions, and constructivists who analyze the impact of the ideational structure of the international system on state interests and behavior.

In direct response to the insights of authors such as Gilpin, Ikenberry, a liberal institutionalist, tends to argue that China's current interests are generally in alignment with the existing Western-dominated liberal economic and political order.[11] To fuel its prosperity, China needs access to the global capitalist system and wants the protections that the Western order's rules and institutions provide.[12] In Ikenberry's words, the Western international liberal order is "easy to join, but hard to overturn," and China benefits significantly from the current system, so for now, cooperating as a rising power serves China's interests best.[13] In response to Gilpin's theory, Ikenberry would argue that China is satisfied with the current order and that a rising China will not come into conflict with the United States and the rest of the West in the Middle East, sub-Saharan Africa, or elsewhere in the world. Ikenberry's arguments would lead one to expect cooperation and norm convergence between China's behavior and liberal international norms in the Middle East and sub-Saharan Africa. Or perhaps China is setting up its own institutions that are still underpinned by the norms of the liberal international order.[14] That said, he does acknowledge a potential for tension between a rising China and the hegemonic United States, especially as the norm of sovereignty erodes and the United States attempts to renegotiate aspects of the hegemonic liberal order in the post–Cold War era.[15] He also highlights that it is essential to consider that China may be satisfied with the liberal order now and the United States is ceding its support for the system.[16]

Other scholars who examine the integration of states into the international order focus on the socialization of states, emphasizing ideational rather than material factors in international relations. They therefore tend to examine China's behavior in international institutions and socialization into those institutions over time. In general, their studies do not speak to China's overall behavior as a rising power. Still, they do examine how China is integrating into the existing international order in contrast with the expectations of offensive realism and Gilpin's work. Among the scholars who analyze China's socialization into the liberal international order are Johnston, Kim, Kent, Foot and Walter, and Carlson.[17] Many of these authors tend to argue that China is increasingly cooperating with Western powers and that its behavior in general is converging with international norms.

A vibrant debate is now emerging among liberals and realists about the degree to which China's behavior converges with or diverges from aspects of the contemporary international order and how to characterize that behavior.[18] One important aspect of that debate is promulgated by scholars who provide conceptual clarity to the meaning of the international order and contemplate the ways in which China's behavior toward it may vary significantly across elements of the order. For example, Johnston's newest work proposes that there are at least eight elements of international order against which to evaluate China's behavior: the constitutive order (e.g., sovereignty and territorial integrity), the military order, the political development order, the social development order, the international trade order, the international financial and monetary order, the international environmental order, and the international information order.[19] He argues that China's approach varies significantly across these orders.

Finally, related to the socialization literature, a wide range of constructivists argue that what matters most for understanding the behavior of states is the ideational structure of the international system as opposed to its material structure. The insights of these works indicate that China will not necessarily become competitive because of material factors. It could instead become cooperative and integrated into the international system. Constructivist scholars such as Wendt and Ruggie stress that states mutually constitute their interests and identities through interactions with other states and that those interests can change because of those interactions.[20] They argue that the international system is indeed anarchic, but that structure does not determine state interests. It is important to note that the impact of those ideational factors could result in either cooperative or competitive behavior. For example, as China interacts with other states in the system, it could develop an identity as a non-Western, Global South, developing country that advocates for change in the international order or constructs an alternative world order with like-minded states.[21]

Clearly there is no unified conventional wisdom about the behavior of a rising China. Theoretical analysis and predictions regarding China's rising power behavior vary widely among scholars. Empirical observation of China's actual behavior in the Middle East and sub-Saharan Africa exhibits aspects of cooperation and convergence, as well as competition and divergence. Its behavior varies dramatically across functional areas and over time. China's actions in the Middle East and sub-Saharan Africa could support either conclusion: China is a competitive, norm-divergent power, or China is a cooperative, norm-convergent actor.

China's behavior analyzed in this book indicates that in the post–Cold War era, it is not attempting to maximize power in the Middle East and sub-Saharan Africa as Mearsheimer would predict, but it is also not being socialized into the rules of the liberal international order as liberalists would argue. Instead, in alignment with the insights of Gilpin's work and power transition theories, this book argues that although China is not seeking to change the international distribution of territory in the Middle East and sub-Saharan Africa, it is increasingly building spheres of influence as its power grows and challenging the rules of the liberal international system in these regions.[22] China is constructing an alternative international order that could one day challenge the existing international order.[23]

What Is the Current International Order?

One significant contribution of this book is to provide an assessment of China's approach to the international order in the Middle East and sub-Saharan Africa. Often scholarship about China's rise vaguely refers to the international order and China's attempts to integrate into, change, or overthrow that order. For the analysis in this book, two often conflicting sets of norms and institutions constitute the current international order: the Westphalian order and the liberal international order.[24] It is important to be clear that these norms exist apart from the behavior of the United States or other states. These are not the only norms of the international system, but they serve as its contemporary foundation.

The norms of the Westphalian order are sovereignty, territorial integrity, noninterference in the domestic affairs of states, self-determination, and nondiscrimination.[25] Although signatories of the Treaty of Westphalia introduced the Westphalian system to Europe in 1648 and the United Nations Charter enshrines it in the contemporary order, the Westphalian order has been a global order only since the end of colonization in the 1960s. Arguably the Westphalian order is the bedrock of the contemporary international system and represents the most universally accepted norms of the international order. That said, competing liberal norms such as universal human rights and the responsibility to protect constantly challenge norms of the Westphalian order.

The liberal international order, which coexists and interacts with the Westphalian order, is open and rules based. Norms include free markets, international institutions, cooperative security, democracy, collective problem solving, shared sovereignty, and the rule of law. In a post–World War II environment, examples of specific institutions embodying those norms include the United Nations (Security Council and General Assembly), World Trade Organization (WTO; previously the General Agreement on Trade and Tariffs), the Bretton Woods institutions (the World Bank and International Monetary Fund, IMF), and the Universal Declaration of Human Rights. Although the United States and the rest of the West established many elements of this order after World War II, the liberal order did not become a truly global order until after the fall of the Soviet Union in 1991. Before that event, the liberal international order was a Western (not global) order competing with an alternative Soviet-led communist order.[26] Also, until the 1970s, colonialism and imperialism coexisted with the liberal order, and Western states were the predominant members of that order.

Even today, due to contestation among norms, some scholars question the universal existence of the liberal order. Barma, Ratner, and Weber write, "Today, we have an international order that is neither orderly nor liberal."[27] They further assert, "The liberal order can't be under siege in any meaningful way (or prepped to integrate rising powers) because it never attained the breadth or depth required to elicit that kind of agenda. The liberal order is today still largely an aspiration, not a description of how states actually behave or how global governance actually works."[28]

Although analysts question the universal nature of the liberal order, these two international orders, Westphalian and liberal, coexist, overlap, often contradict each other, and change over time. They exist independent of states in the international system. This book seeks to understand how China behaves toward the norms and institutions of these orders. As a result, throughout this book, each foreign policy tool that China uses in the Middle East and sub-Saharan Africa is examined in comparison to the relevant norms and institutions of these orders and categorized as convergent with or divergent from the liberal order.

Who Is the Revisionist?

Much of the literature on rising powers characterizes states as revisionist or status quo oriented. This book takes another approach: it examines China's rise in terms of cooperation versus competition with the United States and norm convergence with versus divergence from the liberal order over time and across functional areas and regions. These are two distinct concepts. *Competition* means China is attempting to gain power or influence relative to another great power. *Power* refers to economic, political, military, and technological capabilities.[29] A great power therefore is a state with the ability to exert influence globally through military, economic, and political power. *Cooperation* indicates China is working together with another great power to achieve a goal in the region.[30]

Divergence or convergence in this book refers to China's behavior in relation to the liberal international normative order. *Norm divergent* means China's behavior differs from a norm, and *norm convergent* characterizes alignment between China's behavior and an international norm or institution. This concept explores the degree to which China's behavior converges with or diverges from specific norms of the liberal international order, not the behavior of the United States or other states. Although the United States or the West in general may champion certain aspects of the liberal order and often refers to it as the Western-led or United States–led liberal order, the concept of the liberal order exists independent of those states. Great power behavior that diverges from the liberal order may weaken it, but does not necessarily destroy it because it exists independent of the great powers that advocate for it.

It is important to note that China's competitive behavior is not always norm divergent and its cooperative behavior is not always norm convergent. Sometimes it competes with norm-divergent behavior, but sometimes

Table 2.1. Combinations of Behavior

	Competitive with the United States	*Cooperative with the United States*
Divergent from the liberal order	Competitive and divergent	Cooperative and divergent
Norm neutral	Competitive and norm neutral	Cooperative and norm neutral
Convergent with the liberal order	Competitive and convergent	Cooperative and convergent

it leverages norm convergence. Also, some of China's behavior neither converges with or diverges from the liberal international order because there are not applicable elements of the liberal order related to a behavior or foreign policy tool. This book labels that type of behavior as norm neutral. In this book, there are six possible combinations of behavior, identified in Table 2.1.

There are several reasons for using these separate concepts of competition with the United States and norm divergence from the liberal order instead of status quo versus revisionist. First, in today's world, it is increasingly unclear what the status quo is. International norms are continually evolving and often contradict each other. For example, considering the international norm of Westphalian sovereignty, what state is the revisionist in the Middle East and sub-Saharan Africa in a post–Arab awakening environment? The United States or China? One can assert that the United States and other Western countries are the revisionists through the evolving emphasis on the limits of sovereignty, including the need for humanitarian intervention, the responsibility to protect, and the promotion of military-backed regime change in certain countries.[31]

To interpret China's behavior as a rising power in these regions, what is most important is not to determine which is revisionist and which is status quo supporting, but rather to understand when and why China is cooperating with the United States and when and why its behavior is converging with or diverging from liberal international norms. Lack of cooperation between the United States and China and divergence between China's behavior and the liberal norms of the international system could potentially lead to tensions and affect relations.

Also, the terms *revisionist* and *status quo* are laced unnecessarily with normative connotations that can be partially avoided by conceptualizing

China's behavior as cooperative versus competitive with the United States and converging with versus diverging from liberal international norms. If one uses the terms *revisionist* or *status quo*, readers often assume that those words describe a state's intent or preferences rather than state behavior regardless of motivation. When labeling states as revisionist or status quo supporting, analysts tend to generalize that behavior at the state level. In the literature, there are revisionist states and status quo states. However, the real world is not that simple. State behavior can and often does vary widely across functional areas. A state may be revisionist in the realm of politics but status quo supporting in military relations. There could even be variation within functional areas. Revisionist is not necessarily bad, and supporting the status quo is not always good. Those distinctions are important, especially when one is considering whether a rising state's behavior will result in conflict, military confrontation, and, potentially, war. For example, China may be attempting to compete with the United States in the Middle East and sub-Saharan Africa, but that does not necessarily mean that it is also challenging the rules of the international system in those regions. China can compete inside and outside the international order with convergent or divergent behavior. Moving away from the term *revisionist* makes it easier to highlight those nuances.

Finally, another problem with the term *revisionist* is that in a unipolar system, balancing against the hegemon is always a revisionist as opposed to status-quo-supporting policy.[32] This phenomenon makes use of the term *revisionist* problematic when examining the current transition of the international system from unipolarity to multipolarity or bipolarity.[33]

For all of these reasons, rather than labeling China as revisionist or status quo oriented, this book looks at specific foreign policy tools by functional area over time and across regions to understand China's cooperative or competitive behavior with the United States and behavior that converges with or diverges from liberal international norms and institutions.

Evaluating China's Interests, Perceived Threats, and Behavior

This book examines China's interests, perceived threats, and behavior over time and across functional areas to understand it as a rising power in the Middle East and sub-Saharan Africa. Examining this rise over time offers opportunities for identifying how China's changing interests and threat perception have influenced its behavior. For example, in the mid-2000s, the international system started to exhibit signs of multipolarity or potentially reemerging bipolarity. One would expect that variations in the balance of power of this magnitude would result in changes in rising power state behavior. Analyzing China's behavior from 1991 to 2019 shows how shifting polarity in the system influences China's interests, threat perception, and behavior.

Examining this time frame also offers the opportunity to analyze China's behavior at points in time when it had very different economic interests and to understand the manifestations of those changing interests. Comparing China's behavior over time provides insight into how its changing economic needs affected its behavior in these regions.

Finally, since this book examines China's behavior toward the liberal international order, this long time frame allows an exploration of how China's engagement with elements of the liberal international order have changed over time.

I collected the vast majority of research materials for this book during extensive fieldwork in China, Washington, DC, Egypt, South Africa, Belgium, France, Kuwait, Qatar, the Netherlands, Oman, Saudi Arabia, the United Arab Emirates, and the United Kingdom. Sources include interviews with approximately two hundred Chinese, Middle Eastern, African, US, and European government officials and scholars;[34] PRC government-issued white papers, declarations, communications, action plans, and press releases; top leaders' speeches (mainly focused on Xi Jinping, Hu Jintao, Jiang Zemin, Deng Xiaoping, and Mao Zedong); quantifiable statistics regarding China's relations—economic, political, foreign aid, and military—with these regions; and scholarly analysis and media reports from China, the Middle East, and sub-Saharan Africa.

The next chapter explores China's post–Cold War interests, threat perceptions, and behavior. It derives China's contemporary interests and perceived threats from primary sources of Chinese government documents and speeches as well as interview data. The rest of the book examines the behavior that results from those interests and perceived threats. For each foreign policy tool analyzed, comprehensive data are examined over time. Each chapter describes data sources, and they vary by tool. China's behavior with each foreign policy tool is summarized and then categorized as cooperative versus competitive with the United States and norm divergent versus convergent with the liberal order. The book aggregates those findings by functional area to make overall claims regarding China's behavior over time.

Finally, the concluding chapter brings together the findings on all the foreign policy tools examined in the book to make claims about broader patterns in China's behavior as a rising power. In particular, it discusses how China is competing with the United States, how it challenges the liberal order, how it portrays and differentiates itself as a great power, how it is building spheres of influence, and the international order it is constructing in the Middle East and Africa. This qualitative approach presents a complicated picture about China as a rising power. Even within functional areas, China's behavior may be contradictory. Its behavior is complex, and this book seeks to shed light on some characteristics of that complexity. Nevertheless, this nuanced qualitative approach produces deep insights into China's rising power behavior in the Middle East and sub-Saharan Africa, as well as the developing world, more broadly.

CHAPTER 3

WHAT DOES CHINA WANT IN THE MIDDLE EAST AND SUB-SAHARAN AFRICA?

To better understand China as a rising power in the Middle East, sub-Saharan Africa, and globally requires a deep appreciation of China's interests. This chapter therefore analyzes China's interests in the Middle East and sub-Saharan Africa during the post–Cold War era. What are those interests? How and why have they changed over time? How do those interests vary between the Middle East and sub-Saharan Africa? Since the beginning of the Arab awakening, how have China's interests in these regions changed? Is increasing competition between the United States and China in Pacific Asia and globally affecting China's interests in the Middle East and sub-Saharan Africa? As argued in chapters 1 and 2, China's domestic economic and political systems, together with perceptions of external threats, shape its interests in these regions, which then drive whether China cooperates or competes with the United States in these regions and the degree to which China's behavior converges with or diverges from liberal international norms. An understanding of China's interests provides insights into why and how China engages in competition with the United States, builds spheres of influence, and challenges the rules of the international system.

China's interests in the Middle East and sub-Saharan Africa have shifted dramatically over time. In stark contrast with today, China's interests in the Middle East and sub-Saharan Africa during the Mao era (1949–1976) were minimal—primarily political and military. China was promoting revolutions through national liberation movements;[1] advocating for fellow third world states; seeking support for China on the international stage, particularly for recognition of the People's Republic in the United Nations; and balancing against great powers (both the United States and the Soviet Union at different times) in these regions.

After the death of Mao in 1976 and the rise of Deng Xiaoping in 1978, China's interests changed with its new economic and political orientation as well as external threat perception. As a result, during the 1980s, China's economic, political, and security interests in the Middle East and sub-Saharan Africa were all minimal.

In the post–Cold War era from 1991 to the present, China's primary interests in the Middle East and sub-Saharan Africa have been to promote its domestic economic growth, foster support in the international arena, ensure its domestic stability, advocate for developing country causes, safeguard its citizens and businesses abroad, and protect its territorial integrity and sovereignty from the United States. An understanding of those interests sheds light on the root causes of China's competitive, norm-divergent behavior and attempts to change the international system. It also provides context for China's objectives as it builds spheres of influence in these regions, competes against the United States, and portrays and differentiates itself as a great power. Thoughtful analysis of China's interests is critical because ultimately they drive the characteristics of the international orders it is creating to interact with these regions, and those orders may one day serve as an alternative international order.

This chapter examines primary sources such as PRC State Council–issued white papers on national defense,[2] peaceful development,[3] the Middle East and Africa,[4] energy,[5] foreign trade,[6] foreign aid,[7] and Xinjiang;[8] People's Republic of China (PRC) Ministry of Foreign Affairs–issued China's Foreign Affairs annual yearbooks;[9] Chinese Communist Party (CCP) National Party Congress Reports,[10] top leader speeches, and writings about the Middle East and sub-Saharan Africa (focused on Xi Jinping, Li Keqiang, Hu Jintao, Wen Jiabao, Jiang Zemin, and Deng Xiaoping); scholarly analysis from Chinese analysts; and interviews with Chinese, Middle Eastern, sub-Saharan African, US, and European government officials and scholars. Much of the analysis relies heavily on Chinese government documents, which provide a deep understanding of how China conceptualizes and articulates its interests. After this analysis of China's post–Cold War interests (1991 to the present), chapters 4 to 9 assess the foreign policy behavior resulting from those interests.

Promoting China's Domestic Economic Development

Much of China's competitive and norm-divergent behavior in the Middle East and sub-Saharan Africa discussed later in the book stems from its escalating economic interests in these regions since 1991. In stark contrast with its pre-1976 ideological, revolutionary interests in these two areas, China's predominant interest in these regions and globally since then is supporting its domestic economic development and the need for international peace and stability to support that development.[11]

Peace and Development

After 1978, China pursued an export-oriented development strategy. To maintain its domestic growth rates through interactions with the global economy, it wanted a peaceful and stable international environment. Beginning in the early 1980s, Deng Xiaoping asserted that the two significant issues confronting the world and China were peace and development.[12] Since 1991, statements about China's need for development and international stability have been prominent in China's white papers; the Chinese Foreign Ministry's annual publication regarding the state of the world (*China's Foreign Affairs*); and speeches by such leaders as Jiang Zemin, Hu Jintao, Wen Jiabao, Xi Jinping, and Li Keqiang.[13] These publications and statements often describe development and peace as the dominant, irreversible themes of the times and identify them as fundamental interests.[14] In the words of Xi Jinping's 2017 work report to China's National Party Congress (NPC), "China will continue to hold high the banner of peace, development, cooperation, and mutual benefit and uphold its fundamental foreign policy goal of preserving world peace and promoting common development. . . . peace and development remain irreversible trends."[15] China's 2019 white paper "China and the World in the New Era" also emphasizes the role of peace and development in China's interactions with the rest of the world.[16]

China's interest in its economic development and a peaceful international environment to support that development has remained constant since 1978. What has changed during this time is the importance of the Middle East and sub-Saharan Africa to that development and the level of international and domestic stability in these regions over time. In the 1980s and early 1990s, China's economic interests in these regions were limited because it was focusing its efforts internally on transforming into a market-driven economy and starting to interact with the global economy to attract foreign direct investment.

During the post–Cold War era, its economic interests in the Middle East and sub-Saharan Africa substantially expanded due to its desire to acquire natural resources and overseas markets for goods and services to support the growth of its economy as its export-oriented economy developed. With the onset of the Arab awakening in 2011, threats from within and between states in the region constantly challenged peace in the Middle East. Concurrently, civil war, piracy, and terrorism endangered sub-Saharan Africa's stability.

This section provides an analysis of the role of the Middle East and sub-Saharan Africa in China's economic development from 1991 to the present. Highlighted are China's needs for resources (both energy and non-energy resources) and markets for goods and services, economic security, and regional stability to support that economic development.

Natural Resources and Markets for Goods and Services

During the Mao era, the Chinese Communist Party (CCP) pursued economic autarky and did not require resources or markets in the Middle East and sub-Saharan Africa. As a result, economic relations were minuscule and mostly related to foreign aid. Domestic economic reforms within China changed those relations significantly. China's pursuit of an export-oriented industrialization model for economic growth in the post-Mao era resulted in its growing need for Middle Eastern and sub-Saharan African natural resources and markets for its goods and services.

China became a net oil importer in 1993 and surpassed the United States as the world's largest net oil importer twenty years later. As China's industrial output grew in the late 1990s and early 2000s, it required, in addition to energy, a wide range of industrial minerals to fuel production, including cooper bauxite, iron ore, and aluminum. China's needs for agricultural products also increased as the per capita income of its population rose. Since the Middle East is rich in energy resources and sub-Saharan Africa has an abundance of a wide range of energy, industrial, and agricultural resources, both regions grew in importance to China as its economy developed.[17] Sub-Saharan Africa also became increasingly significant as China attempted to diversify away from Middle East oil.

The Middle East and sub-Saharan Africa are promising markets for Chinese goods and services. As China's domestic economy matured, its state-owned and private companies started seeking out market opportunities globally. China sees the Middle East and sub-Saharan Africa as regions where

Chinese goods and services, including manufacturing, construction, telecommunications, and finance, are very competitive. In addition to providing export opportunities for Chinese goods and services, many countries in these regions are attractive destinations for China's growing foreign direct investment.

Chapter 4 on cooperation forums discusses aspects of economic cooperation incorporated into those forums. Chapter 6 on economic relations provides an in-depth analysis of China's trade with, services to, and investment in these regions over time. That chapter also introduces many of the foreign policy tools China uses to facilitate those economic relations, including state support for Chinese companies, foreign aid, free trade agreements, special economic zones, and agricultural technology demonstration centers. The primary purpose of this section is to point out that China's interests in securing resources and markets in these regions have been a significant driver of its foreign policy behavior since the end of the Cold War. As China's domestic economy slows over the coming decades and its firms continue to need lower-cost labor markets to outsource production and opportunities to address domestic excess capacity issues, its interests in trade and investment in these regions will likely intensify. Also, if economic relations with the United States continue to deteriorate, market opportunities in the Middle East and sub-Saharan Africa will become even more important to Chinese firms.[18]

Economic Security

Closely related to China's quest for natural resources and markets is economic security, a rising concern. As the role of Middle Eastern and sub-Saharan African resources and markets grew in importance for China, China's official discourse about economic security intensified in government white papers; Chinese Ministry of Foreign Affairs publications; speeches by Hu Jintao, Wen Jiabao, and Xi Jinping; and Chinese scholarly analysis of relations with these regions.

Around the time that China began increasing its imports from the Middle East and sub-Saharan Africa, its 1998 National Defense white paper emphasized the rising importance of economic security for state security.[19] White papers issued in 2000 and 2002 articulated similar concerns.[20]

After the United States invaded Iraq in 2003, China's expressed sensitivities about economic security escalated, with energy security as its core concern. Through 2010, government-issued documents and top leaders' speeches particularly emphasized worries over rising resource prices, potential struggles with other powers for strategic resources, and volatility in vital energy-producing regions.[21] Chinese scholars provided a detailed analysis of China's energy security worries.[22] Although China was actively attempting to diversify its oil suppliers away from the Middle East to sub-Saharan Africa due to perceived risks in the region,[23] the Middle East, according to Chinese scholars, was the most vital region for its energy security. They characterized its energy resources as the "blood of the world's economic development."[24]

China's concerns about energy security in the Middle East and sub-Saharan Africa have only grown since the beginning of the Arab awakening in 2011.[25] The 2013 issue of *China's Foreign Affairs* stressed, "Global issues such as food security, energy, and resource security and cyber security became more acute."[26] Military strategy white papers articulate similar concerns.[27] Those worries continued as China faced challenges to its energy security, such as dependence on foreign sources, maritime transportation routes in need of protection, price fluctuations, and instability in resource-rich areas of the world.[28]

Although the bulk of China's economic security interests revolve around energy resources in the Middle East, at the end of the 2000s, there was an increased prevalence of discussion of food security issues in official Chinese government discourse, especially by Hu Jintao.[29] Due to agricultural production capacity, China's food security concerns tend to involve sub-Saharan Africa rather than the Middle East. Hu's speeches from 2008 through 2011 indicated this concern. One speech during the 2008 global financial crisis included a particularly poignant statement: "Food issues not only concern the economy and people's well-being of each country but also bear on the development and security of the whole world. . . . China always attaches great importance to agriculture and especially the food issue"[30]

Although the Hu administration particularly highlighted food security during the 2008 spike in global food prices, the Xi administration continues to emphasize the issue.[31] If the trade war between the United States and China intensifies, food security may become more of an issue for China in these regions as it attempts to identify alternative suppliers. For example, in the short term, finding alternative soybean suppliers or building up domestic capacity quickly could be a challenge, and African countries could become more important suppliers. Also, significant events such as the recent African swine flu deaths of millions of pigs in China may make food security cooperation with Africa more critical in the future.

Regional Stability

China's concerns about economic security have escalated over the past thirty years. Its economic security requires regional stability in the Middle East and sub-Saharan Africa. As a result, parallel to its economic security concerns is its desire for stability in the Middle East and sub-Saharan Africa.

International stability is key to China's continued development, required to ensure the continued flow of natural resources to China and ongoing access to markets. In terms of regional stability, China views the Middle East and sub-Saharan Africa very differently. It perceives the Middle East to be a turbulent region that is within the US sphere of influence. In contrast, it sees sub-Saharan Africa as a relatively stable region that is not within the sphere of influence of the United States.

China has long considered the Middle East to be a region ridden with turbulence and conflict. In the year 2000, Jiang Zemin described the situation there: "In the Middle East, ethnic conflicts, territorial disputes and endless flames of war have over the years taken countless lives and displaced numerous people. That has severely dampened the economic and social development of the region and affected world peace and stability."[32]

The US invasion of Iraq in 2003 heightened China's unease about instability in the region.[33] In 2004, China's concerns regarding instability in the region continued to mount. *China's Foreign Affairs* described the regional situation as "highly tumultuous with significant changes in the region's geopolitical and security landscape as a result of the Iraqi War."[34] Referring to the Iraq War in 2003, the same publication stated, "By unleashing the war against Saddam and engaging in Iraqi post-war reconstruction, the United States unveiled its ambitious plan to 'reshape' the Middle East."[35] Throughout the rest of the 2000s, Chinese official documents expressed concern over turbulence and conflict in the Middle East.[36] Similar to official publications, contemporary Chinese scholarly analysis consistently portrayed the area as a region of instability and upheaval.[37]

Since the beginning of the Arab awakening in 2011, China's concerns about regional stability in the Middle East have only escalated. China already viewed the region as plagued by turbulence and instability, and developments there intensified that perception. As regimes changed, regional power competition grew: Syria descended into civil war, proxy wars emerged, and great power competition in the region became a growing concern. In 2013, *China's Foreign Affairs* summarized the regional situation: "West Asia and North

Africa experienced a prolonged period of turbulence, with regional issues becoming more complex and internationalized. This exerted a major impact on the international political, economic and security landscape, and drew close attention from the international community."[38] It also expressed worries that conflict in the Middle East could spread to other parts of the world. These concerns about escalating regional turbulence continued through 2019.[39]

A significant part of China's discourse regarding chaos in the Middle East revolves around hot spot issues in the region. Throughout the 2000s, the most frequently discussed ones were the Palestinian-Israeli conflict, the Iraq War, and the Iranian nuclear issue.[40] China perceived the Middle East to be more of an area of hot spot issues than sub-Saharan Africa. The only sub-Saharan African problems in the 2010s that China framed as hot spot issues with any frequency were war crimes and crimes against humanity in Darfur, civil war in Sudan,[41] political crisis and violence in president Mugabe led- Zimbabwe,[42] and Somali piracy.[43]

After the beginning of the Arab awakening, China's concerns about hot spots in the Middle East dramatically intensified. Although Chinese government documents continued the discussion of the Palestinian-Israeli conflict, Iran, and Iraq, they also started expressing concerns about stability in Tunisia, Egypt, Libya, Yemen, and Syria, including the rise of ISIS.[44] Over time, the Syrian war appears to be the most crucial addition to China's concerns. The initial concern was over the civil war there more broadly, including regional implications of regional power rivalries in the conflict. Starting in 2015, ISIS and other terrorist groups thriving in Syria, such as the Turkistan Islamic Party (TIP), became a significant worry for China.[45] In sub-Saharan Africa, together with Sudan and South Sudan, China highlighted hot spot issues such as Guinea-Bissau, Mali, Democratic Republic of the Congo, Central African Republic, terrorism in Nigeria, piracy in the Gulf of Guinea, and the spread of Ebola.[46] Although it emphasized hot spots in both regions, China expressed much greater concern with those in the Middle East.

China perceives the Middle East to be a region of historical and contemporary great power conflict. Mainly, competition between the United States, European countries, and Russia has been acute. Chinese scholars tend to not portray China as a great power in the Middle East but highlight the impact of this competition on China's energy security.[47] China consistently characterizes the region as within the sphere of influence of the United States. Chinese scholars assert that since the end of the Cold War, the United States has attempted to dominate the Middle East and maintain a hegemonic role in the region.[48] China considers control of the Middle East to be a core national interest of the United States, and it perceived increased US meddling in the region after the 2003 Iraq invasion.[49] Regarding energy security and competition in the Middle East, Chinese analysts portray the United States as the most important power.[50]

After the Arab awakening began, China increased its complaints about the role of the United States and Europe in the Middle East, especially in relation to Libya, Syria, Iran, and intervention in sovereign states.[51] Although Russia's involvement in the Middle East has expanded since the beginning of the awakening, China appears to be most worried about interference by the United States and western Europe. It does not tend to criticize Russia's meddling, including military intervention in Syria.[52]

Since 2017, Chinese government documents increasingly highlight the negative impacts of great power competition between the United States and Russia in the region. *China's Foreign Affairs 2017* edition states, "The United States and Russia tried to outmaneuver each other in the region, which was a major factor influencing the regional situation and its development."[53] In 2018, the same publication said, "Rivalry between the US and Russia weighed on the regional situation."[54]

Another emerging threat to regional stability that endangers China's interests in the Middle East is regional powers struggling with each other for power and influence. These include competition between Saudi Arabia and Iran, Saudi and the United Arab Emirates against Qatar,[55] Iran and Israel competition, Egypt and Turkey, and the Sunni-Shia split.

In contrast to the turbulence, great and regional power competition, and US dominance of the Middle East, China has viewed sub-Saharan Africa as a relatively stable region since the 1990s, experiencing economic growth,[56] although its government assessments often mention local domestic issues such as AIDs, underdevelopment, and civil war.[57] From 2014 to 2018, the Chinese Ministry of Foreign Affairs consistently described the situation in sub-Saharan Africa as moving toward stability and economic growth.[58] It considers the region as much more stable than the Middle East and therefore is less of an economic security threat for it.[59] Compared to worries about conflicts in the Middle East generated by great and regional powers, there is no indication that China has increasing concerns about foreign interference or great or regional power competition in sub-Saharan Africa. Recent Chinese government documents highlight cooperation between great powers in Africa and the increased positive attention they are paying to the region.[60] They also portray US involvement in the region in a positive light. In response to the US focus on great power competition between it and China in Africa,[61] China may place more emphasis on those elements of rivalry in official documents in the future.

Seeking Support in the International Arena

During the post–Cold War era, a primary Chinese political interest in these regions is gaining support in the international arena during emerging global multipolarity. During the Mao era, PRC interests in international support centered on admission to the United Nations, struggles with Taiwan for international recognition, and gaining political support against the United States and the Soviet Union. Since 1991, its interests in international support have shifted to fostering support from developing countries in a newly emerging post–Cold War multipolar order.[62]

With the end of the Cold War in the early 1990s, China began forecasting that a multipolar international order would develop and China would be a pole. Deng Xiaoping provided one of the first assessments of the emerging multipolar system and China's role in that system in 1990.[63]

Although some scholars assert that China reduced its emphasis on emerging multipolarity in the early 1990s and accepted the hegemonic position of the United States in the international system in the short term,[64] as early as 1998 China began to make strong statements regarding the evolving multipolar order and the role of developing countries in that order. For example its first National Defense white paper in 1998 emphasized the shift to multipolarity.[65] Throughout the early to mid-2000s, Chinese government publications and top leader speeches continued to stress these shifts and the future role of developing countries.[66]

Starting in the mid-2000s, in the context of this emerging multipolarity, China heavily stressed coordination with other developing countries (South-South cooperation) as a significant foreign policy goal. For example, *China's Foreign Affairs 2004* describes expanding cooperation with developing countries as a major foreign policy activity.[67]

During and after the 2008 global financial crisis, China's rhetoric about the transition to multipolarity became more pronounced.[68] In 2008, official Chinese discourse started highlighting the inevitability of the change to multipolarity, describing a "profound readjustment brewing in the international system" with an intensified role for developing countries.[69] China increasingly made forceful comments on the issue of multipolarity and the new role for developing countries in forming the new system and described the trend toward multipolarity as irreversible. International strategic competition was intensifying, and the balance of power was shifting to emerging powers and developing countries.[70]

Through 2019, *China's Foreign Affairs*, as well as other official government publications and leader speeches, contain statements about the growing foreign policy priority of South-South cooperation with developing countries in the emerging multipolar order.[71] For example, China's 2019 white paper on China's role in the world frames multipolarity and South-South cooperation as an opportunity for it.[72]

Some Chinese scholars predict that the world is moving toward a bipolar configuration with the United States and China as the two poles, especially after Russia began its confrontation with Western powers regarding Syria in 2011.[73] Chinese scholar Yan Xuetong also argues that this bipolar competition in the international order will not be over strategic hot spots but about the rules of the world order.[74]

Regardless of whether the world is moving toward multipolarity or bipolarity, in China's view, support for it from states in the developing world will be necessary. The Middle East and sub-Saharan Africa, which encompass many of the developing countries of the world, are critical sources of support for China in the emerging world order.

Ensuring China's Domestic Stability

Another interest of China in the Middle East is protecting its domestic stability from Muslim separatists in Xinjiang and the radicalization of Muslims throughout China. China does not appear to perceive any threat to its domestic stability radiating from sub-Saharan Africa. Still, due to religious and ethnic strife in Xinjiang, China's Muslim-majority province, and terrorist attacks in China, it perceives the Middle East as a potential source of domestic instability. Such concerns as containing tensions in Xinjiang and preventing terrorism throughout the country strengthen its advocacy the Five Principles of Peaceful Coexistence, which includes principles such as noninterference in the domestic politics of other states and respect for territorial integrity and sovereignty. Also,

China's desire for support for its activities in Xinjiang is a driver of its advocacy for Arab political causes and developing positive relations with Muslim countries. (chapters 4 to 9 discuss China's actual behavior with the Five Principles.)

Over the years, China has made it very clear that one of its most significant core interests is safeguarding its unity and territorial integrity.[75] In the eyes of its leaders, separatist activities in Xinjiang by Uyghur groups, who are of Turkic ethnic heritage, directly threaten China's territorial integrity. Although official Chinese statistics likely underreport the population of Muslims in China, it is widely believed to be well over 20 million (mostly composed of Hui, Uyghurs, and Kazakhs). Approximately 50 percent of China's Muslim population are Uyghurs, who primarily reside in the western Xinjiang Autonomous Region.[76] For many years, a limited number of Uyghurs engaged in a series of terrorist acts against Han Chinese in Xinjiang and other provinces.[77] Their main insurgent movement is known as the Eastern Turkestan Islamic Movement (ETIM). The US State Department and INTERPOL officially named it a terrorist organization after the attacks in the United States on 9/11.

China has long expressed concern about the impact of international terrorism on domestic insurgency activity in Xinjiang and throughout the rest of the country, including the effect of the return of Uyghur mujahedeen from Afghanistan to China in the 1980s.

After the September 2001 terrorist attacks on the United States, China's rhetoric regarding the threat of terrorist elements in Xinjiang noticeably intensified. Its 2002 National Defense white paper expresses concerns about terrorist activities in Xinjiang and highlights the threat it sees from perceived "East Turkistan" terrorist forces.[78]

Over the past twenty years, China's worries regarding the potential impact of international groups on Muslim insurgency groups within China have noticeably increased.[79] From 2001 through 2008, official discourse and scholarly analysis highlighted the separatist threat posed by Muslims in Xinjiang.[80] In July 2009, large-scale violence between ethnic Han Chinese and Uyghurs in Xinjiang resulted in 137 Han killed, 46 Uyghurs, and 1 from the Hui ethnic group.[81] After the violence, China's fears of domestic instability due to potential external support from Muslim separatist groups spiked. Its 2010 National Defense white paper argued, "Separatist forces working for 'East Turkistan Independence' and 'Tibet Independence' have inflicted serious damage on national security and social stability" and vowed to " crack down on separatist forces . . . and defend [China's] national sovereignty and territorial integrity."[82]

Both Chinese and Middle Eastern interviewees for this book identified stability in Xinjiang as one of China's critical interests in the Middle East. Those interviewed said that China sees the Middle East as the origin of Muslim fundamentalism and seeks support from Middle Eastern governments for its initiatives to suppress Uyghur separatist activities. For example, a high-level Middle East analyst with the Chinese Institute of International Studies in the Ministry of Foreign Affairs emphasized that one of China's most important interests in relations with the Middle East was ensuring the suppression of domestic terrorism in Xinjiang. He stressed that China perceived that the sources of terrorism radiate from the Middle East and sought support from Middle Eastern countries to prevent terrorism in China.[83] A Beijing University Middle East scholar also commented that China's concerns over the Middle East as a source of domestic terrorism were increasing and becoming a higher-priority issue in relations with Middle Eastern countries.[84]

Chinese interviewees frequently indicated that China is most concerned regarding Turkish support for Uyghur separatists due to ethnic and religious ties between the Turkish population and the Uyghurs. One Chinese interview respondent from the Chinese Institute of Contemporary International Relations emphatically argued that Turkey had become one of the top five most important countries for China in the Middle East, mainly due to concerns over the impact of Turkish support for Xinjiang separatist activities.[85] Since 2009, the situation in Xinjiang has increasingly worried Chinese leaders and influenced relations with the Middle East, especially Turkey.[86]

Middle Eastern interviewees stressed China's interests in Middle Eastern states' support for ensuring domestic stability in Xinjiang as well as preventing funding from the Middle East for violent activities of Uyghurs and other Muslim groups in China. A Jordanian embassy official stressed that China sought his country's political support for its actions in Xinjiang.[87] A former Egyptian ambassador to China highlighted that shortly after the 2009 Xinjiang riots, the Chinese government hosted a group of representatives from the Organization of Islamic Cooperation to visit Xinjiang and better understand the Chinese version of events on the ground. The purpose of this organized tour was to solicit support from Islamic countries and Middle Eastern embassy officials based in China for suppression of insurgency activities.[88] A former League of Arab States ambassador to China also stressed that the 2009 riots amplified China's interests in Middle Eastern support for the suppression of domestic insurgency in China.[89]

China's sensitivity to the potential impact of international terrorism on domestic stability in China has escalated, especially since the outbreak of riots and violence in Xinjiang in 2009, the Arab awakening in 2011, and a string of high-profile terrorist attacks within China's borders. Attacks included a suicide bombing under Mao's portrait in Tiananmen Square, a mass knife attack in a Kunming train station, and several violent incidents in Xinjiang.[90] In particular, China is concerned that Uyghurs and other Chinese Muslims will join transnational terrorist organizations such as ISIS, al-Qaeda, and TIP in Syria and return to China radicalized and ready to disturb the social order. They also worry that external funding will be funneled to Muslim insurgency groups within China by sympathetic outside groups. (Chapter 5 discusses those specific concerns in more detail.)

A Chinese government white paper in 2015 on Xinjiang describes the challenge to China's domestic stability in this way:

> Since the 1990s, the three forces (ethnic separatism, religious extremism, and violent terrorism) working from bases both inside and outside China have planned and staged a series of incidents of terror and violence, such as explosion, assassination, poisoning, arson, assault and riot, in Xinjiang and elsewhere, causing great loss to the lives and property of innocent civilians of all ethnic groups. . . . These violent and bloody crimes show clearly that the perpetrators are anything but representatives of "national" or "religious" interests. They are a great and real threat to ethnic unity and social stability in Xinjiang.[91]

Since 2009, in the name of preventing terrorism and ensuring social stability, China has engaged in a crackdown in Xinjiang and nationwide. Examples of increased repression in the name of preventing domestic terrorism include China's new national security law[92] and counterterrorism law,[93] as well as a wide range of policing activities and tightening of social control in Xinjiang.[94] The extreme manifestation of this interest is China's extrajudicial incarceration of over 1 million Uyghurs in camps in Xinjiang.[95] As China attempts to secure domestic stability, it continues to seek Middle Eastern state support for this treatment of Muslims within its borders. (Subsequent chapters discuss ways in which it attempts to gain the support of Middle Eastern countries and prevent linkages between international terrorist groups and Chinese Muslims.)

Advocating for Developing Country Causes

China's interests as a developing country also affect its behavior. During the Mao era, one of its primary interests in the Middle East and sub-Saharan Africa was advocating for third world country causes. That interest drove a great deal of its behavior during that era, including support for anticolonial movements, as well as armed insurgencies and promoting political cooperation among third world countries. China's support for developing country causes is one of the most consistent aspects of its interests over time.

Although many Western analysts and governments push back on the assertion that China is a developing country, the Chinese government claims that it is one, and that narrative significantly shapes how it characterizes its relations with the developing world. This section demonstrates that supporting developing country causes continues to be a significant narrative for China.

China as a Developing Country

Since the founding of the PRC in 1949, China has considered itself an integral part of the third world. China in fact was instrumental in developing the concept of the third world: Mao Zedong proposed his three worlds theory in 1974.[96] China's self-identification as a third world country led to Mao-era interests in supporting anticolonial and anti-imperial activities in the Middle East and sub-Saharan Africa,[97] shaped China's foreign aid approach to these regions, and ultimately resulted in China's support for calls for a New International Economic Order (NIEO) in the early 1970s.[98] This enduring legacy of China's role in the third world continues to influence China's foreign policy toward these regions to this day.

In a 1974 UN speech, Deng Xiaoping explained China's role as a developing, third world country.[99] During the reform era after 1978, he continued to emphasize that China was a developing country and would always belong to the third world.[100] Over time, the term *developing country* has replaced *third world* in China's official discourse, which encompasses the shared experiences of non-Western, formerly colonized underdeveloped countries.[101]

Although China occasionally mentioned its interests as a developing country in official documents and speeches during the 1990s and 2000s,[102] these references became more frequent after Hu Jintao assumed office in 2002.[103] In this official discourse, China continues to refer to itself as the largest developing country in the world.[104] The emergence of this emphasis during the

Hu administration may be due to his broader focus on the developing world internationally and attempts to address imbalances within China that were in many ways caused by its rapid development.

On the eve of China's gross domestic product surpassing Japan to become the world's second-largest economy in 2009, Premier Wen Jiabao passionately maintained that China was indeed still a developing country,[105] an emphasis that continues to this day despite the phenomenal growth of its GDP and per capita income. Xi Jinping's work report to the Nineteenth National Party Congress states, "The basic dimension of the Chinese context—that our country is still and will long remain in the primary stage of socialism—has not changed. China's international status as the world's largest developing country has not changed."[106] Other Chinese official documents and academic analysis also emphasize China's status as a developing country.[107]

Many internal factors drive this enduring affiliation with the developing world. One is the simple fact that although a number of its cities and regions have achieved prosperity and its GDP has grown dramatically over the years, China's per capita GDP is still quite low. In 2019, it was a mere $10,261 compared to $65,297 in the United States.[108] In many rural areas of China, the standard of living for residents is much closer to less developed African and Middle Eastern countries than developed countries. Another root cause is that the Chinese Community Party's (CCP) legitimacy continues to be partially based on the ability to improve the quality of life for all PRC citizens. Although in many ways, China has moved toward state-led capitalism, socialist aspects of its economy remain. Fighting for the rights of developing countries, including itself, is one way to ensure that China is not disadvantaged in global economic interactions due to past exclusion from the system. Another cause of China's identification with developing countries is the legacy of cooperation and shared historical experiences with fellow postcolonial, exploited countries. Finally, this continued identification with the interests of the developing world could come from the impact of Marxist-Leninist teachings on CCP leadership.

Although it is impossible to determine the exact root cause of China's continued identification with the developing world or to prove China perceives itself as a developing country, an interest in advocating for developing country causes does appear to influence its behavior toward both the Middle East and sub-Saharan Africa. Regardless of whether Chinese leadership actually believes China is still a developing country, it uses this rhetoric to its political advantage and to differentiate itself from other great powers.

Just and Equitable New Economic and Political Order

Over the past forty years, China has consistently expressed a desire to establish what it calls a just and equitable new political and economic order. In a famous speech at the United Nations in 1974, Deng Xiaoping began advocating for this concept.[109] At the heart of this envisioned order is addressing economic and political inequalities between the developing world and the developed world, between the Global South and the Global North.[110] Deng's calls for a new order continued through the 1980s, and official statements reflected his aspirations in the 1990s.[111] China's first National Defense white paper in 1998 discussed its desire for these new orders.[112]

Although the need for establishing this new order was often mentioned during the Jiang Zemin era,[113] starting with the Hu Jintao administration in 2002, China's noticeably amplified its emphasis on building a just and equitable new international political and economic order together with concerns over the gap between the Global North and South.[114]

China's call for the establishment of this new political and economic order (with specific recommendations regarding the structure of that order) and demands for the representation of developing countries in the new order dramatically increased after the beginning of the 2008 global financial crisis and have continued.[115] After the crisis, China's calls for establishing a new order became more assertive; for example, *China's Foreign Affairs* in 2009 stressed the need for establishing a new order.[116] In 2012, Hu Jintao emphasized that China is a friend to developing countries and works to make the international order more just and equitable for them.[117]

In the past few years, China has diversified the language it uses to describe the order it seeks. Although it does not always explicitly assert that it is seeking a new just and equitable international economic and political order, it continues to stress the role of coordination with other developing countries in shaping the international order. For example, China's 2016 Arab policy paper states, "We will keep closer cooperation and coordination in international organizations and defend the common interests of the two sides and all developing countries."[118] Also, "Arab states are China's important partners in following the peaceful development path, strengthening unity and cooperation among developing countries and establishing a new type of international relations with win-win cooperation at its core."[119]

Some scholars assert China is moving away from its old phrasing toward a more nuanced approach to the international order. For example, Wang Jisi argues that China is moving toward the wording "pushing the international political and economic order to a more just and rational direction."[120] Nevertheless, in some communications, China has continued to use the phrase *just and equitable new international economic and political order.*[121] For example, Xi Jinping in a speech to the BRICS (Brazil, Russia, India, China, and South Africa) in 2017 called for a more just and equitable international order and the need to increase the representation and voice of developing countries in that order.[122]

Xi Jinping's 2017 report to the National Party Congress stressed China's desire to advocate for developing country causes and efforts to shape global governance to meet the needs of China and fellow developing countries.[123] He even began to make statements indicating that China wanted to provide a model for other developing countries to follow as they modernize.[124]

Finally, China's 2019 white paper on its role in the world continued to elaborate on ways its development could serve as a model for other developing countries. It also provided insight into some of China's thoughts on the current manifestations of the new and equitable world order it is working to build. It included discussion of proposed concepts and initiatives such as "a global community of shared future, a new model of international relations, the Belt and Road Initiative, the principle of upholding the greater good and pursuing shared interests, a vision of common, comprehensive, cooperative, and sustainable security, the principles of extensive consultation, joint contribution and shared benefits in global governance, and the principles of equality, mutual learning, dialogue and inclusiveness between civilizations."[125]

Safeguarding China's Citizens and Businesses Abroad

As China's global economic, political, and security footprint grows, its interest in protecting its citizens and businesses abroad has expanded, concerns that have escalated since the beginning of the Arab awakening. Four of the biggest threats to China's citizens and businesses abroad are internal conflict within states where Chinese companies operate, international terrorists targeting Chinese firms and citizens overseas, threats of piracy toward Chinese commercial ships, and anti-Chinese backlash within local populations that result in harm to Chinese business and citizens.[126]

In the first round of interviews for this project between 2009 and 2011, these concerns of protecting Chinese citizens and businesses were not prominent. Interviewees often highlighted the fact that Chinese companies were willing to operate in environments that many Western businesses considered too dangerous. But the great pride that interview respondents appeared to have that Chinese firms were operating in those environments has changed over time. Beginning in January 2013, interview subjects started to stress worries about the need to protect Chinese citizens and businesses in these countries.[127]

The first mention of the need to protect China's overseas interests in China's defense white papers appeared in 2013.[128] China's 2015 "Military Strategy" also emphasized those overseas interests.[129] In 2019, China's National Defense white paper stressed, "China's overseas interests are endangered by immediate threats such as international and regional turmoil, terrorism, and piracy. Chinese diplomatic missions, enterprises and personnel around the world have been attacked on multiple occasions."[130]

Since the beginning of the Arab awakening, deteriorating local security conditions in countries that quickly descended into civil war have forced China to evacuate a number of its citizens. For example, in 2011, China evacuated over 35,000 citizens from Libya as NATO-led airstrikes began.[131] Other examples of noncombatant evacuations in the Middle East and sub-Saharan Africa include Lebanon's war with Israel in 2006 (167 evacuated), riots in Tonga in 2006 (193), the civil war in Chad in 2008 (411), the Arab awakening in Egypt in 2011 (1,800), the Central African Republic civil war in 2012 (300), and Syria's civil war in 2011 and 2013 (2,000).[132] China also evacuated 600 Chinese from Yemen when civil war erupted in 2015.[133] These high-profile incidents increased awareness of the need for China to be able to respond quickly to these sorts of emergencies throughout the Middle East and sub-Saharan Africa.

China also has increasing concerns regarding risks associated with investments in many of the countries in these regions. There are worries about how these environments affect the profitability of and risks for both Chinese state-owned and private businesses throughout the Middle East and Africa.[134] For example, one interviewee with a long career in the Chinese oil industry described how all of the major Chinese oil companies operating in the Middle East and Africa started seriously weighing the risks of investing in countries that could be prone to conflict.[135] The findings of scholar Zeng Ka on Chinese Belt and Road investment globally also support this assertion. Her analysis of recent survey data on Chinese company decisions to invest in particular countries indicates that firms (state owned and private) increasingly factor these risks into their investment decisions.[136]

International terrorism also increasingly threatens China's citizens and businesses in the Middle East and sub-Saharan Africa. In a March 2017 video, ISIS pledged to "shed blood like rivers" in attacks against Chinese targets.[137] Over the past two decades, international terrorists have targeted Chinese citizens, businesses, peacekeepers, and government facilities. Between 2004 and 2014, Chinese citizens died in terrorist attacks in Afghanistan, Cameroon, Jordan, Kenya, Malaysia, Mali, Pakistan, Syria, Thailand, and the United States.[138] In 2016, international terrorists killed several Chinese citizens abroad. ISIS executed two Chinese teachers in Pakistan.[139] In two separate Mali attacks, al-Qaeda killed a Chinese citizen at a luxury resort[140] and a Chinese UN peacekeeper.[141] A terrorist with supposed links to Uyghur separatists in China conducted a suicide attack on the Chinese embassy in Kyrgyzstan.[142] ISIS killed a Chinese businessperson in a bombing of Belgium's Brussels airport.[143] As these attacks occur, the Chinese public and government are increasingly concerned about the deaths of Chinese citizens abroad.[144]

Kidnappings of Chinese nationals are also worrying. Two prominent examples included abductions in 2012. Rebels kidnapped twenty-nine Chinese road workers in South Kordofan, Sudan, and twenty-four Chinese cement workers in Sinai, Egypt.[145] Recent examples in early 2021 include the kidnapping of Chinese miners in Ethiopia, Niger, and Nigeria, as well as railway workers in Nigeria.[146]

Since the mid-2000s, pirates in the Gulf of Aden have threatened China's commercial vessels.[147] Although the piracy in the Gulf of Aden is now less prevalent due to successful efforts of multilateral antipiracy initiatives, Chinese citizens and businesses in the Middle East and Africa are still threatened by it. Related to this concern regarding piracy, as China's economic footprint in the Middle East and sub-Saharan Africa grows, its leaders worry about the security of trade routes to these regions.[148]

Finally, China wants to protect its citizens and businesses against any local anti-Chinese backlash, which is particularly acute in sub-Saharan Africa. For example, there have been violent clashes between the local population and Chinese workers in Algeria, Iraq, and Angola.[149] Chinese citizens have been killed in Zambia,[150] Senegal,[151] and the Central African Republic.[152] These incidents often involve the murder of Chinese merchants or factory owners or riots against Chinese enclaves within these societies.

Another driver of the increased salience of the need to protect Chinese citizens and businesses is the role of public opinion in Chinese foreign policy decision making. According to interviewees for this project, public pressure on the central government to protect Chinese citizens and businesses abroad has been intensifying.[153] Although this study does not analyze in depth the role of public opinion, many interviewees have emphasized the rising impact of this factor, especially related to China in the Middle East and sub-Saharan Africa.

Protecting China's Sovereignty and Territorial Integrity from the United States

China's main interests in the Middle East and sub-Saharan Africa are promoting its own domestic economic growth, fostering support for it in the international arena, ensuring its internal stability, advocating for developing country causes, and safeguarding its citizens and businesses abroad. China also has a new interest in these regions: increasingly, the Middle East and sub-Saharan Africa are becoming regions important to China's protection of its sovereignty and territorial integrity from the United States. This emerging interest was a response to the US Obama-era Rebalance to Asia initiative in the early 2010s focused on strengthening US military, economic, and political relations and engagement across Asia-Pacific; increasing competition between the United States and China in Pacific Asia; tensions over territorial disputes in the South China and the East China Seas; and fears about neo-interventionist activities of the United States and other Western states in the Middle East and sub-Saharan Africa. As a result, China is strengthening relations with countries to its west, which include those in the Middle East and Africa. Chinese scholarly writings, government documents, and interview data collected for this book provide evidence of this linkage.

The first significant public articulation of the need for China to start to look west in reaction to souring relations with the United States in Pacific Asia occurred in 2012 when prominent Chinese international relations scholar

Wang Jisi, former dean of Beijing University's School of International Studies and a leading instructor at the Chinese Central Party School, argued in the *Global Times* that China should "march West" in reaction to a growing US threat in the Asia Pacific.[154] In his words, "China which is located at the center of the Asia-Pacific region should not confine its vision to its own coastal areas, its traditional competitors and partners. Instead, China should have a strategic plan of `looking westward' and `going westward.'"[155] Also, in reaction to New Silk Road initiative the United States announced in 2011 to integrate Central Asia and Afghanistan and enhance its potential as a transit area between East Asia and Europe, Wang Jisi stated, "The United States has already begun 'chess.'"[156] In 2015, Wang Jisi started to write more concretely about a March West grand strategy for China:[157] "It is time for China to reevaluate the 'East Asian' framework and redefine itself with reference to all of its border areas, thereby drawing closer to the heartland of Eurasia."[158] One of Wang's primary arguments for a March West strategy was that this approach could reduce tensions with the United States and Japan in Pacific Asia.[159]

Wang Jisi is a well-connected scholar within the Chinese political system. It is often hard to know whether his views help to shape Chinese leadership's thinking on foreign policy or whether his writing reflects foreign policy decisions leadership has already made. Either way, over the past several years, China has pursued a foreign policy approach to the West closely aligned with Wang's argument.

Other Chinese scholars contest the wisdom of Wang Jisi's views and China's focus on the West. For example, another prominent Chinese international relations scholar, Yan Xuetong, stresses that China should continue to focus on its immediate periphery rather than look west: "If China looks beyond its own neighborhood and puts its strategic resources into regions such as Europe, Africa, the Middle East and Latin America, it will only reap a limited harvest."[160]

One of the primary manifestations of this March West approach by the Chinese government is the Belt and Road Initiative (BRI), which includes the Middle East and sub-Saharan Africa, as well as Central Asia, South Asia, Europe, Latin America, and the Arctic. (Chapter 9 discusses China's BRI behavior in the Middle East and Africa.) Although Chinese government documents do not tend to articulate a direct linkage between the BRI's westward focus and rising tensions in Pacific Asia, the announcement of BRI in 2015 occurred in parallel with increasing Chinese rhetoric about rising tensions to its east. For example, "China's Military Strategy 2015" highlighted the PRC's concerns with the increasingly competitive dynamic within the rest of Asia and on its borders.[161]

Linkages between the US rebalance and China's approach to the Middle East and Africa first emerged in interviewing for this book in early 2013. Before that time, interviewees always stressed how China's compartmentalized relations with the Middle East and sub-Saharan Africa from the broader US-China relationship and that there was no linkage between US-China relations in one region and another. That dynamic has now changed. For example, as early as January 2013, there was so much interest in the potential impact of the US rebalance on China's relations with the Arab world that I was asked to present on the rebalance and the current state of US-China relations to a gathering of representatives of all member states of the League of Arab States in Beijing.

Over the past several years, interviewees have started to stress that China's BRI, including its enhanced relations with the Middle East and sub-Saharan Africa, is a direct response to the US rebalance and that BRI is a significant part of China's global strategy.[162] They emphasize that as the United States shifts east, China is going west to the Middle East and Africa to avoid future conflict with the United States.[163]

Interviewees often express views very similar to those of Wang Jisi.[164] They stress that to prevent conflict, China needs to find more opportunities for cooperation with the United States. In their view, the Middle East is a region where that cooperation could occur. One respondent argued that China is both an East Asia and a Eurasian power.[165] In that context, he said that the March West strategic approach challenges the United States to make a choice. Will the United States only stress tensions in East Asia, or will it embrace opportunities for cooperation? If the United States does not seize opportunities to cooperate in the Middle East, its intentions will be apparent, and China can react accordingly. In the mind of this scholar, the March West approach is a test for the United States.[166]

Some scholars have argued that although BRI and China's current approach to its West is a response to the US rebalance and China must consider itself opposed to the United States in the Middle East, China does not need to compete with the United States in that region.

Many interviewees indicated that in response to the US rebalance, China must balance to its west through its relations with the Middle East and sub-Saharan Africa.[167] Some asserted that China needs to support Russia's stance in Syria to strengthen China-Russia relations in response to America's efforts to internationalize US-China relations and incite countries in Asia against China through the rebalance.[168]

Often interviewees highlighted the importance of the Middle East in China's overall BRI. Several interviewees discussed the importance of the Middle East as a route to Europe through BRI.[169] Others argued that the Middle East is the end destination of BRI, and through this westward push, China is trying to establish a voice against the United States, and Middle East states are useful in this effort.[170]

Increasingly, China conceptualizes its approach to the Middle East and sub-Saharan Africa as part of a balancing strategy against the United States. As this competitive dynamic has developed, China wants to balance against the United States not only in Asia but also in countries that are part of its broader March West as operationalized through BRI. China sees itself as a Eurasian power with a need to balance its East and its West.[171] Therefore, its approach to these regions is now much more than economic; it is genuinely geostrategic.[172] Belt and Road, encompassing both the Middle East and sub-Saharan Africa, is now China's grand strategy,[173] and these regions are particularly relevant to that new strategy.[174]

American scholars have observed related dynamics. For example, Scobell and Harold highlight links between China's foreign policy assertiveness over the past several years and perceived threat from the United States in its actions in the rebalance to Asia.[175] Michael Swaine argues that BRI and China's recent focus on westward peripheral diplomacy is a direct response to the US rebalance.[176] Jon Alterman asserts that China is increasingly using relations with Iran as a way to balance against the United States in the Middle East because of Iran's strained relations with the United States.[177] Scobell and Nader argue that China now has a geostrategic interest in the Middle East and an actual Middle East strategy.[178] They do not agree that the Rebalance to Asia is a significant driver of that strategy, but they do argue that this strategy seeks to provide ways for China to break out of US encirclement. [179] (Chapter 9 discusses this topic in detail.)

One particular policy issue now linking Pacific Asia and the Middle East and sub-Saharan Africa is China's territorial claims in the South China and East China Seas. China wants support for its claims from countries in the Middle East and sub-Saharan Africa, an interest closely related to its desire to respond to the US rebalance to Asia.

Multiple interviewees mentioned China's desire to seek support for its stance on these territorial disputes from countries in the Middle East and sub-Saharan Africa.[180] One interviewee pointed out that China hates the internationalization of the South China Sea and East China Sea territorial disputes. Still, if the United States does choose to internationalize the issue, China will seek support for its position from Middle Eastern states.[181]

Chinese government publications have also highlighted this linkage. For example, *China's Foreign Affairs 2014* states, "The African side valued China's positions on issues related to its core interests such as the Diaoyu Islands and the South China Sea."[182] The 2016 China-Arab States Cooperation Forum Declaration first referred explicitly to the issue:

> Arab states support China and relevant countries to peacefully settle of territorial disputes and maritime issues using friendly consultations and negotiations through bilateral agreements and regional consensus; emphasize the need to respect the right of sovereign States and States parties to the United Nations Convention on the Law of the Sea to choose dispute settlement methods.[183]

The 2018 and 2020 CASCF declarations contain similar wording.[184]

Related to this interest is the emerging desire to have Russian support for China's claims in the South China Sea. China's cooperation with Russia in the Middle East, primarily related to Syrian intervention, is a way China is currying favor with Russia for support of China's territorial claims in the South China Sea.[185]

Another aspect of China's desire to protect its sovereignty from the United States and the rest of the West is its interest in preventing what it calls neo-interventionism. In the wake of the Arab awakening, China is concerned about the United States and other Western states using political upheaval in the Middle East as an excuse to insert themselves into political processes and forcibly pursue regime change. A turning point in China's thinking about this issue occurred with the 2011 NATO action against Libya that ultimately resulted in the execution of Muammar Gadaffi.[186] The level of foreign intervention in the Syrian civil war has reinforced these concerns.[187] Western internal meddling in countries in the Middle East after the Arab awakening has changed the way China looks at foreign power intervention.[188] Those developments forced it to reflect on its stance on intervention and the potential long-term impact on the Middle East and China.

Since the beginning of unrest with the Arab awakening, China has continuously harped on rising neo-interventionism and the need to more strictly interpret sovereignty to protect against that type of interference.[189] China does not want the West to shape the outcome of upheavals in the Middle East.[190] It also does not want Western countries to be encouraged to engage in forcible regime change and interfere in China's domestic politics.[191] In contrast to China's increasing receptivity to norms such as the responsibility to protect during the mid-2000s, Western actions in Libya and Syria caused China's desire to maintain a strict interpretation of sovereignty to harden.

The first *China's Foreign Affairs* after the beginning of the Arab awakening described threats of external influence in the Middle East as the United States and some European countries intervening in Libya, demanding Assad step down, and increasing sanctions on Iran.[192] *China's Foreign Affairs 2013* states that in West Asia and North Africa, "Major Western countries and emerging market economies contended frequently and fiercely with each other over the principle of non-interference in internal affairs and other important principles of international relations in addressing regional hotspot issues. The US and Europe continued their practice of 'neo-interventionism' in the region."[193]

China's concerns regarding neo-interventionism continue to the present day. (Chapters 4 and 5 discuss how China attempts to differentiate itself from interventionist powers.) China more explicitly speaks of neo-interventionism in the Middle East. This specific term is not often used to express concerns about foreign involvement in sub-Saharan Africa.

Conclusion

In the post–Cold War era, China is mostly a competitive and norm-divergent power in the functional areas of politics, economics, and foreign aid. The next six chapters analyze manifestations of that behavior and how it has escalated.

China's primary interests in the Middle East and sub-Saharan Africa are promoting its domestic economic growth, fostering support for it in the international arena, ensuring its domestic stability, advocating for developing country causes, safeguarding its citizens and businesses abroad, and protecting its territorial integrity and sovereignty from the United States. These interests shape the international order China is constructing and how it is building spheres of influence. They also provide insight into why and how China is competing with the United States in the Middle East and sub-Saharan Africa and how it differentiates itself from other great powers.

By far, China's most significant interest in the Middle East is promoting its economic development, an interest that is a direct result of its transition from economic communism to an export-oriented market economy in the late 1970s. This domestic change fundamentally shifted China's approach to the Middle East and sub-Saharan Africa. Rather than instability, China now promotes stability. This interest has also shifted its behavior from a primarily political and military focus to a heavy emphasis on economic interactions. Natural resources acquisition and export markets for Chinese goods and services are at the heart of this new interest. The Middle East and sub-Saharan Africa are vital regions from which to acquire needed resources. The Middle East possesses much of the world's energy products, and sub-Saharan Africa provides a broad array of resources required to fuel China's economic growth, including industrial minerals and agricultural products.

Although China's natural resource acquisition needs are a crucial component of its interests in promoting its economic development, its search for goods and services export markets in these regions is equally significant. Due to their level of economic development, these regions are important markets for a wide range of China's exports and services.

Related to China's interest in promoting its economic growth are its concerns about economic security and regional stability in the Middle East and sub-Saharan Africa. China is particularly worried about energy security in the Middle East. It views this region as a turbulent, US-dominated region that is a hotbed of great power and regional competition, especially after the United States invaded Iraq in 2003. These worries regarding stability are particularly acute in the post-Arab awakening environment. In contrast, China perceives sub-Saharan Africa as a relatively stable and growing region that does not pose major economic security threats to China.[194] China also does not portray sub-Saharan Africa as a continent plagued by great and regional power competition. Its concerns about instability there tend to center on domestic issues such as civil war, terrorism, and the spread of disease.

China's second most crucial interest in the Middle East and sub-Saharan Africa is fostering international support from these regions for China in an emerging multipolar or bipolar world order. Since the end of the Cold War, China has perceived an emerging multipolar order. Its proclamations regarding the inevitability of the trend toward multipolarity intensified after the 2008 global financial crisis. It envisions developing countries, including those in the Middle East and sub-Saharan Africa, as playing an increasingly important role in this new order. China considers the Middle East and sub-Saharan Africa to be important parts of the Global South. As a result, one of its significant interests in these regions is gaining political support through South-South cooperation.

China's third most important interest is ensuring its domestic stability. This interest does not include sub-Saharan Africa because China does not perceive that region to threaten its domestic stability. In contrast, China considers Middle Eastern Muslim extremist groups as a potential source of support for China's Muslim Uyghur separatists and other terrorism within China. Turkish support for the insurgency in Xinjiang, due to shared ethnic heritage with the Uyghurs, is a crucial concern. This domestic stability interest in the Middle East intensified after September 11, 2001, and became particularly acute after the Xinjiang riots and bloodshed in 2009. Due to this interest, China seeks support from Middle Eastern governments for its suppression of insurgency activities in Xinjiang to maintain its domestic stability. For the same reason, China wants to pursue counterterrorism efforts with Middle Eastern states to prevent the spread of transnational terrorist groups into Xinjiang and other parts of China. As China attempts to stamp out terrorism and insurgency in Xinjiang and throughout the country with crackdowns on religion and the extrajudicial incarceration of over 1 million Uyghurs, it increasingly seeks support from Middle Eastern states for its treatment of Muslims within its borders.

China's interests as a developing country also motivate its behavior in the Middle East and sub-Saharan Africa. Although China's behavior to support this interest has changed dramatically over time, the interest itself has remained constant since 1949. Because of this interest, in the post–Cold War era, China has consistently called for the establishment of a just and equitable new international economic and political order that better represents the needs of developing countries. During the Hu Jintao administration, China's self-identification as a developing country and calls for establishing this new order escalated. The 2008 global financial crisis also amplified demands for a new, more inclusive order. Although some of the verbiage regarding these issues has changed during the Xi administration, China continues to advocate for a just and equitable political and economic order. There are even some indications that China wants to serve as a model for other developing countries.

As China's footprint in the Middle East and sub-Saharan Africa has grown to support its domestic economic growth, it increasingly needs to safeguard its citizens and businesses in these regions. The primary threats to the individuals and organizations are terrorism, political instability, piracy, and anti-Chinese backlash against its citizens. China worries about these issues escalating with both the Arab awakening and the increasing pressure they receive from the Chinese population at home and abroad for protection.

Perceptions of external threats increasingly shape China's interests in these regions. In an era of growing great power competition, China now finds a need to protect its sovereignty from the West through its interactions with the Middle East and sub-Saharan Africa. Partially in response to the US rebalance to Asia and increasing tensions with the United States and Japan in Pacific Asia, it is pursuing a strategy to march west and strengthen its power as a Eurasian country. This competition is reinvigorating the role of these regions in China's global strategy. China wants to use its relations with countries in the Middle East and sub-Saharan Africa to balance against the United States. It wants support from these states as it asserts its territorial claims in South China and East China Seas. It also urges them to support the "one-China" principle in the international arena.

Another way in which China wants to protect its sovereignty from the United States is by pushing back against US and Western neo-interventionism in the Middle East. China has an interest in preventing Western meddling and intervention in these societies to uphold the norms of sovereignty and noninterference that China holds so dear to protect its internal political system. It pushes back on neo-interventionism and interference in these regions to preserve the norms protecting is own sovereignty from the U.S. and Western powers.

This chapter described the interests that shape China's post–Cold War behavior in the Middle East and sub-Saharan Africa. It answered the questions: What are China's post–Cold War interests in the Middle East and sub-Saharan Africa? How and why have those interests changed over time? How do those interests vary between the Middle East and sub-Saharan Africa? Since the beginning of the Arab awakening, how have China's interests in these regions changed? Is increasing competition between the United States and China in Pacific Asia affecting China's interests in the Middle East and sub-Saharan Africa?

Chapters 4 through 9 examine behavior resulting from China's interests to address the remaining questions of this book: Is China cooperating or competing with the United States in these regions? Is China's behavior converging with or diverging from liberal international norms? Is it building an alternate international order in these regions? If yes, what are the characteristics of that order? How does China portray and differentiate itself as a great power? How is it building spheres of influence? Ultimately, what does China's behavior in the Middle East and sub-Saharan Africa indicate about its rise globally?

CHAPTER 4

COMPETING WITH COOPERATION FORUMS?

The China–Arab States Cooperation Forum and the Forum on China-Africa Cooperation

China's primary post–Cold War interests in the Middle East and sub-Saharan Africa are to promote its domestic economic growth, foster support in the international arena, ensure its domestic stability, advocate for developing country causes, safeguard its citizens and businesses abroad, and protect its territorial integrity and sovereignty from the United States. To support all of these interests, China is building an institutional order to facilitate interaction with these regions. This chapter analyzes an element of that new institutional order: China's cooperation forums in the Middle East (the China-Arab States Cooperation Forum, CASCF) and Africa (the Forum on China-Africa Cooperation, FOCAC). It also briefly compares those two forums to China's longest established forum, the Shanghai Cooperation Organization (SCO).

The primary questions driving this chapter and the rest of the book are: Is China cooperating or competing with the United States in the Middle East and sub-Saharan Africa? Is its behavior converging with or diverging from liberal international norms? Is it building an alternative international order in these regions? If yes, what are the characteristics of that order? Ultimately, what does China's behavior in the Middle East and sub-Saharan Africa indicate about its rise globally? A comparison of FOCAC and CASCF over time generates essential insights about how China is competing in these regions and diverging from liberal international norms, how it is developing spheres of influence, and the specific characteristics of the alternative order it is constructing to manage its relations with the Global South. Due to the robust nature of these forums and their wide scope, including all functional areas of interactions, they provide insights into how China is designing regional institutions globally. China's activities in these forums also shed light on how it is portraying and differentiating itself from other great powers in these regions and globally.

Around the world, China has established cooperation forums with regional groups of countries. For example, in addition to FOCAC and CASCF, it has founded forums with Central Asia (2001), Portuguese-speaking states (2003), central and eastern Europe (2012), and Latin American and Caribbean states (2015).[1] Today, China's cooperation forums and similar mechanisms govern much of its relations with the developing world.[2]

Created in the early 2000s, the FOCAC and CASCF are China's primary multilateral coordination mechanisms with Middle Eastern and African countries. They are also significant because they are the first regional organizations established by China outside its territorial periphery. They therefore provide an opportunity to examine China's multilateral interaction with these two regions across a variety of functional areas over time. This examination offers rich content for analyzing China's behavior as a rising power toward these regions and the rest of the developing world. Also, Western scholarly analysis of these forums is limited, and analysis of these two forums in a comparative perspective is almost nonexistent.[3] This chapter strives to fill that empirical gap in the literature.

This chapter introduces China's cooperation forums with these regions and analyzes the similarities and differences between them across various functional areas and over time. The comparison is primarily based on official documents generated by the forums (declarations and action plans)[4] from 2000 to 2020 and interviews in China, the Middle East, and sub-Saharan Africa. Member countries held ministerial meetings for the FOCAC every three years: 2000, 2003, 2006, 2009, 2012, 2015, and 2018. The 2006, 2015, and 2018 meetings were summits that included most of the top leaders from African countries and China's President Xi. The rest of the FOCAC meetings were ministerial conferences. The CASCF meets every two years (2004, 2006, 2008, 2010, 2012, 2014, 2016, 2018, and 2020). To date, all of these meetings were at the ministerial level.

The meetings have produced a wealth of primary source data associated with these cooperation forums. Materials include official documents generated from the ministerial meetings of each of these cooperation forums, (e.g., communiqués, action plans, and declarations); speeches by high officials at the ministerial meetings; Chinese, Middle Eastern, and African news reporting associated with these ministerial meetings; scholarly work from China, the Middle East, and sub-Saharan Africa; and interviews with Chinese, Middle Eastern, and African government officials and scholars. Most of the chapter focuses on official documents from the forums to better understand agreements among members, how the institutions are designed, how activities of these organizations have changed over time, and how parties to these organizations officially portray their relations. This analysis produces deep insight into the institutional order China is building to facilitate its interactions with the Middle East and Africa.

The purpose of the chapter is to understand China's behavior in these forums and to categorize that behavior as competitive versus cooperative with the United States and norm divergent versus convergent with the liberal order by functional area.

Membership and Structure

Established in 2000, the FOCAC includes the entire continent of Africa, including North Africa. The current members are the PRC, fifty-three African nations that recognize the PRC, and the Commission of the African Union (AU). Only one African country is not a member of FOCAC, eSwatini (formerly Swaziland).[5] In North Africa, several states are members of both FOCAC and CASCF due to their affiliation with the Arab League. Those dual members are Algeria, Djibouti, Egypt, Libya, Mauritania, Morocco, Somalia, Sudan, and Tunisia.

In contrast with CASCF, in which the Arab League officially represents participating Arab states as a relatively unified body, the FOCAC does not have a central organizing body on the African side. The African Union did not even join as a member until 2012. As a result, each African state represents itself in the forum, and all activities are implemented bilaterally between China and the participating country. Increasingly, the African Union is playing a more official coordinating role in FOCAC. Previously Morocco was not a member of the AU, but it rejoined in 2017. In the past, Morocco's exclusion from the AU served as a barrier to a more coordinated approach from African states. Many African countries were hopeful that once the AU was more actively involved in the coordination of FOCAC, projects involving multiple countries in Africa would be prioritized in the organization.[6] There are already indications that the AU is now pursuing a more robust role in promoting regional projects in FOCAC. For example, in June 2020, the AU and FOCAC cohosted a summit on COVID-19.[7]

Chinese and African interviewees for this project claim China established FOCAC in response to the urging of African ambassadors in Beijing during the late 1990s.[8] Although the forum was supposedly initiated by African states, China has taken the lead throughout the life of the organization,. In addition to African pressure, according to interview respondents, China had its own reasons for wanting to establish a cooperation forum with these African states at that time. Some interviewees asserted that in the late 1990s, China observed other great powers and rising powers establishing cooperation mechanisms with Africa, spurring it to preemptively set up a mechanism to ensure future economic and political influence on the continent.[9] For example, two interviewees claimed that China wanted to counterbalance Japan's influence in Africa resulting from the Tokyo International Conference for African Development established in 1993.[10] Also, in the same time frame, the European Union (EU) was pursuing a formal cooperation mechanism with Africa and held its first EU-Africa summit in 2000. Interviewees noted that China wanted to counteract this rising EU influence.[11] Finally, some interviewees stated that China wished to counterbalance against emerging India-Africa and Turkey-Africa cooperation organizations.[12]

China established the CASCF in 2004. Interviewees claim that it created this forum at the urging of the League of Arab States (Arab League) and its members.[13] The Arab League represents its twenty-two members in this forum: Algeria, Bahrain, Comoros, Djibouti, Egypt, Iraq, Jordan, Kuwait, Lebanon, Libya, Mauritania, Morocco, Oman, Palestine,[14] Qatar, Saudi Arabia, Somalia, Sudan, Syria, Tunisia, United Arab Emirates, and Yemen. All of these states recognize the PRC rather than Taiwan. Due to coordination by the Arab League, in CASCF, the Arab states have the ability to negotiate actively for the inclusion of collective projects involving multiple Arab countries (e.g., railway projects, nuclear power projects, and Dead Sea initiatives).[15] This forum provides Arab states the opportunity to communicate with China with a unified voice.[16] That said, it is important to note that as of 2011, Libya and Syria were suspended from the Arab League though they still participate in CASCF. Post–Arab awakening developments, including differing views on the Syrian war and the embargo of Qatar, have significantly degraded the ability of the league to speak with a unified voice and coordinate among its members within the CASCF.

CASCF was the first cooperation forum between the Arab League and another country or region. Since CASCF was formed, the Arab League has established cooperation forums with other countries, including a grouping of South American nations (2005),[17] Turkey (2007),[18] Japan (2007),[19] Russia (2013),[20] and India (2016).[21] According to an Arab League official, CASCF inspired all of these forums.[22]

Political Cooperation

Both FOCAC and CASCF emphasize political cooperation between China and these regions. The foundational norms of political cooperation in the forums are China's Five Principles of Peaceful Coexistence and South-South cooperation.[23] China's second-most-important interest in the Middle East and sub-Saharan Africa is promoting international support for China in an emerging era of multipolarity. In different ways, China uses these forums to gain that support. Political cooperation in the forums also supports China's interests in ensuring its domestic stability, advocating for developing country causes, and protecting China's territorial integrity and sovereignty from the United States.

China's political behavior in these forums is competitive with the United States, because it established them excluding the United States. It uses them as a mechanism to promote South-South cooperation in opposition to the developed world and it leverages them to build influence in these regions. This book categorizes some of China's behavior in these forums as norm divergent from the liberal order and some as norm neutral.

China's Five Principles of Peaceful Coexistence (the Five Principles) are the core political norms advocated within these forums:[24]

- Mutual respect for territory and sovereignty
- Mutual nonaggression
- Mutual noninterference in internal affairs
- Equality and mutual benefit
- Peaceful coexistence

The Five Principles represent a very conservative interpretation of the Westphalian norms of sovereignty, territorial integrity, and noninterference. They diverge from norms of the Western liberal political order but converge with the Westphalian order. China has incorporated these principles in its interactions with the Middle East and sub-Saharan Africa since the 1955 Asian-African Conference in Bandung, Indonesia (Bandung).[25] At the conference, 29 nonaligned states from Asia, Africa, and the Middle East met to condemn colonialization, imperialism, and racism, as well as express reservations about the growing Cold War between the United States and the Soviet Union. At that conference, China advocated for the Five Principles as a basis for cooperation among the Bandung participants.

As opposed to the international liberal political order that focuses on promoting democracy, protecting human rights, and encouraging good governance in interacting with these countries, China explicitly vows to respect the sovereignty of and not interfere in the internal affairs of countries in these regions. There is an inherent tension between these Westphalian norms and liberal norms.

According to interviews for this book over a number of years, China's advocacy of the Five Principles distinguishes it from the United States and other great powers in the minds of many African and Arab elites. Interview respondents indicated that many states in these regions appreciate this normative stance. The three principles most important for these states are respect for sovereignty, mutual noninterference, and equality and mutual benefit.

Arguably, after the beginning of the Arab awakening and NATO intervention and regime change in Libya in 2011, China's advocacy for this strict interpretation of Westphalian norms intensified. One example where adherence to that principle has caused tensions within the CASCF is China's voting behavior in the UN Security Council about Syria (discussed in chapter 7). Although some Arab states criticized China over its stance on Syria, in general, the League of Arab States members continue to support China's advocacy for the Five Principles.

Although the two forums share a similar political cooperation basis (e.g., the Five Principles of Peaceful Coexistence and South-South Cooperation), their political emphasis is markedly different. Interview respondents from the Arab states and China frequently commented that CASCF is a more political organization than FOCAC.[26] By "more political," they mean more focused on international and regional political issues. The Egyptian Foreign Ministry even strongly asserted that CASCF was primarily a political cooperation forum between China and the Arab world.[27] Many Arab states see China as a great power that can assist them in amplifying their voice in the international community, especially in the UN Security Council.[28]

Because of heavy pressure from Arab states, the CASCF explicitly includes cooperation on key Arab political issues. The most prominent issue is the Middle East peace process targeted at resolving Arab-Israeli conflict, including the Palestinian-Israeli conflict and Syria's and Lebanon's territorial disputes with Israel[29] Even after the beginning of the Arab awakening, China's stance regarding the Arab-Israeli conflict including the Palestinian-Israeli conflict via the CASCF remained consistent.[30] What has changed is the fact that many other political issues have emerged in a post–Arab awakening environment. CASCF now highlights additional issues as part of political cooperation in CASCF, including the Syrian war, Iraq, Libya, Yemen, Sudan, and Somalia.[31] China's support for Arab causes in the CASCF is classified as competitive because it is supporting these causes in direct opposition to US support for Israel and US interventionist policies in Iraq and other countries in the region.

Starting at Bandung in 1955, particularly crucial to Arab states was China's first expression of support for the Palestinians.[32] In poignant language, Zhou Enlai declared at Bandung that "there was a parallel between the problems of Palestine and Formosa; neither could be solved peacefully unless intervention by outside forces was excluded; China was suffering from the same problem as the Arab countries."[33]

During the Mao era, China provided various types of support and training to Palestinian groups. Even after Mao's death, China provided support to the Palestinian Liberation Organization and the Popular Front for the Liberation of Palestine against Israel throughout the late 1970s and 1980s.[34]

For Arab states, the most critical aspect of political cooperation with China in the CASCF is support for the Palestinian people in the Middle East peace process. In the words of a Chinese scholar interviewed for this project, "To support Palestine is to support the Arab world."[35] In the founding declaration of the CASCF in 2004, the second principle of China-Arab cooperation after the Five Principles was "China stresses support for the Middle East peace process, land for peace principle and the Beirut Summit Arab Peace Initiative."[36] The 2004 CASCF action plan provided even more concrete details regarding the thrust of China-Arab cooperation on this issue, calling for strengthening the role of the UN in the peace process and establishing an independent state for the Palestinians.[37]

Throughout the development of the CASCF, Arab states urged China to strengthen its support for the Palestinians via the forum. The results of this lobbying are evident in the evolving text in forum documents over the years. The 2008 CASCF communiqué contained more assertive wording associated with the Middle East peace process. In addition to wording from the 2004 action plan, the 2008 CASCF declaration calls on Israel to end the occupation of lands occupied since 1967 and for the international community to lift the blockade on the Palestinians, improve the humanitarian situation in Gaza, and stop the construction of settlements.[38]

To the great pleasure of Arab states (and particularly Palestine), the wording of the 2010 CASCF communiqué further urged the international community to take action on the Middle East peace process in support of the Palestinians and for the first time explicitly referred to East Jerusalem:

> Israel should restore legitimate Arab rights by completely ending the occupation of Arab territories since 1967, including in East Jerusalem, to achieve a comprehensive, just and lasting peace in the Middle East . . . demands that Israel halt the construction of settlements in occupied Arab territories, including in East Jerusalem; . . . and demands that Israel cease all actions that exacerbate tensions in order to maintain regional stability and create favorable conditions to move the Middle East Peace Process forward.[39]

Speaking about this wording, a Palestinian embassy official in Beijing commented that China's position on the conflict was more evident than before in support of the Palestinians due to the inclusion of wording addressing the issue of Israeli settlements in East Jerusalem.[40] According to this official, at the 2010 forum, all Arab states united in their views about the status of East Jerusalem. They made their position clear to China, which resulted in the inclusion of this wording.[41] A scholar from Kuwait University also noted that inclusion of the East Jerusalem wording in the communiqué created a significant controversy at the 2010 forum due to Chinese concern over the text. Still, ultimately the parties agreed to retain the verbiage.[42]

The 2012 CASCF continued to stress the same stance on the Palestinian-Israeli conflict.[43] One new addition to the text of the declaration was support for Palestine to become a full member of the United Nations and UNESCO. It also declared support for the 2011 Palestinian National Reconciliation agreement between Fatah and Hamas and called on Israel to release Palestinian detainees and improve living conditions for all Palestinians.[44] CASCF's 2014 declaration highlighted Israel's illegal actions in East Jerusalem and further welcomed Palestine to join international treaties and organizations.[45] The 2016 declaration stressed support for specific Arab leaders who were standing up for Palestinian rights in Jerusalem.[46]

The 2018 CASCF declaration continued to emphasize the violation of Palestinian rights and called on all states to implement UN Security Council Resolution 2334 (2016), which " condemn[s] all measures aimed at altering the demographic composition, character and status of the Palestinian Territory occupied since 1967, including East Jerusalem," including settlements, transfers of Israeli settlers, demolishing homes, and displacing Palestinian civilians.[47] It also welcomed UN General Assembly Resolution A/RES/ES-10/20 (2018) on the protection of Palestinian civilians.

The 2018 declaration explicitly criticized the United States for moving its embassy to Jerusalem. It stated that CASCF members strongly oppose recognizing Jerusalem as the capital of Israel and that relocating the embassy set a dangerous precedent and violated international law.[48] The 2018 declaration also expressed appreciation for President Xi Jinping's 2017 "four-point proposition" on promoting the settlement of the Palestinian issue and China's efforts to promote the Middle East peace process.[49] Finally, the 2020 CASCF declaration expressed support for the peace plan proposed by Palestinian president Mahmoud Abbas at the UN Security Council.[50]

Another aspect of China's support for Arab stances on the Middle East peace process is CASCF statements about issues related to Syria's and Lebanon's tensions with Israel over territorial disputes. In 2008 and 2010, China expressed its support for Syria to recover the occupied Golan Heights.[51] In the same years, CASCF documents added text about conflicts between Lebanon and Israel that began in 2006. The 2008 declaration emphasized solidarity with Lebanon as well as political and economic support.[52] In the 2010 CASCF communiqué, member states called for implementing UN Security Council resolutions regarding occupied territory in southern Lebanon.[53] Emphasis on Syria's claims against Israel continued through 2014; then Syrian comments shifted to the Syrian civil war. Through 2020, CASCF documents continued to express support for Lebanon[54] and Syria[55] in territorial claims related to Israel.

Although China also has strong and growing relations with Israel, interview respondents appear to believe that China supports the Arab side of the Arab-Israeli conflict, including the Palestinian-Israeli conflict.[56] For example, a former African Union official commented that China had assured the Arab world of its support for the Palestinians.[57] A Palestinian embassy official in Beijing declared, "China has good relations with Israel, but this did not change the hearts of China toward the Palestinian issue. China's position has not changed since 1967, but it has become clearer and clearer."[58]

In CASCF, China's support for the Middle East peace process is categorized as competitive but norm convergent. It is competitive because it is in direct opposition to strong US support for Israel in the peace process and it is norm convergent with the liberal order because it urges all parties to abide by UN resolutions about the issues and encourages multilateral mechanisms to facilitate peace.

China's political support for the Arab states' objectives in the Middle East peace process is by far the most crucial aspect of its political backing for states in the CASCF. That said, as the forum evolved, its scope broadened to include other Arab causes. In 2006, CASCF documents began to stress support for Iraq's sovereignty and independence.[59] Documents from meetings from 2008 to 2020 included similar statements.[60] The forum also started calling for respect for Sudan's and Somalia's national unity and sovereignty in 2006, 2008, and 2010.[61]

After the beginning of the Arab awakening in 2011, the political issues discussed in the CASCF declarations proliferated. The Palestinian- Israeli conflict was still clearly the political priority, but other subjects also became prominent. For example, in 2012, the documents started strongly reiterating the need to respect the sovereignty of all Arab countries and practice noninterference in internal affairs.[62] Declarations continued to express concerns about the protection of Iraq, Sudan, and Somalia's sovereignty. Still, with the Arab awakening and the NATO-led campaign against Libya, even more countries were experiencing internal upheavals, and the documents highlight external interventions. Documents from 2012 to 2020 highlighted the need to protect Libya's unity, sovereignty, and independence. Other hot spots frequently discussed include the United Arab Emirates' maritime territorial disputes with Iran, the need to safeguard Comoros's sovereignty, and political reforms in Tunisia and Egypt.

Since 2011, the three most important political issues discussed in the CASCF documents after the Palestinian-Israeli conflict have been the Syrian war, the Yemen war, and Iran's relations with the Arab world. In the 2012 CASCF, documents started including pointed statements about the Syrian conflict. The 2012 declaration said China attached importance to the role played by the Arab League in facilitating a political solution for the war in Syria. Both sides stressed that Syria suffered from external interference and its sovereignty should be respected. The statement also condemned massacres and attacks against Syrian civilians. Finally, the declaration encouraged China to play a more significant role in solving the Syria crisis.[63]

According to interview respondents, because of China's stance on Syria and vetoes in the UN Security Council, some Arab states were reluctant to have closer relations with China at the 2012 CASCF.[64] In particular, Gulf Cooperation Council (GCC) countries were more critical of China at the 2012 CASCF compared to those in transition, such as Egypt, Tunisia, and Libya.[65] The same interviewees asserted that was the reason attendance at the 2012 forum was lower than in past meetings. Other interviewees indicated that despite disagreement between the Arab states and China over Syria and China's approach to the Middle East after the Arab awakening more broadly, Arab states understand there is a difference between China and Russia over Syria. Many Arab states respect China's explanation of its desire to advocate for noninterference and stability. As a result, those officials and scholars argued that the Syrian issue had not substantially affected China's cooperation with Arab states at the 2012 CASCF.[66]

According to CASCF participants, several Arab states attempted to pressure China into including a strongly worded statement about Syria in the 2014 CASCF declaration. Still, Arab states increasingly understood China's position about the Five Principles.[67] After 2014, CASCF participant criticism of China over Syria decreased.[68] In 2016 and 2018, declaration documents condemned the use of chemical weapons in Syria. They also urged states to accept Syrian refugees and provide more support for Arab countries that had already welcomed refugees from the conflict.[69]

Discussion of Yemen became pronounced after war broke out in 2015. The CASCF 2016 declaration called for respect for Yemen's unity and territorial integrity and called on states to oppose interference in Yemen's internal affairs.[70] In 2018, CASCF documents stressed the dire humanitarian, health, and education situation in Yemen and called for more humanitarian and medical assistance for the Yemeni people.[71]

Finally, CASCF documents in 2016 explicitly mentioned Iran for the first time. The declaration emphasized that "partnership between the Arab countries and the Islamic Republic of Iran should follow the principle of good-neighborliness, non-interference in internal affairs, respect for national independence, sovereignty and territorial integrity, according to the UN Charter and principles of international law, to resolve their differences through peaceful means, do not use force or threat of force." It also condemned the 2016 attack on Saudi Arabia's embassy in Tehran.[72] The 2018 and 2020 declarations again called for neighborly and peaceful relations between the Arab states and Iran.[73]

On Arab causes outside the Middle East peace process, China's behavior is competitive and norm divergent from the liberal order. China is taking a stand for sovereignty and territorial integrity in the Middle East against US interference and interventions. This strict interpretation of sovereignty is in direct tension with the liberal order and diverges from it.

China also has its own political objectives in fostering political support through the CASCF. As discussed in chapter 3, one of China's interests is to maintain its domestic stability by preventing insurgency activities in Xinjiang and acts of terrorism anywhere in China. China uses the CASCF to solicit support for its suppression of Muslim insurgency activities, especially after the 2009 Xinjiang riots. The text of the 2010 CASCF communiqué reflects these concerns: "[The Arab states are] against religious extremist forces or ethnic separatist forces engaged in terrorism or anti-China separatist activities."[74] Interview respondents also stressed China's desire for support of insurgency suppression activities in Xinjiang through the CASCF.[75]

After the beginning of the Arab awakening, CASCF continued to express support for China's efforts against extremism and insurgency and called on members of the forum to strengthen counterterrorism efforts through bilateral and multilateral mechanisms.[76] Despite the massive crackdown in Xinjiang and the incarceration of hundreds of thousands of Uyghurs in Xinjiang starting in 2017, Arab states continued to include wording in the 2018 CASCF declaration supporting China's efforts against "religious extremist forces, ethnic separatist forces, and violent terrorist forces engaged in anti-China separatist activities."[77] The 2020 declaration expressed support for China's preventive counterterrorism measures and deradicalization efforts. It also stated that the "two sides emphasized that they have made important efforts to care of ethnic minorities" and extended an invitation to delegations for the Arab League and member states to visit the Chinese province of Xinjiang.[78]

China's pursuit of support from Arab states for its suppression of domestic insurgency activities is categorized as norm divergent from the liberal order because it is promoting one of the Five Principles: mutual noninterference in the internal affairs of other countries. This stance is in opposition to liberal norms of the promotion and protection of human rights and responsibility to protect.

Since the beginning of the Arab awakening, it appears that political cooperation between China and the Arab states in CASCF continued to strengthen despite criticism of China over its stance on Syria. Perhaps the most significant change in relations between China and CASCF members is that priorities within the Arab League have changed.[79] Some of the root causes of those changes include domestic upheavals and leadership changes within countries in the region, a more profound desire for protection of the sovereignty of states, and emerging competition between regional powers, including Saudi Arabia, the UAE, Qatar, Iran, and Turkey. There are many disagreements within the league about issues such as Libya, Syria, and Iran.[80] Those shifts are evident in the issues emphasized in the forum before and after the Arab awakening. Although there is text about Iran in the 2016–2020 CASCF documents, according to CASCF participants, China does not want to be drawn into disagreements between the League of Arab States and Iran.[81] The Arab League's internal discord is making it harder for the organization to speak with a unified voice on behalf of its members.

In contrast with CASCF's emphasis on political support for Arab causes in the Middle East, FOCAC focuses less on specific political issues in and between African countries. For example, the CASCF deals with country-specific issues such as the Palestinian-Israeli conflict, the Arab-Israeli conflict, the Syrian war, and Sudan, while FOCAC addresses broader political stances related to Africa. Most of the political cooperation language in FOCAC documents highlights the need for South-South cooperation and China's support for the developing world. China's interests as a developing country to build a just and equitable new international political and economic order significantly influence its behavior toward Africa and the rest of the developing world.

China's promotion of South-South cooperation and advocacy for developing countries' rights is categorized as competitive and norm convergent. It is conducted in direct opposition to the developed countries of the world and advocates for substantial changes to the existing liberal international order to represent the needs of developing countries better. That said, this behavior is categorized as competitive but norm convergent because the change China is seeking is inside the liberal order. China is not attempting to overthrow the current system, but it seeks significant changes in the existing order.

Since its founding, beginning with the initial Beijing Declaration of the Forum on China-Africa Cooperation in 2000, FOCAC documents have strongly emphasized support for the developing countries in Africa. China calls for more robust representation of Africa's developing countries in the political and economic international order, including the UN Security Council and international economic and financial institutions, and the need for South-South cooperation to achieve that goal.[82]

The action plan of the inaugural 2000 forum provided further elaboration on specific methods for South-South cooperation. It asserted, "China and African countries should position themselves to influence the establishment of a new world order which will reflect their needs and interests." Specifically, it stated that FOCAC countries should strengthen cooperation in the UN, the UN Conference on Trade and Development, and WTO; coordinate positions to increase "collective bargaining capacity of developing countries"; and reform the UN and UN Security Council to be geographically representative.[83]

This emphasis on South-South cooperation and providing a voice for developing states in the international system continued through the 2000s. The 2006 FOCAC summit declaration further urged developed countries to increase official development assistance (ODA) and stand by commitments to developing countries.[84] In the wake of the global financial crisis, calls for the need for South-South cooperation increased in the 2009 FOCAC action plan.[85] FOCAC's 2009 documents started to highlight the need for "reform of the international financial system to ensure its development in a fair, just, inclusive and orderly manner, and for increasing the representation and voice of developing countries therein."[86] It also started to mention support for the Doha round of WTO negotiations specifically.

Finally, FOCAC documents from 2012 to 2018 continued to stress the need for South-South cooperation in an era of emerging multipolarity. They include calls for increased representation of the developing world on the UN Security Council, support for the Doha round of the WTO, increased Global South representation in the international financial order including the Bretton Woods system and the BRICS New Development Bank, and a focus on emphasizing the G20 and G77 that have a particular emphasis on the interests of developing countries.[87] The 2018 documents heavily stressed the importance of BRI in South-South cooperation.[88]

Interview respondents also highlighted the importance of South-South cooperation in FOCAC. Chinese scholars often emphasized China's cooperation with African states to oppose US hegemony and establish a fairer international order.[89] These scholars stressed that China provided a voice for developing countries in the international arena.[90] African scholars also highlighted the importance of this South-South cooperation in FOCAC. For example, one South African scholar from the University of London's School of Oriental and African Studies (SOAS) argued that China is using South-South cooperation in FOCAC to position itself as the leader of the developing world and reshape the international system.[91] A scholar with Stellenbosch University's Centre for Chinese Studies stated that FOCAC was a mechanism for China to conduct South-South counterbalancing in a multipolar world order. He argued that within Africa, China is perceived to be defending Africa's interests in the international system.[92] Interview respondents highlighted the fact that China's South-South cooperation with Africa provided African countries an opportunity to balance against the West.[93] China now offered an alternative to the West, and African countries no longer needed to be dependent on developed countries.[94]

Compared to FOCAC, the CASCF does not focus as much on South-South cooperation. That said, in the wake of the 2008 global financial crisis, there did appear to be an emerging emphasis on this issue in that forum as well.[95] The 2010 CASCF Communiqué demonstrated that new development.[96] The 2012 CASCF declaration continued to call for a new international economic and political order that better represented the needs of developing countries, including China and Arab states. It specifically called for a strengthening of oversight of the International Monetary Fund and urged states to resist all forms of protectionism and complete the WTO Doha round as soon as possible.[97] It also called for reform of the UN Security Council with more representation for the Arab states and the developing world.[98] The 2014 and 2016 CASCF declarations continued to call for UN reform, and the 2016 statement explicitly called for more action on the Security Council about the treatment of Palestinians.[99] The 2018 declaration again emphasized South-South cooperation between China and Arab states in the WTO and the United Nations and[100] encouraged Arab states to join the WTO. It also started to highlight the role of BRI in South-South cooperation between China and the Arab World via the CASCF.[101] The 2020 declaration continued to stress the importance of BRI in China-Arab cooperation.

These calls for South-South cooperation in the forums are competitive and norm convergent. The behavior is competitive due to how China frames the struggle between the developing countries and the developed countries, including the United States. That said, all of the changes China seeks in the international order via the cooperation forums appear to call for greater representation and voice in existing liberal institutions. China is seeking change inside the order, but this behavior is convergent with the liberal order.

There are two relatively new developments in China's political cooperation in the forums. One is China's territorial disputes in the South China Sea, and the other is BRI.

China increasingly has a desire to protect its territorial integrity and sovereignty from the United States by soliciting support from states in the Middle East and sub-Saharan Africa. One clear example of this type of behavior was the first inclusion of wording in the 2016 CASCF supporting China's position on territorial disputes in the South China Sea: "Arab states support China and relevant countries to peacefully settle of territorial disputes and maritime issues using friendly consultations and negotiations through bilateral agreements and regional consensus; emphasize the need to respect the right of sovereign States and States parties to the United Nations Convention on the Law of the Sea to choose dispute settlement methods."[102]

Press releases from CASCF in 2016 also started emphasizing the need for forum members to support China's stance on this issue. For example, Xinhua News Agency reported that China's special envoy for the Middle East stated, "It is praiseworthy that Arab League Secretary-General Nabil al-Araby, some Arab countries and the Doha statement confirmed their support for China's stance on the South China Sea issue."[103] The same report noted, "Top diplomats from Algeria, Comoros, Lebanon, Qatar, Saudi Arabia, Sudan, and Yemen, in their separate meetings with Wang on the sidelines of the China-Arab forum, expressed their support for China's position on the South China Sea issue, stressing that related disputes should be solved through negotiations."

The 2018 and 2020 CASCF declarations' wording is almost the same as that on UN Convention on the Law of the Sea (UNCLOS) in the 2016 declaration.[104] UNCLOS and South China Sea are not explicitly mentioned in FOCAC documents. Since China's South China Sea disputes are part of its overall competition with the United States for regional hegemony in Asia, this behavior in the CASCF is categorized as competitive. That said, since there is no particularly relevant norm of the liberal order for which this behavior converges or diverges, this book characterizes this behavior as norm neutral.

Another recent example of China's efforts to protect its territorial integrity from the United States and the rest of the West is seen in the 2020 CASCF declaration, which expresses Arab states' support for China's activities in Hong

Kong—"The Arab countries support China's position on the Hong Kong issue, support China's efforts to maintain national security under the framework of 'one country, two systems'—and opposes interference in internal affairs."[105] The joint statement from the June 2020 PRC-AU-FOCAC summit on solidarity against COVID contains similar wording about FOCAC's support for China on this issue: "The African side supports China's position on Taiwan and Hong Kong, and supports China efforts to safeguard national security in Hong Kong in accordance with law."[106]

China's pursuit of support from Arab and African states for its behavior in Hong Kong through cooperation forums is categorized as norm divergent from the liberal order because it is promoting one of the Five Principles (mutual noninterference in the internal affairs of other countries) and actively dismantling liberal institutions associated with democracy, freedom of the press, freedom of speech, and freedom of assembly in Hong Kong.

The other new emphasis of political cooperation in the forums is the Belt and Road Initiative (BRI). Documents now frame the cooperation forums as falling under the BRI. The 2018 FOCAC declaration states that members "agree to make the Forum a major platform for China-Africa cooperation under the Belt and Road Initiative.[107] The 2018 CASCF issued a separate declaration, specifically discussing Arab-China cooperation under the BRI.[108] The emphasis on BRI continues in 2020 CASCF documents.[109] China's push for BRI in Africa and the Middle East is part of a broader competition for global influence with the United States and an attempt for China to solidify South-South cooperation and build a sphere of influence in these regions. The BRI is also norm divergent in the political realm due to its focus on the Five Principles as opposed to the Western liberal political and economic order. As a result, this political behavior in the cooperation forums supporting the BRI is also categorized as competitive and norm divergent.

China's political behavior in the forums is competitive through establishing regional organizations that exclude the United States and other great powers; promoting South-South cooperation in opposition to the developed world, led by the United States; and the building of spheres of influence, especially via the BRI. In recent years, CASCF has also been competitive in soliciting support from the Arab states for China's position in the South China Sea. China's behavior is norm divergent from the liberal order through its promotion of an alternative normative order of interaction between states through the Five Principles, support for Arab calls for protection of sovereignty, encouraging Arab states to ignore its human rights abuses in Xinjiang, soliciting support for Arab states for its behavior in Hong Kong, and promotion of the Five Principles via the BRI. It is norm convergent in its push for greater representation and voice for developing countries in the current liberal order and its encouragement of the use of the UN and multilateral mechanisms to pursue Middle East peace. Finally, it is norm neutral in encouraging states to recognize jurisdictional interpretations in relation to the South China Sea.

Economic Cooperation

Economic cooperation activities in FOCAC and CASCF also reflect China's competitive behavior. Sometimes that competition is norm divergent, sometimes convergent. In the economic realm, China competes inside and outside the current international order.

China's most significant interests in the Middle East and sub-Saharan Africa are promoting its domestic economic growth by acquiring resources, developing markets, and ensuring stability in these regions. FOCAC and CASCF are the primary multilateral mechanisms through which China coordinates economic activities with these regions to support those interests. The main areas of economic cooperation in these forums are trade, investment, finance, infrastructure, economic security, and BRI. Economic cooperation also supports other Chinese interests, including fostering international support in a multipolar world through South-South cooperation and advocating for developing country causes. China's economic behavior is categorized as competitive and primarily norm divergent. China is competing in these regions by establishing cooperation mechanisms excluding the United States and all other great powers and providing significant state support for these economic activities tied to political support in these forums. China's provision of state support and financing for these economic activities is norm divergent from the liberal economic international order that promotes free market capitalism without active state intervention. That said, certain aspects of its economic cooperation under the forum is competitive but norm convergent—for example, some aspects of trade, financing, and aid.

Trade

Although both forums provide Chinese state support for trade, there are some significant differences in approach between the two regions. The first notable difference in economic cooperation is how China treats trade with African countries. Trade promotion is a high priority in FOCAC and CASCF. China's actions in FOCAC promote exports from least developed countries (LDCs) in Africa to improve their economic situation.[110] This behavior is very much in alignment with China's political pledges to promote the needs of developing countries through South-South cooperation. In the original 2000 FOCAC action plan, China encouraged its enterprises to give preference to the importation of African products.[111] The FOCAC 2003 action plan announced that China would "grant zero-tariff treatment to some commodities of African LDCs for access to [the] Chinese market. The Chinese side will, starting from 2004, negotiate lists of tariff-free goods and the rules of origin with the countries concerned on a bilateral basis."[112] According to FOCAC documents, as of the end of 2004, "substantive progress has been made in the exemption of tariffs for certain commodities exported from 28 least developed African countries that have diplomatic relations with China."[113] In 2006, China pledged to open its markets to African countries further and to increase from 190 to over 440 the number of African products from LDCs eligible for tariff-free treatment.[114] Effective July 1, 2007, in alignment with these FOCAC pledges, China implemented tariff-free treatment of 478 commodities for thirty-one of Africa's LDCs.[115] In 2009 it announced that it would grant tariff exemption treatment to 95 percent of exports from Africa's LDCs. The first phase of this initiative was to provide tariff-free treatment for 60 percent of products originating from these countries in 2010.[116] Starting in 2012, China announced plans for zero-tariff treatment of products under 97 percent of all tariff items for LDC countries recognizing the PRC.[117] The 2019–2021 FOCAC action plan asserted that China was still working toward the 97 percent goal and declared, "China supports Africa in boosting its export and has decided to increase imports, particularly non-resource products, from Africa, with a focus on value added agricultural produce and industrial products" and planned to establish a $5 billion special fund for financing imports from Africa.[118] In the CASCF, Yemen is the only LDC, and CASCF documents do not include mention of tariff exemptions.

China's trade treatment of LDCs via the cooperation forums is convergent with the liberal norms of the international system. Since the early 2000s, the international community has encouraged industrialized countries to provide duty-free trade with LDCs, and today, many developed and developing countries offer preferential trade terms to LDCs. Notable examples include the EU's Anything But Arms program, the US African Growth Opportunity Act, the Canada Least Developed Country Tariff, and programs by Japan, China, Chile, Brazil, India, South Korea, Thailand, and Turkey.[119]

The CASCF also actively advocates for improving trade relations between Arab states and China. In the area of trade, CASCF documents often stress the desire of both parties to complete negotiations on the China-GCC free trade agreement and the China-Palestine free trade agreement. FOCAC documents express an interest in exploring cooperation between China and the African Continental Free Trade Area (AfCFTA).[120] (China's FTAs are discussed further in chapter 6 on economic relations.) This behavior is norm convergent because it converges with norms of the liberal order encouraging free trade and the use of international institutions to facilitate cooperation among states. Regional FTAs are allowed under the WTO and do not conflict with the liberal order.

The CASCF also describes the establishment of a bilateral and collective trade dispute mechanism between China and the Arab states to facilitate trade cooperation. Those mechanisms would also be norm convergent with the liberal order.

Investment and Financing

Another significant aspect of economic cooperation in FOCAC and CASCF is investment and financing. Overall, China pledges much more state support and funding via FOCAC to encourage Chinese companies to invest in Africa compared to the Middle East. The first FOCAC action plan in 2000 stated that the "Chinese side will set aside special funds to support and encourage investment by well-established Chinese enterprises in African countries to set up joint equity or co-operation projects adapted to local need in terms of job creation and transfer of technologies."[121] The 2003 documents continued to state that China would encourage its enterprises (regardless of ownership) to invest in Africa.[122]

At the FOCAC Beijing Summit in 2006, China announced that it would take more concrete steps to encourage Chinese company investment in Africa through the formation of the China Africa Development Fund (CAD) with future funding of US$5 billion.[123] CAD is a Chinese private equity fund solely funded by the China Development Bank, a Chinese government policy bank. China launched the fund in 2007 with initial funding of $1 billion.[124] In the 2009 FOCAC ministerial meeting, China committed $3 billion to expand the CAD.[125] China announced its plan to expand the CAD to $10 billion in 2015.[126]

In 2010, China announced support for Chinese financial institutions to establish a loan of US$1 billion for African small and medium enterprise (SME) development to help the growth of those enterprises.[127] In 2015, it declared it would set up a China-Africa production capacity cooperation fund with an initial pledge of $10 billion.[128] In 2018 plans, China also committed to increasing its stock of FDI in Africa to $100 billion by 2020 (up from $32 billion in 2014)[129] and further expand loans to support SMEs in Africa from $1 billion to $6 billion.[130] In the 2019–2021 FOCAC plan, China committed to extend $20 billion of credit lines and to set up a $10 billion special fund for development financing. That action plan also stated that China would encourage its companies to make at least $10 billion investment in Africa over three years,[131] and China's policy banks[132] and financial institutions to continue to increase support for China-Africa industrial capacity cooperation.[133] China also encouraged its financial institutions to set up branches in Africa[134] and advocated for renminbi settlement of financial transactions in Africa as well as the holding of RMB by African countries as a reserve currency.[135]

Over the years, in FOCAC, both sides have pledged to increase cooperation with financial institutions providing development funds to African countries, such as the African Development Bank Group (AfDB), the Eastern and Southern African Trade and Development Bank, Asian Infrastructure Investment Bank (AIIB), Silk Road Fund, the New Development Bank, and the World Bank.[136]

FOCAC stresses financial cooperation in many ways discussed above. CASCF documentation did not mention financial cooperation until 2008, and in the context of cooperation with the Arab world, it is framed broadly.[137] Although CASCF documents encourage investment (from China to the Arab states and vice versa), CASCF has established no funding mechanisms similar to CAD or special loans to SMEs. That said, the 2018 CASCF action plan announced that under the Belt and Road, China and the Arab states would explore ways to deepen financial cooperation. The China Development Bank and relevant Arab banks would establish a China-Arab Association of Banks to explore the joint provision of financial services for the construction of major China-Arab projects.[138] They would also continue to strengthen cooperation under the Asian Infrastructure Investment Bank (AIIB)[139] and encourage the utilization of funding from China's policy banks.[140] CASCF 2018 documents indicated that China had set up a loan of $15 billion to support industrialization in the Middle East and $10 billion in concessional loans to support BRI projects in the region.[141]

China's bilateral investment and financing within FOCAC and CASCF is competitive and norm divergent from the liberal order. China provides substantial state support and financing through bilateral means to encourage investment and development in Africa through the China Africa Development Fund (CAD), the Silk Road Fund, policy banks, and encouraging financing for SMEs and to develop industrial capacity. Due to heavy state involvement and unilateral financing, this behavior challenges the norms of limited state economic involvement in the international liberal economic order. The CAD, Silk Road Fund, and other bilateral funding from policy banks are important components of the economic order China is building to interact with the Middle East and sub-Saharan Africa. Bilateral and multilateral investment and financing committed in FOCAC and CASCF are competitive with the United States and contribute to China's building of spheres of influence in these regions. That said, China's financing cooperation with AfDB, the World Bank, and other multilateral organizations is more norm convergent with the liberal economic order due to their utilization of international institutions that adhere to liberal norms.

Another difference between FOCAC and CASCF in the area of investment is the establishment of special economic zones (SEZs). As early as 2003, China committed to assisting FOCAC countries with the formation and management of SEZs.[142] In 2006, FOCAC announced that China was ready to encourage well-established Chinese companies to set up three to five SEZs in African countries between 2006 and 2009.[143] As of 2010, according to FOCAC documents, China established six zones in Zambia, Mauritius, Nigeria (two), Egypt, and Ethiopia, and the Chinese government was encouraging its companies to bring their operations to these zones.[144] In 2013, China announced one planned CASCF SEZ in Mauritania.[145] (China's special economic zones in these regions are discussed much more in chapter 6.) Chinese companies are responsible for the construction of all of the zones and are encouraged (together with other foreign enterprises) to form industrial clusters in the SEZs.[146]

SEZs are yet another way in which China is building spheres of influence in these regions. They are competitive but norm neutral. They align with the expectation for developed economies to share their development experiences with developing countries, but there is no specific liberal norm against which to gauge China's behavior.

Infrastructure

Another major area of economic cooperation in FOCAC and CASCF is infrastructure construction. In FOCAC, the Chinese state is heavily involved in supporting infrastructure development. The forum ties infrastructure to promoting the development of African countries.[147] In FOCAC's first action plan in 2000, China offered to assist African countries in infrastructure development by "consider[ing] accepting various forms of payment such as payment in kind, to ease African countries' financial burden and help increase their export to China."[148] In 2003, infrastructure development rose even higher in priority. The action plan committed to "place infrastructure development on top of [the] China-Africa cooperation agenda and actively explore diversified forms of mutually beneficial cooperation."[149] In particular, it wanted to fund infrastructure projects that reduced the negative impact of lack of sea access for landlocked countries and encourage firms to take a more active role in infrastructure projects focused on transportation, telecommunications, energy, water supply, and electricity.

The 2006 action plan had a similar focus.[150] The 2009 action plan provided even more detailed information regarding Chinese state support for infrastructure development in Africa. In that plan, the two sides committed to supporting projects that promote regional integration and to provide $10 billion in preferential loans to African countries to support infrastructure and social development projects.[151]

Extraordinary emphasis on infrastructure in FOCAC continued through the 2012 and 2015 ministerial meetings and the 2018 summit.[152] The 2015 action plan included extensive discussion of infrastructure development, including efforts to build railroads, highways, aviation networks, ports, electricity, power projects, and communications projects, and to establish five universities specializing in transportation infrastructure–related fields including engineering and architecture throughout Africa.[153] The 2015 plan also included $35 billion in concessional loans.[154] The scope of infrastructure projects expanded in the 2019–2021 FOCAC action plan to include aviation and information and communication technology (e.g., cloud computing, big data, and mobile Internet).

In contrast with FOCAC's heavy emphasis on infrastructure, CASCF infrastructure cooperation is less significant. The 2004 CASCF action plan states, "The two sides agreed to encourage their enterprises to participate in contracting projects, especially infrastructure projects. We welcome willing companies from both sides (Chinese and Arab) to provide necessary support and facilities for infrastructure construction in various fields."[155]

Compared to FOCAC's focus on infrastructure development related to foreign aid provision and concessional loans, Arab states are treated as equal partners in CASCF. Two-way infrastructure development is encouraged. CASCF does not publicize state financing for these projects.[156] In 2014, the CASCF began to emphasize infrastructure cooperation more.[157] The 2018–2020 CASCF action plan pledged to strengthen cooperation in ports, maritime administration divisions, airports, land transport stations, logistics centers, railway management, highway, energy, electricity, telecommunications, and water.[158] In 2018, as part of the CASCF, China and the Arab states signed the Declaration of Action on China-Arab States Cooperation under the Belt and Road Initiative. That document stated that it is a priority to "advance cooperation on the planning and development of major infrastructure projects, such as roads, railways, bridges, tunnels, civil aviation, construction, power generation, optical fiber and telecommunications, and push forward cooperation on industrial parks, and in the Gulf Railway and high-speed rails in interested Arab states."[159] The 2020–2022 CASCF action plan also stresses cooperation in building infrastructure, including ports, airports, railways, energy power, telecommunications, and water services.[160]

China's infrastructure behavior in the forums is norm divergent from the liberal order and competitive with the United States. Similar to other areas of economic cooperation, China's support for infrastructure development funded by the state diverges from the liberal norms of free markets and limited state intervention in the economy. Also, China's significant expenditure of funds to support infrastructure development via concessional loans and other state-supported financing is competitive because it is using these tools to build spheres of influence in these regions and improve political relations with countries in these regions at the expense of other great powers, including the United States.

Economic Security

A significant interest for China in the Middle East and sub-Saharan Africa is economic security. Another is gaining support for China in the international system through South-South cooperation. FOCAC and CASCF address economic security through natural resource cooperation, particularly in energy and agriculture. Natural resource cooperation differs between FOCAC and

CASCF in alignment with China's specific resource interests in these regions discussed in chapter 3. Natural resource cooperation is also an essential form of South-South cooperation.

Since its founding, CASCF has stressed energy cooperation between the Arab states and China.[161] To support this cooperation, the CASCF established the China-Arab Energy Cooperation Dialogue in 2006.[162] Through 2020, the CASCF frequently stressed energy cooperation, including the development of renewable energy sources and peaceful nuclear energy cooperation.[163]

FOCAC's focus on energy security is relatively new. In 2018, its documents started to discuss the issue, stressing energy cooperation, including the development of renewable energy, and committing to establishing a China-Africa Energy Cooperation Center and a China-Africa Geoscience Cooperation Center.[164]

Compared to CASCF, FOCAC's natural resource cooperation is broader in scope than energy. It includes agricultural, mineral, and metallurgical resources. The 2000 FOCAC action plan stated, "China agree[s] that Africa needs to beneficiate its agricultural, mineral and metallurgical resources, in order to generate industrial economic activities. In this regard, China agrees to promote investment in, and exploration and beneficiation of metallurgical resources and that such beneficiation should be done in Africa."[165]

The majority of natural resource cooperation in FOCAC addresses food security issues through agricultural cooperation. Both the 2000 and 2003 FOCAC action plans pledge agricultural cooperation due to the importance of agricultural development in eliminating poverty and ensuring food security.[166] In 2006, China announced via FOCAC several agriculture cooperation activities, including sending one hundred senior experts on agricultural technology experts to Africa, setting up ten agricultural technology demonstration centers in Africa,[167] encouraging and supporting Chinese enterprises in expanding their investment in African agriculture, increasing agricultural human resource training for Africans, and strengthening cooperation with African countries in the UN Food and Agricultural Organization's (UNFAO) Special Program for Food Security.[168] In 2009, the two sides further prioritized the issue of agricultural cooperation and food security. In its action plan for that year, the Chinese government escalated FOCAC's activities in this realm. It offered to send fifty agricultural technology teams to Africa and train two thousand agricultural technicians; increase the number of agricultural technology demonstration centers to twenty; continue to run the demonstration centers that had already been built emphasizing crop seed selection, farming, fish breeding, and animal raising; and contribute US$30 million to the UNFAO to establish a trust fund to support South-South cooperation between China and Africa under the framework of the Special Program for Food Security.[169] The 2012 and 2015 FOCAC documents highlighted similar activities, and over time food, security, and agricultural cooperation appear to be more critical areas of collaboration within FOCAC.[170]

One new area of emphasis in agricultural cooperation in 2015 was the ocean or blue economy. The 2015–2018 action plan promotes experience sharing in "offshore aquaculture, marine transportation, shipbuilding, construction of ports and port industrial parks, the surveying and exploitation of offshore oil and gas resources, marine environment management, marine disaster prevention and reduction, marine scientific research, blue economy development."[171]

Finally, the 2018 FOCAC continued to emphasize the need for agricultural cooperation. Its 2019–2021 action plan committed to "implement 50 agricultural assistance programs, provide RMB 1 billion of emergency humanitarian food assistance to African countries affected by natural disasters, send 500 senior agriculture experts to Africa, and train entrepreneurs in agri-business."[172] It also announced plans to establish a China-AU Agricultural Cooperation Commission, a China-Africa Agricultural Cooperation Forum, and a China-Africa Research Center for the Development of Green Agriculture.[173] The 2018 documents continued to promote cooperation in the ocean economy and commit to considering a China-Africa Cooperation Center for Ocean Science and Blue Economy.[174]

Agricultural cooperation is a vital facet of the FOCAC. In contrast, CASCF documents first mentioned agricultural cooperation and food security in 2010.[175] Throughout the 2010s, China's emphasis on agricultural cooperation with Arab countries increased.[176] The 2018 CASCF documents contain an entire section devoted to agricultural cooperation that stressed cooperation in agriculture, organic agriculture/bioagriculture, food security, water-saving agriculture, agricultural product marketing, animal and fishery resources, water technology, water resource utilization and conservation, rainwater harvesting, wastewater treatment and reuse, and water resource management in arid regions.[177] The action plan also announced the establishment of a wholesale market for agriculture, animal husbandry, and fisheries in the United Arab Emirates.[178]

Similar to many of its other economic activities in the forums, China's natural resource cooperation is competitive and norm divergent due to its promotion of cooperation with other states in the Global South while excluding other great powers, including the United States, and its provision of state financial and political resources to develop these relations. Natural resource cooperation in energy and agriculture is an important example of China using South-South cooperation to gain influence in these regions.

Belt and Road

One of the most significant developments in economic cooperation in the FOCAC and CASCF is the launch of China's Belt and Road Initiative (BRI, discussed in chapter 9 in China's relations with the Middle East and sub-Saharan Africa in detail). In 2014, CASCF documents started expressing support for China's Silk Road Economic Belt and 21st Century Maritime Silk Road to promote infrastructure construction, development of industrial cooperation, and deepening energy, finance, and human resources cooperation.[179] The 2015 FOCAC declaration also expressed support for the Silk Road Economic Belt and the 21st Century Maritime Silk Road.[180] CASCF 2016 documents expand the scope of cooperation to infrastructure, railways, finance, industry, minerals, trade, investment, nuclear energy aerospace, satellite, and high-tech areas of new energy.[181] The CASCF in 2018 produced a stand-alone declaration on cooperation under BRI, and FOCAC documents present all aspects of economic cooperation in the forum as part of BRI. The 2020–2022 CASCF action plan also stresses BRI cooperation in energy, infrastructure, logistics finance, industrial and mineral cooperation, trade, investment, nuclear energy, aerospace, satellites and new energy. In both forums, BRI now encompasses all economic interactions.[182]

On the economic front, BRI in these forums is both competitive and norm divergent. It is competitive because it is part of China's attempt to build a sphere of influence in these regions and increase its economic power compared to other great powers. It is also norm divergent because it advocates for heavy state involvement in China's economic interactions with these regions.

Economic Cooperation Conclusion

China's primary economic cooperation through these forums is trade, investment, financing, infrastructure, economic security, and BRI. Overall, its behavior in economic relations is competitive with the United States and norm divergent from the liberal order. China competes with economic cooperation by excluding other great powers for the forums and providing significant state support for economic activities. Economic cooperation is a significant way China is building its spheres of influence in these regions, primarily through South-South cooperation.

China's economic cooperation is also primarily norm divergent from the liberal order. Its trade promotion with LDCs in Africa, the pursuit of FTAs, and the provision of development financing through multilateral institutions are converging with the liberal international norms. China's SEZs in these forums are norm neutral. That said, its other economic cooperation activities are norm divergent from the liberal order. Bilateral investment and financing mechanisms, infrastructure cooperation, economic security cooperation, and BRI are all norm divergent from the liberal order. They promote a dominant role for the state in economic interactions that is fundamentally at tension with the Western liberal economic order's emphasis on free markets and limited state intervention in the economy. The vast majority of China's economic interaction via these forums is competitive and norm divergent. The various mechanisms to support these activities are all part of the institutional order China is building using these forums.

Foreign Aid

One substantial difference between FOCAC and CASCF is foreign aid provision. CASCF documents do not explicitly include foreign aid, but it is a significant area of interaction within FOCAC.[183] This chapter examines China's foreign aid provided through the FOCAC. (Chapter 6 on economic relations analyzes the actual dollar amounts of foreign aid provided by country and region over time.)

China uses foreign aid in FOCAC to build better political relations with African countries.[184] Its desire to advocate for developing country causes and gain support in the international system through South-South cooperation drives its foreign aid. Although many elements of China's foreign aid activities are norm convergent with global foreign aid norms that advocate for the provision of assistance in various forms to less developed countries, its overall approach to foreign aid to Africa is norm divergent. Similar to its behavior from 1949 to 1990, China is critical of global foreign aid norms that interfere in the domestic politics of recipient countries and is actively challenging those norms.[185] Its foreign aid approach stems from its experience as a developing country. It advocates for political condition-free foreign aid provision in alignment with the Five Principles.[186] China also presses for the inclusion of infrastructure development as a component of foreign aid as opposed to Western countries that often do not support that type of aid. China is not merely offering an alternative model of foreign aid; it is directly critiquing the current system and the mistreatment of developing countries in that system. In the FOCAC founding declaration, China offers a robust normative argument supporting changes in existing foreign aid norms: "Each country has the right to choose, in its course of development, its own social system, development model and way of life in light of its national conditions. . . . Moreover, the politicization of human rights and the imposition of human rights conditionalities on economic assistance should be vigorously opposed to as they constitute a violation of human rights."[187]

Based on interviews conducted for this book, it is clear that many African countries genuinely appreciate China's moral stance against political conditions for foreign aid delivery. One Democratic Republic of the Congo scholar noted that aid from the West has failed due to political conditionality and that China provides a better aid model.[188] An Ethiopian interview respondent emphasized that China's foreign aid approach offers African countries with an opportunity to choose their development paths.[189] Discussing Chinese aid activities in his country, a Gabonese scholar noted that the Gabonese people are "fed up with ex-French colonialists and want new partners [such as the Chinese]. . . . China is seen as a part of us. China is seen as a partner. This is a change for developing countries."[190] China presents itself as a development partner rather than an aid donor and is not as patronizing to African countries.[191] A South African scholar stated that having China as an alternative foreign aid provider improved the negotiating position of African countries with other donors.[192] According to interviewees, since the 2012 FOCAC, China has focused more on the quality, effectiveness, and sustainability of the aid it provides to African countries.[193] China also increasingly compares its aid approach to other countries and desires to match Western efforts to remain competitive as a foreign aid provider.

China provides foreign aid in FOCAC in two forms: debt cancellation and development assistance.[194] Debt cancellation is for heavily indebted poor countries and the LDCs in Africa.[195] China offers this forgiveness without any political conditions except for adherence to the one-China principle. China's commitment to debt cancellation has grown throughout the history of the forum. In the 2000 FOCAC action plan, China pledged to "reduce or cancel debt amounting to RMB 10 billion owed by the heavily indebted poor countries [HIPC] and least developed countries [LDC] in Africa in the coming two year[s]."[196] By June 2002, China had already signed debt exemption protocols with thirty-one African states, canceling 156 African debts with a total value of RMB 10.5 billion .[197] China's debt cancellation activities are ongoing. It canceled interest-free loans to African HIPCs and LDCs that were due by the end of 2005.[198] In another ambitious action, China announced in 2009 that it would "cancel due debts of interest-free government loans that will mature by the end of 2009 owed by all heavily-indebted poor countries and the LDCs in Africa having diplomatic relations with China."[199] China made the same announcement in the 2012 FOCAC.[200] FOCAC's 2015 documents expanded the countries with debt cancellation of intergovernmental interest-free loans to LDCs, landlocked countries, and small island developing countries in Africa.[201] Finally, in 2018, China canceled all interest-free Chinese government loans due to mature by the end of 2018 for all LDCs, heavily indebted and poor countries, landlocked developing countries, and small island developing countries.[202]

China's focus on debt cancellation is convergent with the liberal norms of the international system. The G8 encourages members to forgive the debt of HIPC. China goes beyond that expectation by canceling loans for LDCs, heavily indebted and poor countries, landlocked developing countries, and small island developing countries. That said, it should be acknowledged that the actual dollar amount of this relief is small. Also, during COVID, African calls for additional Chinese debt relief are increasing.[203]

In addition to debt forgiveness, China provides development assistance to African countries in FOCAC, mainly through aid grants, concessional loans, and interest-free loans.[204] It provides this aid without any political conditions (other than adherence to the one-China principle).[205] In 2006, China announced that it would double the size of its development assistance to African countries and provide $3 billion in preferential loans and $2 billion in preferential buyer credits to African countries (especially HIPCs and LDCs) by the end of 2009.[206] In 2012, China announced that it had approved concessional loans for $11.3 billion for ninety-two projects.[207] The 2015 pledge increased to $35 billion.[208] Finally, in the 2019–2021 FOCAC action plan, China announced that it would extend $15 billion of grants, interest-free loans, and concessional loans to Africa.[209] Also, it will extend $20 billion of credit lines and set up a $10 billion special fund for development financing.

Related to China's foreign aid to African countries through FOCAC is cooperation in health and medical care, as well as education and human resource development. Although technically included as an area of cooperation since 2006, health and medical cooperation was only briefly mentioned within CASCF.[210] In FOCAC, China is engaged in several activities stressing African medical care and disease control (especially for HIV/AIDS, malaria, and other infectious diseases). As of 2003, China had "signed or renewed protocols with 40 African countries on dispatching Chinese medical teams, pledging continued provision free of charge of pharmaceutics, medical equipment and other hospital materials, and cooperation with Africa in the prevention and treatment of HIV/AIDS, malaria and tuberculosis."[211] At the 2006 FOCAC summit, China announced more assertive actions in this area. It committed to construct thirty hospitals in Africa, provide RMB 300 million of grants for providing anti-malaria drugs, build thirty demonstration centers for the prevention and treatment of malaria, send additional medical teams to Africa, and provide medicines and medical supplies needed by African countries and help them to train medical workers.[212] According to Chinese assessments, by 2009, it had fulfilled these 2006 pledges.[213] At the 2009 FOCAC ministerial meeting, China committed to provide RMB 500 million of medical equipment and malaria-fighting material to the thirty hospitals and thirty malaria treatment centers that China has already built; train three thousand African doctors, nurses, and administrative personnel; and continue to send Chinese medical teams to Africa.[214] The 2012 FOCAC action plan committed to send fifteen hundred Chinese medical workers to Africa over three years.[215] The 2015 FOCAC documents unveiled plans for Chinese support of the establishment of an African Union Disease Control Center[216] and a Ministerial Forum on China-Africa Health Cooperation as part of the FOCAC process.[217] Finally, 2018 FOCAC documents reinforced all of the health cooperation announced in previous forums and committed to upgrading fifty medical and health programs for Africa, including the African Center for Disease Control and Prevention and China-Africa Friendship Hospitals.[218]

Education and human resource development is another functional area that is important for the FOCAC but mentioned only briefly in CASCF declarations and action plans. In the areas of human resource development and education, China has initiated several activities through FOCAC. For example, in 2006, it announced that it had trained over ten thousand African professionals in various fields under the African Human Resources Development Fund and pledged to train an additional fifteen thousand professionals over three years.[219] At the 2006 FOCAC summit, China also announced plans to build one hundred rural schools in Africa, increase the number of Chinese government scholarships to African students from two thousand per year to four thousand per year by 2009, provide annual training for various African education professionals, and establish Confucius Institutes in several African countries.[220]

China's announcements at the 2009 FOCAC ministerial meeting provided even more substantial funding for education development in Africa. It committed to training an additional twenty thousand African professionals by 2012.[221] It pledged to build fifty China-Africa friendship schools in Africa, implement a plan called 20+20 Cooperation to facilitate cooperation between twenty Chinese universities and twenty African universities, admit two hundred middle- and high-level African administrative personnel to master of public administration programs in China, raise the number of Chinese government scholarships for African students to fifty-five, train fifteen hundred African school headmasters and teachers, and continue to promote Confucius Institutes throughout Africa.[222]

The 2012 FOCAC plan encouraged the establishment of Confucius Institutes and Confucius Classrooms in Africa[223] and committed to providing $2 million per year under UNESCO to support education development programs in Africa.[224] Confucius Institutes are Chinese government-funded organizations within universities that teach the Chinese language. Confucian classrooms serve the same purpose in primary and secondary schools. The 2015 FOCAC documents further expanded education cooperation. They promised 30,000 government scholarships to African countries. FOCAC documents highlighted China's new South-South Cooperation and Development Institute at Beijing University, and the further setup of Confucius Institutes was encouraged. The 2015 FOCAC action plan also stressed vocational and technical training facilities in Africa, and China committed to train 200,000 local African vocational and technical personnel and provide 40,000 with training opportunities in China.[225] Finally, plans from the 2018 FOCAC stressed all of the areas of educational cooperation highlighted in past cooperation forums, and China committed to provide Africa with 50,000 government scholarship and 50,000 training opportunities in China between 2019 and 2021.[226]

Although many of the elements of China's foreign aid are norm convergent with behavior that the international aid community encourages, such as debt cancellation for LDCs and assistance for education and health improvement, China's general criticism of the role of political conditionality is divergent from the liberal order. Although much of its behavior is norm convergent, it is also competitive as it uses aid to build China's sphere of influence in Africa. Similar to political and economic cooperation in these forums, the institutions China is forming to support aid to Africa is building an alternative order for China to interact with Africa. This new order more closely aligns with China's needs as a rising power.

Security Cooperation

Although China has established a cooperation forum with another region that emphasizes security cooperation (Shanghai Cooperation Organization, SCO), until recently, security cooperation was not a significant emphasis of either the CASCF or FOCAC. Security cooperation in these forums supports China's interests in regional stability so it can acquire resources and markets and protect its citizens and businesses abroad. Security issues are referred to very broadly, usually just articulating regional support for China's multilateral military activities outside the forums. Both the CASCF and the FOCAC call for establishing nuclear-free zones in these regions.[227] Since 2010, the CASCF communiqués have contained references to a need for a renewed commitment to a nuclear-weapon-free Middle East,[228] most likely due to proliferation concerns about Iran's pursuit of nuclear capability. On other military matters, FOCAC documents praise China for its involvement in African UN peacekeeping operations,[229] past antipiracy initiatives off the coast of Somalia,[230] and potential future antipiracy activity in the Gulf of Guinea.[231] Starting in 2012, when the AU joined FOCAC, there were pledges for China to support the African Union in its peacekeeping efforts and the development of an African peace and security architecture.[232]

In 2018, security cooperation started growing in FOCAC. The most recent FOCAC documents announced that China would launch fifty security assistance programs to advance China-Africa cooperation under the Belt and Road Initiative. These programs will focus on law and order, UN peacekeeping missions, fighting piracy, and combating terrorism.[233] It also states that China will establish a China-Africa peace and security forum within FOCAC and expand defense and military training.[234] The 2019–2021 FOCAC action plan commits China to provide $100 million in military assistance to support the African Standby Force and the African Capacity for Immediate Response to Crisis, as well as establish a China-Africa peace and security fund and provide military aid to the African Union.

The most significant developments in security cooperation in the 2018 FOCAC were the emphasis on security aspects of Belt and Road and the emphasis on the need to protect citizens and businesses operating in Africa and China.[235] This BRI focus is very much in alignment with China's interests in protecting citizens and enterprises discussed in chapter 3.

Although it is a minor emphasis in both forums, CASCF and FOCAC documents do stress the need for cooperation in combating global terrorism. Historically, calls for this type of cooperation were more robust in the CASCF, but the 2018 FOCAC meetings saw an increased focus on counterterrorism action items. CASCF documents call for counterterrorism cooperation through the United Nations and other relevant multilateral organizations.[236] Outside of China's quest for political support in its anti-insurgency activities in Xinjiang, it does not have any bilateral antiterrorism activities with CASCF. The 2018 and 2020 CASCF documents contain a bit less focus on fighting terrorism compared to previous years. Among the many possible explanations for that change are less concern from Arab states about fighting terrorism as ISIS recedes, less consensus among Arab states about fighting terrorism, and a reduced desire to emphasize counterterrorism cooperation with China as it incarcerates over a million ethnic Uyghurs domestically in Xinjiang as part of its counterterrorism activities.

FOCAC documents also declare a need for antiterrorism cooperation through the United Nations and other international organizations.[237] The 2019–2021 FOCAC action plan states that both sides "will strengthen exchanges of intelligence and experience on security issues, and support each other in the prevention and combating of terrorism with equal emphasis on its symptoms and root causes."[238]

Overall, through its cooperation forums, China's security cooperation is norm convergent with the liberal order. It is a minor area of emphasis for the forums. China strongly supports security cooperation through regional multilateral organizations, especially the African Union, the United Nations, and multinational peacekeeping operations. Due to its heavy reliance on multilateral action, this behavior is also categorized as cooperative in Africa because the United States and other Western states are also working through these multilateral mechanisms.

Other Areas of Cooperation

The primary areas for cooperation in both the FOCAC and CASCF are political and economic. As opposed to the CASCF, FOCAC also contains a heavy emphasis on foreign aid, education, human resource development, and health cooperation. Until recently, neither forum included bilateral security cooperation, but in 2018, FOCAC action plans emphasized the establishment of security assistance programs and the foundation of a new peace and security forum under FOCAC. In addition to political, economic, and security cooperation, these forums encompass almost all potential areas of cooperation between regions. Although this book does not discuss them in detail, both FOCAC and CASCF contain clauses for cooperation in areas such as environmental protection, cultural exchange, media, tourism, sports, legislative interaction, climate change, desertification, and building party-to-party ties.

FOCAC, CASCF, and the Shanghai Cooperation Organization: A Comparison

Although this chapter does not provide a detailed case study of the Shanghai Cooperation Organization (SCO), a brief discussion of the similarities and differences among SCO, FOCAC, and CASCF illuminates characteristics of the order China is building more broadly to facilitate interactions with the developing world and some of the differences in its approach to regions.

The SCO was initially formed as the Shanghai Five in 1996 with China, Kazakhstan, Kyrgyzstan, Russia, and Tajikistan. The Shanghai Five officially became the Shanghai Cooperation Organization in 2001 with the signing of the founding charter. The original membership of the SCO was the Shanghai Five plus Uzbekistan. India and Pakistan joined the organization in 2017 as full members. Observer states are Afghanistan, Belarus, Iran, and Mongolia, and dialogue partners are Azerbaijan, Armenia, Cambodia, Nepal, Turkey, and Sri Lanka. Iran applied for full membership in 2008, but SCO has not yet approved that status. China and Russia both issued statements during 2018 supporting Iran's full membership. The past stance of the SCO was that Iran could not become a full member because it was subject to UN sanctions. In

2015, the JCPOA (Joint Comprehensive Plan of Action) resolved that issue. Also, in the wake of US withdrawal from the JCPOA, SCO members may use granting full membership to Iran in the future as a way to demonstrate support for Iran and the nuclear agreement.

The Council of Heads of State, the supreme SCO body, meets once a year to determine SCO priorities and activities. The Council of Heads of Government (Prime Ministries) also meets once a year, approves the budget, and decides on major economic areas of cooperation in the SCO. The Council of Ministers of Foreign Affairs meets once per year approximately a month before the Council of Heads of State to prepare for the meeting. The SCO also has a secretariat that is the permanent executive body of the SCO and a rotating secretary-general.[239]

Although there is a great deal of similarity among these cooperation forums (FOCAC, CASCF, and SCO), there are also some crucial differences. One is that since its beginning in 2001, SCO was established in its founding charter as a formal treaty organization with international legal capacity.[240] The FOCAC and CASCF do not include a similar charter. Another significant difference is that SCO includes another great power, Russia, and is increasingly admitting additional regional powers as its geographic scope expands. India and Pakistan joined in 2017, and Iran aspires to become a member. The FOCAC and CASCF include only China and regional powers with a constant geographic scope since their founding. The SCO also meets more frequently than the other forums and has a more formal institutional structure.[241] It is important to note that the text of the SCO founding charter explicitly states that member states do not need consensus to implement a project. This rule allows for subsets of the SCO members to cooperate in certain areas and not others. FOCAC and CASCF do not require consensus, but they also do not highlight the fact that consensus is not required.

Similar to the CASCF and FOCAC, the Five Principles are the normative underpinnings of the SCO. That said, SCO also stresses in its founding principles that member states will not seek unilateral military superiority in adjacent areas, members will not use force or threat of force in relations with each other, and the SCO will not be directed against other states or international organizations. This verbiage is a clear indication that member states want to avoid military competition within the SCO and do not want the SCO to be perceived or used as a formal military alliance by its members. In this way, the SCO aspires to be a security community in a way that the FOCAC and CASCF do not.[242]

One significant difference among the SCO, FOCAC, and CASCF is the prioritization of areas of cooperation. Since its founding, the SCO's top priority has been security cooperation. This stands in stark contrast to the CASCF and FOCAC, which heavily emphasize political and economic cooperation and only superficially address security issues. The top five areas of cooperation in the SCO since its founding, in order of importance, are maintaining peace and enhancing security in the region; searching for common positions on foreign policy; counteracting terrorism, separatism, and extremism; coordinating disarmament and arms control; and promoting regional economic cooperation.[243] In support of this focus on security, the SCO has built a permanent regional antiterrorism structure with headquarters in Tashkent, Uzbekistan.[244]

Security Cooperation

Although political and economic cooperation in the SCO has grown over the years, the top priority of the organization is security cooperation. The most discussed aspect of security is combating terrorism. Compared to the FOCAC and CASCF, the SCO engages in many concrete actions to combat terrorism throughout member states. Since its founding, it has included a regional antiterrorism structure. Member states have actively cooperated on fighting terrorism, separatism, and extremism. The 2018 SCO declaration even included wording about the threat of foreign terrorists who return from the Middle East to their countries and cooperation among security services.[245] The 2019 declaration highlights the new SCO Convention on Countering Extremism.[246] The 2020 documents refer to the signing of Memorandums of Understanding between the SCO Regional Anti-Terrorism Structure and the UN Office of Counter-Terrorism.[247]

This level of antiterrorism cooperation is significantly higher than activity in the FOCAC and CASCF. Other forms of security cooperation highlighted in the SCO are the desire for a nuclear-weapon-free zone in Central Asia; efforts to keep space free of weapons; support for international chemical weapons conventions; developing an antidrug strategy and combating other nontraditional cross-border threats; and recognizing that corruption is a threat to national and regional security.

Political Cooperation

Political cooperation in the CASCF emphasizes China's support for Arab causes, including the Palestinian-Israeli conflict and the Arab-Israeli conflict, as well as a wide range of issues in the Arab world. FOCAC political cooperation centers on South-South cooperation and advocacy for developing a just and equitable new political and economic order. In contrast, references to political cooperation are focused on regions outside the SCO. The political issues emphasized in the SCO include support for the government and people of Afghanistan, implementation of an inclusive political process for Syria, opposition to the use of chemical weapons anywhere, consistent implementation of JCPOA, settlement of the situation on the Korean peninsula via political and diplomatic means, and the need for a political resolution of the Ukraine crisis.[248] Political cooperation in the SCO appears to emphasize areas of cooperation between the two great powers in the organization, China and Russia. In addition to coordinating positions between China and Russia, the cooperation proposed is often in direct opposition to US and Western approaches to these issues, especially on Syria, JCPOA, Korea, and Ukraine, all indicating a divergence from the United States and the rest of West.[249] This political cooperation is very much in alignment with the original SCO charter that calls for member states to search for common policies on foreign policy issues for mutual interest.

Economic Cooperation

There is more formal economic cooperation in the SCO than the FOCAC or CASCF. The 2018 SCO documents call for "simplifying trade procedures, decreasing the number of customs formalities on imports, exports and transit of goods, increasing transparency, developing cooperation between border agencies, including customs, and expediting the transit of goods, the release of goods and customs clearance to simplify and promote mutual trade between SCO Member States."[250] Since its founding in 2001, the SCO has planned to achieve the free flow of goods, capital, services, and technologies across member state borders.[251] Over time, it is taking steps toward becoming a free trade area and perhaps someday a customs union.

Similar to FOCAC and CASCF documents, the SCO calls for the WTO to serve as the key platform for facilitating international trade.[252] All three forums call for strengthening cooperation in banking and finance, as well as increasing interaction with regional multilateral banking and financial organizations, including the SCO Interbank Consortium, the Asia Infrastructure Investment Bank, the New Development Bank, the Silk Road, and the China-Eurasia Economic Development Fund. They also encourage further infrastructure cooperation to facilitate the interconnectivity of the region.

One difference in economic cooperation between the FOCAC and CASCF versus the SCO is that the organizations covering the Middle East and Africa declare unanimous support for the Belt and Road. In the SCO, all members except India endorse the BRI and encourage efforts to coordinate the development of the Eurasian Economic Union and the BRI.[253] Another difference is that although SCO documents mention agricultural cooperation, it is a much more substantial area of cooperation in FOCAC and CASCF. Also, SCO does not include significant references to foreign aid, economic development, and South-South cooperation, and activities such as special economic zones or agricultural technology demonstration centers are not included.

Conclusion

China competes with the United States in politics, economics, and foreign aid through its cooperation forums in the Middle East and Africa. Both CASCF and FOCAC exclude the United States and other great powers. China uses these forums to gain support in the international system, primarily through South-South cooperation, support for Arab causes, and standing up for sovereignty and nonintervention with the Five Principles. These forums are instruments China uses to develop spheres of influence in these regions. Increasingly, it uses these forums as a way to garner support for itself in opposition to the United States and the West on issues such as the South China Sea, foreign intervention, violations of sovereignty, and China's treatment of Muslims in Xinjiang.

Although some of its behavior converges with liberal international norms, much of its political, economic, and foreign aid behavior diverges. FOCAC and CASCF are important institutions in the alternative order China is building to interact with these regions and the developing world more broadly. The norms that China uses in these forums shed light on the characteristics of that order.

The Five Principles and South-South Cooperation form the political foundation of both forums. CASCF also stresses support for Arab causes and Arab support for China's management of issues in Xinjiang. Although the Five Principles converge with the norm of Westphalian sovereignty, it is in tension with and diverges from the liberal political order. South-South cooperation is norm convergent with the liberal order because it advocates a greater voice in and potential restructuring of that order to better represent the needs of developing countries, but it is competitive because it pits developed countries against developed ones, including the United States. China's support for the Palestinians competes with US support for Israel but is norm convergent because it calls for adherence to UN resolutions about the issue and encourages multilateral mechanisms for peace negotiations. China's support for Arab calls for protection of sovereignty and nonintervention directly competes with the United States and diverges from the liberal order due to its strong emphasis on the Five Principles and standing up to the United States about foreign intervention in the Middle East. Arab tolerance of China's management of Xinjiang is norm divergent because it is in tension with liberal norms of protecting human rights.

China's economic behavior in these forums also mostly diverges from the international order. Although some of this behavior converges with liberal international norms (e.g., trade promotion with LDCs, development finance through multilateral organizations, free trade agreements), China's heavy utilization of state support and financing for most economic activities in the forum (e.g., trade, investment, infrastructure, economic security, and BRI) diverges from liberal international norms of free-market capitalism and limited state intervention in the economy. Its support for SEZs is norm neutral.

Its foreign aid approach is also primarily norm divergent. China's provision of foreign aid in several areas, including concessional loans, education initiatives, and health cooperation, in many ways converges with liberal international norms because they are contributing to the development of many countries around the world. That said, China's overall approach diverges from the liberal international order due to its lack of political conditions in selecting aid recipients. China provides aid to all needy counties, regardless of regime type, human rights abuses, or significant governance issues in society. This approach directly contradicts foreign aid norms of good governance. China's normative stance is that tying aid provision to political conditionality is immoral. It has taken that stand since it started providing aid in the 1950s, and its approach is a deliberate critique of the current foreign aid regime.

As opposed to its norm-divergent behavior in economic cooperation, political cooperation, and foreign aid, China's security cooperation in both forums is cooperative and norm convergent. Security is not a significant focus of these forums, and the security cooperation that does happen is through regional organizations, UN peacekeeping operations, and multilateral anti-piracy initiatives.

Compared to the SCO, FOCAC and CASCF focus on economic and political issues rather than security concerns. They exclude other great powers, while SCO includes Russia as well as India. SCO has a legal personality. In many ways, SCO is an outlier, and FOCAC and CASCF are much closer to all of the other cooperation forums China is operating around the world, especially with the developing world.

Finally, it is important to note how China portrays and differentiates itself from other great powers through its behavior in the FOCAC and CASCF. China portrays itself as a champion of sovereignty, noninterference, and non-intervention. It provides high levels of state support for its economic, political, and foreign aid interactions with these countries. It promotes South-South cooperation and the causes of developing countries. It speaks up for Arab causes, and although it maintains strong bilateral relations with Israel, it uses the CASCF as a way to demonstrate support for the Palestinians. China's priority is economic, political, and foreign activities, and it competes with the West in these regions for those relations but does not want a unilateral military presence. Ultimately, China markets itself as a great power that understands the needs of these countries and is willing to dedicate the resources and energy to fulfill those requirements while still ensuring its own interests.

CHAPTER 5

A RESPONSIBLE POWER?

How China Portrays Itself as a Great Power through Special Envoys for the Middle East, Syria, and Africa

China's primary post–Cold War interests in the Middle East and sub-Saharan Africa are to promote its domestic economic growth, foster support in the international arena, ensure its domestic stability, advocate for developing country causes, safeguard its citizens and businesses abroad, and protect its territorial integrity and sovereignty from the United States. This chapter analyzes China's special envoys for the Middle East, Syria, and Africa from 2002 through 2018. In various ways, China's special envoys to these regions pursue all those interests.

The primary questions driving this chapter and the rest of the book are: Is China cooperating or competing with the United States in the Middle East and sub-Saharan Africa? Is its behavior converging with or diverging from liberal international norms? Is it building an alternative international order in these regions? If yes, what are the characteristics of that order? Ultimately, what does China's behavior in the Middle East and sub-Saharan Africa indicate about its rise globally?

Analyzing China's special envoys in comparative perspective over time generates essential insights about how China is competing in these regions and diverging from or converging with liberal international norms. It shows how China is developing spheres of influence and changing the rules of the system. These envoys provide insights into how China conceptualizes and portrays its role in these regions as a rising great power and how it envisions solving enduring challenges to peace and security in the Middle East and Africa. They show how China approaches what it perceives to be hot spots in these regions. A close examination of China's special envoys also sheds light on how China is differentiating itself from other great powers in these regions and how it is cooperating with Russia.

Since the early 2000s, China has established three special envoys to address hot spot issues in the Middle East and Africa: the China–Middle East issues special envoy in 2002, the China-Africa issues special envoy in 2007, and China's special envoy for Syria in 2016. Examples of China's special envoys outside the Middle East and Africa include special envoys for the Korean peninsula, global climate change, Afghanistan, and Asia (including Myanmar).[1]

Primary sources used in conducting this case study of China's special envoys for the Middle East, Africa, and Syria include speeches by the special envoys; Chinese Ministry of Foreign Affairs press releases; Chinese, Middle Eastern, and sub-Saharan African media reporting;[2] scholarly analysis from China, the Middle East, and sub-Saharan Africa; and interviews with Chinese, Middle Eastern, and sub-Saharan African government officials and scholars. The case studies examine these special envoys from when they were initially appointed through 2018. To date, no Western scholar has produced a detailed case study comparing these envoys. This chapter strives to close that empirical gap in the literature and situate an analysis of these special envoys in a broader context of understanding China's behavior as a rising power in these regions. Due to the strong emphasis on official government statements in this analysis, the primary purpose of this chapter is to construct an argument regarding how China portrays itself as a great power through these envoys. This analysis categorizes China's behavior in these forums as competitive versus cooperative with the United States and norm divergent versus convergent with the liberal order.

As discussed in chapter 4, China's political, economic, and foreign aid behavior in the Forum on China-Africa Cooperation (FOCAC) and China-Arab States Cooperation Forum (CASCF) was primarily competitive with the United States and norm divergent from the liberal order through advocacy for the Five Principles, South-South solidarity, and heavy state intervention in economic activities. That said, some of its behavior was cooperative (e.g., security cooperation) and norm convergent (e.g., pursuing greater representation for developing countries in the liberal institutions, support for UN resolutions and multilateral mechanisms for the Middle East peace process, trade with less developed countries free trade agreements, debt cancellation, lending development finance through multilateral institutions, and security cooperation).

China's behavior through its special envoys is more nuanced. Overall, the behavior of the Middle East envoy and Syria envoy is competitive with the United States and normatively mixed. In contrast, the Africa envoy is cooperative with the United States and norm convergent with the liberal order. Aspects of China's competition and cooperation with the United States, as well as norm divergence from and convergence with the liberal order, are explored in the following case studies.

China's Middle East Issues Special Envoy

During the Mao era, China supported the Palestinians in their struggle against Israel. After China's movement toward reform and the end of the Cold War, the PRC established political relations with Israel and presented itself as a more balanced player in the region in contrast with its past behavior and the approach of the United States.

The special envoy for Middle East issues was the first special envoy ever appointed by China. China established the envoy in 2002, but as early as 1997, China's foreign minister, Qian Qichen, had announced China's Five Principle Standpoints in Support of the Middle East Peace Process:

> 1. Peace talks should proceed on the basis of the implementation of relevant UN resolutions on the Middle East and the land for peace principle forged at the Madrid peace conference (in 1991).
>
> 2. All signed agreements should be implemented seriously and any attempt to hinder the peace process should be avoided.
>
> 3. Terrorism and violence in all forms must be eradicated so that the security of the Mideast countries and the normal lives of their peoples can be assured.
>
> 4. As the peace process makes headway, regional economic cooperation should be strengthened so as to help build confidence and dispel hostility gradually between Arab countries and Israel on their way toward mutual development and prosperity
>
> 5. The international community is obliged to work together with the parties concerned in the Middle East to realize a comprehensive, just and lasting peace in the region, and China is ready to make its own effort to that end.[3]

According to interview respondents (both Chinese and Arab) and press reports, the main reason China established the Middle East special envoy was in response to urging by the Arab states for China to become more involved in Arab-Israeli issues , including the Palestinian-Israeli conflict and territorial disputes among Syria, Lebanon, and Israel.[4] One reason for this Arab pressure was that China was not a member of the Quartet: the United States, Russia, the European Union, and the United Nations.[5] Also, many Arab states perceived China to be a more balanced player in the Middle East peace process than other great powers, especially the United States, due to China's historical support for the Palestinians.[6] Forming the envoy provided China an opportunity to signal that it cared about Arab issues.[7] Similar to China's support for Arab causes in CASCF discussed in chapter 4, advocacy for this issue generates support for China in the international system among many Arab and Muslim countries. According to Israeli officials, Israel welcomed the formation of the envoy and understood that Arab states have an appreciation for what they see as the balanced approach China provides in the Middle East peace process.[8]

China views the Palestinian-Israeli conflict as the core issue in peace and stability in the Middle East because peace would contribute to stability in the region. A stable Middle East ultimately contributes to China's ability to fuel its economic growth through access to resources and markets in the region as well as energy security.

Wang Shijie

China formally announced the appointment of the Middle East issues envoy in September 2002.[9] The first special envoy was Wang Shijie, a veteran Middle East diplomat.[10] He previously served as the Chinese ambassador to Bahrain (1991–1993),[11] Jordan (1993–1995),[12] and Iran (1995–1999).[13]

Shortly after China announced the special envoy, Wang Shijie made several public comments regarding the envoy's purpose—for example, "China supports the relevant UN resolutions on the establishment of an independent Palestinian state with Jerusalem as its capital and Syria's just struggle to recover the Golan Heights and, at the same time, understanding Israel's concerns for its security interests."[14] He also stressed that a peaceful resolution to the conflict was necessary[15] and again highlighted the need for land for peace as a guiding principle of negotiations.[16] In many press statements, China has made clear that its interpretation of the land-for-peace concept is that the borders should be negotiated to pre-1967 lines, the Golan Heights should be returned to Syria, and East Jerusalem should be the capital of Palestine. Further elaborating on China's involvement in the process, he stated, "China, as one of five permanent members of the United Nations Security Council, has a responsibility and an obligation to push ahead with the Middle East peace process."[17]

In May 2003, Wang presented the Five-Point Proposal on the Middle East Peace Process and Road Map:

> 1. China welcomes and supports the "road map" Middle East peace plan officially announced by the "four sides," and thinks the contents of the "road map" are positive and it has provided a good foundation for Israel and Palestine to resume peace talks. China hopes both Israel and Palestine will seize the opportunity, take practical measures to cooperate with the international community in its effort to promote peace, and strive to settle the Palestine issue at an early day.[18]
>
> 2. Israel and Palestine should officially announce accepting and implementing the "road map" as soon as possible. The pressing task at present is that both sides should immediately stop meeting violence with violence and revenging each other so as to create conditions for resuming the peace talks and reaching an agreement. Israel should withdraw its troops to the position before 28 September 2000, stop taking measures of military attacks, political isolation and economic blockade and the policy of "mopping up point by point," freeze the construction of settlement points, alleviate the humanitarian crisis in Palestine, and restore Chairman Arafat's personal freedom. Besides, Israel's security should be fully guaranteed and the Palestinian National Authority has the obligation to take effective measures to stop violence activities. China supports the establishment of an independent Palestine state at an early day, and welcomes a democratic election to be held in Palestine,
>
> 3. In order to ensure the implementation of the "road map," an impartial, authoritative and effective international supervision mechanism should be established earlier.
>
> 4. On the basis of relevant UN resolutions, the principle of "land for peace" set at the Madrid Peace Conference, and the agreements and consensus reached between various sides, the talks between Israel on one side and Syria and Lebanon on the other should be resumed as soon as possible so as to reach

> a final solution plan acceptable to all sides concerned and to finally realize comprehensive and lasting peace in the Middle East.
>
> 5. Promoting the realization of peace and stability in the Middle East is the common responsibility and obligation of the international community. The international community should pay greater attention to and increase input into the Middle East issue and the United Nations should play a greater role. China calls for holding an international meeting on the Middle East issue with the participation of the five permanent member states of the Security Council and relevant parties as soon as possible, and is willing to actively participate in and promote international efforts for the peace process in the Middle East.[19]

The primary differences between the 1997 and the 2003 proposals were that in 2003, China was more specific regarding its expectations about the establishment of a Palestinian state, democratic elections for Palestine, and a call for an international supervisory mechanism for the peace process. The 2003 proposal expressly advocated for the utilization of the new "road map" process, overtly criticized Israel's actions toward the Palestinians, and removed the emphasis on regional economic development.

In June 2004, Wang provided enlightening remarks about China's self-perceived role in the peace process. He stated there were no specific new proposals or initiatives from China on the Middle East issues "because the position of the Chinese side is clear cut and remains unchanged" and "at present, there are numerous proposals and initiatives on the settlement of the Middle East problems . . . but the priority is whether we could kick off negations involving the parties concerned."[20]

In 2004, China also stressed that although it was not part of the Quartet facilitating the road map negotiations, it kept frequent contact with envoys of the Quartet.[21] The first of these talks with the Quartet was held during Wang's first trip as special envoy to the Middle East in November 2002. He met with special envoys from the United States, the EU, Russia, and the UN.

Another example was his visit to meet the Russian special envoy to the Middle East in March 2003. After that visit, Wang Shijie commented that Russia and China held similar or identical views on the Middle East issue and that the role of the United States was critical in the Middle East process since it maintained special relations with Israel.[22] He again stressed, "What is important now is not to raise a new initiative but to implement the already existing understandings and related resolutions of the Security Council. . . .

There are many initiatives to solve the Middle East issue, but many principles are the same."[23]

Wang served as special envoy for three years. In his departure speech, he noted, "Talking about any regret in my tenure, I should say that over three years no satisfactory progress has yet been achieved and the Palestinian and Israeli people are still suffering a lot." He also expressed his opinion that the Chinese envoy "shows the concern and sympathy of the Chinese government and people for the agony suffered by the countries and people in the region" and that China's strategic interest in forming a special envoy to the Middle East is that peace in that region is directly linked to world peace and stability. "China needs a peaceful international environment to continue with its policy of reform and opening up."[24]

Sun Bigan

Wang was replaced by Sun Bigan as special envoy in April 2006. Sun was also a seasoned Middle East diplomat who had served as China's ambassador to Iran from 1999 until 2002[25] and then headed a team responsible for the reestablishment of the Chinese embassy in Baghdad.[26] Upon Sun's appointment, China's stance on the Middle East peace process appeared to be consistent with its 2003 statements. For example, during a June 2006 state visit to Egypt, the comments of Wen Jiabao, China's premier of the State Council, echoed the content of the Five Points proposed in 2003. He stated that China continued to support the road map and political negotiations based on relevant UN resolution and the concept of land for peace. He also mentioned that China was not in favor of political isolation or blockades of the Palestinians and that the international community should provide more assistance to the Palestinians and help President Abbas and the Palestinian government achieve internal stability. Regarding relations with Israel, he stated that China and Israel continued to have normal, friendly state-to-state relations that are "conducive to China's efforts to promote reconciliation and facilitate dialogue and maintain peace and stability in the region."[27]

Shortly after China appointed Sun in 2006, hostilities broke out between Israel and Lebanon. China heavily criticized Israel for disproportionate use of force toward Lebanon in July 2006.[28] In response to the hostilities, Sun stated that draft UN resolutions regarding Lebanon should take into consideration the opinions of Lebanon and the Arab states. He also called on the international community to provide emergency aid and supplies. He expressed China's willingness to intensify further consultation and coordination with Arab countries to alleviate the tense regional situation.[29] In August 2006, the special envoy attended an international conference on Lebanon's reconstruction in Sweden[30] and provided Lebanon with 150 tons of humanitarian assistance,[31] including foodstuffs, medicine, tents, and electric generators.[32]

While the conflict in Lebanon was raging, China's focus continued on the Palestinian-Israeli conflict as the core issue in the Middle East peace process. In August 2006, while exchanging views on the Palestinian-Israeli issue and the current regional situation, Sun stressed, "No matter how the situation may change, China will, as always, support the Palestinian people in their just cause of restoring their legitimate national rights and interests." He also said the Palestinian issue had always been the core of the Middle East issue.[33]

Later, as tensions in Gaza flared in 2009, Sun announced China's five points on the Middle East situation:[34]

> 1. We call on all parties concerned to abide by the UN Security Council Resolution 1860,[35] and cease all military actions immediately to avert more casualties.
>
> 2. Measures should be taken to ease the humanitarian crisis in Gaza. A stable channel for supply of humanitarian aid including food, medicine and fuel for Gaza should be open at the earliest time possible, and parties concerned should provide the necessary guarantee in this regard.
>
> 3. Parties concerned should establish, through negotiation, a ceasefire monitoring mechanism in Gaza and work to create durable security and stability there.
>
> 4. The Palestine-Israel peace talks should resume at the earliest time, and efforts should be made to seek solution to issues related to the final status of Palestine on the basis of mutual-trust, so that an independent Palestinian state will be established as early as possible and the "two states" of Palestine and Israel will co-exist peacefully.
>
> 5. The international community should increase mediating efforts for peace and promote a comprehensive, just and durable settlement of the Middle East issue. China is ready to work with parties concerned and make unremitting efforts in this regard.[36]

Wu Sike

China's third special envoy, Wu Sike, was appointed in March 2009 and served until 2014. Similar to Sun Bigan and Wang Shijie, he possessed a deep working background in the Middle East as ambassador to both Saudi Arabia and Egypt.[37] To move stalled peace negotiations forward, in 2009 he stated, "Israel [can] not achieve its ultimate security until Israel and the Palestinians realize their peaceful coexistence. . . . I have urged the Israeli leaders and politicians to accept the two state solution, stop establishing settlements and negotiate with Syria and Lebanon about concerning issues."[38]

In March 2010, Wu provided an even more detailed account of the stance of the special envoy on the status of the Middle East peace process. According to him, "The Palestinian-Israeli issue is at the heart of Middle East problems. Tackling and resolving the issue will have positive impact on regional and even world stability and developments." He urged Israel to freeze settlements, remove the blockade on the Gaza Strip, and improve the humanitarian situation for the Palestinian people."[39]

During 2010, Wu Sike's dissatisfaction with Israeli activities grew, especially about its blockade of the Gaza Strip and its raid of an aid flotilla in international waters, and his desire to push forward talks amplified.[40]

Overall, China's stance on the Middle East peace process remained constant during Wu Sike's tenure. One significant change in the special envoy's behavior was increased work on issues outside the peace process.[41] For example, the envoy Wu Sike became more heavily involved in the Iran nuclear issue,[42] public relations associated with Xinjiang insurgency suppression activities,[43] and proposals for resolving tensions in Syria.

The envoy's scope expanded as the Arab awakening began to affect countries across the region. Even at the very beginning of political upheaval in the region, Wu stressed that although unrest and regime changes across the region were attracting a great deal of international attention away from the Palestinian-Israeli issue, the peace process continued to be the core issue for comprehensive peace and stability in the Middle East.[44] In May 2011, after Fatah and Hamas reconciled and agreed to negotiate together to advance Palestinian-Israeli peace talks, China urged Israel to adopt a positive and open attitude toward the reconciliation deal.[45] Later in 2011, Wu expressed China's support for Palestine's seeking UN membership and the view that this action could help to break the deadlock in the peace process.[46] Based on Wu's statements in late 2011, China considered the peace talks stalled. Mirroring the wording of the 2010 CASCF declaration discussed in chapter 4, Wu Sike stressed in 2011 that China supported the founding of a fully sovereign Palestinian state with East Jerusalem as its capital.[47]

Starting in 2012, as hostilities broke out in Syria, Wu became more heavily involved. As early as 2011, he stated that China supported Arab League efforts to promote dialogue and reform in Syria.[48] His efforts included meeting with both the Syrian government and opposition groups in Syria about the crisis.[49] In March 2012, China communicated a six-point proposal for resolving the Syria issue:[50]

1. The Syrian Government and all parties concerned should immediately, fully and unconditionally cease all acts of violence, particularly violence against innocent civilians. Various factions in Syria should express political aspirations through non-violent means.

2. The Syrian Government and various factions should bear in mind the long-term and fundamental interests of their country and people, immediately launch an inclusive political dialogue with no preconditions attached or outcome predetermined through impartial mediation of the Joint Special envoy of the United Nations (UN) and the Arab League (AL), agree on a comprehensive and detailed road-map and timetable for reform through consultation and implement them as soon as possible with a view to restoring national stability and public order.

3. China supports the UN' s leading role in coordinating humanitarian relief efforts. China maintains that under the precondition of respecting Syria's sovereignty, the UN or an impartial body acceptable to all parties should make an objective and comprehensive assessment of the humanitarian situation in Syria, ensure the delivery and distribution of humanitarian aid. China is ready to provide humanitarian assistance to the Syrian people. We oppose anyone interfering in Syria' s internal affairs under the pretext of "humanitarian" issues.

4. Relevant parties of the international community should earnestly respect the independence, sovereignty, unity and territorial integrity of Syria and the right of the Syrian people to independently choose their political system and development path, create conditions and provide necessary and constructive assistance for the various political factions of Syria to launch dialogue, and respect the outcome of dialogue. China does not approve of armed interference or pushing for "regime change" in Syria, and believes that use or threat of sanctions does not help to resolve this issue appropriately.

5. China welcomes the appointment of the Joint Special envoy on the Syrian

> crisis by the UN and the AL and supports him in playing a constructive role in bringing about the political resolution of the crisis. China supports the active efforts made by the Arab states and the AL to promote a political solution to the crisis.
>
> 6. Members of the Security Council should strictly abide by the purposes and principles of the UN Charter and the basic norms governing international relations. As a permanent member of the Security Council, China is ready to earnestly fulfill its responsibilities, engage in equal-footed, patient and full consultation with other parties on the political solution to the Syrian crisis in an effort to safeguard the unity of the Security Council.[51]

Later in 2012, Wu started to express concerns regarding the impact of escalating hostilities in Syria and the threat of spillover of the conflict into the region and the world.[52] In apparent reaction to Arab Gulf states' displeasure with China's vetoes of resolutions about Syria in the UN Security Council, Wu Sike started articulating how China's stance on Syria was misunderstood and highlighted the common interests of China and Arab Gulf states in Syria.[53] He stressed that China was trying to promote a political solution in Syria and supported the peacemaking actions of the Arab League and the Gulf Cooperation Council (GCC) and the mediation efforts of the joint UN–Arab League special representative for the Syrian crisis.[54] One of the main differences of opinion between China and the Arab Gulf States was the desire of the Gulf states to provide weapons to the Syrian opposition.[55] In May 2013, China vocally rejected an EU decision to end an embargo on supplying arms to Syrian rebels and announced that it would continue to provide aid to Syrian refugees in Jordan and other countries.[56]

In 2013, China's special envoy refocused efforts on the Palestinian-Israeli issue. For China, this continued to be the core issue in the Middle East.[57] Wu Sike asserted, "Although the United States once gave the Middle East plenty of hope about resolving the Palestinian-Israeli issue, facts have proved that the United States wants to maintain its dominant position in the Middle East even as it seeks to become less invested in the region. At the same time, it has not stopped showing favoritism to Israel. This has greatly affected America's role."[58] In May 2013, China invited the leaders of the Palestinians and Israel to visit China to communicate about peace talks. According to the envoy, "To the Israeli side, we particularly stress the issue of Israel's suspension of building Jewish settlement and of Israel's showing of some goodwill on improving the humanitarian environment in the Gaza Strip and on other issues that are of Palestine's concern. To the Palestine side, we will promote the resolution of problems through talks."[59] To set the stage for this meeting, Xi Jinping announced a four-point proposal for the peace process in May 2013.

> 1. The right direction to follow should be an independent Palestinian State and peaceful coexistence of Palestine and Israel. To establish an independent state enjoying full sovereignty on the basis of the 1967 borders and with East Jerusalem as its capital is an inalienable right of the Palestinian people and the key to the settlement of the Palestinian question. At the same time, Israel's right to exist and its legitimate security concerns should also be fully respected.
>
> 2. Negotiation should be taken as the only way to peace between Palestine and Israel. The two sides should follow the trend of the times, pursue peace talks, show mutual understanding and accommodation, and meet each other half way. The immediate priority is to take credible steps to stop settlement activities, end violence against innocent civilians, lift the blockade of the Gaza Strip and properly handle the issue of Palestinian prisoners in order to create the necessary conditions for the resumption of peace talks. Comprehensive internal reconciliation on the part of Palestine will help restart and advance the Palestinian-Israeli peace talks.
>
> 3. Principles such as "land for peace" should be firmly upheld. The parties concerned ought to build on the existing achievements that include the principle of "land for peace," the relevant UN resolutions and the Arab Peace Initiative to advance the Middle East peace process across the board.
>
> 4. The international community should provide important guarantee for progress in the peace process. Relevant parties of the international community should have a greater sense of responsibility and urgency, take an objective and fair position, make vigorous efforts to encourage talks for peace, and increase assistance to Palestine in such fields as human resources training and economic development.[60]

To further support Xi's four-point proposal, Foreign Minister Wang Yi visited Palestine and Israel in December 2013.[61]

In 2013, Wu also started advocating for economic development as part of the solution for the Palestinian-Israeli conflict. For example, in April 2013, in meetings with Fatah movement leader Abbas Zaki, he discussed attracting

Chinese investment into Palestine and creating job opportunities.[62] In March 2014, he stated that "China would continue its assistance for the economic development of the Palestinians, including enhancing expertise training, prompting the participation of Chinese companies in the infrastructure development, and the development of renewable energy" and encouraged Chinese companies to join a bid for petroleum exploration.[63] China's 1997 Five Principles regarding the Middle East peace process mentioned regional economic cooperation as an important aspect of facilitating an enduring peace. Since then, however, economic development has not been emphasized in official statements. Considering that this renewed focus on economic development surfaced in 2013, it was likely driven by China's announcing land and sea silk roads that later became the BRI.

Late in Wu Sike's term, hostilities between Israel and the Palestinians increased. In June 2014, tensions on the Israel-Gaza border flared after Hamas abducted and murdered three Jewish teenagers.[64] China supported a cease-fire agreement proposed by Egypt, and Wu Sike visited Palestine, Israel, and other countries in the region to attempt mediation.[65] He called on Israel to "immediately stop the military operations against the Gaza Strip and put an end to the blockage it imposes on the coastal enclave."[66] China also urged a cease-fire between Israel and the Palestinians while meeting with Hamas.[67]

As Wu's tenure as special envoy ended, he continued to attempt to make progress on the Syria issue by inviting the Syrian National Dialogue Forum to visit China to discuss ways to resolve the situation in December 2013.[68] Forum participants included Syria's opposition and pro-government groups. He also urged Turkey to communicate and cooperate with China to solve problems in Syria.[69]

Although the vast majority of Wu Sike's energy as special envoy focused on Palestinian-Israeli peace and Syria, he also expressed concerns about several other Middle East issues. In February 2012, he articulated worries that Israel could have intentions to attack Iranian nuclear facilities.[70] In March 2014, he offered China's help with Libya's political transition and economic construction.[71] Wu attended an international meeting in June 2014 to support Lebanese armed forces.[72] In 2014, he also stressed that China stood behind Iraqi efforts to preserve its sovereignty and independence and combat terrorism. At that point, more than ten thousand Chinese nationals had been evacuated from Iraq. In his words, "The stability of Iraq is key to peace and stability of the entire Middle East, as well as that of the world."[73]

Gong Xiaosheng

In September 2014, Wu Sike stepped down, and China appointed Gong Xiaosheng as its fourth special envoy for Middle East issues.[74] He served until September 2019.[75] Another seasoned diplomat, he had previously served as the director of the Chinese Office in Palestine (ambassador level) (2003–2005), ambassador to Jordan (2006–2008), and ambassador to Turkey (2008–2014).[76] His first trip as envoy was to Palestine, Israel, Egypt, Jordan, and Lebanon shortly after taking office.[77] During his first two years (2014–2016), Gong's areas of emphasis were the Palestinian-Israeli peace process, Syria, Yemen, Iran, Libya, and the Belt and Road in the Middle East. After the appointment of a Chinese special envoy for Syria issues in 2016, Gong focused less on Syria.

Similar to all other Chinese Middle East envoys, Gong frequently asserted that the Palestinian-Israeli issue remained the core of conflict in the Middle East.[78] He often emphasized Xi Jinping's May 2013 four-point proposal for solving the Palestinian-Israeli issue and China's support for a Palestinian state with full sovereignty based on 1967 borders with East Jerusalem as its capital.[79] He also continued to point to the importance of economic aid [80] and development for Palestine and met groups such as the Palestine Liberation Organization when visiting Palestine.[81]

Syria was one major focus for Gong before the establishment of a special envoy to deal specifically with the issue in 2016. In November 2015, he began advocating for a three-in-one approach for Syria: advance counterterrorism cooperation, seek political settlement of the Syria issue, and ease the humanitarian crisis.[82] Similar to previous envoys, Gong met with the Western-backed opposition Syrian National Coalition (SNC).[83]

As hostilities broke out in Yemen in 2014, Gong started to press for the resolution of that conflict as well. In April 2015, he met with Iran's deputy foreign minister for Arab-African affairs to discuss the need for peaceful resolution of the Yemen crisis. He also stressed the need to respect countries' sovereignty and regional cooperation to resolve the regional crisis through political means.[84] While in Jordan in May 2015, he discussed the situation in Yemen.[85] In October 2015, he stated that China was in touch with all Yemeni groups and urged them to return to negotiations.[86] Similar to China's stance on Syria, Gong frequently urged all involved parties to find a political solution to the Yemen crisis.[87] In April 2016, after a trip to Saudi Arabia, Egypt, and Oman, he held a press briefing and stressed that China was making efforts to promote peace in Yemen, bolster UN efforts to reach a cease-fire agreement, and helping to start peace talks in Kuwait.[88]

Another hot spot issue for Gong as special envoy was Libya. In May 2015, he praised Morocco's role in facilitating dialogue between Libyan parties in peace talks.[89] In December 2015, he stated that China supported all sides in Libya that were striving to solve the dispute politically.[90] Gong also participated in multilateral talks on Libya's transition in Rome in January 2016.[91]

Since its announcement in 2015, Gong emphasized Belt and Road. In April 2015, he stated that BRI would become an important part of the future solution of the Middle East peace process: "We hope that the initiative can contribute to achieving peace in the region, and bring some hope, opportunities and peace to the Palestinians, the Syrians and the people living in conflict."[92]

In January 2016, Xi Jinping visited Egypt, Saudi Arabia, and Iran. Shortly after this important visit, Gong told the media that the Palestinian-Israeli issue should not be marginalized, and China supported the establishment of a state of Palestine with full sovereignty based on the 1967 borders with East Jerusalem as its capital.[93] Gong asserted, "President Xi Jinping's recent visit to the Middle East could signal the beginning of a new era in relations between China and Palestine as well as other countries in the region."[94] According to Xinhua news agency, Xi's message in Cairo was clear: "What China wants for a region dogged by decades of troubles is peace, development and stability."[95] State-run Chinese media reported, "Xi said the Palestinian issue should not fall into oblivion as it is of fundamental importance to peace in the Middle East, adding that to bring an end to the conflict, the international community should not only promote the resumption of the talks and implementation of the agreements, but also uphold fairness and justice."[96] During Xi's visit, Beijing committed to provide RMB 50 million (US$7.53 million) of grant aid to Palestine and to support a solar power station project in Palestine.[97] Shortly before Xi visited the region, China released its Arab white paper.[98] During Xi's visit, Gong said, "China has called for an all-round solution to the region's hot issues, stressing that China supports the idea of holding an international peace conference in line with the principle of the two-state solution." He also emphasized that economic development, humanitarian assistance, and the Belt and Road all played an important role in promoting social stability in the Middle East.[99]

After China appointed Xie Xiaoyan special envoy for Syria in April 2016, the emphasis of the Middle East envoy shifted back to the Middle East peace process, as well as China's Belt and Road in the Middle East, Iran, and issues affecting the entire Middle East. Gong also stressed cooperation with Russia and the BRICS (Brazil, Russia, India, China, and South Africa) in the Middle East and a holistic approach to addressing all the hot spots in the region, including Syria, Libya, Iraq, and Yemen.[100]

In early 2016, Gong started to highlight how BRI could contribute to Middle East peace.[101] According to Gong, "China seeks comprehensive solutions to the Middle East crisis, and an essential part of it will be economic restoration, where the Belt and Road Initiative will conjoin with restoration plans of regional countries."[102] He also asserted that "the Belt and Road Initiative is highly likely to become China's most significant contribution to the Middle East peace process because it will provide the economic solution the region needs."[103]

The special envoy continued to consider the Middle East peace process as the core of the regional crisis in the Middle East. In 2017, Gong stated, "All the crises in the regions have been entangled, and it is impossible to solve one without solving the others, especially without handling the Palestinian-Israeli conflict properly."[104]

To continue to emphasize the importance of the Middle East peace process, Xi Jinping announced a four-point proposal for promoting the settlement of the question of Palestine in July 2017:

1. Firmly advance political settlement based on the two-State solution. . . . China firmly supports the two-State solution and supports the establishment of an independent State of Palestine with full sovereignty, based on the 1967 borders and with East Jerusalem as its capital. We will, as always, play a constructive role for the settlement of the question of Palestine.

2. Uphold the concept of common, integrated, cooperative and sustainable security. . . . China calls for the earnest implementation of resolution 2334 (2016). There must be an immediate cessation of all settlement activities on the occupied territories and an immediate adoption of measures to prevent violence against civilians. We also call for an early resumption of peace talks in order to expedite a political solution to the question of Palestine, and thereby fundamentally achieve common and lasting security

3. Further coordinate efforts of the international community and strengthening synergy in the interest of peace. . . . The international community should further strengthen coordination and come up with peace-promotion measures that entail joint participation. China is willing to join and support

> all efforts that are favorable to the political settlement of the question of Palestine. China plans to hold a seminar for peace activists in Palestine and Israel within this year to contribute wisdom for the settlement of the question of Palestine.
>
> 4. Take an integrated approach and promote peace through development. While promoting political negotiations, attention should be given to development, especially to the enhancement of the capacities of Palestine for economic development. China views both Palestine and Israel as important partners in the Belt and Road Initiative.[105]

In December 2017, China held a Palestinian-Israeli Peace Symposium in Beijing, the third meeting of its type. The meeting occurred after President Donald Trump had announced the United States would move its embassy to Jerusalem. Special envoy Gong explained that China hosted the symposium to "play an active and constructive role in promoting the settlement of the Palestine-Israel issue" and "China, as a major country, could play an important role" and "create conditions for promoting stronger and effective international endeavors in advancing peace talks." The symposium occurred right after China voted for a nonbinding UN General Assembly resolution rejecting the US decision to move its embassy to Jerusalem. While meeting with the Palestinian delegation during the symposium, Foreign Minister Wang Yi communicated that China believed the final status of Jerusalem should be decided later with the help of the international community.

In May 2018, when Gong revisited Palestine, Majdi al-Khalidi, Abbas's adviser for diplomatic affairs, said, "We hope that it [China's role] will grow and be more effective, especially since there is an opportunity to form a multilateral international mechanism for [peace] negotiations according to the plan proposed by President Mahmoud Abbas in the UN Security Council, which could be formed by the five permanent members of the Security Council."

In addition to his renewed focus on the Middle East peace process, Gong became increasingly vocal about Iran. In response to the United States unilaterally pulling out of the JCPOA (Joint Comprehensive Plan of Action), Gong stated, "We think some deal is better than no deal."[106] The Chinese Foreign Ministry said, "China regrets the decision by the United States to pull out of an international nuclear deal with Iran."[107] In Gong's words, "The JCPOA is a multilateral deal, wrought through talks and backed by a UN resolution. . . . It is pivotal not only to nonproliferation but also to the promotion of peace in the Middle East."[108] He continued, "China's position on the Iran nuclear agreement is very clear-cut: The agreement is a multilateral one negotiated through arduous efforts by the five permanent members of the UN Security Council [UNSC], Germany, the EU, and Iran and was approved by UNSC Resolution 2231; it is a very serious and important agreement."[109]

Gong indicated that China was ready to work with other world powers to salvage the deal and in the meantime would honor bilateral agreements with Iran in various fields.[110] In May 2018, he visited Tehran and urged "all relevant parties to assume a responsible attitude."[111] While there, he also discussed the situation in Syria with Iranian leaders to advance the peace process and play a constructive role in the reconstruction of the country in the future.[112] That same month, Gong also traveled to Saudi Arabia and Turkey to discuss the Iran nuclear deal, regional hot spots, and the situation in Syria.[113]

Another essential feature of Gong's approach as special envoy for Middle East issues was his emphasis on cooperation with Russia and the BRICS in the Middle East. Gong often met with Russian officials to discuss the Middle East. For example, they met in April 2017, March 2018, and June 2018. Their discussions focused on the military-political situation in Syria, Iraq, Yemen, and Libya and prospects for a Palestinian-Israeli settlement.[114] China-Russia coordination in the Middle East includes both bilateral cooperation and working together on different international and regional platforms, including the UN Security Council and the BRICS.[115] The BRICS issued a joint statement on the current situation in the Middle East and North Africa in June 2018.[116]

In September 2019, a new envoy, Zhai Jun, was appointed. This chapter does not analyze his tenure.

Middle East Issues Envoy Conclusion

China established the Middle East issues envoy in 2002 to contribute to the Middle East peace process. China considers the Palestinian-Israeli conflict the core issue influencing peace and stability in the region. After the Arab awakening, the envoy started to expand its focus beyond the Palestinian-Israeli conflict to include Syria, Yemen, Iraq, Libya, Iran, and Belt and Road. Still, the most critical focus of the envoy remains the Middle East peace process.

China has multifaceted strategic interests in the peace process. First, similar to China's behavior in the CASCF, it appears to genuinely support the cause of the Palestinians and other Arabs involved in the conflict in seeking a just solution. Also, it conceptualizes the Middle East conflict as between not only Israel and the Palestinians but also Israel and Syria and Lebanon. Second, regional stability in the Middle East is crucial for China. It wants peace there to ensure a stable international environment for its economic growth and prosperity, as well as energy security. Since China perceives the Palestinian-Israeli conflict as the core problem in the Middle East, solving this dilemma would help to guarantee peace. Third, China considers its involvement to be the appropriate conduct for a responsible great power that is a permanent member of the UN Security Council. Finally, China sees itself as uniquely positioned to function as a balanced liaison and peacemaker between disputing powers because it maintains relatively good relations with all of the parties involved in the conflict and never colonized the region.

Although Arab states may want China to exert more influence in the Middle East peace process on their behalf, the specific role of the special envoy is to gain a deeper understanding of the conflict and serve as a liaison between various parties.[117] China is not making unique proposals; it just wants the issues resolved. At this point, its most important mission is to encourage the parties to negotiate.

As reflected in its official statements about Middle East peace, China supports peaceful negotiations; an end to violence, an independent Palestinian state; the establishment of an international supervisory mechanism; the land-for-peace principle as a basis for talks; negotiations with Israel, the Palestinians, Lebanon, and Syria; greater involvement of the international community in the peace process; and regional economic development as a potential path to peace. China's interpretation of land-for-peace is that borders should be negotiated to pre-1967 lines, the Golan Heights should be returned to Syria, and East Jerusalem should be the capital of Palestine. Also, although China often points out that Israel's statehood is a fact and that its security must be protected, its criticism of Israel's aggression appears to be stronger than its condemnation of terrorist activities perpetrated by Hamas or Hezbollah. China does maintain normal state-to-state relations with Israel, but it seems to support the Arab side of the conflicts more. Since the envoy was initiated in 2002, China's position on these issues has remained relatively constant.

One significant change in its special envoy behavior in the Middle East was the proliferation of issues that it addressed. After the beginning of the Arab awakening, the Middle East issues envoy worked on a wide range of hot spot issues, including Syria, Yemen, Iraq, and Iran.

In 2016, China formed a separate envoy to deal with Syria. After that, the

Middle East envoy shifted its focus back to primarily the Middle East peace process and broader issues of stability in the Middle East, such as the need for BRI development and support for Iran in the JCPOA. Some common themes of the Chinese envoy's approach to issues outside the Middle East peace process were stressing the sovereignty of states in the region, encouraging multilateral approaches to resolve issues through the UN and other international organizations, and a willingness to talk to all relevant states and nonstate actors in the region to solve problems.

China's special envoy for Middle East issues supports many of China's interests discussed in chapter 3. By promoting regional stability, the envoy enables China to pursue its interests in accessing resources and markets in the Middle East and ensuring energy security. China's backing of the Palestinians and Palestine fosters support for China in the international system among many developing countries, particularly Muslim-majority countries. Standing up for the Palestinians is also a way China advocates for developing country causes and demonstrates its support for issues of concern to Arab countries. China's stance against Western foreign intervention in Syria, Yemen, and Libya is part of its broader attempts to protect its sovereignty from the West and stand up for Arab causes. China also uses the special envoy to cooperate with Russia and pursue shared interests in the Middle East.

Through the special envoy for Middle East issues, China portrays itself as a responsible permanent member of the UN Security Council that serves as a balanced actor in the Middle East peace process and other regional issues, including Iran's nuclear issues. It differentiates itself from other great powers by advocating for nonintervention and noninterference. Although it leans to the side of Arabs and Palestinians in the Arab-Israeli conflict and Palestinian-Israeli conflict, it distinguishes itself from the United States by stressing that it is a balanced actor and not taking sides compared to US support for Israel. China also consistently highlights its desire to use multilateral mechanisms for addressing all hot spot issues in the region in contrast with the unilateral intervention of the West historically and today.

China's behavior is competitive with the United States via this envoy in the Middle East. China's support for the Arab stance on the Middle East peace process, in opposition to US support for Israel, is competitive. China is presenting itself as a different kind of great power from the United States that is willing to work with all regional states to address the Middle East peace process as well as issues in Syria, Yemen, and Libya. It is competing by standing up to the United States for its promotion of foreign intervention and interference in other hot spot issues. China's behavior is also competitive in criticizing the United States for its treatment of Iran by withdrawing from the multilateral JCPOA agreement and regime change motives in the region more broadly. In addition, pursuing shared interests with Russia in this region could be interpreted as competitive against the United States and the rest of the West.

China's normative behavior through the special envoy for Middle East issues is mixed. Most of China's behavior in the envoy is norm convergent with the liberal order. China's promotion and utilization of multilateral mechanisms for pursuing peace in regional conflict is categorized as norm convergent. As part of this behavior, China advocates for the role of the United Nations in resolving disputes in the Middle East and calls on all parties to respect UN resolutions. In other hot spot issues addressed by the special envoy, China's strict interpretation of Westphalian sovereignty and its stance against foreign intervention and taking sides are norm divergent from the liberal order.

China's Special Envoy for Syria

In 2016, China appointed an envoy solely focused on resolving the Syria issue to promote peace and stability in the Middle East. Xie Xiaoyan was appointed special envoy for Syria in March 2016. He previously served as Chinese ambassador to Iran (2007–2010), Chinese ambassador to Ethiopia, and concurrently head of the Chinese mission to the African Union (2011–2015).[118] In his past diplomatic roles, he was involved in talks on the Iran nuclear program and South Sudan.[119] At the time of his appointment, the United Nations and the United States also had special envoys for Syria, Staffan de Mistura, and Michael Ratney, respectively.[120]

Xie Xiaoyan

During this tenure, Xie Xiaoyan has spent most of his energy on Syria focused on: achieving a cease-fire, seeking a political solution to the conflict, encouraging counterterrorism activities, facilitating humanitarian assistance, planning reconstruction activities, and condemning chemical weapons use in Syria while emphasizing that a full investigation of alleged chemical weapons use by the Assad regime is needed.[121] He frequently warns that China and the rest of the international community need to learn from the lessons of Iraq and Libya and prevent regime change by foreign intervention. To encourage a resolution to the Syria issue, Xie represents China in all significant peace talks on Syria, including the Geneva, Astana, and Vienna processes. His efforts to promote peace include meeting with opposition groups in Syria as well as the Syrian government. Xie also seeks cooperation with Russia, Iran, and Hezbollah to resolve the Syrian situation.

When Xie was appointed, China's Foreign Ministry stated that the purpose of the Syria envoy was to "better promote peace talks and negotiations, contribute Chinese wisdom and proposals, and enhance communication and coordination with relevant parties more effectively, so that China can continue to play a constructive role in seeking a final proper settlement of the Syrian issue."[122] Although the government has not explicitly stated why it formed a separate Syrian envoy, several factors likely influenced its creation. First, with the Arab awakening, Syria began to occupy a great deal of the time of the special envoy for Middle East issues. Establishing a special envoy focused exclusively on Syria freed up the Middle East issues special envoy to work on the Middle East peace process and other regional issues. Second, in November 2015, ISIS killed a Chinese hostage in Syria, [123] an incident that increased public awareness within China of dangers to Chinese citizens in Syria and Chinese government fears about the risk of terrorism emanating from Syria. It also underscored concerns about terrorism spreading from Syria to China. Third, in January 2016, Xi Jinping visited the Middle East (Saudi Arabia, Iran, and Egypt), and an important topic of discussion during his trip was Syria. That visit could have increased his awareness of the need for two Middle East envoys: one focused on the Middle East peace process and one on Syria. Finally, creating two separate envoys provides China the opportunity to treat the Middle East peace process and Syria as different issues. China labels some opposition groups in Syria as terrorists (e.g., Turkistan Islamic Party), and counterterrorism efforts are a significant thrust of that envoy. In contrast, China does not refer to Palestinians as terrorists. Separating these two issues allows China to differentiate between terrorism concerns in Syria that could potentially threaten Chinese abroad and at home from historical and contemporary support for the Palestinians and their quest for self-determination.

Xie stresses that China's stance on Syria is to advocate for a political solution in alignment with the principles of noninterference in internal affairs, sovereignty, and territorial integrity.[124] This stance closely aligned with China's promotion of the Five Principles. China is advocating for Syria's right to sovereignty, noninterference, and nonintervention, but it was not taking sides in the dispute. Xie's position is that "preconditioning the ouster of Assad to start negotiations is not a solution as it will obstruct any peacemaking efforts."[125] China proposes a four-track approach to resolving the Syria issue: cease-fire, political peace talks, counterterrorism cooperation, and humanitarian cooperation.[126] In November 2017, Chinese Foreign Minister Wang Yi emphasized similar themes with his three pillars for resolving the Syria crisis: fight terrorism, engage in dialogue, and begin reconstruction.[127]

China has made clear that it views Syria as much more than a domestic problem for Syria; rather, it is an issue that "has affected the security and stability of the region and the entire world, and all relevant parties should seek common ground while resolving differences to promote the establishment of an effective political settlement."[128] It frames the issue as one that could significantly influence regional security in the Middle East.

In May 2018, Xie elaborated on China's specific position on the Syria issue. Its Five Point approach is:

1. Continue maintaining communication with all relevant parties, and deeply call on various parties to promote peace talks.

2. Continue supporting the UN's role as the main channel for mediation and the mediation efforts of special envoy for Syria of the UN Secretary-General.

3. Continue actively participating in Geneva Peace Talks, the International Syria Support Group and other peace-promotion mechanisms, and support all peace-promotion initiatives that are conducive to advancing the political settlement of the Syrian issue and accepted by various parties.

4. Continue offering assistance within capacity to the Syrian people.

5. Support Syria's reconstruction process in proper ways.[129]

China announced these five points during the first international symposium on Syria held by China. Attendees included the representative of the special envoy for Syria of the UN secretary-general, the special envoy for Syria of the government of the United Kingdom , the special envoy for Syria of the French government, and experts as well as scholars from twelve countries: China, the United States, Syria, Egypt, Qatar, Turkey, Iraq, Iran, Saudi Arabia, Jordan, Lebanon, and the United Kingdom. At the meeting, they conducted in-depth discussions on three topics: "the way out for the settlement of the Syrian issue, the major factors influencing the settlement of the Syrian issue and the role of the international community in the Syrian issue."[130]

Consistently, Xie calls for a political solution and counterterrorism efforts to continue in parallel. In his words, "The efforts to counter terrorists and extremists within Syria will also facilitate the political settlement of the Syria issue. It is also a good thing for counterterrorism endeavors in the wider region."[131] He also says, "The fight against terrorism is an important issue because terrorism hinders a cease-fire and leads to the continuation of chaos, and it is a common enemy to all mankind. Therefore, all terrorist organizations listed by the United Nations on the black list must be hit with an iron fist."[132] He stresses that "terrorism is a common enemy of mankind and it should not be exploited to forward special agendas."[133]

Often he refers to the need for international efforts to fight terrorism in Syria.[134] He specifically stresses that although terrorism must be countered, intrafactional fighting within Syria was not helpful for conflict resolution.[135] Xie frames Russia's military intervention in Syria as a counterterrorism effort: "Russia's anti-terrorist operations in Syria are part of international counter-terrorism efforts. Russia's military operations in Syria in the past six months have effectively curbed the spread of extremists and terrorists there. I think this is encouraging progress."[136] He stresses that Syrian factions, regional countries, and the international community should all unite to fight terrorism.[137]

One major driver of China's concerns regarding terrorism in Syria is the operations of the Turkistan Islamic Party (TIP). PRC leaders believe that TIP was partially to blame for the uptick of terrorist violence in China from 2012 to 2015. They are concerned that TIP has connections with Uyghurs in China's Xinjiang province.[138] Many countries recognize TIP as a terrorist group, and China has even convinced Turkey to categorize it as one.[139] Scholars estimate that in 2017, there were approximately 2,000 Uyghur jihadists in TIP fighting in the Syrian provinces of Idlib, Latakia, and Hama.[140] As of 2018, according to special envoy Xie, there was no accurate figure of the number of ethnic Uyghurs who had gone to fight with militant groups in Syria. "As for how many Uyghur terrorists there are, I've seen all sorts of figures. Some say 1,000 or 2,000; 2,000 or 3,000; 4,000 or 5,000, and some say even more," Xie said.[141]

There are reports that Chinese military advisers have trained the Syrian military in Damascus and are working with the Syrian military to target TIP activities there. According to one report, a senior diplomat at Deutsche Welle news agency was quoted as stating, "Whenever [Syrian] troops capture TIP or ISIS jihadists, these officers collect from militants first-hand information about individuals who are of interest to the Chinese special services." According to that same report, Syrian government troops and Hezbollah, backed by Russia and Iran, delivered Uyghur militants in Syria to Chinese advisers, and they were sent to China after interrogation.[142] Voice of America reported that in late 2017, Syrian and Chinese government officials were discussing the possibility of deploying Chinese special forces to Syria to fight TIP. China has not publicly discussed this issue.[143]

There is also reporting that China is providing direct military assistance to Syria. In August 2016, reports indicated that the Chinese military would provide aid and training to the Syrian government. According to those reports, a People's Liberation Army (PLA) delegation headed by Rear Admiral Guan Youfei, director of international cooperation at China's Central Military Commission, met Syrian government representatives. During the visit, "They reached consensus on improving personnel training, and the Chinese military offering humanitarian aid to Syria." It was reported that the PLA was willing to continue exchanges and cooperation with the Syrian military. It also claimed that Guan met Lieutenant General Sergei Chvarkov, chief of Russia's reconciliation center, in Syria. [144] Despite multiple reports in 2016, 2017, and 2018 of Chinese military cooperation with Syria, the Chinese government claims that China has no military presence in Syria. Still, it does plan to participate in the reconstruction of the country after the war.[145]

China's concern about TIP explains why it continues to emphasize counterterrorism heavily in Syria, even as the ISIS presence decreases. In January 2018, the special envoy stated, "Although the Islamic State terror group . . . has been defeated in Syria, its remaining members, as well as other terrorist groups, such as Jabhat al-Nusra . . . and the East Turkestan independence movement, still exist, so the war on terror is far from being over."[146] In light of the continued TIP presence, China continues to call on all countries of the world to fight terrorism in Syria.[147]

In addition to often highlighting the need for a cease-fire, political solution, and counterterrorism efforts in Syria, Xie also stresses humanitarian relief. Shortly after Xie was appointed special envoy, he stated that China had already provided RMB 680 million (about US$104.97 million) in aid for Syria and would continue to contribute.[148] In August 2016, he announced that in

2016, China provided Jordan with RMB 130 million (US$20 million) to help with Syrian refugees.[149] That year, China also offered Lebanon aid for Syrian refugees.[150] China gave ten thousand tons of food assistance to the refugees, as well as medical equipment and medicine.[151]

Starting in 2017, China's focus on humanitarian aid emphasized the need to support reconstruction in Syria after the war. In Xie's words, "All groups should make joint efforts to start reconstruction in the near future and China as a UN Security Council member is ready to act upon its responsibility to reconstruct Syria and we are prepared for it."[152] China estimates that Syria will need $200 billion for reconstruction efforts.[153] When he speaks about reconstruction in Syria, Xie stresses that it is not just economic reconstruction but also cultural, societal, and security reconstruction.[154] One potential barrier to the participation of Chinese companies in Syria's reconstruction is the settlement of past debts. According to the envoy, if left unresolved, this issue could prevent Chinese companies from working on future reconstruction projects.[155]

Related to China's broader humanitarian concerns about Syria, it strongly condemns and opposes the use of chemical weapons.[156] According to Xie, China's position is that it is "firmly against and strongly condemn any use of chemical weapons by any country, any organization or any individual under any circumstances in any place at any time" and in the case of accusations about Syrian chemical weapons use in 2017 China called for "an independent, impartial, professional and thorough investigation into the case to find out the perpetrators, catch them, condemn them and punish them according to international law and conventions."[157]

Again in 2018, China strongly voiced its opposition to the use of chemical weapons and called for a comprehensive, just, and objective probe into the alleged gas attacks.[158] Although opposed to chemical weapons use, China does express concern that the use of chemical weapons by nonstate groups in Syria could be used as a pretext for foreign powers to carry out military action against Syria.[159] Both China and Russia condemned the retaliatory strikes conducted against Syria by the United States in April 2018 without a UN Security Council resolution.[160] According to news reporting at the time, at a meeting between special envoys on Syria, Russia and China agreed that the "alleged chemical attack in Syria was staged in order to prepare the ground for striking that country without the consent of the UN Security Council."[161]

To pursue the goal of achieving a cease-fire and political solution to the Syrian issue, Xie began meeting with both the Syrian government and opposition immediately after he was appointed special envoy.[162] Numerous meetings have been held with representatives of opposition groups at intra-Syrian talks at international locations as well as in Syria.[163] China is taking an active role in negotiating for peace in Syria's civil war.

One theme the special envoy frequently stressed is that the international community should learn from experiences in Iraq, Libya, and Yemen and not pursue regime change in Syria.[164] In April 2017, Xie explicitly criticized the United States and the rest of the West for intervention and regime change:

> External players of the Syria crisis should draw lessons from Iraq and Libya if they are mulling a "regime change." . . . External forces do have a role to play, but there is a line beyond which is meddling in the internal affairs of another country. . . . It is not our job to make prejudgment and it is not our duty to decide the future of that particular person. . . . Past experiences have told us the mere change of regime will bring disaster for a country, the case being Iraq, Libya, and elsewhere. . . . Just look at these two countries, have peace and stability returned? Have people benefited from the removal of figures like Saddam Hussein or Gaddhafi?[165]

Concerning foreign interference, he also emphasizes that it "has led to the reinvigoration of the terrorists in Syria and the spread of their presence to other areas"[166] and that foreign "military strikes not only fail to solve problems, but incur turmoil and suffering to those living in the region."[167] In his words, "We will never tolerate a repeat of historical tragedy."[168]

To promote a political solution to the situation in Syria, China participates in several multilateral Syria peace process negotiations, including Geneva, Vienna, and Astana.[169] China has not proposed its own mechanism for negotiating peace in Syria. The UN sponsors the Geneva process that facilitates negotiations between the Syrian government and Syrian opposition groups. China has participated in the Geneva process since its first meeting in June 2012.[170] Other representatives at the initial meeting in 2012 included the League of Arab States, France, Russia, the United Kingdom, the United States, Turkey, Iraq, Kuwait, Qatar, and the European Union. China also attended Geneva II (January 2014)[171] and Geneva III (February 2016). Xie participated in several meetings since he was appointed special envoy. For example, he attended Geneva IV in April 2016[172] and Geneva V in January 2017.[173] According to Xie, China's stance is that the United Nations should remain the main channel of mediation for reaching a political solution in Syria. [174] In 2018, the

Geneva process hosted the first negotiations of the Syrian cease-fire guarantor states: Iran, Russia, and Turkey.[175]

China also participated in the Vienna process from its beginning in November 2015. The United States and Russia lead that process. Participants are called the International Syria Support Group (ISSG). They include the Arab League, Australia, Canada, China, Egypt, the European Union, France, Germany, Iran, Iraq, Italy, Japan, Jordan, Lebanon, the Netherlands, the Organization of Islamic Cooperation, Oman, Qatar, Russia, Saudi Arabia, Spain, Turkey, the United Arab Emirates, the United Kingdom, the United Nations, and the United States.[176] After his appointment, Xie started attending ISSG meetings.[177] The Vienna process produced an agreement to bring the Syrian government and the opposition to the negotiating table under UN auspices. Members of the Vienna process affirmed their commitment to enforcing the 2012 Geneva Communiqué for political transition and a nationwide cease-fire.

The Astana peace process, sponsored by Russia, Turkey, and Iran, was initiated after Xie assumed his role as special envoy. The talks facilitate discussion between the Syrian government and opposition groups. When the first meeting was held in January 2017, China sent a delegation, and Xie stressed that the UN and China welcomed the talks as part of the broader effort to find a political solution to the crisis in Syria.[178] China views the Astana and Geneva talks as complementary. According to Xie, "I think the two platforms, each having its own special role to play, but can also be mutually supportive."[179] In July 2017, he noted that deescalation zones were an important achievement of the recent Astana talks.[180] As of September 2017, China was not an official observer of the Astana process but was open to a proposal to join the process officially.[181]

China also has pursued bilateral cooperation with interested states and nonstate actors in attempting to seek political resolution of the Syrian issue. For example, it has engaged in significant cooperation with Russia, Iran, and Hezbollah.

China frequently meets with Russia about Syrian issues. Xie often emphasizes that China coordinates positions with Russia on a political solution to the Syrian crisis,[182] values the efforts that Russia puts on fighting terrorism and promoting peace talks,[183] and is ready to work with Russia on postwar reconstruction efforts in Syria.[184] After a January 2017 trip to Moscow, Xie stated, "This is our third visit to Moscow; the situation on the ground has been changing very rapidly, and Russia and China, being strategic partners, should have an opportunity to exchange opinions and to exercise coordination on the Syria issue."[185] In 2017 alone, Xie met with Russian government officials in Moscow at least three times, in January, April, and September.[186] China and Russia share many interests in Syria. In April 2018, Xie stated that both Russia and China's key goals in Syria were "the fight against terrorism, preventing the return of foreign militants from the Middle East and post-war restoration of Syria."[187] Russia and China are cooperating on Syria in many international institutions, including the United Nations, BRICS, and the Shanghai Cooperation Organization (SCO).[188]

China is also working closely with Iran on Syria. Xie often travels to Tehran to meet with Iranian government officials.[189] The two countries stress the need for cooperation on counterterrorism and humanitarian aid for Syria.[190] Both countries also warn against foreign intervention in Syria. For example, while meeting with Iranian government officials in Tehran, in reaction to a US announcement that it planned to send 250 additional special forces to Syria, Xie stated, "No foreign power must interfere in issues related to Syria's future. We must allow the Syrian people to decide for themselves about writing a new constitution and choosing a president"[191] In preparation for a July 2017 trip to Tehran, Xie stated that "Iran and China enjoy common positions not only on Syria but also on other regional and international issues."[192]

In addition to Russia and Iran, Xie frequently meets with Hezbollah about Syria. In December 2016, while Xie met with Hezbollah's head of international relations, he stressed that both sides agreed to seek solutions to the Syrian crisis that fight terrorism and rescue civilians.[193] One purpose of that trip to Lebanon was to "clarify the role of Hezbollah movement in the Syrian conflict, and to express China's appreciation of Lebanese authorities' efforts to aid the humanitarian efforts in Syria."[194] Xie met with Hezbollah again in June 2017 to discuss efforts to fight terrorism in Syria and the importance of reaching political solutions there.

Although the level of interaction was lower than that of Russia, Iran, and Hezbollah, China also meets bilaterally with other regional powers about the situation in Syria, including Turkey, Egypt,[195] the Arab League,[196] the Gulf Cooperation Council,[197] Saudi Arabia,[198] and Israel.[199]

Syria Envoy Conclusion

The focus of the Syria special envoy is to achieve a cease-fire, seek a political solution to the conflict, encourage counterterrorism activities, facilitate humanitarian assistance, plan reconstruction activities, and condemn chemical weapons use in Syria while emphasizing that a full investigation of alleged chemical weapons use by the Assad regime is needed.[200] The envoy frequently warns that China and the rest of the international community need to learn from the lessons of Iraq and Libya and prevent regime change by foreign intervention. To encourage a resolution to the Syria issue, Xie represents China in all significant peace talks on Syria, including the Geneva, Astana, and Vienna processes. His efforts to promote peace include meeting with opposition groups in Syria as well as the Syrian government. Xie also has sought cooperation from Russia, Iran, and Hezbollah to resolve the Syrian situation.

Similar to China's Middle East issues envoy, the Syria envoy pursues many of China's interests in the Middle East. China views the Syrian civil war and potential spillover into broader conflict as threatening peace and stability. This envoy thus works to facilitate peace in Syria for China to continue to access resources and markets in the broader Middle East. The Syrian envoy also provides China an opportunity to foster support in the international arena by acting as a balanced player on the issue. The envoy meets with all relevant regional state and nonstate parties, as well as intergovernmental organizations, to promote resolution of the issue while still protecting Syria's sovereignty.

The special envoy also facilitates China's pursuit of its own domestic stability. By encouraging counterterrorism activities toward TIP in Syria through cooperation with the Syrian government and vocally supporting Russia's counterterrorism efforts, China attempts to eradicate TIP and other terrorist groups as a threat to it at home and abroad. This action also contributes to China's ability to protect its citizens and businesses abroad. This focus on counterterrorism is different from how China approaches the Middle East and Africa envoys. Neither the Middle East peace process nor Sudan and South Sudan are framed as terrorism issues that threaten China's domestic stability.

China fulfills its interests by advocating for developing country causes. Through the envoy, China expresses its desire to contribute to humanitarian challenges encountered by Syria as well as participate in reconstruction efforts. Finally, China uses the envoy to protect its sovereignty from the United States and the rest of the West. Through the special envoy, China champions sovereignty and struggles against foreign intervention.

China's Syria envoy competes with the United States and cooperates with Russia. Due to its firm stance against foreign intervention, interference, and refusal to choose sides in the conflict, China differentiates itself from other great powers. (China's competitive behavior on the Syria issue is also clearly seen in chapter 7 during the discussion of its UN Security Council voting.) Most of China's competitive behavior in this special envoy is through demonstrating that it is a different kind of great power from the United States. It is standing up to the United States to prevent Iraq or Libya-style regime change by the United States in Syria. That said, China is also cooperating with the West by participating in the multilateral Geneva and Vienna peace talk processes.

Although it is often competing with the United States through the special envoy for Syria, China's normative behavior is mixed. China is enthusiastically supporting multilateral institutions aimed at resolving the Syrian crisis and providing humanitarian aid and reconstruction assistance, support for counterterrorism, and criticism of the use of chemical weapons in Syria. All of that behavior converges with liberal norms of the international system. That said, its behavior diverges from the liberal order, especially the responsibility to protect (R2P) citizens from mass atrocities such as genocide, war crimes, ethnic cleansing, and crimes against humanity, through its strong focus on the Five Principles, Westphalian sovereignty, and criticizing foreign intervention in Syria.

How does China portray and differentiate itself as a great power with the Syria envoy? It portrays itself as a balanced actor in Syria, standing up against foreign intervention and meddling. It sees itself as a responsible permanent member of the UN Security Council and supports all major peace processes for Syria. It does its best to contribute to Syrian peace though unilateral and multilateral channels. China does not try to create its own mechanisms to deal with the conflict. It prefers to use multilateral mechanisms led by others. To achieve peace, China is willing to interact with all relevant parties, including those with strained relations with the United States, such as Russia, Iran, and Hezbollah.

China's Africa Issues Special Envoy

As opposed to the competitive and mixed normative behavior of China's Middle East issues special envoy and Syria envoy, China's behavior in the special Africa issues envoy has been cooperative with the United States and norm convergent with the liberal order. The origin of the African special envoy was pressure from the broader international community, especially the United States and the EU. The original purpose of this envoy was to focus on the resolution of issues in Darfur that were drawing international concern and criticism of China.[201] One main objective of the envoy was to demonstrate to the international community that China was concerned about the violence in Darfur.[202]

Liu Guijin

In May 2007, China appointed a special envoy for African Issues, Liu Guijin. He previously held posts as the ambassador to Zimbabwe (1995–1998) and South Africa (2001–2007).[203] In July 2007, he announced the objectives of the special envoy about the Darfur situation:

> Firstly, the position and policy of the Chinese government on the Darfur issue are widely recognized by the international community, particularly African countries, AU and LAS.[204] The African countries all agreed with the basic opinion of China on how to resolve the Darfur issue, that is, seeking for a long-term and ultimate solution to the issue by political means and through consultations and dialogues on an equal footing. . . .
>
> Secondly, it is the general agreement of African countries and the wide consensus of the international community that the current three-party mechanism, that is, equal consultations among AU, UN and the Sudanese government, is the main channel, whose role should be continuously played. . . .
>
> Thirdly, we, whether EU, AU, LAS or the international community, all have one common goal, that is, the early resolution of the Darfur issue.[205]

In the same speech, he claimed credit for China's contribution to the resolution of the Darfur issue: "The Chinese government played a responsible role in resolving the Darfur issue. We have taken many positive actions. It should be said that obvious results were achieved. The Sudanese government has explicitly declared the unconditional acceptance of the third phase of Annan Plan, that is, hybrid peacekeeping operation."[206] Other sources also noted that the envoy was instrumental in convincing Khartoum to accept the deployment of the UN-African Union Mission to Darfur (UNAMID).[207]

China portrayed the appointment of this African special envoy as a response to requests from the international community. For example, the envoy declared, "Because the Darfur issue draws worldwide attention and the international community hopes China plays a bigger role, the Chinese government, at the request of the international community, appoints a special representative on the issue."[208]

In describing his activities to resolve the Darfur issue, Liu Guijin often emphasized China's coordination with the AU, EU, United States, and UN. He highlighted the approval of these states of China's approach. For example, in September 2007, he stated that "the UN and US spoke positively of the constructive role played by China in resolving the Darfur issue and commented that the commitments of the Chinese government to dispatch multifunctional engineering unit to Darfur are a strong support to the hybrid peacekeeping operations."[209]

Most of Liu's activities as special envoy for Africa revolved around Sudan and Darfur. One exception was his involvement in debates associated with imposing sanctions on Zimbabwe in 2008.[210]

Zhong Jianhua

Upon resolution of the Darfur issue, the activities of the envoy became relatively limited. After South Sudan formed in 2011, China appointed Zhong Jianhua as the next special envoy in 2012.[211] As is true of all of China's special envoys, he had a long and distinguished career in China's foreign service. He was China's ambassador to South Africa 2007 to 2012.[212] During his tenure as special envoy, he mostly worked on issues related to South Sudan. Other topics addressed include Mali, the African Great Lakes region, promoting positive economic engagement between China and African states, and articulating China's approach to peace and security in Africa.

Most of Zhong's emphasis was managing China's involvement with South Sudan. His efforts focused on facilitating mediation, protecting Chinese company interests, and encouraging cooperation between the United States and China. To promote mediation, he stressed bilateral relations with South Sudan in the areas of economics, infrastructure, agriculture, and basic services.[213] Regarding oil clashes between Juba (South Sudan) and Khartoum (Sudan), he continually stated that China supports the African Union High Implementation Panel's efforts to resolve issues between the two states.[214] China's stance on the conflict between the two countries was if "asked by South Sudan and Sudan to intervene and help them solve the dispute they would be glad to do so, however they declared their position as neutral on the issues involving the two countries. Because it is a Chinese policy that no interference with other countries' domestic affairs."[215] As tensions between Sudan and South Sudan grew in 2012, special envoy Zhong visited both countries to promote peace talks and negotiations.[216]

Closely linked with China's interests in protecting Chinese citizens and businesses abroad, a critical aspect of China's involvement in South Sudan was Beijing's desire to protect Chinese companies operating in the country. When Sudan and South Sudan split in July 2011, Sudan was exporting most of its oil to China. Upon South Sudan's independence, the South took 75 percent of the oil reserves but continued to be dependent on the North's pipelines to export crude because it does not have a seaport of its own.[217] As hostilities broke out in 2012, China urged Sudan and South Sudan to protect the rights and interests of Chinese oil companies.[218]

China's concerns regarding stability in Sudan also grew when twenty-nine Chinese workers building a road in South Kordofan Province in Sudan were abducted in January 2012. Although the workers were released in February, the incident raised Chinese public awareness regarding the situation in Sudan.[219] Similar to the execution of a Chinese hostage in Syria shortly before the special envoy for Syria was established, this incident created popular pressure on the Chinese government to protect Chinese citizens and businesses in Sudan.

One enduring theme of China's Africa and Middle East envoys is that China differentiates itself as a balanced actor willing to deal with all interested parties and one that respects the sovereignty of other countries. According to an editorial in May 2012 in the *South China Morning Post*, "Half a world separates China from the bickering Sudans, but there is no country better placed to stop the two African nations from going to war."[220] In the words of Jean Ping, chairperson of the African Union Commission, "China with its good relations with Sudan and South Sudan, is in a 'unique position to play a constructive role in the search for a peaceful solution to the crisis between both states.'"[221] One way China demonstrates this balanced approach is by supporting the AU-sponsored process negotiating peace between Sudan and South Sudan.[222] China actively encourages both sides of the conflict to enter into negotiations and reach a settlement.[223]

After his appointment, Zhong Jianhua stressed cooperating with the United States on Sudan and South Sudan. As tensions between Sudan and South Sudan heated up in 2012, China's vice foreign minister, Cui Tiankai, stressed that China was working with the United States to try to end the crisis: "Both of our countries have special envoys who are in very close touch. . . .

China and the United States are working on the issue through our own channels. We hope Sino-U.S. cooperation on this issue will pay off."[224] In 2012, China and the United States seriously considered sending US Secretary of State Hillary Clinton and China's foreign minister, Yang, to travel together to Khartoum and Juba to attempt to normalize relations and persuade South Sudan to resume oil production. Ultimately the plan was aborted. Although it failed, this is a good example of the level of cooperation that was occurring between the United States and China on this issue.[225]

As special envoy, Zhong frequently traveled to both countries to encourage peace, and leaders of both countries visited Beijing.[226] During 2013, he frequently met with both countries to prevent Sudan from shutting down a pipeline that transports South Sudan's oil to external markets.[227] Partially because of his efforts, the Sudanese government agreed in July 2013 to delay the shutdown of the oil pipeline used to transport South Sudan's oil to Port Sudan.[228] According to a Sudanese diplomat, "China sees itself in partnership with north and south Sudan in oil production and therefore it stepped into the row in a timely manner."[229] Zhong was also instrumental in securing delays in a pipeline shutdown later in the year. Working with AU mediator Mbeki regarding the deadline, he "convinced Bashir to hold it off while committees work to verify rebel support claims made by Khartoum and Juba."[230]

After a failed December 2013 coup attempt in South Sudan that eventually evolved into civil war,[231] Zhong urged all relevant parties to remain calm, show restraint, and resolve their differences through dialogue. He also called on the South Sudanese government to protect the "personal and property safety of Chinese people and institutions in South Sudan."[232] He traveled to South Sudan and neighboring countries to mediate between factions in the dispute and administer emergency humanitarian aid.[233]

From the beginning of South Sudan's civil war in 2013, the Intergovernmental Authority on Development (IGAD), whose members are Djibouti, Ethiopia, Somalia, Eritrea, Sudan, South Sudan, Kenya, and Uganda, requested China's engagement in mediation.[234] Zhong expressed China's support for the IGAD efforts to resolve the crisis in South Sudan.[235] As part of his attempts to cooperate with regional powers to resolve the crisis in South Sudan, he met with government officials from other IGAD countries, including Ethiopia, Uganda, and Kenya.[236]

In reaction to the situation in South Sudan, Zhong stated, "We will be happy to be mediator. If any party has any message to want to bring to the other side, as long as it is toward a peaceful solution, we would be happy to do that. And of course, we have admitted that this is an African problem; it must be solved by the African people in African way. We fully respect that."[237]

Zhong saw China as playing a unique role by facilitating communications among all parties: "Beijing can play this role well because African nations such as South Sudan trust China, as it has never invaded African countries or hurt the self-esteem of African people." He also frequently notes that African and Western nations have spoken highly of China's role.[238] Zhong asserted that China's approach to South Sudan marks a "'new chapter' in Beijing's foreign policy that will seek to engage more in Africa's security."[239]

Zhong, who met with the South Sudanese opposition on December 15, 2013, noted that this was the first time China had met with the opposition in an African conflict:

> That was pretty dramatic for us. I think for the last two or three decades we were quite rigid about non-interference in the internal affairs of other countries. . . . This is a typical domestic conflict. Usually when this happens, we try to avoid making direct contact with the opposition because to some extent we think it's a rebel force. When you talk to a rebel force that means stepping into internal affairs.[240]

Outside observers also considered China's proactive attempts to encourage a cease-fire in South Sudan to deviate from its long-held noninterference approach.[241]

In January 2014, Foreign Minister Wang Yi called for an immediate end to hostilities in South Sudan as he began a six-day tour of Africa in Ethiopia where South Sudan factions were beginning peace talks. He urged South Sudan's government and the rebels attempting to overthrow it to accept an immediate cease-fire. Wang identified China's position on the situation in South Sudan as, "first, . . . calling for immediate cessation of all hostilities and violence. Second . . . political dialogue should start as soon as possible. Third, the international community should make vigorous mediation efforts. And fourth . . . China called on the international community to provide help and support to South Sudan because of the humanitarian situation."[242] Zhong accompanied Wang Yi on that trip to Ethiopia to engage in negotiations and met with both government and rebel delegations.[243] By June 2014, China was preparing to send a battalion of troops to join the UN peacekeeping mission in Sudan and had already given more than $1 million to an IGAD-proposed monitoring mechanism to record violations of the cease-fire deal.[244]

Wang Yi decided that in this conflict, China needed to meet with the opposition due to previous pledges in the Forum on China-Africa Cooperation that China would do more to establish peace and stability in Africa.[245] Starting in January 2015, Wang became even more outspoken about why China was mediating in South Sudan.[246] He argued that China was behaving as a responsible power in issues related to Sudan and South Sudan. In response to reporters' questions about whether China was mediating in South Sudan due to its oil interests in the country, he replied,

> China's mediation of the Sudan and South Sudan issues is out of the responsibility and obligation that a responsible power should undertake, and is not for China's self-interest. . . . In the recent years, at the request of Sudan and in accordance with a consensus reached by the international community, including a relevant resolution of the UN Security Council, China has played a positive role in resolving dispute involving the Sudan issue. . . . As a good friend of Sudan and South Sudan, we will continue to work toward this end.[247]

Although Zhong Jianhua's top priority was Sudan and South Sudan as special envoy, he worked on several other issues. One was Mali. In 2012, a Tuareg separatist group, the National Movement for the Liberation of Azawad (MNLA), together with other Islamist militant groups—Ansaw Dine, al-Qaeda in the Islamic Maghreb (AQIM), and the Movement for Unity and Jihad in West Africa—took over portions of north Mali and declared independence. MNLA and the Islamist groups split, and the Islamist groups continued to push toward the center of the country, prompting French military intervention at the request of the Mali government.[248]As the situation deteriorated and the French intervened in January 2013, Zhong Jianhua attended a donors' conference on Mali at African Union Headquarters in Addis Ababa. The African Union (AU) hosted the meeting to raise funds for the African-led International Support Mission in Mali (Afisma) and the Malian army, as well as humanitarian aid.[249]At the conference, China began discussing offering support and aid to the International Support Mission for Mali under the framework of China-Africa peace and security cooperation. Reportedly, he committed $1 million in monetary aid as well as $3 to $5 million in material support.[250] He also stated that China supports African countries and regional organizations' efforts to safeguard Mali's unity, regional peace, and security.

China called for the early implementation of UN Security Council Resolution 2085, which emphasizes the importance of political dialogue and the pursuit of negotiations and authorized deployment of an African-led force to respond to the growing security threats on the ground.[251]

Another hot spot requiring Zhong's attention was the African Great Lakes region that includes Burundi, the Democratic Republic of the Congo (DRC), Kenya, Malawi, Rwanda, Tanzania, and Uganda. In February 2013, he traveled to Burundi, DRC, and Rwanda and said, "China will be more active mediating regional affairs and finding solutions to security issues, which also serves China's interests."[252] In 2015, protests erupted in Burundi when President Pierre Nkurunziza announced plans for a disputed third term as president, resulting in violent clashes between police and protestors. A coup attempt failed and the Burundi government engaged in a brutal crackdown against opposition groups and leaders. Fears of a full-blown civil war grew. In November 2015, Zhong traveled to Kenya to discuss this unrest and conflict in Burundi. While there, he stated that the deteriorating in Burundi was a threat to development in the region. He called on President Nkurunziza to be "more receptive to dialogue in the search for a solution to the Burundi conflict." He also stressed that China and the international community were ready to provide the support needed to resolve the Burundi conflict.[253] While meeting with African Union Commission chair, Nkosazana Dlamini-Zuma, Zhong suggested holding a dialogue with the stakeholders in the country.[254] In January 2016, when Zhong visited Zambia, President Lunga urged China to help resolve internal conflicts in some states in the African Great Lakes region, and Zhong expressed China's support for Zambia's engagement in the region to promote peace.[255]

In addition to Zhong Jianhua's attempts to promote peace in Sudan, South Sudan, Mali, and the Great Lakes, he emphasized China's economic engagement with Africa. Shortly after taking office, he started stressing that the world's attention was shifting from aid to business opportunities in Africa, and "it's now a good time for investment as the regional economy is on track of fast development." In his words, "Economic transformation in Africa has been effective in the past decade which has boosted economic growth . . . No doubt that Africa will be the next growth pole for the global economy, and everyone should get ready to embrace the boom." He urged Chinese companies to increase their knowledge of Africa and engage in business activities on the continent.[256] In his words, "With the last underdeveloped continent coming to its peak, it will bring huge potential for the world economy. For this reason, you'll see the future of China is the future of world economy. The world future economy involves the most important part, the African continent."[257]

In April 2013, a Nigerian central banker publicly stated, "China takes from us primary goods and sells us manufactured ones. This was also the essence of colonialism. China is no longer a fellow underdeveloped economy. China is the second biggest economy in the world, an economic giant capable of the same forms of exploitation as the West. China is a major contributor to the de-industrialisation of Africa and thus African underdevelopment."[258] Likely, in response to growing criticism from Nigeria, as well as Botswana, Zambia, and other countries across the continent, about some of China's more mercantilist activities in Africa, Zhong started publicly insisting that Chinese companies should comply with local laws. According to Zhong, "If Chinese traders engage in activities that violate your laws, we would not seek to shield them. We would not protect Chinese citizens' illegal behavior."[259] In 2013, he also started highlighting the economic exploitation of underdeveloped countries, including African countries and China, and pointing out how China's experience developing infrastructure and export markets could serve as a model for fellow developing countries in Africa.[260]

In 2015, as trade volumes between China and Africa started to fall, Zhong expressed that the "slide in trade between China and Africa is not due to falling demand but falling resource prices. I don't think we need to panic about fluctuations in trade volumes."[261]

China portrays and differentiates itself from other great powers' behavior in Africa by stressing its support for the sovereignty and equality of African states. China's Ministry of Foreign Affairs deputy director-general of the Department of West Asia and North Africa, Chang Hua, articulated China's four policies toward African countries in 2012:

> One is that to China all countries are of equal importance and each has a right to choose its own path. They have never interfered in any countries' domestic affairs, imposed anything on them or did anything in China's own interest.
>
> Secondly, they support peace and interest of African countries, this means they respect independence and sovereignty of African Countries.
>
> Thirdly, China also promotes a win-win cooperation and development dedicated to promoting mutual development between African countries.
>
> Lastly but not least, is that China's policy promotes openness and mutual exchange. Here people can openly discuss issues of concerning them and only through openness can there be progress.[262]

In March 2013, Xi Jinping embarked on his first trip abroad as president to Africa to attend the BRICS summit in South Africa.[263] He also visited Tanzania and the Republic of Congo. During an interview about Xi's trip to Africa, Zhong Jianhua stated, "Africa wants to be treated as an equal, and this is what many Western countries do not understand, or are at least are not willing to do."[264] Laying the groundwork for Xi's trip, he stressed that China does not want African countries to perceive it as an imperial master. Rather, he said, "The legacy of [the] West is the feeling that Africa should thank them, and that Africa should recognise that it is not as good as the West. . . . That is not acceptable."[265]

Zhong often highlighted that China and Africa share a history of exploitation at the hands of the West and denies China is acting as a colonizer.[266] "In the colonial system, Africans were forced to sell material at such a minimum price, it would be barely enough for them to feed themselves with," he explained. "Now they sell to China at a proper market price—US$200 a barrel for oil, for example—and not only is this enough for Africa to feed itself with, but it gives it money for other things, like building infrastructure."[267] He also stressed, "While Chinese companies sometimes bring in Chinese labor for economic reasons, it is also sometimes due to a skill shortage at the local level." He said that government-to-government projects running in Africa often have skills transfers built in and encouraged all foreign investors, not just the Chinese, to do more to help build local skills. He added that China's economic success story was with "sweat, tears and some blood" and that China was very willing to share lessons it learned along the way.[268] Although China has been sensitive in recent years about accusations that it is promoting the use of a China model in other countries characterized by significant role for the state in economic development coupled with authoritarian political leadership, it is increasingly advocating for African countries to learn from China's experiences.

Regarding China-Africa relations, in March 2013, Zhong said, "We'll do the best to serve the interests not only for China, but also for the developing countries, including African countries. Until that day every country becomes strong enough to perform on your own behalf, you'll probably don't need our support. What we hope is that not only relying on China but also working together with China."[269] Zhong also stressed that China wants to help Africa learn how to compete. In his words, "Africa is strong enough to fight economically . . . but this is the first time we are hearing that it is willing to do so. I welcome this kind of attitude." [270]

China wanted to share its experience with Africa in the area of peace and security. Zhong said that in his mediation work in Africa, he approached the issues "by using China's own example to convince the leaders of the importance of peace and stability for development."[271] In his assessment, the conflicts in Somalia, Sudan/South Sudan, Mali and the African Great Lakes region "each has its own complexities, but all share the same root cause: underdevelopment, which makes it hard for governments to gain the support of the unprivileged and results in a fragile security environment."[272] China's contributions to mediating these conflicts are part of a broader effort to strengthen its role in African security.[273] Referring to China's 2012 FOCAC meeting, Zhong stated, "President Hu Jintao on behalf of the Chinese government pledged that we will do more in the field of stability and peace on this continent ... on the basis that we understand that sometimes this is also crucial to the development of the continent. And so we need to contribute also in this field. This was the first time our leaders talked about doing something on peace and security for Africa."[274] In October 2014, he noted, "We have actively conducted peace and security, anti-terrorism dialogues and cooperation with AU and African countries within the framework of FOCAC. We support peace-keeping operations led by Africa, provided capacity building assistance in this regard and launched the 'Initiative on China-Africa Cooperative Partnership for Peace and Security.'"[275]

Despite this new emphasis on contributing to African peace and security, Zhong warned that security threats in Africa are exaggerated. According to him, China would not be drawn into arranging "special security" for its citizens doing business in Africa because they were not "prime targets" for violence.[276] In discussing general peace and security in Africa, he also stressed that China did not want to see a repeat of Libya.[277]

Zhong also focused on nontraditional security threats in Africa, such as piracy and Ebola. At the 2014 Third International Counter-Piracy Conference in Dubai and New Deal for Somalia Conference in Brussels, Zhong committed to bringing greater stability to the Gulf of Aden.[278] During the 2014 Ebola outbreak, China played an active role. China sent more than 170 medical workers to affected areas to fight the epidemic. In August 2014, China offered RMB 30 million ($4.86 million) worth of humanitarian assistance to Liberia, Sierra Leone, and Guinea. In September, President Xi Jinping announced an additional package of support totaling RMB 200 million and offered cash assistance to the World Health Organization and African Union, each worth

$2 million.[279] In Zhong's words, "It is China's responsibility to join hands with Africans and face this disaster threatening humanity."[280]

Xu Jinghu

Zhong stepped down as special envoy in 2016. The next special envoy for Africa appointed was Xu Jinghu (2016–present).[281] Ambassador Xu Jinghu is a veteran diplomat who once served as director-general of the Department of African Affairs of the Foreign Ministry and Chinese ambassador to Madagascar, Morocco, and Switzerland.[282] During her tenure as a special envoy, her emphasis has been South Sudan, general peace and security in Africa, building relations with various countries in Africa, maritime security, and responding to debt trap allegations that accuse China of purposely encouraging developing countries to accrue unsustainable amounts of debt from China to increase leverage over the borrower country and gain future economic and political concessions, including strategic assets.

In March 2017, she traveled to Uganda for talks on South Sudan after Chinese peacekeepers were killed on the UN Mission in South Sudan in October 2016.[283] During those meetings, she expressed China's interest in resolving the conflict in South Sudan but opposed sanctions.[284] In support of China's continued efforts to support the UN-led IGAD process, she attended the High-Level Revitalization Forum on the South Sudan Peace Agreement aimed at promoting the implementation of the South Sudan peace agreement. China signed the agreement as an international witness.[285] During the meeting, she "made extensive contacts with representatives of all the warring parties in South Sudan and representatives of all relevant parties in the region and international community, exchanging in-depth views on the current situation and the peace process in South Sudan."[286]

Similar to her predecessors as special envoy, Xu articulates China's broader approach to peace and security in Africa and China's relations with the continent. In November 2017, she attended the Fourth Dakar International Forum on Peace and Security in Africa held in Senegal. At that meeting, she stressed, "The Chinese side is willing to, together with the international community, continuously support Africa's efforts in realizing peace and security, and jointly make due contributions to pushing forward the construction of a new type of international relations and a community of common destiny for mankind."[287] In July 2018 at the Oslo Forum, she "stressed that China has always adhered to taking a constructive part in peace and security affairs of Africa, actively fulfilled responsibilities as a major country, and promoted peace talks, so as to make positive contributions to the realization of peace, stability and development in Africa." [288]

At a conference in August 2018, she said, "Implementation of projects had faced head winds in the past two years due to rising anti-globalization sentiments, natural disasters that disrupted the priorities of African governments, and falling commodity prices. . . . Increased efforts are therefore needed in designing strategies that would enhance sustainable China-Africa cooperation. China does meet its commitments and we aim to continue with this trend."[289] After the FOCAC meeting in September 2018, she noted that "China has contributed to Africa's peace and security affairs in an active and constructive way, and put into place its military aid plan for Africa."[290]

During her tenure, she has promoted strengthening relations between China and Mauritius,[291] the Seychelles,[292] and Rwanda.[293] She has also continued China's emphasis on maritime security in Africa.[294]

Finally, during 2018, as debt trap allegations against China mounted, she spent significant energy defending China against those claims. For example, in September 2018 at a FOCAC meeting, she said, "It is the international economic situation that has raised the costs of financing. Most of the African countries (facing a debt problem) have been exporting raw materials for which the price on the international markets has been decreasing. This has added to the debt problem of these countries. Where African countries are in debt, China is not their creditor. So it is wrong to shift the blame on the Chinese side."[295] She also said, "China would conduct studies to avoid causing debt problems as it rolled out Xi's plan." In her words, "These projects will take into account their development prospects so as to help African countries achieve sustainable development and avoid debt or financial problems."[296]

China's Special Envoy for Africa Conclusions

China's special envoy for Africa pursues many of the nation's interests in Africa. Through attempting to resolve conflict in Darfur and between Sudan and South Sudan, China is promoting its economic growth through stability in Sudan and Darfur, as well as Mali and the Great Lakes region. Regional stability is essential for China's continued access to resources and markets in Africa. Stabilizing these conflicts also works to safeguard China's businesses and citizens. Moreover, mediating African conflicts provides China an opportunity to foster support in the international arena.

China's promotion of economic growth through the envoy and criticism of other countries for past colonial behavior allows China to advocate for developing country causes. As opposed to the BRI focus of the Middle East and Syria envoys, the Africa envoy rarely mentions BRI but stresses South-South economic cooperation between China and Africa.

As opposed to the Middle East and Syria envoys, the African envoy does not deal with issues thought to affect China's domestic stability. It also does not harp on the need to protect the territorial integrity and sovereignty of African countries from the United States.

China's behavior in the special envoy for African issues is categorized as cooperative with the United States and norm convergent with the liberal order. China's activities in this envoy appear to be strongly driven by a desire to be perceived as a responsible power in the international system. Since its founding, the African envoy has stressed cooperation with the West. In large part, China formed the envoy because of direct pressure from the United States and the European Union. The envoy explicitly coordinates with Western countries as well as international and regional organizations to seek peace in Africa. Since its establishment in 2007, China's special envoy for Africa issues has cooperated with the United States and the rest of the West to find solutions in Sudan and South Sudan. This behavior differs from China's special envoys for Middle East issues and for Syria. Those envoys focus more on cooperating with Arab states and Israel to resolve the Middle East peace process and Russia, Iran, Turkey, Arab states, Israel, and the United Nations to resolve the crisis in Syria.

Overall, China's actions are norm convergent through the Africa envoy. In alignment with the liberal order, China is promoting multilateralism and seeking negotiated solutions to conflicts. When it aims to contribute to conflict resolution activities, it engages through and with international and regional organizations. It works with the UN, EU, and AU as well as other regional organizations to resolve conflicts. It is also willing to speak to any interested parties, including opposition groups. In contrast with China's Middle East envoys, the Africa envoy is more involved in negotiations between states in Africa, especially Sudan and South Sudan.

How does China portray itself as a great power? Through the Africa envoy, China acts as a mediator within and between countries. It uses multilateral mechanisms and is willing to meet any interested parties to pursue conflict resolution. Its message is that China is a responsible power in Africa and treats the African states as equals. It differentiates itself from states with a legacy of colonization in Africa. Repeatedly, it stresses that it never colonized Africa. It vows respect for the sovereignty and territorial integrity of the African states. On the economic front, China emphasizes that Africa is an economic opportunity, encourages companies to obey local laws, and pushes back against accusations of debt trap diplomacy.

Conclusion: A Responsible Power?

Is China cooperating or competing with the United States through its special envoys? In the Middle East, China competes with the United States and cooperates with Russia through its special envoys for Middle East Issues and Syria. Through its Africa envoy, it cooperates with the United States and the West.

In the Middle East, China takes a firm stand against US and other Western intervention and regime change. It presents itself as a different kind of great power that does not meddle in the domestic politics of Middle Eastern countries and does not pick sides. It stands up to the United States for its preferential treatment of Israel in the Arab-Israeli conflict and Palestinian-Israeli conflict and picking favorites in Syria's civil war. It also actively criticizes the United States for its treatment of Iran and withdrawal from the JCPOA. Unlike other great powers, China cooperates with all interested parties in the Middle East, including state and nonstate actors with strained relations with the United States such as Russia, Iran, Syria, and Hezbollah.

In contrast, China's Africa envoy explicitly cooperates with the United States and the West. Since its foundation, the envoy has stressed its desire to work with the United States and the rest of the West to solve issues in Sudan and South Sudan.

One difference between the special envoys in the Middle East and sub-Saharan Africa is that in the Middle East, China cooperates with great power Russia and regional power Iran and competes with the United States and the rest of the West. In sub-Saharan Africa, China is more focused on cooperating with the AU rather than great or regional powers. In Africa, it does indicate a willingness to coordinate with the United States regarding South Sudan, and the Africa envoy was arguably initially established at the urging of Western states. Cooperation with Russia is not emphasized in Africa.

Is China's behavior through these envoys converging or diverging with liberal international norms? China's normative behavior in the Middle East special issues and Syria envoy is mixed, but its Africa envoy's behavior converges with liberal international norms.

China's support for the Arab and Palestinian stance in the Palestinian-Israeli and Arab-Israeli conflicts competes with the strong US support for Israel. Although China does maintain good relations with Israel and Israel appreciates China's attempts to act as a balanced actor in negotiations, it can be argued that China leans toward the Palestinian and Arab side. On other hot spot issues in the region, the Middle East issues envoy diverges from the liberal order due to its strict interpretation of Westphalian sovereignty and its firm stance against foreign intervention and regime change by the United States and the rest of the West. That said, in the Middle East issues envoy, China's behavior is norm convergent in its utilization of multilateral mechanisms for conflict resolution and support for the leading role of the UN in conflict resolution for the Middle East peace process.

The Syria envoy's normative behavior is also mixed. It converges with the liberal order when it promotes the utilization of multilateral mediation mechanisms as well as humanitarian aid, reconstruction assistance, support for counterterrorism, and criticism on the use of chemical weapons. That said, it diverges from the liberal order when it stands up for sovereignty and against foreign intervention and aligns with Westphalian norms.

China's behavior through the Africa envoy converges with liberal international norms: it is promoting multilateralism and seeking negotiated solutions to conflicts. When it aims to contribute to conflict resolution, it does so through international and regional organizations.

Is it building an alternative international order in these regions? If so, what are the characteristics of that order? Although China is building alternative orders through its cooperation forums and other foreign policy tools in the Middle East and sub-Saharan Africa, it is not constructing an order with its special envoys. These special envoys explicitly leverage existing international and regional organizations and mechanisms to participate in mediation activities. It stresses the role of the UN, AU, LAS, EU, and other organizations in facilitating conflict resolution.

What does China's behavior through these envoys indicate about its rise in the Middle East, sub-Saharan Africa, and globally? In the Middle East and sub-Saharan Africa, China's special envoys provide insights into the type of great power China wants to be in these regions. As China attempts to build spheres of influence in these regions, it uses these envoys to demonstrate how it is different from other great powers. China claims to be a responsible great power in these regions. It frequently emphasizes that a member of the UN Security Council must seek peace in these regions. In particular, through these envoys, China attempts to address the root causes of regional hot spots of concern. It also emphasizes China's desire to engage in mutually beneficial economic cooperation with these regions and serve as a model for future development.

China conceptualizes and portrays itself as a balanced player that never colonized these regions. China is a champion and defender of sovereignty and stands up against US and other Western interference, intervention, and regime change. It sees itself as a mediator seeking to resolve issues in these regions that threatened its interests. Although China advocates noninterference, it is willing to meet with all interested parties in conflicts, including opposition groups in Syria and South Sudan, as well as the PLO and Hezbollah. Aiming for stability, China acts as a mediator in civil wars and between states. It is not picking sides; it is just working toward the resolution of issues that endanger peace and stability. It orchestrates most of its meditation work through international and regional organizations and promotes the critical role of the UN in resolving these regional hot spots.

China stresses the role of economic development in the longer-term peace in the Middle East and Africa. It emphasizes the role of BRI in helping to resolve long-term Middle East conflicts, but it seldom brings up the issue of the BRI with the special envoy for Africa issues. That said, in all of these conflicts, China appears to believe that domestic economic development and regional economic cooperation could lessen conflict in the future.

Through all three of these envoys, China portrays and differentiates itself as a great power. It demonstrates that it seeks to facilitate peace in these regions and fulfill its obligations as a responsible great power. It strives to resolve hot spot issues. It pursues interests in promoting its domestic economic growth, fostering support in the international arena, ensuring its domestic stability, advocating for developing country causes, safeguarding its citizens and businesses abroad, and protecting its territorial integrity and sovereignty from the United States. It differentiates itself as a great power that stands up for the countries in these regions, respects their sovereignty and territorial integrity, and acts as a balanced actor in resolving conflict.

CHAPTER 6

COMPETING FOR INFLUENCE?

Economic Relations

Economic relations are the most robust aspect of China's post–Cold War interactions with the Middle East and sub-Saharan Africa. Over the past twenty years, China has become one of the most important economic actors in these regions and is increasingly competing, challenging the rules of the international system, building spheres of influence, and constructing an alternative order to support its interests. China's most important interests in the Middle East and sub-Saharan Africa related to economic behavior are promoting China's domestic economic growth, fostering support for China in the international arena, and advocating for developing country causes.[1]

The primary questions driving this chapter and the rest of the book are: Is China cooperating or competing with the United States in the Middle East and sub-Saharan Africa? Is its behavior converging with or diverging from liberal international norms? Is it building an alternative international order in these regions? If so, what are the characteristics of that order? Ultimately what does China's behavior in the Middle East and sub-Saharan Africa indicate about its rise globally? Analyzing China's bilateral economic relations with these regions in a comparative perspective over time generates important insights about how China is competing in these regions and diverging from or converging with international norms. It shows how China is developing spheres of influence, changing the rules of the system, and building an alternative economic order in these regions. It also provides insights into how China is portraying itself as a great power.

This chapter examines China's bilateral economic relations with countries in the Middle East and sub-Saharan Africa.[2] It describes the broad contours of China's trade, services, and investment interactions with these regions in the post–Cold War era to provide an overview of China's economic relations with these regions over time and then analyzes the specific economic foreign policy tools China uses to pursue its interests: Chinese government support for companies operating in these regions, foreign aid, free trade agreement negotiations, special economic zones, and agricultural technology demonstration centers. This chapter categorizes each of these behaviors as competitive versus cooperative with the United States and norm convergent with versus divergent from the liberal order. This chapter in particular focuses on norms associated with the Western liberal economic order such as free markets, limited state intervention, and cooperating through multilateral organizations. The chapter examines a wide range of economic foreign policy tools over time and across regions to draw broad conclusions about China as a rising power in these regions.

This chapter uses primary sources to examine China's bilateral economic relations with the Middle East and sub-Saharan Africa. They include International Monetary Fund (IMF) country-level data on trade, Chinese government-issued data on China's services and investment in these regions, annual reports of national champion companies operating in these regions, China Aid Data project data collected on China's overseas development assistance, various government and news reports, as well as academic analysis of China's free trade agreement negotiations, special economic zones, and agricultural technology demonstration centers, and interviews with Chinese and regional government officials and scholars.

This chapter asserts that overall, China's behavior is competitive in all of the foreign policy tools examined. Sometimes it competes inside the current order, sometimes outside. Its state support for Chinese companies is divergent from the norms of free trade and limited stated intervention in the liberal economic order. Foreign aid behavior diverges from liberal international norms by explicitly excluding political and good governance conditions in aid allocation. That said, China's free trade agreements are norm convergent with the liberal order and its special economic zones and agricultural technology demonstration centers are norm neutral.

Trade, Services, and Investment

By far, China's most significant interest in the Middle East and sub-Saharan Africa is fueling its domestic economic growth. These regions are essential for meeting China's needs for access to natural resources and markets for goods and services.

Searching for Resources

Over the past two decades, China's quest for natural resources has increased. It requires overseas natural resources, especially from the Middle East and sub-Saharan Africa, to fuel its domestic economic growth. In 1993, China became a net oil importer. In the late 1990s and the early 2000s, its resource needs were expanding beyond energy to a more extensive set of natural resources such as copper, bauxite, iron ore, aluminum, and agricultural products. Both the Middle East and sub-Saharan Africa are vital natural resource suppliers for China. The Middle East is well endowed with energy resources, and sub-Saharan Africa provides a wide variety of natural resources, including not only energy but also minerals required for industrial growth and agricultural products.

China's overall imports from the Middle East and sub-Saharan Africa were minimal from 1991 to 1999. In 1999, they were $3.82 billion and $2.18 billion, respectively. As shown in figure 6.1, the dramatic growth of China's imports from these regions began in 2000. China's Middle East and sub-Saharan Africa imports both exceeded US imports from these regions starting in 2012. In 2014, China's total imports from the Middle East peaked at $169 billion and sub-Saharan African at $112 billion. Because of dramatically falling commodity prices and decreasing Chinese demand associated with its economic slowdown, 2015 imports plunged to $108 billion from the Middle East and $52 billion from sub-Saharan Africa. By 2019, China's imports from these regions recovered and were $166 billion from the Middle East and $87 billion from sub-Saharan Africa.[3] Despite these fluctuations, China's imports from these regions are still much higher than US imports, which from the Middle East in 2019 were only $71 billion and from sub-Saharan Africa $21 billion.[4]

China's need for natural resources (oil and other resources) to fuel its economic development has been a significant driver of this extraordinary growth in imports from both of these regions.[5]

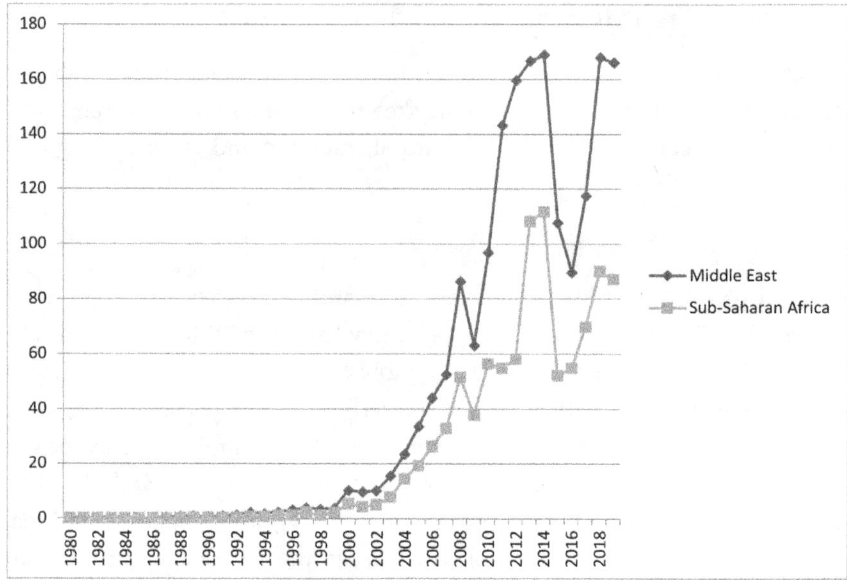

Figure 6.1. China's Total Imports from the Middle East and Sub-Saharan Africa, 1980–2019, in billion USD (CIF). Source: Data compiled by author from International Monetary Fund, *Direction of Trade Statistics Database*, www.imfstatistics.org. Accessed February 2, 2011, May 22, 2013, June 8, 2016, August 26, 2018, and January 29, 2021.

China's Thirst for Oil

Since China became a net oil importer in 1993, its energy needs have grown substantially, and in 2012, it became the world's largest net petroleum importer.[6] In 2014, it exceeded the United States in net crude oil imports. One significant reason for the decrease in US imports per year is the increased capacity of fracking in the United States. Finally, in 2016, China surpassed the United States in gross crude oil imports.[7] As of 2019, China imported over 10 million barrels of oil per day and is the world's largest oil importer.[8]

Analyzing a breakdown of China's crude oil import sources by country over time provides greater clarity regarding specific trends in energy trade with these regions. In 2000, 83 percent ($10.35 billion) of China's crude oil imports originated from the Middle East and sub-Saharan Africa (55 percent from the Middle East and 27 percent from sub-Saharan Africa). China's top five crude oil suppliers from the Middle East and sub-Saharan Africa were Oman (26 percent, $3.26 billion), Angola (15 percent, $1.84 billion), Iran (12 percent, $1.46 billion), Saudi Arabia (9 percent, $1.18 billion), and Sudan (6 percent, $0.73 billion).[9]

China's 2019 crude oil imports from the Middle East and sub-Saharan Africa combined decreased to 63 percent of its global oil imports.[10] Forty-seven percent of imports were from the Middle East and 16 percent from sub-Saharan Africa. China's top crude oil suppliers from the Middle East and sub-Saharan Africa were Saudi Arabia ($40 billion), Iraq ($24 billion), Angola ($22 billion), Oman ($16 billion), Kuwait ($11 billion), United Arab Emirates ($7 billion), and Iran ($7 billion).[11]

In percentage terms, Middle Eastern and sub-Saharan African countries account for seven out of ten of China's top oil suppliers in 2019. China's top ten oil suppliers at that time were Saudi Arabia (17 percent of China's global total crude oil imports), Russia (15 percent), Iraq (10 percent), Angola (10 percent), Brazil (8 percent), Oman (7 percent), Kuwait (5 percent), Iran (3 percent), United Arab Emirates (3 percent), and the United Kingdom (3 percent).[12]

The volume of China's total oil imports from the Middle East and sub-Saharan Africa has increased rapidly since 2000. It is now more dependent on the Middle East and sub-Saharan Africa for oil than the United States is. In 2019, 63 percent of China's $239 billion of global crude oil imports originated in the Middle East and sub-Saharan Africa. In contrast, only 20 percent of the United States' $132 billion in global crude oil imports come from these regions.[13] One striking example of the increasing importance of these regions for China is the fact that starting in 2009, China imported more oil from Saudi Arabia (in dollar and percentage terms) than the United States did. Also, US domestic production capacity is much higher than China's, and the development of fracking capability in the United States has only reinforced this disparity. Compared to China, US production capacity makes it less dependent on the Middle East and sub-Saharan Africa to meet its energy needs.

In summary, the majority of China's global oil supplies originate in the Middle East and sub-Saharan Africa. The volume and dollar value of China's crude oil imports from these regions significantly increased from 2000 to 2019. That said, China's percentage of worldwide oil imports from the Middle East and sub-Saharan Africa decreased from 82 percent in 2000 to 63 percent in 2019 as it diversified its sources to suppliers outside these regions. Over time, Oman, Iran, and Sudan have become less critical sources as a percentage of total imports. Angola has remained relatively constant, and Saudi Arabia's and Iraq's importance increased. Current and future sanctions on Iran,

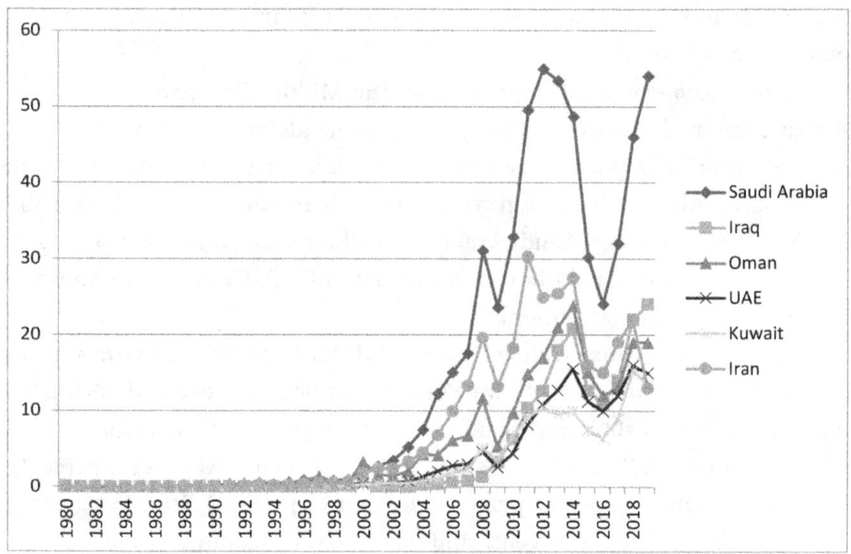

Figure 6.2. China's Total Imports from the Middle East Broken Down by Top Six 2019 Suppliers, 1980–2019, in billion USD (CIF). Source: Ibid.

as well as stability in Iraq, will shape China's oil import composition from the Middle East. It could be argued that China is buying oil on world markets, and therefore, the geographical composition of supply may not be as important as it appears. That said, China's lack of domestic capacity, together with such a large percent of its imports originating from turbulent regions of the world, does add to China's risk, at least in the short term.

Regional Breakdown of Imports

China's imports from the Middle East tend to be heavily composed of oil and gas. As of 2019, crude oil alone accounted for 67 percent of China's total imports from the Middle East. China's top import partners from the Middle East are all energy-exporting countries. As seen in Figure 6.2, China's top six import origin countries in the Middle East in 2019 were Saudi Arabia ($54 billion), Iraq ($24 billion), Oman ($19 billion), UAE ($15 billion), Kuwait ($13 billion), and Iran ($11 billion). The vast majority of imports from these countries are energy resources (oil and natural gas).

In contrast to the Middle East, imports from sub-Saharan Africa represent a more diverse set of natural resources, including not only energy but also minerals and agriculture. For example, only 45 percent of China's imports

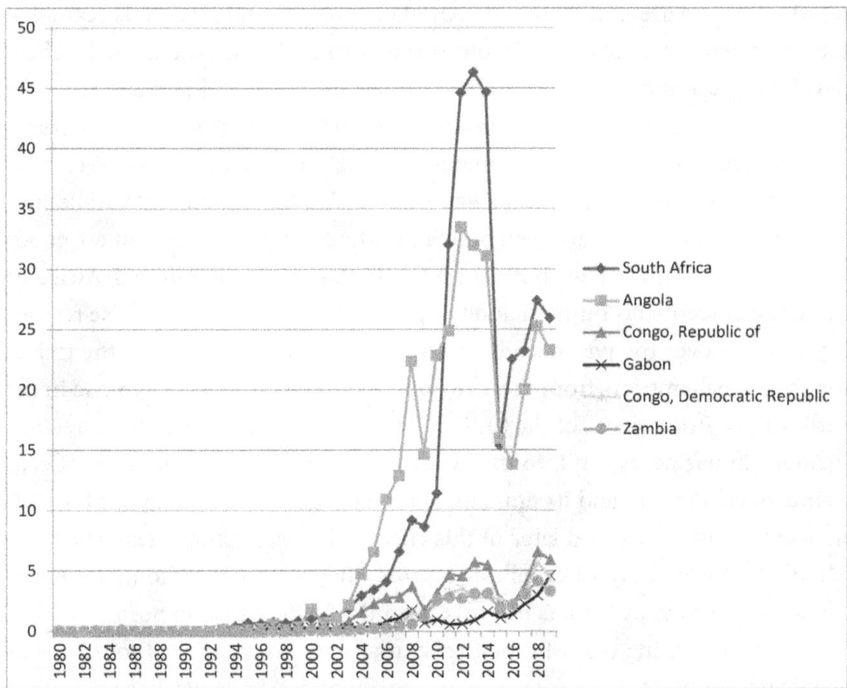

Figure 6.3. China's Total Imports from Sub-Saharan Africa Broken Down by Top Six 2019 Suppliers, 1980–2019, in billion USD (CIF). Source: Ibid.

from sub-Saharan Africa are crude oil. Natural resource imports from sub-Saharan Africa include energy, iron ore, copper, cobalt, and agricultural products. Figure 6.3 shows China's top import supplier countries in sub-Saharan Africa. China's top import partner in 2019 in sub-Saharan Africa was South Africa ($25.9 billion), which is not an oil exporter but provides an assortment of minerals, such as iron and chromium, required to fuel China's domestic growth. China's second-, third-, fourth-, and fifth-largest import sources are all energy suppliers: Angola ($23.3 billion), the Republic of Congo ($5.9 billion), Gabon ($4.6 billion) and the Democratic Republic of Congo ($4.4 billion). Finally, import supplier number six, Zambia, was not an oil producer. Zambia ($3.3 billion) primarily exports copper to China.

Searching for Markets

Although much of the literature on China's relations with the Middle East and sub-Saharan Africa examines the acquisition of natural resources, China's economic interests are much broader. Another fundamental interest is searching for markets for Chinese goods and services to fuel domestic growth. These developing economies demand a wide range of goods and services China is particularly well positioned to produce due to its current stage of economic development and the goods it is manufacturing for its domestic markets. Now that China is engaged in a trade war with the United States, the Middle East and sub-Saharan Africa are even more important as markets for Chinese goods and services. China views both the Middle East and sub-Saharan Africa as immense current and future market opportunities. Its exports to these regions skyrocketed over the past decade. As seen in Figure 6.4, similar to the trajectory of China's imports from these regions, China's exports began to rise in the early 2000s. Root causes of the timing of this surge in exports to these regions include China's accession into the World Trade Organization, its level of economic development, and its emphasis on going global and going out for Chinese companies discussed later in this chapter. In 1999, China's exports to the Middle East were only $6.47 billion; by 2019, they were $151 billion. This figure is almost as much as China's imports from the Middle East in 2019 ($166 billion), demonstrating that Middle East markets are just as crucial for China as acquiring resources. China's exports to sub-Saharan Africa also have increased rapidly since the 1990s. In 1999, China's exports to sub-Saharan Africa equaled $2.8 billion; in 2019, they had climbed to $86 billion (as compared to China's imports from sub-Saharan Africa at $87 billion). It is also important to stress that these regions are also larger export markets for China than for the United States. In 2019, US exports to the Middle East were only $87 billion and to sub-Saharan Africa a mere $16 billion.[14]

Chinese import and export markets in sub-Saharan Africa and the Middle East tend to involve different countries due to an import focus on resources and an export composition driven by manufactured goods. China's primary exports to both the Middle East and sub-Saharan Africa are consumer goods, capital goods, machinery and electronics, intermediate goods, and textiles and clothing.[15] China's top import markets from the Middle East in 2019 were Saudi Arabia, Iraq, Oman, the UAE, Kuwait, and Iran. In contrast, as shown in Figure 6.5, China's 2019 top six export partners in the Middle East were the UAE ($33.5 billion),[16] Saudi Arabia ($23.9 billion), Turkey ($17.3 billion), Egypt ($12.2 billion), Iran ($9.6 billion), and Israel ($9.5 billion).[17] These countries are some of the most populous in the region and therefore have significant consumer demand for goods.

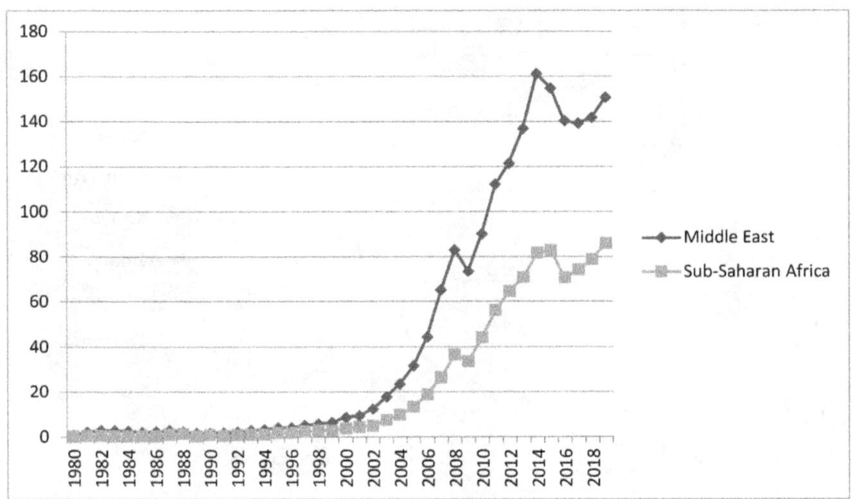

Figure 6.4. China's Total Exports to the Middle East and Sub-Saharan Africa, 1980–2019, in billion USD (FOB). Source: Ibid.

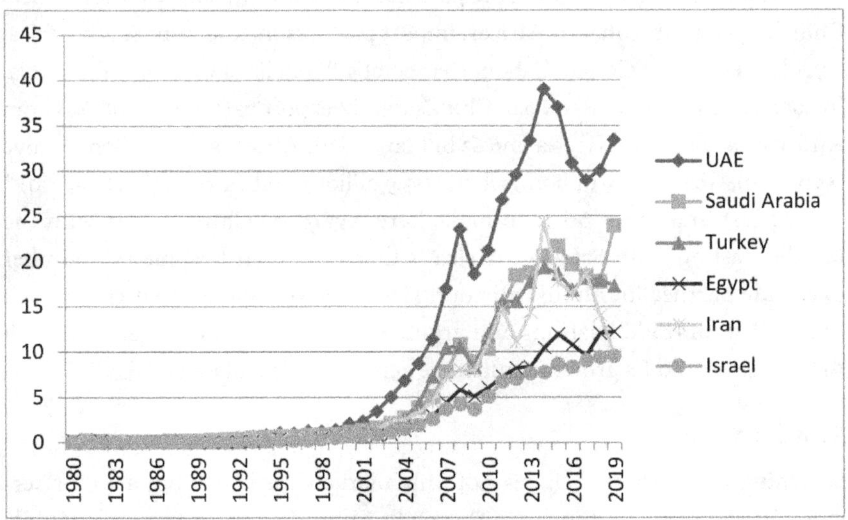

Figure 6.5. China's Exports to the Middle East Broken Down by Top Six 2019 Export Destinations, 1980–2019, in billion USD (FOB). Source: Ibid.

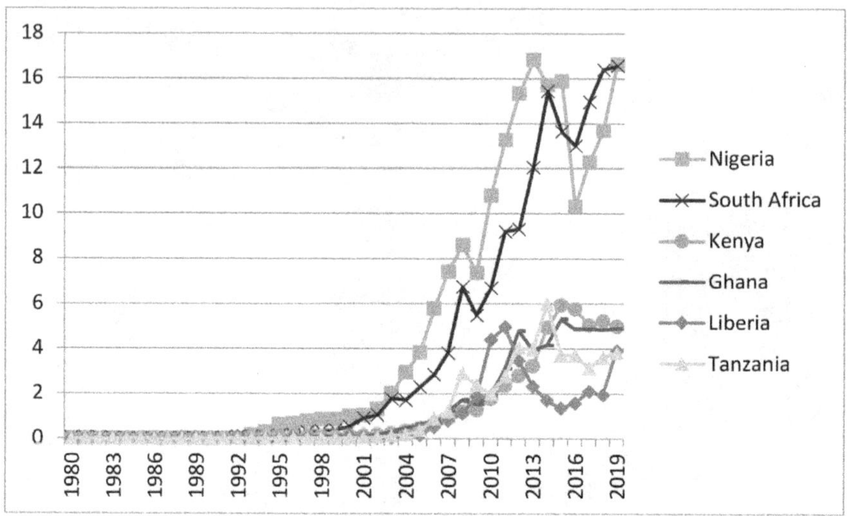

Figure 6.6. China's Exports to Sub-Saharan Africa Broken Down by Top Six 2019 Export Destinations, 1980–2019, in billion USD (FOB). Source: Ibid.

China's top import and export partners also differ in sub-Saharan Africa. China's largest sub-Saharan African import partners in 2019 were South Africa, Angola, Republic of Congo, Gabon, Democratic Republic of Congo, and Zambia. In contrast, as seen in Figure 6.6, China's top six export partners in sub-Saharan Africa as of 2019 were Nigeria ($16.63 billion), South Africa ($16.56 billion), Kenya ($5 billion), Ghana ($4.9 billion), Liberia ($3.9 billion), and Tanzania ($3.8 billion).[18]

The last important point to make here regarding China's trade with the Middle East and sub-Saharan Africa is that China has become the number one trade partner for almost all countries in these regions. That change is a titanic shift in trade relations and arguably shapes China's interactions with these regions and its growing influence across functional areas.

Contract Services

Searching for markets includes not only markets for goods but also for services. In addition to China's rapid growth in product exports to the Middle East and sub-Saharan Africa, its export of services expanded at an impressive pace during the post–Cold War era. China's primary service export markets in these regions are construction, telecommunications, and finance. China's goods exports and contract services exports summed together are much larger in dollar value than China's imports from these regions. Although these regions

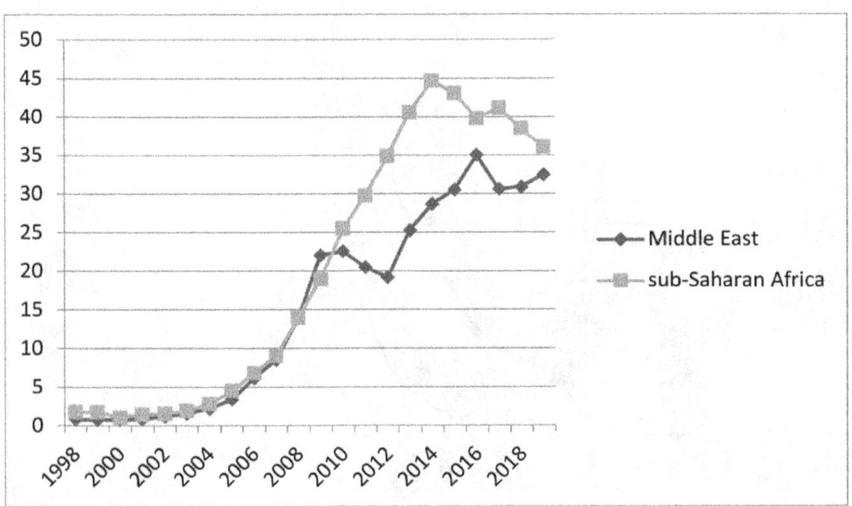

Figure 6.7. China's Overseas Contract Services in the Middle East and Sub-Saharan Africa, 1998–2019, in billion USD. Sources: Data compiled by author from "Turnover of Economic Cooperation with Foreign Countries or Territories" in *China Statistical Yearbooks*, 2000-2010, and "Economic Cooperation with Foreign Countries or Regions," in *China Statistical Yearbooks, 2011-2020*.

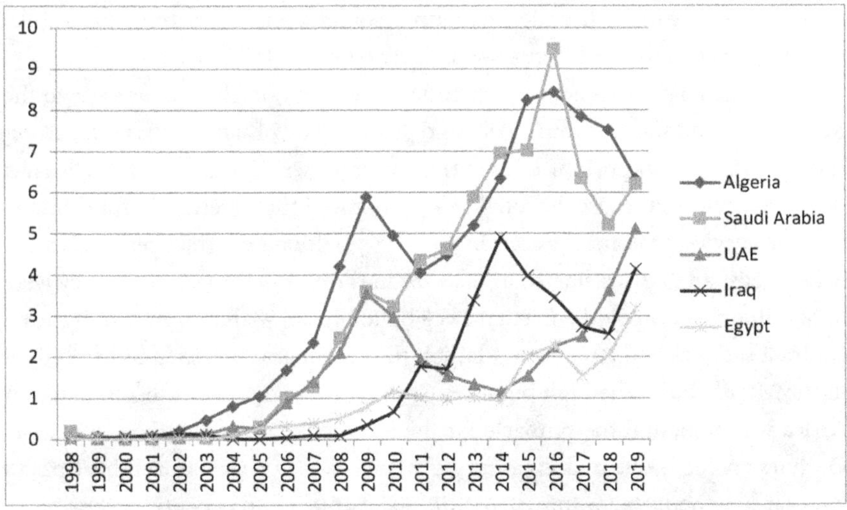

Figure 6.8. China's Overseas Contract Services in the Middle East by Country, Top Five, 1998–2019, in billion USD. Sources: Data compiled by the author from ibid.

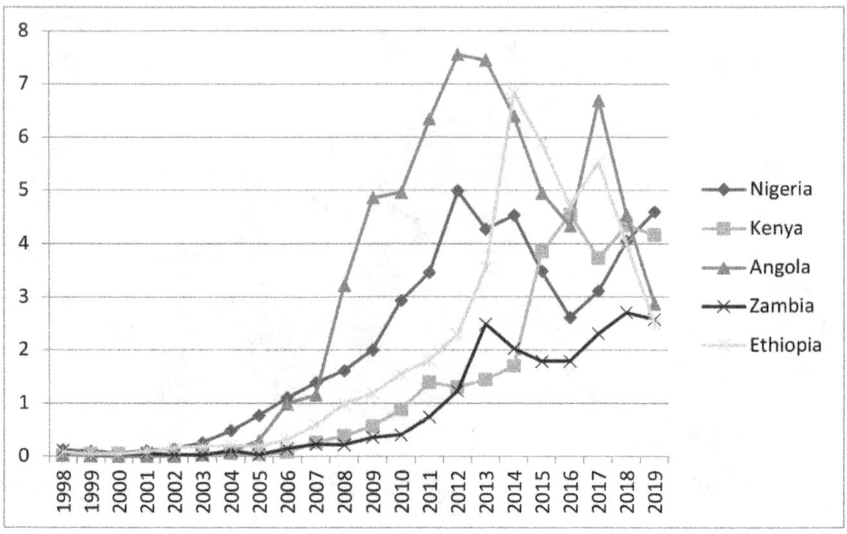

Figure 6.9. China's Overseas Contract Services in Sub-Saharan Africa by Country, Top Five, 1998–2019, in billion USD. Sources: Data compiled by author from ibid..

are essential sources of energy and minerals, the volume of China's exports of goods and services to these regions demonstrates that its economic interests in these regions are much broader than just resources. Also, over time due to BRI, contract services to these regions will likely continue to increase.

Contract services constitute a significant segment of Chinese services to the Middle East and sub-Saharan Africa and primarily involve firms in the construction sector.[19] It is important to note that contract services are not investments; they are services. It is also essential to keep in mind that foreign aid funds many of these service projects. As seen in Figure 6.7, China's contract services in the Middle East and Africa started to increase in the early 2000s. In 1998, they were $788 million in the Middle East and $1.8 billion in sub-Saharan Africa. By 2014, contract services had risen to $45 billion in sub-Saharan Africa and $29 billion in the Middle East. The high point for China's contract services to sub-Saharan Africa was 2014, and the pinnacle for the Middle East, at $35 billion, was 2016. Declines are likely due to decreasing global oil prices and the impact those prices have on state budgets for infrastructure. As of 2019, China's contract services to sub-Saharan Africa were $36 billion and to the Middle East $32 billion.

To provide a global context, the Middle East component of contract services as a percentage of China's total worldwide contract services increased from 8 percent in 1998 to 18 percent in 2019.[20] sub-Saharan Africa's percentage increased from 19 percent to 21 percent during the same period.[21] Constituting close to 40 percent of China's worldwide contract services, the Middle East and sub-Saharan Africa are unquestionably essential markets for Chinese service firms.

As shown in Figure 6.8, China's 2019 top contract service markets in the Middle East were Algeria ($6.3 billion), Saudi Arabia ($6.2 billion), United Arab Emirates ($5.1 billion), Iraq ($4.1 billion), and Egypt ($3.2 billion). China's 2019 top contract services markets in sub-Saharan Africa were Nigeria ($4.6 billion), Kenya ($4.2 billion), Angola ($2.9 billion), Zambia ($2.6 billion), and Ethiopia ($2.5 billion).[22] (See Figure 6.9.)

China's Outbound Foreign Direct Investment

Natural resource acquisition and searching for markets for goods and services are fundamental interests for China in these regions. Although Western media portrayals often emphasize China's investments in sub-Saharan Africa and the Middle East, especially in the resource sector, China's outbound foreign direct investment (OFDI) activity is minimal compared to its trade with these regions, service contracts, and its global OFDI.[23] One reason for this misperception may be that observers conflate FDI with service projects funded with foreign aid.(This chapter covers only OFDI in which the Chinese investor owns 10 percent or more of an enterprise operating in a recipient country.)[24]

Figure 6.10 shows China's total OFDI flows to the Middle East and sub-Saharan Africa from 2003 through 2019. In 2003, China's FDI flows to the Middle East were only $25 million, and sub-Saharan Africa only $70 million.[25] Although China's FDI in these regions did increase in the 2000s and early 2010s, these increases were not impressive compared to China's phenomenal growth in imports from and exports to these regions. In the Middle East and sub-Saharan Africa, China's trade and services are high but investments are low. The substantial increase in 2008 sub-Saharan Africa FDI flows was due to China's acquisition of 20 percent equity in South Africa's Standard Bank that was an anomaly. In 2019, China's total FDI flows into the Middle East were a mere $2.5 billion, and into sub-Saharan Africa $3 billion.

From 2003 to 2019, China's top FDI flow destinations in the Middle East were United Arab Emirates ($5.9 billion), Israel ($2.9 billion), Saudi Arabia ($2.6 billion), Iran ($2.2 billion), and Algeria ($2 billion). In sub-Saharan Africa, the top destinations were South Africa ($7.3 billion),[26] Democratic

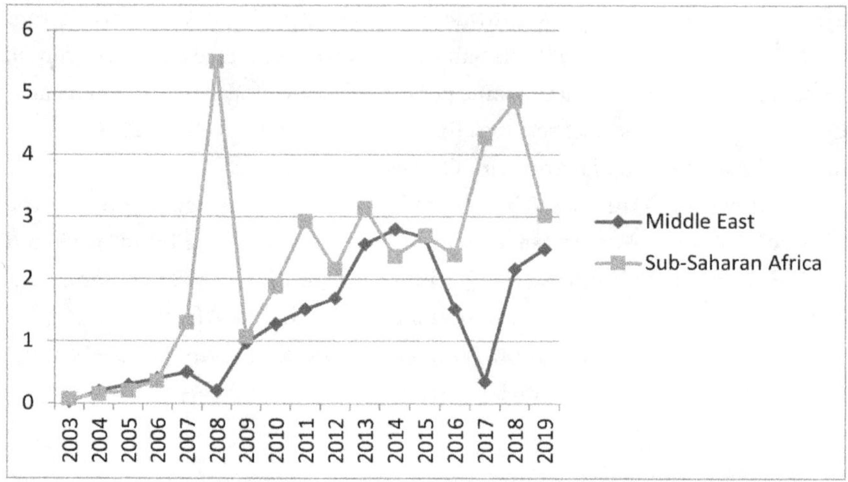

Figure 6.10. China's Overseas Foreign Direct Investment Flows in the Middle East and Sub-Saharan Africa, 2003–2019, in billion USD. Source: Data compiled by author from *Statistical Bulletin of China's Outward Foreign Direct Investment*. China Ministry of Commerce: 2011 edition, 78–83; 2015 edition, 82–84; 2016 edition, 86–90; and 2020 edition, 146–149.

Republic of Congo ($3.3 billion), Zambia ($3.2 billion), Nigeria ($2.6 billion), and Ethiopia ($2 billion).

China's 2019 top five FDI flow destinations in the Middle East were United Arab Emirates ($1.2 billion), Iraq ($887 million), Saudi Arabia ($654 million), Israel ($192 million), and Jordan ($31 million). China's top 2019 net FDI flow destinations in sub-Saharan Africa were Democratic Republic of Congo ($931 million), Angola ($383 million), Ethiopia ($375 million), South Africa ($339 million), and Mauritius ($186 million).

Compared to other regions of the world, the Middle East and sub-Saharan Africa are not particularly important areas for China's overseas investment. In 2003, its FDI to the Middle East represented only 0.87 percent of its worldwide OFDI, and sub-Saharan Africa represented 2.4 percent. As of 2019, the portion of Middle East OFDI was 1.8 percent and sub-Saharan Africa 2.2 percent. China's net outflows as a percentage of world FDI flows in 2019 were Hong Kong, 66 percent; Asia (minus Hong Kong), 12 percent; North America, 3 percent; Europe, 8 percent; Oceania, 1.5 percent; and Latin America (including the Cayman Islands and the British Virgin Islands), 4 percent.[27] As is widely known, a large portion of the Hong Kong figure is due to round-tripping by Chinese firms. FDI figures for potential tax havens such as the Cayman Islands and the British Virgin Islands could also include funds for round-tripping and onward journeying. That said, the argument still holds regarding Chinese investments in the Middle East and sub-Saharan Africa compared to other regions. Although China's investment in sub-Saharan Africa and the Middle East has grown over the past decade, it is still a small part of its global OFDI. For example, in 2016, Chinese firms invested $17 billion in the United States compared to less than $4 billion for the Middle East and sub-Saharan Africa combined. As economic tensions with the United States escalated during the Trump administration, China's ODFI started to shift to other regions, including the Middle East and sub-Saharan Africa. Chinese FDI flows to United States by 2019 dropped to $4 billion (compared to $5.5 billion in the Middle East and sub-Saharan Africa) due to both China's capital controls and Chinese concerns about the investment climate in the United States due to the Committee on Foreign Investment in the United States and other investment restrictions.[28] Chinese companies that previously looked to the United States for investment opportunities are starting to consider the Middle East and sub-Saharan Africa more favorably. One example of this impact is the recent increase in Chinese investment in Israel's technology sector due to more limited opportunities in the United States. The substantial increase in Israel is due to Chinese companies that are seeking opportunities in Internet, cybersecurity, and medical device start-ups as the investment climate in the United States for Chinese companies worsens.[29]

Examining the composition of Chinese OFDI into these regions highlights the diversification of China's investments. As of the end of 2019, the primary industries of China's FDI stocks in Africa (including North Africa) were construction (31 percent), mining (25 percent), manufacturing (13 percent), financial services (12 percent), and leasing and business services (4 percent).[30] These statistics indicate that China's OFDI interests in sub-Saharan Africa and North Africa are both to pursue resources (oil and other natural resources) and establish markets for a wide range of Chinese goods and services.

Trade, Services, and Investment Conclusions

By far, China's most significant interest in the Middle East and sub-Saharan Africa from 1991 to 2019 was promoting China's domestic economic development. Natural resources acquisition and export markets for Chinese goods and services were at the heart of this interest. China's imports from the Middle East and sub-Saharan Africa have increased rapidly since 1991. China became a net oil importer in 1993. By the late 1990s, importing from these regions began to skyrocket. Imports from the Middle East tended to be composed of energy products, and sub-Saharan Africa provided a more extensive array of resources required to fuel China's economic growth, including industrial minerals and agricultural products.

Although China's natural resource acquisition needs were a key component of China's interests in promoting its economic development, China's search for goods and services export markets in these regions was equally significant. In addition to product exports, the Middle East and sub-Saharan Africa were great services export markets for China's construction, telecommunication, and finance industries. In comparison to China's imports and exports to the Middle East and sub-Saharan Africa and investment in other regions of the world, China's FDI in these regions was minimal.

China's trade with, services to, and investment in the Middle East and sub-Saharan Africa have increased since the end of the Cold War as China's economic interests in these regions expanded. Exports, imports, and services have all increased at an impressive pace.

The rest of this chapter explores the foreign policy tools China uses to increase those interactions. Specifically, it looks at Chinese government support for Chinese companies, foreign aid, special economic zones, free trade agreements, and agricultural technology demonstration centers. This chapter categorizes those tools as competitive versus cooperative and norm convergent versus divergent.

Chinese Company Activities, 1991–2017

One of the most active and vigorously criticized facets of China's interactions with the Middle East and sub-Saharan Africa is the engagement of Chinese companies. Analysts, journalists, and nongovernmental organizations (NGOs) often accuse China of neocolonial behavior. Based on a review of available data, "neocolonial" is an exaggeration and misrepresentation. The terms *mercantilist* or *neomercantilist* would be more accurate.[31] Mercantilism is norm divergent from the liberal order. China is using state power through a variety of foreign policy tools to promote the export of manufactured goods to these regions, facilitate resource imports on advantageous terms, and secure market access for Chinese firms. This mercantilist behavior is competitive with the United

States and norm divergent from the liberal international order. In contrast, the liberal order stresses support for free markets and limited state intervention in the economy.

China's economic interests in these regions for resources and markets have dramatically increased from 1990 to the present. In the Middle East and sub-Saharan Africa, the vast majority of company activity is in three sectors: energy, construction, and telecommunications. This section describes the behavior of specific representative Chinese companies and analyzes what this company behavior indicates about China as a rising power in these regions.

This chapter began with examining China's aggregate FDI flows per country in the Middle East and sub-Saharan Africa. Unfortunately, comprehensive data for Chinese FDI and contract services at the company level by country in these regions are not available. As a result, this section examines the behavior of specific representative companies between 1991 and 2017. During my field research for this book, I obtained detailed company operation information over time and by country for a number of the Chinese enterprises engaged in these regions, obtained from company annual reports and various annual yearbooks of specific companies and industries. Many annual reports are also available online. I collected the data by company and then supplemented that material with additional information available from Chinese company websites and other sources.[32]

It is important to note that contract services are not foreign investment. China's overall contract services to these regions, which have significantly increased since 1999, involve a limited duration project where a company provides a service, for example, construction of a dam or building a telecommunications network. Chinese companies in these regions are involved in both contract services and FDI. Often, Chinese aid in the form of concessional loans funds contract services. An examination of Chinese state support for companies and company activities in these regions finds that investment, services, and aid are intertwined.

The State's Role in Chinese Company Behavior in the Middle East and Sub-Saharan Africa

Chinese state-owned enterprises (SOEs) conduct the vast majority of Chinese enterprise activity in the Middle East and sub-Saharan Africa.[33] Over the past two decades, the Chinese government has actively encouraged these enterprises to pursue opportunities globally and specifically in the Middle East and sub-Saharan Africa. In addition to the fact that these enterprises are ultimately owned and controlled by the Chinese state, the state guides the behavior of these enterprises through many initiatives. These companies receive direct and indirect government subsidies, favorable financing in the form of generous credit lines and low-interest loans from state-owned banks, preferential awarding of construction contracts tied to China's foreign aid and concessional loans, and expedited approvals for large-scale OFDI activities. These companies have been encouraged to pursue overseas opportunities in target industries and regions through the creation of national champions and the Chinese government's going out/going global programs. In the Middle East and sub-Saharan Africa, companies have been encouraged to pursue economic engagement through initiatives announced in the FOCAC and CASCF and through Belt and Road. The government provides strong political support encouraging economic interactions through its cooperation forums as well as BRI, including initiatives to improve relations with countries in these regions using foreign aid, concessional loans, agricultural cooperation, and cultural cooperation.

Going Out and National Champions

As early as 1985, China's Ministry of Foreign Economy and Trade passed a resolution stating that "any entity can apply for setting up overseas joint ventures if it had the relevant financial resources, a certain level of technology and business specialty, and joint partners."[34] The government started aggressively promoting overseas foreign direct investment (OFDI) in the early 1990s.[35] President Jiang Zemin declared during the Fourteenth Chinese Communist Party (CCP) Congress in 1992, "To open wider to the outside world . . . we should encourage enterprises to expand their investments abroad and their transnational operations."[36] During this phase, the government's motivation to promote OFDI was driven by the state's recognition of natural resource constraints to further national economic development.[37]

In support of this going out initiative, between 1991 and 1997, the Chinese State Council assembled a national team of 120 state-owned industry groups charged with leading the internationalization of Chinese enterprises. To build the national team, these companies were provided high levels of protection and state financial support, as well as OFDI encouraging special rights in management autonomy, profit retention, and investment decisions.[38] Firms that received this support were state owned and referred to as "National Champions." In addition to financial support from the Chinese government, the government provided National Champions with political advice and support regarding operating in various foreign environments.[39] The Chinese government also helped National Champions coordinate their activities abroad.[40]

The illustrative examples of National Champions analyzed in this section of the book are in the following sectors:

- Energy (CNOOC, China National Offshore Oil Corporation; CNPC, China National Petroleum Company; Sinochem Group; and SINOPEC, China Petrochemical Corporation)
- Construction (CRBC, China Road and Bridge Corporation; CRCC, China Railway Construction Corporation; CSCEC, China State Construction Engineering Corporation; NORINCO, China North Industries Corporation, controlled by the People's Liberation Army; and SINOHYDRO, China Hydraulic and Hydroelectric Construction Corporation)
- Telecommunications (Huawei, currently privately owned but previously state owned)
- Finance (Agricultural Bank of China; Bank of China; China Construction Bank; ICBC, Industrial and Commercial Bank of China)
- Manufacturing (Chery, state owned; Haier partially state owned)

China further strengthened its encouragement of OFDI of Chinese enterprises in the early 2000s as part of the go global campaign.[41] For example, in the oil industry, the goal of the going global initiative was to encourage oil companies to develop equity oil and seek income and rent from the upstream sector and create internationally competitive firms, especially in pillar industries.[42]

The primary difference between the official OFDI policy of the 1990s and 2000s was that the initiatives in the 1990s heavily focused on encouraging the OFDI behavior of state-owned enterprises. It was not until the 2000s that the emphasis shifted to the inclusion of nonstate-owned enterprises. Since the mid-2000s, the percentage of China's global OFDI provided by SOEs has been decreasing.[43] In the Middle East and sub-Saharan Africa, OFDI continues to be SOE dominated, but there is a trend toward more financial support for private companies investing in these regions. Although private companies are not entitled to the same level of financial support from the Chinese government for overseas activities as SOEs, many private companies can obtain private loans.[44] Also, small businesses are eligible to apply for funds such as monies from the China Development Bank and other development banks.[45]

(See chapter 4 for a discussion of the various funding mechanisms that are encouraged via China's cooperation forums.) It is important to note that starting in 2017, Xi Jinping implemented capital controls to rein in China's global OFDI, an action that resulted in steep declines in Chinese OFDI globally. That said, with China's BRI initiative, National Champions going out to the Middle East and Africa continues to be an important policy priority for the Chinese government.

Energy Sector

One of China's most significant interests in the Middle East and sub-Saharan Africa is promoting its economic development by acquiring natural resources and ensuring energy security. The energy sector is the most important economic sector for China in these regions to support that goal. With substantial support from the state, China's state-owned National Champion energy companies (CNOOC, CNPC, SINOPEC, and SINOCHEM) all pursue economic opportunities to meet those needs. All of these companies launched activities in these regions in the late 1990s in alignment with China's go global policies. During the 1990s and 2000s, many Chinese energy companies were willing to invest in relatively risky environments in the Middle East and Africa. Increasingly, Arab awakening events and incidents of terrorism in countries where national oil companies (NOCs) operate are influencing their risk assessments. As a result, many NOCs are rethinking how they deal with host countries and regional issues. This reconsideration has resulted in a more cautious approach in recent years to investment and contract opportunities in the Middle East and sub-Saharan Africa.[46] Also, for the NOCs, it is important to highlight that decisions to invest in blocks versus merely providing services are often driven by host country national and local regulations rather than the desires of the companies or the Chinese state.

Of China's national oil companies, CNPC (China National Petroleum Corporation) is the most active in the Middle East and sub-Saharan Africa. In the Middle East, it owns blocks in Algeria, Iran, Iraq, Libya, Oman, Qatar, Syria, Tunisia, and the United Arab Emirates. It also provides services in Egypt, Saudi Arabia, and Yemen. In sub-Saharan Africa, CNPC's blocks are in Chad, Equatorial Guinea, Mauritania, Niger, Nigeria, South Sudan, and Sudan. CNPC also provides services to Angola, Cameroon, Republic of Congo, Ethiopia, Ghana, Kenya, Madagascar, Mozambique, Tanzania, and Uganda.[47]

China Petroleum Corporation (SINOPEC) is the second most active NOC in the Middle East and sub-Saharan Africa. In the Middle East, it owns blocks in Algeria, Egypt, Iran, Kuwait, Oman, Saudi Arabia, Syria, and Yemen. It also provides services in the United Arab Emirates. SINOPEC's block ownership in sub-Saharan Africa is in Angola, Gabon, Ghana, Kenya, Mali, Nigeria, São Tomé and Principe, and Sudan. SINOPEC also provides services in Liberia.[48]

China National Offshore Oil Corporation (CNOOC) is also active in these regions. In the Middle East, it owns oil blocks in Algeria, Iraq, Qatar, and Yemen. Its oil blocks in sub-Saharan Africa are in Equatorial Guinea, Gabon, Kenya, Liberia, Nigeria, Republic of Congo, and Uganda. CNOOC has service projects in Iran and Somalia.[49]

Finally, Sinochem has limited operations in the Middle East and no reported operations in sub-Saharan Africa. It owns oil blocks in Syria, Tunisia, United Arab Emirates, and Yemen.[50] It also has agricultural investments in Israel.[51]

Chinese NOCs are responsible for securing supplies to meet their customers' needs. The Middle East and sub-Saharan Africa are both long-term strategic regions for these companies. In the eyes of these oil companies, the most important strategic energy suppliers in the Middle East are Saudi Arabia, Kuwait, Iran, and Iraq. Both Saudi Arabia and Kuwait are relatively closed to foreign investment, so Chinese companies primarily pursue service contracts with these countries to ensure access to supply. In contrast, Iraq and Iran are open to foreign investment. Nevertheless, Chinese companies are cautious with their investments in Iran due to current and future international sanctions against the country. Although the Middle East is the most important energy market for China, Chinese companies are actively seeking opportunities in sub-Saharan Africa to ensure the security of supply. Also, China perceives the Middle East to be a turbulent region that endangers its energy security. This concern is another reason for these companies to diversify away from the Middle East to other regions, including sub-Saharan Africa.

Construction Sector

The construction sector provides immense service export opportunities for Chinese companies. These services are directly related to China's needs to secure international markets for its services to fuel its economic growth. Similar to the energy NOCs, China's National Champion construction companies contribute to those goals of the Chinese state. These companies receive overall support from the Chinese government available for all National Champion SOEs, but they especially benefit from the tying of concessional infrastructure loans to Chinese company providers.[52] The National Champion construction companies analyzed in this section are CRBC (China Road and Bridge Corporation), CRCC (China Railway Construction Corporation), CSCEC (China State Construction Engineering Corporation), NORINCO (China Northern Industries Corporation), and SINOHYDRO (China Hydraulic and Hydroelectric Construction Group Corporation).

The most active of these construction companies in the Middle East and sub-Saharan Africa is SINOHYDRO. Although it does have some investments in the Middle East and sub-Saharan Africa, the vast majority of its activities are services. Throughout the two regions, SINOHYDRO builds irrigation projects, highways, dams, housing units, stadiums, power stations, schools, hotels, sewage treatment facilities, bridges, mines, airports, and water distribution systems. In the Middle East, it has completed projects in Algeria, Iran, Kuwait, Libya, Oman, Qatar, Saudi Arabia, the United Arab Emirates, and Yemen. Sub-Saharan African projects have been completed in Angola, Botswana, Cameroon, Republic of Congo, Democratic People's Republic of Congo, Equatorial Guinea, Ethiopia, Gabon, Ghana, Ivory Coast, Kenya, Kuwait, Mauritania, Madagascar, Mali, Mozambique, Namibia, Niger, Nigeria, Sudan, Tanzania, Togo, Zambia, and Zimbabwe.[53]

After SINOHYDRO, the second most active SOE construction company examined in this section is CRCC. Despite its name, this company is involved in many projects outside of railways. In the Middle East and sub-Saharan Africa, its projects include railways, roads, airports, power distribution systems, hospitals, buildings, bridges, transformers, stadiums, and water supply projects. Their Middle East projects have included Algeria, Egypt, Israel, Libya, Oman, Qatar, Saudi Arabia, Turkey, and the United Arab Emirates. sub-Saharan projects have occurred in Angola, Benin, Botswana, Chad, Djibouti, Ethiopia, Madagascar, Mali, Niger, Nigeria, Rwanda, Senegal, Sierra Leone, Sudan, Tanzania, Zambia, and Zimbabwe.[54]

Although not as extensively involved as SINOHYDRO and CRCC, the CRBC has conducted significant projects in sub-Saharan Africa. Its Middle East operations are more limited (only in Kuwait) than its sub-Saharan African operations. Its projects include building roads, bridges, harbors, and plants. Its sub-Saharan African projects were conducted in Angola, Burundi, the Republic of Congo, the Democratic People's Republic of Congo, Gabon,

Equatorial Guinea, Ethiopia, Kenya, Malawi, Mali, Mauritania, Mozambique, and Rwanda.[55]

China State Construction Engineering Corporation (CSCEC) engages in a large number of Middle Eastern construction projects. In this region, it tends to build structures such as universities, living units, airports, refineries, hotels, government buildings, office buildings, and malls, as well as roads. CSCEC has launched projects in Algeria, Kuwait, Qatar, and the United Arab Emirates. Projects in sub-Saharan Africa include Botswana, Republic of Congo, Ghana, Mauritius, and Nigeria.[56]

Finally, NORINCO, which is owned by the PLA, has engaged some major construction projects in these regions. In Iran, it has completed several projects, including the building of the Tehran subway system and other rail projects. In Ethiopia, it provided engineering service for a highway and a hydropower plant. It also provided services in Guinea-Bissau, Iraq, and Kenya.[57]

Telecommunications Sector

The primary service markets for Chinese companies in the Middle East and sub-Saharan Africa are construction, telecommunication, and finance. Huawei is the most important Chinese telecommunications company in these regions.[58] ZTE also has established operations, but a detailed country-by-country breakdown of their services is not available. Huawei's activities in the Middle East and sub-Saharan Africa are increasingly linked to security competition between the United States and China in these regions as tensions flare between the two countries over potential security concerns about Chinese telecommunications companies building 5G and other networks globally. These tensions are not discussed in detail in this book, but it is an important example of how Chinese state support for a company can generate security concerns.

Since the late 1990s, Huawei has built telecommunication networks and provided services throughout sub-Saharan Africa and the Middle East. In the Middle East, the company has branch offices in Algeria, Bahrain, Iraq, Kuwait, Oman, Qatar, Saudi Arabia, Turkey, and United Arab Emirates.[59] Its Middle East headquarters are in Bahrain, and Huawei North Africa is in Egypt.[60] It also has extensive operations in Tunisia.[61] Huawei branches in sub-Saharan Africa are in Ethiopia, Nigeria, and South Africa.[62] Its East and South Africa headquarters is in South Africa, and its West African headquarters is in Nigeria.[63] It also has extensive operations in Angola, Botswana, Burundi,

Gambia, Ghana, Kenya, Madagascar, Mauritania, Mauritius, Mozambique, Namibia, Senegal, Sierra Leone, Uganda, Zambia, and Zimbabwe. In South Africa, Huawei has an R&D center and seven training centers in Angola, the Democratic Republic of the Congo, Egypt, Kenya, Morocco, Nigeria, and South Africa.[64]

Finance Sector

Financial services are another essential emerging service sector for China in these regions. China's four largest banks have operations in the Middle East and sub-Saharan Africa. The leading Chinese bank with operations in sub-Saharan Africa and the Middle East is ICBC (Industrial and Commercial Bank of China).[65] In 2008, ICBC purchased a 20 percent stake in South Africa's Standard Bank for $5 billion. This purchase was the single most substantial investment by any Chinese company in Africa in history. ICBC also established branch offices in Kuwait, Qatar, Turkey, and the United Arab Emirates.[66] Bank of China (BOC) has opened branches and representative offices in Bahrain, Kenya, South Africa, United Arab Emirates, and Zambia.[67] Agricultural Bank of China (ABC) operates in the United Arab Emirates.[68] Finally, China Construction Bank (CCB) has established a presence in South Africa and the United Arab Emirates.[69]

Manufacturing Sector

Finally, to develop markets for Chinese goods in the Middle East and sub-Saharan Africa, Chinese manufacturing companies have been encouraged to establish operations in these regions. China has provided incentives for the establishment of special economic zones (SEZs) to support Chinese manufacturing investment in these regions. Compared to the energy sector and the services sector, Chinese manufacturing operations in the Middle East and sub-Saharan Africa are more limited.

Two high-profile Chinese manufacturing companies with operations in the Middle East and sub-Saharan Africa are Chery and Haier. The automotive sector and home appliances are particularly important sectors for Chinese exports to these regions. To establish itself in Middle Eastern automotive markets, state-owned Chery automotive has opened plants in Egypt, Iran, Jordan, and Syria.[70] It has no plants in sub-Saharan Africa but has established many distributors throughout the continent.

Haier produces household appliances and is also partially state owned.

One of the largest appliance companies in the world, it acquired GE's home appliances division in 2016. To access markets in these regions, it has opened plants in the Middle East (Algeria, Egypt, Jordan, and Tunisia) and sub-Saharan Africa (Nigeria and South Africa).[71]

Chinese Company Activities Conclusions

China's state support for its companies' activities in the Middle East and sub-Saharan Africa is competitive with the United States and norm divergent from the liberal order. It is categorized as competitive toward the United States because these primarily state-owned National Champion companies with substantial state support are actively pursuing opportunities for resources, markets, and contract services throughout these regions. This behavior is directly related to the Chinese state's desire to secure energy resources for China and market opportunities for these state-owned companies. Most of these companies are state owned and are provided immense encouragement and support, financial and political, to make inroads into these markets to serve state interests. At its core, this is neomercantilist behavior aimed at increasing China's economic power in these regions. Assuming that economic power is a finite resource, this behavior is directly at the expense of the United States and other great powers involved in these regions.

This section provided some illustrative examples of companies benefiting from Chinese state support in key industries from 1991 to 2017. Upon analysis of where China is engaged in investment and services, there is no indication that it is explicitly targeting rogue regimes or any other type of state with this behavior. It is merely securing resources and markets wherever they exist.

As China's overall power is increasing, so is this competitive behavior. China is building spheres of influence in these regions. Chinese companies, both state owned and other National Champions, are important actors in building that influence. As demonstrated by recent US government statements about Huawei and China's economic activities in these regions, it is clear the United States increasingly views China's support for companies operating in the energy, construction, and telecommunications sectors as engaging in competition and endangering US national interests.[72]

China's behavior supporting these companies is also categorized as norm divergent from liberal international economic norms. Those norms are free-market capitalism and limited state involvement in economic interactions. China's mercantilist, state-led model directly contradicts those rules.

Together with China's cooperation forums and other economic foreign policy tools discussed in this chapter, China's substantial state support for companies operating the Middle East and sub-Saharan is an important aspect of the economic and political order China is building in these regions.

Foreign Aid

China's history of foreign aid provision in sub-Saharan Africa and the Middle East dates back to the 1950s. The purpose of this section is to provide an understanding of the magnitude and distribution of China's bilateral overseas development assistance over time in these regions. It explores how these programs are competitive with the United States and the rest of the West and norm divergent from the liberal order governing aid.[73]

China initiated its global foreign aid program in 1953[74] with aid to the Middle East and sub-Saharan Africa that included grants, loans, agricultural assistance, technicians, and rural medical teams.[75] As a poor country itself, China was a unique donor:[76] the only poor country in the world that was providing outbound aid.[77] Two of China's most crucial aid programs were grants (donations) and interest-free and low-interest loans. Its first foreign aid recipient in the Middle East was Egypt during the Suez Canal crisis in 1956.[78] Its first recipient in sub-Saharan Africa was Guinea in 1959 (during China's own economically disastrous Great Leap Forward) to assist the country in building its infrastructure after declaring independence from France.[79] Another notable feature of China's foreign aid during this period was that it often assisted countries possessing a higher per capita income than it had.[80]

In 1964, China proposed Eight Principles of Aid to oppose existing hegemonic foreign aid norms of the time directly. Zhou Enlai most famously articulated China's principles for aid to the third world in 1964 during his trip to Ghana:

> 1. The Chinese government always bases itself on the principle of equality and mutual benefit in providing aid to other countries. It never regards such aid as a kind of unilateral alms but as something mutual.
>
> 2. In providing aid to other countries, the Chinese government strictly respects the sovereignty of recipient countries, and never attaches any conditions or asks for any privileges.
>
> 3. China provides economic aid in the form of interest-free or low-interest

> loans, and extends the time limit for the repayment when necessary so as to lighten the burden on recipient countries as far as possible.
>
> 4. In providing aid to other countries, the purpose of the Chinese government is not to make recipient countries dependent on China but to help them embark step by step on the road of self-reliance and independent economic development.
>
> 5. The Chinese government does its best to help recipient countries complete projects which require less investment but yield quicker results, so that the latter may increase their income and accumulate capital.
>
> 6. The Chinese government provides the best-quality equipment and materials manufactured by China at international market prices. If the equipment and materials provided by the Chinese government are not up to the agreed specifications and quality, the Chinese government undertakes to replace them or refund the payment.
>
> 7. In giving any particular technical assistance, the Chinese government will see to it that the personnel of the recipient country fully master the technology.
>
> 8. The experts dispatched by China to help in construction in recipient countries will have the same standard of living as the experts of the recipient country. The Chinese experts are not allowed to make any special demands or enjoy any special amenities.[81]

China's approach to foreign aid, exemplified in these eight principles, diverged from international aid norms and was intended to expose the shortcomings of Soviet and Western assistance and provide an alternative aid model.[82] One of the most fundamental underpinnings of this approach was that China would not seek economic profit in its foreign aid programs. As a result, China (as opposed to Western and Soviet donors at the time) offered interest-free or low-interest loans to countries in sub-Saharan Africa and the Middle East.[83] China, as a critique of Western and Soviet aid provision, also emphasized that Chinese aid was different because it provided learning opportunities to African and Middle Eastern countries based on China's own development experience. China's aid programs often encouraged low-investment, labor-intensive, and cottage industry projects reflecting its development experience.[84] Finally, China's aid approach was different from Western and Soviet aid models because it required that Chinese experts dispatched to these regions have living similar to experts in the local population, as opposed to Western expatriates who received special treatment and living standards better than local residents.[85]

In many ways, these Mao-era principles remain in operation. This section examines one element of China's foreign aid in the post–Cold War era: overseas development assistance (ODA).

Chinese aid is notoriously opaque. It does not report its foreign aid provisions in alignment with the expectations of the international aid community. In 2017, the China Aid Data project released comprehensive data on China's foreign aid by project from 2000 to 2014. The data they collected is the first in-depth look at Chinese aid broken down by region and over time.[86] Based on China Aid Data's information, figure 6.11 shows that China's assistance to the Middle East is minimal, and most of its aid in these two regions is provided to sub-Saharan Africa. Examination of the data shows that the top recipients of China's aid in the Middle East from 2000 to 2014 were Yemen (US$282 million), Jordan (US$8 million), Algeria (US$63 million), Palestinians (US$58 million), Egypt (US$43 million), Tunisia (US$38 million), Lebanon (US$20 million), and Morocco (US$11 million). In sub-Saharan Africa, top recipients were Côte d'Ivoire (US$3.967 billion), Ethiopia (US$3.659 billion), Zimbabwe (US$3.606 billion), Cameroon (US$3.403 billion), Tanzania (US$3.024 billion), Ghana (US$2.627 billion), Mozambique (US$2.430 billion), and Republic of Congo (US$2.095 billion). sub-Saharan Africa receives significantly more Chinese aid than the Middle East (including North Africa).

The provision of overseas development assistance provides the Chinese state an opportunity to link its political and economic activities in these regions.[87] That said, the state is not a monolith in its allocation of foreign aid. From 2000 to 2014, Chinese aid allocation decisions could be understood as a competition among China's Ministry of Commerce (MOFCOM), Ministry of Foreign Affairs (MFA), and Ministry of Finance.[88] In 2018, China announced the creation of the International Development Cooperation Agency, which reports directly to the State Council and oversees foreign aid programs across the government. Its purpose is to improve strategic planning and coordination between China's foreign aid and BRI.[89] It coordinates with MOFCOM, MFA, and the Ministry of Finance to ensure that China's political goals and foreign assistance are better aligned.

China pursues several interests with its foreign aid programs. The provision of foreign aid promotes China's economic growth because such aid is

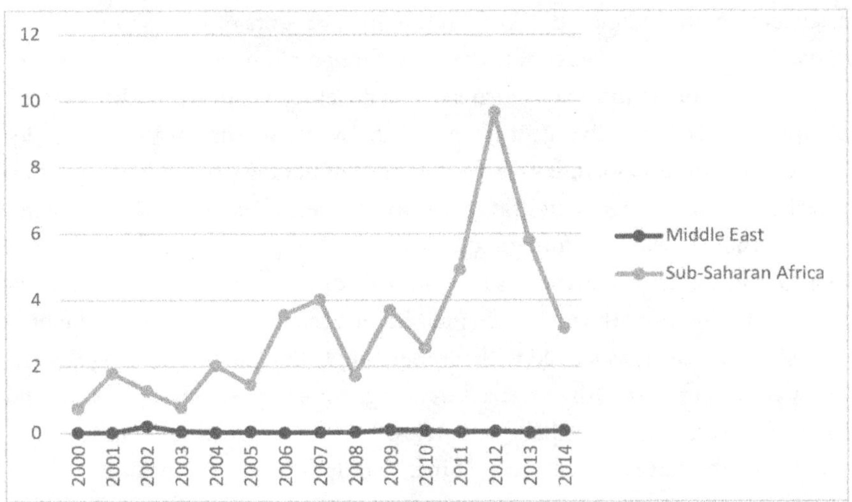

Figure 6.11. China's Official Development Assistance, 2000–2014, in billion USD deflated 2014 dollars. Source: Data compiled by author from Axel Dreher, Andreas Fuchs, Bradley Parks, Austin M. Strange, and Michael J. Tierney, "Aid, China, and Growth: Evidence from a New Global Development Finance Dataset," AidData working paper 46 (Williamsburg, VA: AidData, 2017).

contingent on the utilization of Chinese companies for the contracts. These service projects provide business opportunities for Chinese companies, including SOEs and national champions. Many of the companies discussed in the last section of this chapter benefit from the projects generated by China's concessional loans to countries in these regions. China's foreign aid programs also support China's economic interests because they fund the construction of much-needed infrastructure in countries where China is seeking resources or markets.

Foreign aid is a tool China uses to foster support in the international arena and advocate for developing country causes. It is one of the ways China demonstrates it is a responsible great power in these regions. That said, there is some criticism that China overpromises and underdelivers on its aid pledges. The gap in pledged versus delivered aid is causing dissatisfaction in some countries and could erode the effectiveness of using foreign aid to build goodwill with countries in these regions and demonstrating that China advocates for developing country causes.[90]

China's norms of foreign aid provision are divergent from liberal norms associated with foreign aid.[91] Although many elements of China's foreign aid activities are norm convergent with global foreign aid norms that advocate for the provision of aid in various forms to less developed countries, China's overall approach is norm divergent from the liberal order. Similar to its behavior between 1949 and 1990, today China is critical of liberal foreign aid norms that interfere in the domestic politics of recipient countries and is actively challenging those norms. Its foreign aid approach stems from its experience as a developing country. It advocates for political condition-free foreign aid provision in alignment with the Five Principles of Peaceful Coexistence. The only political condition associated with Chinese aid is that countries recognize the one-China principle. Otherwise, China is agnostic regarding regime type and internal governance of recipient countries. This aid often comes with financial requirements that recipients use Chinese companies for the projects. It also presses for the inclusion of infrastructure development as a component of foreign aid as opposed to Western countries that do not support infrastructure development.

Over time, China's overall foreign aid approach has not changed. What has changed is that as its own economic development needs have grown, it has also expanded its foreign aid to developing countries around the world. From China's perspective, it is not merely offering an alternative model of foreign aid; it is directly critiquing the current system and the mistreatment of developing countries in that system.

Together with the other economic tools discussed in this chapter and chapter 4 cooperation forums, China's approach to foreign aid provision is an important component of the overall economic order it is building in these regions and the rest of the developing world.

This chapter categorizes China's foreign aid as competitive with the United States and the rest of the West. In both absolute dollar terms and as a percentage of gross national income, Chinese foreign aid is much lower than the United States, the United Kingdom, Germany, and Japan.[92] That said, foreign aid programs are one of the main ways in which China is attempting to increase its sphere of influence in sub-Saharan Africa and the Middle East.

Although China is often accused of using its foreign aid programs to secure natural resources or support authoritarian regimes, recent research indicates that although political considerations play into any great power's foreign aid provision, China's ODA allocation is mostly independent of a recipient country's natural resource endowments and regime type.[93] That said, it does appear that China's foreign aid has decreased the ability of the United States to manipulate UN General Assembly voting of recipient countries.[94] Chinese support weakens recipient countries' dependence on US aid and therefore makes it harder for the United States to coerce or induce voting behavior in the General Assembly.[95]

Free Trade Agreements

In contrast to the competitive, norm-divergent foreign policy of Chinese support for its companies operating in the Middle East and sub-Saharan Africa and its foreign aid to countries in these regions, this chapter characterizes China's pursuit of free trade agreements (FTAs) as competitive but norm convergent with the liberal order. Setting up these FTAs is competitive because it is building a sphere of influence for China at the expense of other great powers but convergent because FTAs are in alignment with the liberal norms of the international system of encouraging free trade and utilizing multilateral institutional mechanisms to facilitate cooperation among states. Establishing FTAs is norm convergent with the liberal order because the WTO explicitly allows states to establish regional preferential trade agreements.

This section introduces China's FTA negotiations with regional organizations and bilateral FTAs in these regions. In the Middle East, China is negotiating FTAs with the GCC (Gulf Cooperation Council), Israel, and Palestine.[96] In sub-Saharan Africa, it has signed an FTA with Mauritius.[97] It previously negotiated an unsigned FTA with the Southern African Customs Union (SACU). In addition to FTAs, China provides unilateral tariff-free trade benefits to all LDC countries in Africa and the Middle East. (That tariff treatment is discussed in more detail in chapter 4 on cooperation forums.) As a point of comparison, as of the beginning of 2021, the United States has FTAs with the Middle East countries of Bahrain, Israel, Jordan, Morocco, and Oman. It does not have any FTAs in sub-Saharan Africa,[98] but its African Growth Opportunity Act (AGOA) provides preferential treatment for many African countries.[99]

To provide a global context for these FTAs, as of the beginning of 2021, outside of the Middle East and sub-Saharan Africa, China already had established agreements with ASEAN, the Association of Southeast Asian Nations (2005), Pakistan (2007), Chile (2006), New Zealand (2008), Singapore (2008), Peru (2010), Costa Rica (2010), Iceland (2014), Switzerland (2014), Korea (2015),

Australia (2015), Georgia (2018), Maldives (2018), Cambodia (2020), and the Regional Comprehensive Economic Partnership, which is an FTA including ASEAN, Australia, China, Japan, New Zealand, and South Korea (2020). Ongoing FTA negotiations outside the Middle East and sub-Saharan Africa were occurring with Moldova, Mauritius, Norway, Sri Lanka, Japan, and Panama. China was considering FTA negotiations with Mongolia, Bangladesh, Canada, Papua New Guinea, Nepal, Fiji, and Columbia.[100] In contrast, outside of the Middle East and sub-Saharan Africa, the United States has free trade agreements with Australia, Canada, Chile, Columbia, Costa Rica, Dominican Republic, El Salvador, Guatemala, Honduras, the Republic of Korea, Mexico, Nicaragua, Panama, Peru, Singapore, and the United States- Mexico- Canada agreement (USMCA).[101]

Since the beginning of the post–Cold War era, China has pursued formal FTAs with two regional organizations in the Middle East and sub-Saharan Africa: the Cooperation Council for the Arab States of the Gulf (GCC) and the Southern African Customs Union (SACU). China pursued these FTAs to increase its exports to these crucial markets through the tariff-free entry of goods to its own main export markets in these regions. The SACU FTA is no longer viable due to the emergence of other regional organizations in Africa, but China does likely want to pursue a broader regional African FTA with the new formed continent-wide African Free Trade Area (AfFTA). The AfFTA was established only in late 2020, so formal negotiations for an FTA have not yet started, but future trade cooperation with the AfFTA is mentioned in the FOCAC 2019–2021 action plan.[102] This chapter discusses the GCC FTA, which is in the process of negotiation.

The GCC was established in 1981 as a customs union. Its member states are the United Arab Emirates, Bahrain, Saudi Arabia, Oman, Qatar, and Kuwait.[103] China's economic interests motivate FTA negotiations with the GCC. Saudi Arabia, Oman, Kuwait, and the UAE are four of China's top global crude oil suppliers. Qatar is also one of China's top natural gas suppliers. The GCC countries are also incredibly important export markets for China in the Middle East. China's GCC members were among China's top export destinations in the Middle East. Saudi Arabia and the United Arab Emirates are also two of China's largest construction services markets in the Middle East.

In July 2004, China and the GCC signed the Framework Agreement on Economic, Trade, Investment, and Technological Cooperation, and China announced the launch of FTA negotiations.[104] The proposed FTA would include goods, services, and investment.[105] Between 2004 and 2016, China and the GCC held nine rounds of talks. In April 2005, the first round held in Saudi Arabia focused on formulating a working outline of the FTA negotiations and beginning discussions regarding tariff reduction for goods. During the second round of talks in June in China, the two sides reached an agreement on a tariff reduction method for goods and began talks on market access and rules of origin. The third round of negotiations, held in Beijing in January 2006, focused on continued negotiations about tariff reductions, market access, rules of origin, customs procedures, and trade remedies. Round 4 occurred in July 2006 in China when the two sides began to negotiate bilateral services trade.[106] In February 2009, Chinese president Hu Jintao visited Saudi Arabia, met with GCC Secretary-General Abdul Rahman Al-Attiya, and pledged to pursue progress in completing the FTA.[107] Shortly after Hu Jintao's visit, after three years of delay, the fifth round of talks was held in June 2009 in Saudi Arabia. Chinese press releases appear to indicate that one reason behind the delay was the effect of the global financial crisis of 2008.[108]

After a seven-year pause in negotiations after 2009, negotiations restarted in 2016, and rounds 6 to 9 were held that year.[109] There appear to be many root causes for the delays associated with concluding this FTA. One interviewee with the Ministry of Commerce, an expert on China-GCC relations, stated that part of the delay was that the China-GCC FTA was much more complicated than other FTA negotiations for the GCC (e.g., the Singapore-GCC FTA).[110] Another reason that interviewees frequently mentioned was the impact of the Arab awakening on GCC unity.[111] In many ways, it appears that disagreements within the GCC are stalling progress. For example, the UAE wants the central bank supporting the FTA to be headquartered in Dubai, while Saudi Arabia wants it to be in Riyadh.[112] Feuding among some GCC members (e.g., Saudi Arabia and UAE versus Qatar) aggravated tensions, which resulted in an embargo on Qatar starting in 2017. Several interview respondents indicated that China planned to sign the FTA during Xi's visit to the Middle East in 2016, but those plans were abandoned when that trip was postponed.[113] The CASCF 2016–2018 and 2020–2022 action plans stressed the need to speed up China and the GCC FTA agreement negotiations.[114] Although significant progress was made over the years, and China and the GCC were very close to signing a deal in 2016,[115] an agreement is unlikely until internal GCC issues between Qatar and other members are resolved.[116]

In addition to its attempts to negotiate FTAs with GCC, China is also pursuing bilateral FTAs with countries in the Middle East and sub-Saharan Africa, Mauritius, Israel, and Palestine.

China initiated a joint feasibility research study on an FTA with Mauritius in 2016, and the two sides launched official trade negotiations in late 2017. This agreement, the first bilateral FTA negotiations China has ever pursued with an African country, is meant to expand trade and investment relations further and support the Belt and Road Initiative. The two countries signed the FTA in October 2019.[117]

Negotiations with Israel were initially announced in 2016, and as of 2019, six rounds of talks had been conducted. In scope for this FTA are goods, services, movements of persons, rule of origin and customs procedures, sanitation procedures, trade remedies, economic and technical cooperation, e-commerce, and dispute resolution. It is also meant to support Belt and Road.[118]

Finally, China is negotiating an FTA with Palestine focused on trade and investment. A feasibility study started in December 2017,[119] and the first round of negotiations was held in 2019. Although China does not frame it in this way, it is likely pursuing the Palestine FTA concurrent with the Israel FTA to continue to demonstrate its balanced relations with both parties of the Palestinian-Israeli conflict.

China pursues its interests through these FTA negotiations. Successfully concluded FTAs would promote its domestic economic growth through access to resources and markets. Negotiating these FTAs also helps China to build support in the international system. According to recent research, China's selection of FTA negotiation partners is heavily influenced by political considerations. Although China FTAs with these regional organizations and countries will improve access to resources and markets, evidence supports the assertion that China selects FTA partners for political reasons, not economic ones.[120] Also, it is important to note that Chinese FTAs in general have a low level of trade liberalization and legal obligations and exclude sensitive sectors. In that respect, China is relatively conservative in how it pursues FTAs.

China's FTA negotiations in the Middle East and sub-Saharan Africa are competitive because it is building a sphere of influence for China in these regions. These FTAs will contribute to China's economic and political clout with the GCC, Mauritius, Israel, and Palestine. Despite their competitive nature, these FTAs are norm convergent because FTAs are in alignment with the norms of the liberal order and allowed by the WTO. These FTAs are yet another element of the economic order China is building in the Middle East and sub-Saharan Africa.

Special Economic Zones, 1991–2018

China's special economic zones (SEZ) in the Middle East and sub-Saharan Africa are competitive and norm neutral. China is using them to build spheres of influence. It is promoting economic development by sharing China's successful SEZ model with other developing countries. That said, there is not an applicable liberal norm for this foreign policy tool in the liberal order, so it is considered norm neutral.

Between 1990 and 2018, Chinese companies launched eleven SEZs in sub-Saharan Africa and the Middle East in Algeria, Djibouti, Egypt, Ethiopia, Kenya, Mauritius, Mauritania, Nigeria (two), Oman, and Zambia.[121] FOCAC highly publicizes these zones.

China's first overseas SEZs were initiated to facilitate the offshoring of China's labor-intensive, less competitive, and mature industries.[122] Particular industries targeted were textiles, leather goods, and building materials.[123] The Kenya, Oman, and Zambia zones focus on natural resources (see table 6.1). The rest promote investment in Chinese manufacturing.[124] Today, China's SEZs aim to transfer China's development successes to other countries, increase business opportunities for China manufacturing companies, avoid trade barriers by setting up zones in countries with preferential trade access to important markets, and create a positive business environment for Chinese small and medium-sized enterprises investing in these regions.[125]

In general, the Chinese government relies on Chinese enterprises to establish the zones and takes a relatively hands-off approach. Outside of various financial incentives, the Chinese government does not directly become involved in the design or direct operation of the zones. The enterprises are responsible for constructing the zones and attracting Chinese and other foreign enterprises to establish operations and form industrial clusters.[126] That said, the government does provide some support for the projects. For example, zone developers can access grants, loans, and subsidies from the Chinese government, including mechanisms such as the China Africa Development Fund (CADF).[127] Finally, African small and medium enterprises interested in investing in the zones can apply for funds from the Chinese government.[128]

Table 6.1. Chinese Special Economic Zones (SEZs) in the Middle East and Sub-Saharan Africa, 1990–2018

Country	*Region*	*Planning Initiated*	*Location*[1]	*Name*	*Developers*	*Home Province*	*Industry Focus*
Algeria	Middle East	2006 (Tender year 2007)	Oran City	Jiangling	Jiangling Economic and Trade Cooperation Zone in Mostaganem[2] Jiangling Automobile, Zhongding International. Jianxing Coal Corporation Group[3]	Jiangxi	Automotive assembly, construction materials
Djibouti	Sub-Saharan Africa	2018	Djibouti	Djibouti International Free Trade Zone	Djibouti Ports and Free Zones Authority; China's Merchants Holdings Company; Dalian Port Authority; and IZP.[4]	Liaoning	Trade and logistics, export processing, business, and financial support services; manufacturing; and duty-free merchandise
Egypt	Middle East	1994	China-Egypt Suez	Suez	Egypt Suez Canal Cooperation Zone[5] Tianjin TEDA, CADF, Egypt-China Corporation for Investment (ECCI), Tianjin Suez International Cooperation Corporation Company	Tianjin	Textiles and garments, petroleum equipment, automobile assembly, electronics assembly
Ethiopia	Sub-Saharan Africa	2006 (Tender 2007)	Eastern	Dukem, Addis Adaba	Yongguang, Qiyuan Investment Group, Jianglian International Trade, Yangyang Asset Management, Zhangjiagang Free Trade Zone	Jiangsu	Electric machinery, steel and metallurgy, and construction materials

Table 6.1. Chinese Special Economic Zones (SEZs) in the Middle East and Sub-Saharan Africa, 1990–2018 (*continued*)

Country	*Region*	*Planning Initiated*	*Location*[1]	*Name*	*Developers*	*Home Province*	*Industry Focus*
Kenya	Sub-Saharan Africa	2017	Africa Economic Zone[6]	Eldoret	China's Guangdong New South Group	Guangdong	Agro-processing, chemical and construction sectors, technology, hospitality[7]
Mauritania	Sub-Saharan Africa	2015	Nouadhibou	Nouadhibou Free Economic Zone[8]			Announced in 2016–2018 action plan for FOCAC.[9] Fishing, mining, construction, infrastructure, social housing, residential housing, health care, plant construction, renewable energies, telecommunications, water treatment, information and communication technology, logistics, and agricultural processing [10]
Mauritius[11]	Sub-Saharan Africa	2006	Jinfei	Terre Rouge	Jinfei Special Economic Zone[12] Shanxi-Tianli Group, Shanxi Coking Coal Group, Taiyuan Iron and Steel Company	Shanxi	Manufacturing (textile, garments, machinery, hi-tech), information and communication technology, trade, services (tourism, finance, and education), solar equipment, seafood processing[13]

Table 6.1. Chinese Special Economic Zones (SEZs) in the Middle East and Sub-Saharan Africa, 1990–2018 (*continued*)

Country	*Region*	*Planning Initiated*	*Location*[1]	*Name*	*Developers*	*Home Province*	*Industry Focus*
Nigeria	Sub-Saharan Africa	2003-Lekki	Lekki	Lagos State	CECC (China Civil Engineering Construction,) Jiangning Development Corporation, Nanjing Beyond, China Railway, Lagos State, Lekki Worldwide Investments Limited	National	Transportation equipment, textile and light industries, home appliances, and telecommunications; possible oil refinery
Nigeria	Sub-Saharan Africa	2004-Ogun	Ogun-Guangdong	Ogun State	Guangdong Xinguang, South China Developing Group, Ogun State Government	Guangdong	Construction materials and ceramics, ironware, furniture, wood processing, medicine, computers, lighting
Oman	Middle East	2017	Duqm Special Economic Zone[14]	Duqm	Ningxia Provincial Government	Ningxia	Port, oil refinery, menthol plant, solar equipment manufacturing, automotive, oil and gas equipment, building material distribution. Sino-Oman Industrial City with tourism zone[15]
Zambia	Sub-Saharan Africa	2003	Zambia-China	Chambishsi/ Lusaka	China Nonferrous Mining Group (CNMC group)	National	Copper, cobalt processing, garments, food, appliances, tobacco, electronics

China's economic behavior establishing these SEZs is categorized as competitive with the United States and norm neutral. China is exporting its model of economic development by setting up SEZs, which have been successful within China. Both the Middle East and sub-Saharan Africa are promising markets for Chinese manufactured goods, so the Chinese government

Notes

1. Many locations from Tang, "How Do Chinese."

2. "Algeria-Egypt-China: Zoning In and Zoning Out," *Africa-Asia Confidential*, June 5, 2012.

3. "Algeria-Egypt-China."

4. Abdi Latif Dahir, "Thanks to China, Africa's Largest Free Trade Zone Has Launched in Djibouti," *Quartz Africa*, July 9, 2018; Justina Crabtree, "While China Slaps Tariffs on the US, It's Also Championing Free Trade in Africa," *CNBC*, July 6, 2018.

5. "Algeria-Egypt-China."

6. "Chinese Firm to Construct Sh200b Industrial Park in Eldoret after Beijing Deal," *Daily Nation*, May 18, 2017.

7. Roland Njoroge, "Kenya Launches Special Economic Zone Project," Xinhua, July 8, 2017.

8. CASCF, "2018 to 2020 Action Plan," section 3.13.

9. FOCAC "Johannesburg Action Plan (2016–2018)."

10. http://www.idainternational.org/projects/mauritania-free-zone/.

11. As of 2015, not many businesses had expressed interest in participating in the zone, and it has not yet started operations.

12. Eric Olander, Cobus van Staden, and James Wan, "China's Special Economic Zones in Africa: Lot of Hype, Little Hope," August 20, 2015, www.chinafile.com.

13. "'Rise and Stall' China's Stepping Stones to Nowhere," *African Business Magazine*, April 8, 2015; and "Chinese Plan to Develop Economic Zone Faces Problem in Mauritius, Algeria," *Africa-Asia*, June 5, 2012.

14. Interview, US Embassy in Oman, August 2016.

15. Wade Shepard, "Why Is China Building a New City Out in the Desert of Oman?" Forbes, September 8, 2017; and Duqm government website ""Invest in Duqm" Moves to Second Phase in China and Meets with Investors," October 9, 2017, Duqm.gov.om/sezad/media/news/invest-in-duqm-moves-to-its-second-phase-in-china-and-meets-with-investors

Sources

China Aid Data. http://china.aiddata.org/projects/30052; Lu Jiang, Angela Harding, Ward Anseeuw, and Chris Alden, "China Agricultural Technology Demonstration Centres in Southern Africa: The New Business of Development," in *Public Sphere* (2016); "China-Africa Trade and Economic Relationship Annual Report 2010"; Brautigam, *Dragon's Gift*, 249; and Deborah A. Brautigam and Xiaoyang Tang. "China's Engagement in African Agriculture: 'Down to the Countryside,'" *China Quarterly*, no. 199 (2009), 702.; Xu et al., "Science, Technology"; and various news reports.

support for these zones is based on its interest in ensuring its economic growth through the development of export markets in these regions and its support to developing countries by exporting successful aspects of its economic development model. The Chinese government provides limited financial support for these zones and relies on Chinese companies to establish and operate these zones. Overall, this behavior appears to rely on the initiative of individual manufacturing companies. That said, SEZs fall into the category of China's broader support for its companies to go out and go global to seek opportunities around the world and to become competitive globally. Also, several of these SEZs (e.g., Egypt, Oman, and Djibouti) are in critical strategic locations due to proximity to the Suez Canal and the Straits of Hormuz.

These zones also support China's interests in fostering support in the international system and advocating for developing country causes. They serve as important symbols of South-South cooperation and help China to demonstrate it is acting as a responsible great power in these regions.

This behavior is competitive because it works toward building China's influence in these regions and is an important example of how China uses South-South cooperation to differentiate itself from other great powers. It is very much in alignment with the behavior of more developed states to share their development experiences with developing countries. Also, although the state does provide some funding for these SEZs, their establishment overall is reliant on Chinese companies interested in these markets taking the initiative to request funding. All that said, since there is not an applicable liberal economic norm with which to compare China's behavior for the foreign policy tool, it is considered norm neutral.

Agricultural Cooperation

China's contemporary agricultural cooperation with the Middle East and sub-Saharan Africa, like the SEZs, is also competitive and norm neutral. China is using agricultural technology demonstration centers as another way to build a sphere of influence and compete with other great powers in Africa. This behavior has aligned with international expectations of promoting economic development for less developed economies and sharing development lessons with countries in need. That said, since there is not an applicable liberal international norm with which to compare China's behavior, it is labeled norm neutral.

China's long history of agricultural cooperation with sub-Saharan Africa started in the 1960s. Most of China's agricultural cooperation activities with Africa and the Middle East in the post–Cold War era have been with sub-Saharan African countries. Since 1991, China's agricultural cooperation has included sending agricultural experts to African countries, establishing agricultural technology demonstration centers, encouraging and supporting Chinese enterprises in expanding their investment in African agriculture, increasing agricultural human resource training for Africans, and strengthening cooperation with African countries in the UN Food and Agricultural Organization's (UNFAO) Special Program for Food Security.

Much of China's agricultural cooperation is publicized through FOCAC. For example, by the end of 2009, China had helped build 142 agricultural projects in Africa, including plans mainly for "pilot agro-technical stations, stations for popularizing agricultural techniques, farms, and agricultural technology demonstration centers."[129] Chinese government documents also emphasize that the two sides have conducted cooperation in "agricultural infrastructure construction, food production and breeding industry, exchange and transfer of agricultural practical techniques, and processing, storage and transport of agricultural products" and that the Chinese government encourages its businesses to invest in product processing and agricultural development projects in Africa.[130] Between 2006 and 2009, China sent 104 senior agricultural experts to work in thirty-three African countries.[131] At the 2009 FOCAC meeting, China committed to expanding agricultural cooperation further. In the 2010–2012 action plan, it specifically vowed to send 50 additional agricultural technology teams to Africa, train 2,000 agricultural technicians from African countries, increase the total number of African agricultural technology demonstration centers from fifteen to twenty, contribute US$30 million to UNFAO to set up a trust fund, and use the trust fund to support South-South cooperation between China and African countries under the framework of UNFAO's Special Program for Food Security.[132] The 2016–2018 FOCAC action plan committed to send 20 Chinese teams of agricultural experts and increase the number of Africans trained on agriculture in China.[133] The 2019–2021 FOCAC plan committed to send 500 agricultural experts to Africa and a wide range of other agricultural cooperation activities.[134] The CASCF action plans for 2016–2018 and 2018–2020 also emphasized agricultural cooperation between Arab states and China.[135]

Agricultural Technology Demonstration Centers, 2006–2018

One of the essential contemporary components of China-Africa agricultural cooperation is agricultural technology demonstration centers. These centers are a highly visible aspect of China's agricultural cooperation, and data are available for an in-depth comparison.[136] The purpose of the centers is to transfer agricultural technology and expertise to developing countries and create market opportunities for China's agriculture companies. China first announced its plans to promote agricultural technology demonstration centers at the 2006 FOCAC meeting. Between 2006 and 2018, it launched centers in nineteen countries, all in sub-Saharan Africa: Angola, Benin, Cameroon, Democratic Republic of Congo, Ethiopia, Gabon, Liberia, Mauritania, Mozambique, the Republic of Congo, Senegal, South Africa, Sudan, Tanzania, Togo, Uganda, Zambia, and Zimbabwe.[137] (See table 6.2.) Fourteen of the demonstration centers have been established in LDCs. Most of them focus on a diverse set of agricultural needs, including rice, corn, soy, livestock, and fisheries. None are in the Middle East. Chinese agricultural companies (e.g., the China National Agricultural Corporation) or province-level agriculture institutes run the centers. The Chinese Ministry of Commerce allocates three years of grant support to the enterprises and institutes to provide them with an opportunity to adjust to operating in a commercially viable way. The enterprises and institutes are then expected to run the centers for an additional five to eight years (dependent on the consent of the host country).[138] After nine years, the Chinese companies are supposed to transfer the centers to the host governments.

China's agricultural technology demonstration centers are competitive but norm neutral. China is building a sphere of influence through these state-supported centers. Developing that influence is competitive with the United States and the rest of the West. From 1991 to 2018, its interests in African agriculture were growing. China's interests in securing long-term food security and fueling its economic growth by facilitating market opportunities for its agricultural enterprises drive its agricultural cooperation. It is also motivated by its ideological interests as a developing country in fostering South-South cooperation, gaining the support of developing countries, and advocating for developing countries' causes.

During the 2000s, China's food security concerns were increasing. The "red line" for China's own food security is 120 million hectares, to ensure 95 percent self-sufficiency in grain. As of 2006, China only had 122 million hectares of arable land remaining[139] and was increasing its focus on agricultural cooperation

Table 6.2. China's Agricultural Technology Demonstration Centers, 2006–2018

Country	*Details*
Angola	Established in 2012. Focus on developing new plants essential to cereal production. Xinjiang Production and Construction Corps.
Benin	Established in 2009. Focus on crop cultivation demonstration, and farming technology training. Grains (e.g., maize), vegetables, livestock (e.g., chicken). Run by China National Agricultural Development Corporation.[1]
Cameroon	Established in 2009. Focus on research, technology demonstration, and training on technology. Rice cultivation. Run by Shaanxi's Nongken Agricultural Company.[2]
Congo, Republic of	Established before 2009. Focus on crop cultivation demonstration and training. Run by Hainan-based Chinese Academy of Tropical Agricultural Sciences. Grains (e.g., maize, cassava), vegetables, livestock (e.g., chicken), fodder production and processing, agricultural mechanization.
Congo, Democratic Republic of	Established in 2012 ZTE energy.
Ethiopia	Established in 2009. Focus on horticultural plants cultivation, livestock and farming technology demonstration and training. Grains, vegetables, and livestock (e.g., pigs, cows, and chicken). Run by Guangxi province's Bagui Agricultural Technology Company.[3]
Gabon	Announced in 2016.[4]
Liberia	Established in 2009. Focus on rice and corn cultivation technology training and development of plant varieties. Research and training will initially focus on rice, corn, and vegetable growing at the initial stage and may be extended to animal husbandry at a later period. Run by Hunan's Yuan Longping High Tech Company.[5]
Mauritania	Established in 2015. Run by Yanlinzhuanyuan Technology.
Mozambique	Established in 2009. Focus on soybean and corn cultivation, processing, demonstration, and training. The scope of the center also includes vegetable and fruit tree growing, animal and poultry raising, farm produce processing., rice, and cotton. Run by Hubei's Lianfeng Overseas Agricultural Development Company.[6]
Senegal	Established in 2011. Started with vegetable training classes. Now emphasis on subsistence farming and increasing yields of small farms.

Table 6.2. China's Agricultural Technology Demonstration Centers, 2006–2018 (*continued*)

Country	*Details*
Rwanda	Established before 2009. Focus on rice, grains, jun-cao, mulberry cultivation, silkworms, soil, and water conservation technology demonstration and training. Run by Fujian's Agricultural and Forestry University.
South Africa	Established before 2009. Focus on research, technology demonstration, and training on freshwater aquaculture. Run by China National Agricultural Development Corporation.
Sudan	Established in 2009. Focus on crop cultivation and irrigation technology demonstration and training. Improved strains of rice, production demonstration, and personnel training. Grains (e.g., wheat, maize), vegetables, cotton, peanuts, water conservancy. Run by Shandong's Academy of Agricultural Science.
Tanzania	Established in 2009. Focus on crop cultivation demonstration, development of improved plant varieties, and training. Grains (e.g., rice, maize, soybeans), vegetables, flowers, livestock (e.g., chicken). Run by Chongqing's Agricultural Technology Company
Togo	Established before 2009. Focus on research and training on agricultural technology. Rice and maize. Run by Jiangxi's Huachang Infrastructure Construction Company
Uganda	Established in 2009. Focus on aquaculture technology demonstration, technology transfer, and training. Run by Sichuan's Huaqiao Fenghua Group, which specializes in fisheries.[7]
Zambia	Established before 2009. Focus on agricultural technology demonstration and training, especially on crop improvement for corn, soya beans, wheat, maize, and vegetables. Run by Jilin's Agricultural University.
Zimbabwe	Established in 2009. Focus on corn cultivation technology transfer and training as well as soya beans and cotton. Agricultural mechanization and irrigation. Run by Research Institute of China Agricultural Mechanization. Partner province is Anhui.[8]

Notes

1. http://www.fmprc.gov.cn/eng/wjb/zzjg/fzs/gjlb/2919/,

2. http://www.fmprc.gov.cn/eng/wjb/zzjg/fzs/gjlb/2949/.

3. See "China Attaches Great Importance to Ties With Ethiopia: Top Legislator," Xinhua, November 10, 2008.

4. "China to Help Gabon Build Agricultural Demonstration Center," CGTN, April 15, 2016.

5. "A Brief Introduction to the China-aided Agricultural Technology Demonstration Center," Embassy of the People's Republic of China in the Republic of Liberia, http://

to meet its food security needs. The agricultural technology demonstration centers provide a concrete example of China's expanding involvement in this realm. As a contribution to China's food security, these agricultural technology centers focus on essential agricultural products for China, including rice, corn, soybeans, cotton, livestock, and fish. Building up local capability in African countries to produce these agricultural commodities contributes to local food security as well as China's longer-term need for reliable food suppliers.

Notes

1. http://www.fmprc.gov.cn/eng/wjb/zzjg/fzs/gjlb/2919/,

2. http://www.fmprc.gov.cn/eng/wjb/zzjg/fzs/gjlb/2949/.

3. See "China Attaches Great Importance to Ties With Ethiopia: Top Legislator," Xinhua, November 10, 2008.

4. "China to Help Gabon Build Agricultural Demonstration Center," CGTN, April 15, 2016.

5. "A Brief Introduction to the China-aided Agricultural Technology Demonstration Center," Embassy of the People's Republic of China in the Republic of Liberia, http://lr.china-embassy.org/eng/sghdhzxxx/t720776.htm, accessed February 28, 2012; "Bilateral Relations with Liberia," *Chinese Ministry of Foreign Affairs,* August 22, 2011; "China to Construct 100-Bed, 10M-Dollar Modern Hospital in Liberia—Envoy," *Star Radio,* March 28, 2008.

6. "Chen Shun, "New Impetus to China-Africa Agricultural Cooperation," Xinhua, December 22, 2007; "China Economic News in Brief: Sino-African Agro-Tech Center; Beijing House Price; Hainan Duty-Free Imports; Jiangxi Gold Output," Xinhua, July 20, 2011.

7. http://www.fmprc.gov.cn/eng/wjb/zzjg/fzs/gjlb/3109/.

8. Gretinah Machingura, "Chinese-Built Demonstration Center to Revolutionize Zimbabwe's Agriculture," Xinhua English News, September 16, 2011; Tichaona Chifamba, "Zimbabweans Place High Hope on Chinese-Funded Agricultural Center," Xinhua, July 19, 2010; and "Bilateral Relations with Zimbabwe," *Chinese Ministry of Foreign Affairs,* August 22, 2011.

Sources

China Africa Economic and Trade Cooperation, white paper (Beijing: Information Office of the State Council of the People's Republic of China, December 23, 2010); Deborah Brautigam and Xiaoyang Tang, "African Shenzhen: China's Special Economic Zones in Africa," *Journal of Modern African Studies* 49, no. 1 (2011): 32; Deborah Brautigam and Tang Xiaoyang, "Going Global in Groups: Structural Transformation and China Special Economic Zones Overseas," *World Development* 63 (2014); and various news reports noted in end notes.

These demonstration centers serve China's interests in promoting opportunities for its agricultural enterprises abroad. Since the mid-1990s, the Chinese government has officially encouraged its agricultural enterprises to pursue opportunities as part of its broader go out/go global initiatives.[140] Chinese enterprises are encouraged to invest in specific agricultural industries. Those prominently featured in Chinese government policy guidance are agro-industrial crops like rubber, fuel oils (oil palm) and cotton, vegetable cultivation, animal husbandry and aquaculture, and agricultural machinery assembly.[141]

Finally, these agricultural technology demonstration centers (and China's agricultural cooperation with Africa more broadly) are part of China's emphasis on South-South cooperation, which is greatly influenced by its interests as a developing country. The tools and magnitude of cooperation have been changing over the past twenty years. Still, China's commitment to assisting African countries in establishing their food security and raising their living standards appears to have been constant since the 1950s. China is sharing its development experiences with less developed countries and promoting economic development. This agricultural cooperation is yet another way it demonstrates it is a responsible great power in this region. It is also another facet of the economic order China is building in these regions.

Conclusion

China pursues its interests of promoting its domestic economic growth and fostering support for China in the international arena by using all of the economic foreign policy tools discussed in this chapter: state support for Chinese companies, foreign aid, free trade agreements, special economic zones, and agricultural technology demonstration centers. It also advocates for developing country causes with its foreign aid, special economic zones, and agricultural technology demonstration centers.

China's need for resources and markets in the Middle East and sub-Saharan Africa to fuel its economic growth has expanded significantly since the end of the Cold War. Although its investment in these regions is still limited, China's trade in goods and services has dramatically increased.

China competes with the United States and other great powers with all of the tools discussed in this chapter. This competition with the United States, as well as tensions with the Western liberal order in China's state support of companies and foreign aid provision, are important aspects of China's behavior in the regions as well as globally. Increasingly, the United States is concerned about the relationship between the Chinese state and economic actors, as well as divergence from the liberal order. Those worries are particularly acute about Chinese economic activity abroad.

China's economic approach to these regions is neomercantilist and norm divergent from the liberal order. It is using state power through a variety of foreign policy tools to promote the export of manufactured goods to these regions, facilitate resource imports on advantageous terms, and secure market access for its own firms—behavior that is competitive with the United States and the rest of the West. All the tools discussed in this chapter not only increase China's economic power in these regions but also contribute to developing China's goodwill and political power. China uses its bilateral economic relations to build spheres of influence in the Middle East and sub-Saharan Africa.

China differentiates itself as a great power in these regions through its use of South-South cooperation, respect for the sovereignty of states in these regions and advocacy of noninterference, and its substantial commitment to aid in the development of countries through direct assistance and to share its experience as a developing country.

Although all of China's behavior in this chapter is competitive, some foreign policy tools are norm divergent from the liberal order, some convergent, and some norm neutral. China's state support for companies is divergent from the liberal economic order that emphasizes the importance of free markets and limited state involvement in the economy. Foreign aid is also divergent because it directly confronts the political and good government conditionality of Western assistance.

In contrast, China's FTAs are norm convergent. Regional FTAs are allowed under the WTO and promote the liberal norms of free trade. Great powers frequently pursue them to complement WTO commitments. SEZs and agricultural technology demonstration centers are very much in alignment with encouraging sharing development experience with less developed countries, but they are norm neutral because there are no relevant norms of the liberal order in relation to them.

All of the foreign policy tools discussed in this chapter should be considered elements of the economic order China is building in these regions. They must also be considered together with China's cooperation forums, special envoys, and Belt and Road to fully understand how China is managing its economic relations with these regions and the order China is constructing.

CHAPTER 7

MAKING FRIENDS AND BUILDING INFLUENCE?

Political Relations

China has a long history of political relations with many countries in the Middle East and sub-Saharan Africa. Although its interests in these regions have changed over time, the Five Principles of Peaceful Coexistence introduced at Bandung in 1955 and South-South cooperation continue to be the bedrock of political interactions between China and these regions.[1] Building on China's political relations through its cooperation forums and special envoys discussed in chapters 4 and 5, this chapter explores some other aspects of China's post–Cold War political relations with the Middle East and sub-Saharan Africa. It examines China's voting behavior in the United Nations Security Council (UNSC) and strategic partnerships with countries throughout these regions.[2]

The primary questions driving this chapter and the rest of the book are: Is China cooperating or competing with the United States in the Middle East and sub-Saharan Africa? Is its behavior converging with or diverging from liberal international norms? Is it building an alternative international order in these regions? If so, what are the characteristics of that order? Ultimately, what does China's behavior in the Middle East and sub-Saharan Africa indicate about its rise globally?

Analyzing China's political relations with these regions through UNSC voting and strategic partnerships in comparative perspective over time generates essential insights about how it is competing in these regions and diverging from or converging with international norms. It shows how China is developing spheres of influence, changing the rules of the system, and building an alternative political order in these regions. It also provides insight into how China is portraying itself as a great power.

Of the interests described in chapter 3, China's most important political interests in the Middle East and sub-Saharan Africa are fostering support for China in the international arena, advocating for developing country causes, and protecting China's territorial integrity and sovereignty from the United States.[3] China works to promote its domestic economic growth by building strong relationships with countries in these regions and linking political, economic, and security relations. It also tries to ensure stability in these regions by protecting state sovereignty and working toward solving enduring challenges to peace and security such as the Palestinian-Israeli conflict. This chapter analyzes specific political foreign policy tools China uses to pursue all those interests.

The primary sources used in examining China's UNSC voting behavior and strategic partnerships in the Middle East and sub-Saharan Africa are documents associated with Security Council votes; media reports and government statements about strategic partnerships; and interviews with Chinese and regional government officials and scholars. All of these activities are high profile and require the dedication of important resources. As a result, they provide essential signals regarding China's foreign policy priorities. These tools also provide data to analyze within and between regions as well as over time.

As with all other chapters in this book, this one examines whether China's political behavior through UNSC voting and strategic partnerships diverges from or converges with norms governing these interactions and whether China competes or cooperates with the United States in its relations with these regions. This chapter in particular focuses on norms associated with the liberal political order. Together with chapters on China's cooperation forums and special envoys, it examines political foreign policy tools over time and across regions to draw broad conclusions about China as a rising power in these regions.

In alignment with the findings in other chapters about China's political behavior in the Middle East and sub-Saharan Africa, this chapter asserts that overall, China's behavior is competitive in all of the foreign policy tools examined. Some behavior is norm divergent from the liberal order, some is norm convergent, and some norm neutral. Similar to China's cooperation forums and special envoys, the main points of difference between China and the United States in political relations discussed in this chapter are stances on foreign intervention and support for the Palestinians. China's behavior is norm divergent in UNSC voting on sovereignty issues, norm convergent in UNSC voting on Palestinian-Israeli issues, and norm neutral in strategic partnerships.

Although the vast majority of the time there is alignment between China's voting and the rest of the permanent members on the Security Council, China's voting does differ from that of the United States on issues of territorial integrity and sovereignty, as well as the Palestinian-Israeli conflict. China's UNSC voting is categorized as competitive because it is standing up to the United States on issues related to sovereignty as well as the Palestinians. Normatively, China differs from the United States and other Western permanent five members on the Security Council with its strict interpretation of sovereignty, negative views of sanctions, and opposition to other intrusions into the internal affairs of states in support of the liberal order promoting responsibility to protect or regime change.

Strategic partnerships are also competitive behavior with the United States. They contribute to China's building spheres of influence in sub-Saharan Africa and the Middle East. They are also norm neutral.

United Nations Security Council Voting Behavior

The majority of China's voting in the UNSC is in alignment with the other permanent members: Russia, France, the United Kingdom, and the United States.[4] Nevertheless there are some significant differences between China and the United States explored here because it provides an opportunity to consider China's behavior on core issues of international peace and security in comparison to the United States and international norms. Table 7.1 provides a lists all UNSC votes from 1990 to 2020 in which the votes of China and the United States differed.

In the 1990s, China's vote differed from the United States in fifty cases. Twenty-two percent of those votes involved Middle East issues and 10 percent sub-Saharan Africa. In the 2000s, there was a dramatic increase in the percentage of differing votes involving these regions. Out of thirty-two cases where votes differed between China and the United States, Middle East and sub-Saharan Africa issues accounted for 84 percent of differing votes, 53 percent involved the Middle East, and 31 percent involved sub-Saharan Africa, including a veto regarding applying sanctions to Zimbabwe.

Before 2011, China rarely used its veto power in the Security Council, but instead often employed abstention to voice disapproval without directly confronting the United States and other permanent members.[5] That pattern changed with the beginning of the Arab awakening and the NATO invasion of Libya in 2011. Between 2010 and 2020, China vetoed ten resolutions about Syria and one on Venezuela.[6] Overall, in those ten years, 79 percent of votes that differed between the United States and China involved the Middle East and sub-Saharan Africa (53 percent Middle East, 26 percent sub-Saharan Africa).

As evidenced by China's abstention and veto behavior from 1991 to 2020, disagreement between China and the United States was primarily over Middle East and sub-Saharan Africa issues. The level of differences increased over time.

Further examination of China's voting behavior from 1990 to 2020 provides clarity about which specific rules and norms China is advocating or protesting. Table 7.1 provides a detailed description of differing votes about the Middle East and sub-Saharan Africa. During the entire time under consideration, the vast majority of China's abstentions and all of its vetoes were over issues of territorial integrity, particularly sanctions and jurisdiction of international criminal courts. These votes directly correspond to China's promotion of the Five Principles, especially the principles of mutual respect for territory and sovereignty and mutual noninterference in the internal affairs of other states. From 1990 to 2020, China's support for these norms was relatively constant, although there are a few inconsistencies in China's behavior. In the 1990s, China abstained from several cases in votes concerning actions against Iraq. In the 2000s, none of China's Security Council votes on Iraq differed. Also, in direct conflict with its general opposition to sanctions, it voted for sanctions targeting Iran's developing nuclear program on numerous occasions. For example, China voted yes on seven resolutions implementing sanctions on Iran.[7] One possible explanation for these discrepancies is that China did not want to oppose the United States on issues that involved vital national interests for the United States.[8] China perceives the Middle East to be in the US sphere of influence and does not want conflict with the United States in the region. As a result, it may be

Table 7.1. Disagreement between China and the United States on UN Security Council, Votes Concerning the Middle East and Sub-Saharan Africa, 1991–2020

Year	*Region*	*Country*	*Resolution Number*	*Brief Summary of Content*	*China*	*United States*	*United Kingdom*	*France*	*Russia*
1991	Middle East	Iraq	686	Demands Iraq withdraw from Kuwait	A	Y	Y	Y	Y
1991	Middle East	Iraq	688	Demands halt of repression of the Iraqi civilian population, including Kurds	A	Y	Y	Y	Y
1992	Middle East	Iraq	778	Distribution of proceeds of sales of Iraqi petroleum and petroleum products	A	Y	Y	Y	Y
1993	Middle East	Libya	883	Sanctions in response to Libya's bombing of Pan Am Flight 103	A	Y	Y	Y	Y
1994	Sub-Saharan Africa	Rwanda	955	Structure of International Criminal Tribunal for Rwanda	A	Y	Y	Y	Y
1994	Sub-Saharan Africa	Somalia	946	Extending mandate of UNOSOM	Y	A	Y	Y	Y
1994	Sub-Saharan Africa	Rwanda	929	Mandate of UNAMIR	A	Y	Y	Y	Y
1995	Middle East	Palestinian-Israeli Conflict	Draft 394	Confirms that the expropriation of land by Israel in East Jerusalem is invalid	Y	N	Y	Y	Y
1996	Sub-Saharan Africa	Sudan	1070	Imposing air sanctions against Sudan	A	Y	Y	Y	Y

Table 7.1. Disagreement between China and the United States on UN Security Council, Votes Concerning the Middle East and Sub-Saharan Africa, 1991–2020 (*continued*)

Year	*Region*	*Country*	*Resolution Number*	*Brief Summary of Content*	*China*	*United States*	*United Kingdom*	*France*	*Russia*
1996	Sub-Saharan Africa	Sudan	1054	Sanctions. Demanded Sudan extradite to Ethiopia three suspects wanted in connection with the June 1995 assassination attempt on Egyptian President Mubarak. Diplomatic sanctions imposed.	A	Y	Y	Y	A
1996	Middle East	Palestinian-Israeli Conflict	1073	On the situation in Jerusalem and the areas of Nablus, Ramallah, Bethlehem, and the Gaza Strip	Y	A	Y	Y	Y
1997	Middle East	Palestinian-Israeli Conflict	Draft 241	Calling on Israel to refrain from construction of a new housing settlement in the Jabal Abu Ghneim area of East Jerusalem	Y	N	Y	Y	Y
1997	Middle East	Palestinian-Israeli Conflict	Draft 199	Israel called on to refrain from building a new settlement in the Jabal Abu Ghneim area of East Jerusalem.	Y	N	Y	Y	Y
1997	Middle East	Iraq	1134	Sanctions. Restrict the travel of Iraqi officials	A	Y	Y	A	A
1999	Middle East	Iraq	1284	Established (UNMOVIC) to undertake the responsibilities of the former (UNSCOM), which was charged with monitoring the elimination of weapons of mass destruction in Iraq.	A	Y	Y	A	A
1999	Middle East	Iraq	1280	Sanctions. Extension of oil-for-food program sanctions	A	Y	Y	Did not vote	A

Table 7.1. Disagreement between China and the United States on UN Security Council, Votes Concerning the Middle East and Sub-Saharan Africa, 1991–2020 (*continued*)

Year	*Region*	*Country*	*Resolution Number*	*Brief Summary of Content*	*China*	*United States*	*United Kingdom*	*France*	*Russia*
2000	Middle East	Palestinian-Israeli Conflict	Draft 1171	Establish a United Nations force of military and police observers in the occupied Palestinian territories.	Y	A	A	A	A
2000	Middle East	Palestinian-Israeli Conflict	1322	Deplored the provocation carried out at Al-Haram Al-Sharif in Jerusalem on September 28	Y	A	Y	Y	Y
2001	Middle East	Palestinian-Israeli Conflict	Draft 270	Establish a United Nations observer force to protect Palestinian civilians	Y	N	A	A	Y
2001	Middle East	Palestinian-Israeli Conflict	Draft 1199	Condemned all acts of extrajudiciary executions, excessive use of force, and wide destruction of property, and looked to the establishment of a monitoring mechanism to help the parties.	Y	N	A	Y	Y
2001	Sub-Saharan Africa	Sudan	1372	Diplomatic sanction in resolution 1054 lifted.	Y	A	Y	Y	Y
2002	Middle East	Palestinian-Israeli Conflict	Draft 1385	Condemned the killing by Israeli forces of several United Nations employees, as well as the "deliberate destruction" by those forces of a United Nations World Food Programme warehouse in the occupied Palestinian territory	Y	N	Y	Y	Y

Table 7.1. Disagreement between China and the United States on UN Security Council, Votes Concerning the Middle East and Sub-Saharan Africa, 1991–2020 (*continued*)

Year	*Region*	*Country*	*Resolution Number*	*Brief Summary of Content*	*China*	*United States*	*United Kingdom*	*France*	*Russia*
2002	Middle East	Palestinian-Israeli Conflict	1435	Demanded that Israel immediately cease measures in and around Ramallah, "including the destruction of Palestinian civilian and security infrastructure"	Y	A	Y	Y	Y
2003	Middle East	Palestinian-Israeli Conflict	Draft 980	Declared illegal Israel's construction of a wall in the occupied territories departing from the armistice line of 1949	Y	N	A	Y	Y
2003	Middle East	Palestinian-Israeli Conflict	Draft 891	Demanded that Israel desist from any act of deportation and cease any threat to the safety of the elected president of the Palestinian Authority	Y	N	A	Y	Y
2003	Middle East	Libya	1506	Lifts sanctions against Libya, imposed after terrorist acts against Pan Am flight 103 1988, and France's Union de transports aeriens flight 772 1989	Y	A	Y	A	Y
2004	Middle East	Palestinian-Israeli Conflict	Draft 783	Demanding end to Israeli military offensive in Gaza	Y	N	A	Y	Y
2004	Middle East	Palestinian-Israeli Conflict	Draft 240	Condemned the most recent extrajudicial execution of Sheikh Ahmed Yassin along with six other Palestinians would have called for a complete cessation of extrajudicial killings	Y	N	A	Y	Y

Table 7.1. Disagreement between China and the United States on UN Security Council, Votes Concerning the Middle East and Sub-Saharan Africa, 1991–2020 (*continued*)

Year	*Region*	*Country*	*Resolution Number*	*Brief Summary of Content*	*China*	*United States*	*United Kingdom*	*France*	*Russia*
2004	Sub-Saharan Africa	Sudan	1564	Declares intention to consider sanctions to obtain Sudan's compliance in Darfur	A	Y	Y	Y	A
2004	Middle East	Lebanon	1559	Declares support for free, fair presidential election; calls for withdrawal of foreign troops.	A	Y	Y	Y	A
2004	Sub-Saharan Africa	Sudan	1556	Demanded that the government of the Sudan disarm the Janjaweed militias	A	Y	Y	Y	Y
2004	Middle East	Palestinian-Israeli Conflict	1544	Calls on Israel to stop the demolition of Palestinian homes	Y	A	Y	Y	Y
2005	Sub-Saharan Africa	Sudan	1593	Refers situation in Darfur to the prosecutor of International Criminal Court	A	A	Y	Y	Y
2005	Sub-Saharan Africa	Sudan	1591	Sanctions. Imposes travel ban and an assets freeze on those impeding peace process in Darfur	A	Y	Y	Y	A
2006	Middle East	Palestinian-Israeli	Draft 878	Condemning Israeli military operations in Gaza "which have caused loss of civilian life," as well as Palestinian rocket fire into Israel, while calling for an immediate withdrawal of Israeli forces from the Gaza Strip and a cessation of violence from both parties in the conflict	Y	N	A	Y	Y

Table 7.1. Disagreement between China and the United States on UN Security Council, Votes Concerning the Middle East and Sub-Saharan Africa, 1991–2020 (*continued*)

Year	*Region*	*Country*	*Resolution Number*	*Brief Summary of Content*	*China*	*United States*	*United Kingdom*	*France*	*Russia*
2006	Middle East	Pales-tinian-Israeli Conflict	Draft 508	Demands Israel halt its two-week military offensive in Gaza Strip.	Y	N	A	Y	Y
2006	Sub-Sa-haran Africa	Sudan	1706	Expand UN Mission to include Darfur	A	Y	Y	Y	A
2006	Middle East	Syria	1680	Encourages Syria to respond positively to Lebanon's request to delineate common border and est. full diplomatic relations	A	Y	Y	Y	A
2006	Sub-Sa-haran Africa	Sudan	1672	Sanctions. Imposed travel restrictions and financial sanctions on four Sudanese individuals	A	Y	Y	Y	A
2007	Middle East	Lebanon	1757	Establishment of a Special Tribunal for Lebanon	A	Y	Y	Y	A
2008	**Sub-Sa-haran Africa**	**Zimba-bwe**	**Draft 447**	**Intended to impose sanctions against Zimbabwe's President Robert Mugabe**	**N**	**Y**	**Y**	**Y**	**N**
2008	Sub-Sa-haran Africa	Sudan	1828	Extension of the mandate of the African Union-United Nations Hybrid Operation in Darfur (UNAMID)	Y	A	Y	Y	Y
2009	Sub-Sa-haran Africa	Eritrea and Somalia	1907	Arms embargo against Eritrea because it provided support to armed groups undermining peace and reconciliation in Somalia and that it had not with-drawn its forces following clashes with Djibouti in June 2008	A	Y	Y	Y	Y

Table 7.1. Disagreement between China and the United States on UN Security Council, Votes Concerning the Middle East and Sub-Saharan Africa, 1991–2020 (*continued*)

Year	*Region*	*Country*	*Resolution Number*	*Brief Summary of Content*	*China*	*United States*	*United Kingdom*	*France*	*Russia*
2010	Sub-Saharan Africa	Sudan	1945	Sanctions. Extended the mandate of the panel of experts that monitors the arms embargo and sanctions on those who impede peace in Sudan	A	Y	Y	Y	Y
2011	Middle East	Palestinian-Israeli Conflict	Draft s/2011/24	Settlements. On the cessation of all settlement activities by Israel in occupied Palestinian territory, including East Jerusalem.	Y	N	Y	Y	Y
2011	Middle East	Libya	1973	Demanded an immediate cease-fire, including an end to the current attacks against civilians, which it said might constitute "crimes against humanity." Imposed a no-fly zone and tightened sanctions on the Gaddhafi regime and its supporters.	A	Y	Y	Y	A
2011	Sub-Saharan Africa	Eritrea	2023	Sanctions. Targeting the mining sector.	A	Y	Y	Y	A
2011	**Middle East**	**Syria**	**Draft s/2011/612**	**Threatened sanctions and condemned "grave and systematic human rights violations."**	**N**	**Y**	**Y**	**Y**	**N**
2012	**Middle East**	**Syria**	**Draft s/2012/538**	**Extended the mandate of the United Nations Supervision Mission in Syria (UNSMIS) and threatened sanctions.**	**N**	**Y**	**Y**	**Y**	**N**
2012	**Middle East**	**Syria**	**Draft s/2012/77**	**Demanded that all parties in Syria—both government forces and armed opposition groups—stop all violence and reprisals.**	**N**	**Y**	**Y**	**Y**	**N**

Table 7.1. Disagreement between China and the United States on UN Security Council, Votes Concerning the Middle East and Sub-Saharan Africa, 1991–2020 (*continued*)

Year	*Region*	*Country*	*Resolution Number*	*Brief Summary of Content*	*China*	*United States*	*United Kingdom*	*France*	*Russia*
2013	Sub-Saharan Africa	Kenya	Draft S/2013/660	Requested the International Criminal Court, under Chapter VII of the United Nations Charter, to defer the investigation and prosecution of Kenyan leaders.	Y	A	A	A	Y
2014	**Middle East**	**Syria**	**Draft S/2014/348**	**Referral of Syria to the International Criminal Court.**	**N**	**Y**	**Y**	**Y**	**N**
2014	Middle East	Palestinian-Israeli Conflict	Draft S/2014/916	Impose twelve-month deadline on negotiated solution to Israeli-Palestinian conflict.	Y	N	A	Y	Y
2016	Sub-Saharan Africa	Burundi	S/RES/2303	Establish police component in Burundi to monitor security situation	A	Y	Y	Y	Y
2016	Sub-Saharan Africa	South Sudan	S/RES/2304	Authorizes expanded peacekeeping force to bolster civilian protection efforts.	A	Y	Y	Y	Y
2016	Middle East	Syria	S/2016/846	Council demanded an immediate halt to all aerial bombardments and military flights over the city of Aleppo. Urged the immediate implementation of a cessation of hostilities as well as immediate, safe, and unhindered humanitarian access throughout the country, and demanded that parties to the conflict—in particular, the Syrian authorities—fully implement all previous council resolutions. (Draft proposed by France and Spain)	A	Y	Y	Y	N

Table 7.1. Disagreement between China and the United States on UN Security Council, Votes Concerning the Middle East and Sub-Saharan Africa, 1991–2020 (*continued*)

Year	*Region*	*Country*	*Resolution Number*	*Brief Summary of Content*	*China*	*United States*	*United Kingdom*	*France*	*Russia*
2016	Middle East	Syria	S/2016/847	Urged an immediate cessation of hostilities, particularly in Aleppo, demanded that all parties prevent materiel and financial support from reaching groups associated with al-Qaeda, Islamic State in Iraq and the Levant (ISIL/Da'esh) or Jabhat al-Nusrah. (Draft proposed by Russia on the same date as 846 above)	Y	N	N	N	Y
2016	Sub-Saharan Africa	Somalia and Eritrea	S/RES/2317	Extend arms embargoes on Somalia, Eritrea.	A	Y	Y	Y	A
2016	**Middle East**	**Syria**	**S/2016/1026**	**Resolution to end attacks on Aleppo**	**N**	**Y**	**Y**	**Y**	**N**
2016	Sub-Saharan Africa	Sudan and South Sudan	S/2016/1085	Imposing arms embargo on South Sudan, designating key figures for targeted sanctions.	A	Y	Y	Y	A
2016	Middle East	Palestinian-Israeli Conflict	S/RES/2334	Declared Israel's establishment of settlements in Palestinian territory occupied since 1967, including East Jerusalem, had no legal validity, constituting a flagrant violation under international law and a major obstacle to the vision of two states living side-by-side in peace and security, within internationally recognized borders.	Y	A	Y	Y	Y
2017	**Middle East**	**Syria**	**S/2017/172**	**Impose sanctions for the use of chemical weapons in Syria**	**N**	**Y**	**Y**	**Y**	**N**

Table 7.1. Disagreement between China and the United States on UN Security Council, Votes Concerning the Middle East and Sub-Saharan Africa, 1991–2020 (*continued*)

Year	*Region*	*Country*	*Resolution Number*	*Brief Summary of Content*	*China*	*United States*	*United Kingdom*	*France*	*Russia*
2017	Middle East	Syria	S/2017/315	Condemning chemical weapons use in Syria	A	Y	Y	Y	N
2017	Middle East	Syria	S/2017/884	Renew the Mandate of Joint Investigative Mechanism on Chemical Weapons Use in Syria	A	Y	Y	Y	N
2017	Sub-Saharan Africa	Somalia and Eritrea	S/2017/2385	Extending arms embargoes on Somalia, Eritrea	A	Y	Y	Y	A
2017	Middle East	Syria	S/2017/962	Security Council Fails to adopt 2 draft resolutions on extending mandate of joint mechanism investigating chemical weapons attacks in Syria	A	Y	Y	Y	N
2017	Middle East	Syria	S/2017/970	Renew the Mandate of Joint Mechanism Investigating chemical weapons attacks in Syria	A	Y	Y	Y	N
2017	Middle East	Palestinian-Israeli Conflict	S/2017/1060	Calling on states not to establish diplomatic missions in Jerusalem	Y	N	Y	Y	Y
2017	Middle East	Syria	S/2017/2393	Renews authorization for cross-border, cross-line humanitarian access to Syria	A	Y	Y	Y	A
2018	Middle East	Yemen	S/2018/156	Renews sanctions against Yemen, rejects alternative draft after veto by Russian Federation	A	Y	Y	Y	N
2018	Middle East	Syria	S/2018/321	Chemical weapons attack in Syria, Security Council fails to agree on independent investigative mechanism	A	Y	Y	Y	N

Table 7.1. Disagreement between China and the United States on UN Security Council, Votes Concerning the Middle East and Sub-Saharan Africa, 1991–2020 (*continued*)

Year	*Region*	*Country*	*Resolution Number*	*Brief Summary of Content*	*China*	*United States*	*United Kingdom*	*France*	*Russia*
2018	Middle East	Syria	S/2018/355	Following air strikes against suspected chemical weapons sites in Syria, Security Council rejects proposal to condemn aggression	Y	N	N	N	Y
2018	Middle East	Western Sahara	S/RES/2414	Renewed Efforts to End decades-old Western Sahara Conflict, Security Council extends mission	A	Y	Y	Y	A
2018	Sub-Saharan Africa	South Sudan	S/RES/2418	Renew sanctions against officials in South Sudan	A	Y	Y	Y	A
2018	Middle East	Palestinian-Israeli Conflict	S/2018/516	Resolutions on Israeli Force, Hamas role in conflict	Y	N	A	Y	Y
2018	Sub-Saharan Africa	South Sudan	S/RES/2428	Sanctions on South Sudan	A	Y	Y	Y	A
2018	Middle East	Libya	S/RES/2441	Mandate extension to panel of experts on Libya sanctions	A	Y	Y	Y	A
2018	Sub-Saharan Africa	The Central African Republic	S/RES/2448	Renews the mandate of the United Nations Multidimensional Integrated Stabilization Mission in the Central African Republic (MINUSCA)	A	Y	Y	Y	A
2018	Middle East	Syria	S/RES/2449	Authorizes one-year extension of cross-border aid deliveries	A	Y	Y	Y	A

Table 7.1. Disagreement between China and the United States on UN Security Council, Votes Concerning the Middle East and Sub-Saharan Africa, 1991–2020 (*continued*)

Year	*Region*	*Country*	*Resolution Number*	*Brief Summary of Content*	*China*	*United States*	*United Kingdom*	*France*	*Russia*
2019	Sub-Saharan Africa	South Sudan	S/RES/2471	Renews sanctions against South Sudan	A	Y	Y	Y	A
2019	**Middle East**	**Syria**	**S/2019/756**	**Rejects Two draft resolutions on situation in Syria amid divisions over Idlib truce, armed groups**	**N**	**Y**	**Y**	**Y**	**N**
2019	Sub-Saharan Africa	Somalia	S/RES/2498	Renews mandate for panel of experts, sanctions regime on Somalia	A	Y	Y	Y	A
2019	**Middle East**	**Syria**	**Draft S/RES/916**	**Authorizing cross-border, cross-line humanitarian access in Syria (DCM: Also, Russia Federation proposal vetoed by US, UK, and France.)**	**N**	**Y**	**Y**	**Y**	**N**
2020	Sub-Saharan Africa	Central African Republic	S/RES/2507 (2020)	Extends Central African Republic sanctions regime, panel of experts mandate	A	Y	Y	Y	A
2020	Middle East	Yemen	S/RES/2511 (2020)	Sanctions imposed on those threatening security, stability in Yemen	A	Y	Y	Y	A
2020	Sub-Saharan Africa	South Sudan	S/RES/2521 (2020)	Renews mandate of expert panel overseeing South Sudan arms embargo	A	Y	Y	Y	A

Table 7.1. Disagreement between China and the United States on UN Security Council, Votes Concerning the Middle East and Sub-Saharan Africa, 1991–2020 (*continued*)

Year	*Region*	*Country*	*Resolution Number*	*Brief Summary of Content*	*China*	*United States*	*United Kingdom*	*France*	*Russia*
2020	**Middle East**	**Syria**	**S/2020/654**	**First resolution renewing cross-border mechanism for humanitarian aid delivery into Syria (second draft submitted by Russia, China ,and Russia for, other Security Council permanent members against) document S/2020/658). (There were two separate votes on the same issue. China and Russia vetoed both times.)**	**N**	**Y**	**Y**	**Y**	**N**
2020	**Middle East**	**Syria**	**S/2020/667**	**Second resolution renewing cross-border mechanism for humanitarian aid delivery into Syria**	**N**	**Y**	**Y**	**Y**	**N**
2020	Middle East	Syria	S/2020/ 2533	One-year extension of mechanism for cross-border aid delivery into Syria	A	Y	Y	Y	A
2020	**Middle East**	**Iran**	**Draft S/2020/803**	**Extend arms-related restrictions on Iran (not enough votes to pass, so not technically a veto)**	**N**	**Y**	**A**	**A**	**N**
2020	Middle East	Libya	S/ RES/2542 (2020)	Extend mandate of United Nations mission in Libya for 12 months	A	Y	Y	Y	A
2020	Sub-Saharan Africa	Somalia	S/ RES/2551 (2020)	Extend mandate for expert panel on Somalia, renew partial lifting of arms embargo	A	Y	Y	Y	A

Source: Data compiled by author from United Nations, United Nations Documentation Research Guide, http://www.un.org/Depts/dhl/resguide/scact.htm (accessed September 23, 2011, and February 15, 2013) and http://research.un.org/en/docs/sc/quick/meetings/ (accessed June 15, 2016; June 1, 2017; May 29, 2018; November 12, 2019; and January 24, 2021) and https://www.un.org/securitycouncil/content/meetings-2020-vtc (accessed January 25, 2021) Note: Entries in bold were vetoed. This table shows differences between votes by China and the United States on issues in the Middle East and sub-Saharan Africa.

more cooperative on issues such as the 2003 Iraq War and actions against Iran's nuclear program.

Another critical shift to note in China's UNSC voting related to sovereignty is the impact of NATO's 2011 invasion of Libya.[9] Arguably, in the mid-2000s, China was increasingly open to the concept of responsibility to protect (R2P), especially related to Sudan and Darfur.[10] That receptivity dramatically reversed with the NATO invasion of Libya. China voted yes for UNSCR 1970, referring Gaddafi to the International Criminal Court (ICC), and then abstained on UNSCR 1973 authorizing sanctions and a no-fly zone in Libya.[11] Shortly after this vote, NATO initiated military action against Libya. The result of that action was the overthrow of Gaddafi's regime, his televised execution in the streets, and a civil war in Libya that continues to this day. Many interview respondents indicated that Libya was a turning point for China on sovereignty.[12] After the NATO intervention, China held up Libya as an example of the United States and the rest of the West using humanitarian concerns to justify aggression and regime change by force.[13] After 2011, China's views on sovereignty hardened. It increasingly feels a need to protect itself and others, including Syria, from Western neo-interventionism.[14] China started vetoing resolutions on Syria and taking a more vocal stand on the protection of sovereignty more broadly in the UN to ensure Libya does not become a model for future Western interventions.[15] China is concerned that intervention in Syria will result in chaos and potentially a regional power war in the Middle East.[16] In particular, China worries about the potential for conflict in Syria to spill over into greater Sunni-Shia competition regionally.[17]

Although China does not have significant material interests in Syria, these vetoes also provided it an opportunity to support and cooperate with Russia in the Middle East.[18] Interview respondents noted that part of why China supports Russia on Syria is that it wants Russia's support for its territorial claims in the East China and the South China Seas.[19] China is also using this opportunity to demonstrate support for Russia in opposition to the West and to balance with Russia in the Middle East.[20] That said, China is seen as a very different actor in Syria compared to Russia by countries in the Middle East.

Shortly after the beginning of the Arab awakening, China's voting behavior on Syria issues caused tensions with some Gulf Cooperation Council (GCC) countries, such as Saudi Arabia and the United Arab Emirates.[21] After a few years, though, those concerns dissipated. Several interview respondents noted that China's position on noninterference has been consistent over time.[22]

Although their governments do not agree with China's specific stance and action on Syria, they do respect China's principled stance and consistency.[23]

One area of difference between United States and China is UNSC voting on sovereignty issues. Another is voting on the Palestinian-Israeli conflict. In contrast with China's no and abstain votes on proposed violations of sovereignty, its yes votes that differ from those of the United States tend to indicate its support for the Palestinians. These yes votes, which significantly increased in the 2000s, directly correspond to China's pledges via the China-Arab States Cooperation Forum (CASCF) and the China–Middle East special envoy to support the Palestinians in the international arena.[24] Interview respondents indicated that Arab states have been pressuring China to use its vote in the Security Council to support their causes.[25] This increase in votes in support of the Palestinians may be a result of this Arab pressure via the CASCF.[26]

Before the beginning of the Arab awakening in 2011, the Palestinian-Israeli conflict was the central political issue of emphasis by states across the Middle East. Since then, many political issues have risen in importance, including civil wars in Syria, Yemen, and Libya; concerns regarding a rising Iran; and efforts to counter ISIS and similar groups. That said, Chinese officials still consider the Palestinian- Israeli conflict to be the core political issue in the region.[27] As a result, China perceives taking a stand against the United States on UNSC votes related to this issue as a concrete way to demonstrate its support for the Palestinians and differentiate itself from the United States as a more balanced great power in the Middle East.[28]

China's support for the Palestinians differs from US support for Israel. Although China currently has strong relations with both Israel and Palestine, it continues to stand up for the Palestinians in the UNSC against the United States. France, Russia, and the United Kingdom's votes tend to align with China's, so the difference is between the United States and the rest of the Security Council. China's support for the Palestinians in the UNSC is very much tied to its historical advocacy for the Palestinians and national liberation movements. Outside the UNSC, the United States and China also continue to differ on issues associated with Israel. For example, as the United States moved its embassy from Tel Aviv to Jerusalem in 2017, China articulated its support for Palestinian claims to East Jerusalem. (See chapter 5 on special envoys for a more detailed discussion of this issue.)

China's behavior in UNSC voting regarding the Middle East and sub-Saharan Africa differs from the United States in two ways. First, its use of abstentions and vetoes to voice opposition to interference in the internal affairs of other states directly contradicts the Western political liberal international order and is divergent from it. It is competing with the United States through this norm-divergent behavior on sovereignty votes.

Second, China's yes votes in support of the Palestinians are in direct conflict with US support for Israel in the UNSC. China's support for the Palestinians in the UNSC is therefore competitive with the United States, although it is also norm convergent because in the votes, China is encouraging states to comply with resolutions of a liberal organization, the United Nations, to resolve the conflict between Israel and the Palestinians.

Chinese voting behavior is competitive with the United States. It is using its veto in the UNSC to stand up to the United States about foreign intervention and US support for Israel. It also uses its votes to differentiate itself from the United States and the rest of the West. As a defender of sovereignty and the Palestinians, China attempts to foster support for itself through South-South solidarity in a world with emerging multipolarity or bipolarity. It also uses its status as a permanent member of the Security Council as a way to advocate for developing country causes and protect its sovereignty from the United States by protesting against foreign interventions more broadly. Indirectly, China's voting in the UNSC fuels its domestic economic growth by helping to ensure the Middle East and sub-Saharan Africa remain stable, so it can continue to access their resources and markets.

Strategic Partnerships

Starting in the mid-1990s, China introduced a new diplomatic mechanism, strategic partnerships, that it develops with individual countries and groups of countries. This section examines these partnerships with individual Middle Eastern and sub-Saharan African countries between 1991 and 2020. China also established strategic partnerships with Africa as a continent at the 2006 Forum on China-Africa Cooperation (FOCAC) Summit[29] and with the League of Arab states via the CASCF at the 2018 Eighth Ministerial Meeting.[30]

China has established over seventy strategic partnerships globally, but those partnerships in no way compare to America's sixty full-fledged treaty allies that involve military cooperation.[31] China's strategic partnerships are not military alliances or quasi-military alliances involving security and military cooperation. The Chinese government labels these relationships as strategic because they include all aspects of bilateral relations (e.g., economic, political, cultural, and security), and both sides make a long-term commitment to bilateral ties.[32] China started establishing strategic partnerships in 1993. As of March 2021, it had established twelve in the Middle East and fifteen in sub-Saharan Africa. (See table 7.2.)

China's first strategic partnership in the Middle East, established in 1999, was with long-time friend Egypt.[33] From the beginning, this partnership encompassed a broad range of political, economic, social, and cultural relations.[34] Additional agreements were signed in 2006 to boost strategic ties.[35] In 2009, Egypt's minister of international cooperation, Faiza Abou el-Naga, described the partnership as "a genuine wide-ranging strategic cooperation that covers industry, agriculture, transportation, health, technology training, and education."[36] According to an official with the Egyptian Ministry of Foreign Affairs, a new world order was evolving, and Egypt wanted a better position in both the current and future orders. Egypt viewed China as a rising power that was a friendly country in this evolving world order.[37] In his words, "FOCAC is helping China to have its own camp. Egypt can help in that endeavor."[38] Egypt's strategic partnership with China was one component of providing that support.

China's first sub-Saharan African strategic partner was South Africa. During the development of China–South Africa relations, they upgraded relations from partnership to strategic partnership to a comprehensive strategic partnership.[39] In 2000, the Pretoria Declaration on the Establishment of a Partnership between the People's Republic of China and the Republic of South Africa initiated the partnership.[40] In 2004, they relabeled relations as a strategic partnership. China formed a comprehensive strategic partnership with South Africa in 2010[41] that includes political and economic cooperation and advocates for cooperation between China and South Africa in the regional and international arenas.[42] Similar to international cooperation in the FOCAC, the China–South Africa comprehensive strategic partnership stresses supporting the needs of developing countries and promoting a greater voice for developing countries in the world system.[43] An official with the South Africa embassy in Beijing identified China as a major strategic partner, especially after overtaking the United States as South Africa's largest trading partner. According to this official and other interview respondents, when they formed the partnership, China viewed South Africa as a gateway to the rest of Africa due to the country's leading political and economic role on the continent.[44]

Table 7.2. China's Strategic Partnerships in the Middle East and Sub-Saharan Africa, 1999–2020.

Year	*Region*	*Country*
1999	Middle East	Egypt[1]
2000	Sub-Saharan Africa	South Africa[2]
2004	Middle East	Algeria[3]
2005	Sub-Saharan Africa	Nigeria[4]
2010	Sub-Saharan Africa	Angola[5]
2010	Middle East	Turkey[6]
2012	Middle East	UAE[7]
2014	Sub-Saharan Africa	Ethiopia[8]
2014	Middle East	Qatar[9]
2015	Middle East	Jordan[10]
2015	Sub-Saharan Africa	Sudan[11]
2015	Middle East	Iraq[12]
2016	Middle East	Iran[13]
2016	Sub-Saharan Africa	Gabon[14]
2016	Sub-Saharan Africa	Sierra Leone[15]
2016	Sub-Saharan Africa	Republic of Congo[16]
2016	Middle East	Morocco[17]
2016	Sub-Saharan Africa	Mozambique[18]
2016	Sub-Saharan Africa	Guinea[19]
2016	Sub-Saharan Africa	Senegal[20]
2016	Middle East	Saudi Arabia[21]
2017	Sub-Saharan Africa	Kenya[22]
2017	Sub-Saharan Africa	Djibouti[23]
2018	Sub-Saharan Africa	Zimbabwe[24]
2018	Sub-Saharan Africa	Namibia[25]
2018	Middle East	Oman[26]
2018	Middle East	Kuwait[27]

Notes

1. "PRC's Wang Gang Heads Delegation to Egypt on Friendship, Bilateral Ties," Xinhua, June 6, 2010; and "Chinese Magazine Lauds Development Of Egyptian-Chinese Relations," *MENA,* June 20, 2007.

2. "Beijing Declaration on the People's Republic of China and the Republic of South Africa Establish-

ing a Comprehensive Strategic Partnership," Xinhua Domestic Service, September 1, 2010.

3. "Zhang Dejiang, Algeria Premier Discuss Developing Ties 14 Oct," Xinhua, October 15, 2004.

4. "China, Nigeria to Strengthen Cooperation on UN Reform: Joint Communique," Xinhua, April 15, 2005.

5. Wang Bingfei and Song Xu, "Wu Bangguo Holds Talks with Speaker of Angola's National Assembly," Xinhua Domestic Service, May 24, 2011.

6. "Today's Zaman: 2012: A Year of Growth in Turkish-Chinese relations," *Today's Zaman Online Sunday*, December 30, 2012.

7. "Premier Wen: China-UAE Strategic Partnership to Create Broader Prospect for Bilateral Cooperation," Xinhua, January 18, 2012.

8. Wang Yi, "China-Ethiopia Relations: An Excellent Model for South-South Cooperation," Chinese Ministry of Foreign Affairs Website, December 1, 2014, www.fmprc.gov.cn.

9. "China, Qatar Announce Strategic Partnership," Xinhua, November 4, 2014.

10. "Jordan, China Sign Strategic Partnership Agreement," *Jordan Times*, September 10, 2015.

11. "China, Sudan to Establish Strategic Partnership," Xinhua, September 1, 2015.

12. "China, Iraq Establish Strategic Partnership," Xinhua, December 22, 2015.

13. "China, Iran Lift Bilateral Ties to Comprehensive Strategic Partnership," *China Daily*, January 23, 2016.

14. "Wang Yi Meets with President Ali Bongo Ondimba of Gabon," Chinese Ministry of Foreign Affairs Website, January 15, 2018, www.fmprc.gov.cn.

15. "Sierra-Leone and China Continue Strengthening Their Partnership, Which Brexit Opens New Opportunities for Historical Ties with the UK," *World Folio*, May 2017.

16. "China's Top Political Advisor Visits Republic of Congo to Further Ties," Xinhua, June 14, 2018.

17. "Morocco, China Give New Impetus to bilateral partnership in 2017," *Global Times*, December 31, 2017.

18. "China intends to reinforce the strategic partnership with Mozambique," *Macao Magazine*, May 2, 2018.

19. "Xi Jinping Holds Talks with President Alpha Conde of Guinea and the Two Heads of State Decide to Establish China-Guinea Comprehensive Strategic Partnership of Cooperation," Embassy of the People's Republic of China in Grenada website, November 2, 2016.

20. "China, Senegal to advance comprehensive strategic partnership," Xinhua, September 2, 2016.

21. "KSA, China Agree on Strategic Partnership," *Arab News*, January 21, 2016. In 1999, China and Saudi signed a strategic oil cooperation agreement. See "Jiang Zemin Concludes Visit to Saudi Arabia," Xinhua, November 3, 1999.

Similar to interview respondents in Egypt, South African interviewees indicated that South Africa viewed China as a rising global power in an emerging multipolar world, and establishing a strategic partnership with it provided South Africa an opportunity to increase its potential power in that evolving new order.[45] South Africa wanted a role in the future of global governance, and strategic partnership with China is part of fulfilling that aspiration.

China slowly began developing partnerships with other states in these regions. In the mid-2000s, it launched strategic partnerships with Algeria and Nigeria and announced strategic partnerships with Angola and Turkey in 2010 and the UAE in 2012. These partnerships, which targeted some of China's most important economic partners in these regions, were established at a time when China's economic interests in these regions were growing. .

After Xi Jinping took power in 2012, China's use of strategic partnerships increased substantially in both of these regions starting in 2014 (see table 7.2). Although each strategic partnership has many root causes, based on the patterns observed, it could be argued that the uptick in these partnerships is due to Xi Jinping's greater use of this foreign policy tool and changes in China's approach to these regions. Some of those changes include China's need to establish partnerships in a post–Arab awakening environment, a desire to solicit support for BRI, and a goal of gaining support in the international system in an era of increasing multipolarity and competition with the United States.

In the Middle East, China appears to be very cautious to ensure it continues to be seen as a balanced player among regional powers. For example, it has established partnerships with key predominantly Sunni states (Saudi Arabia, Egypt, UAE, Oman, Qatar, Jordan, Kuwait), Shia states (Iran and Iraq),

---

22. "Xi Jinping Meets with President Uhuru Kenyatta of Kenya," Chinese Ministry of Foreign Affairs, May 15, 2017, www.fmprc.gov.cn.

23. "China, Djibouti Agree to Establish Strategic Partnership," Xinhua, November 23, 2017.

24. "China, Zimbabwe Agree to Establish Comprehensive Strategic Partnership of Cooperation," Xinhua, April 3, 2018.

25. "China, Namibia Agree to Establish Comprehensive Strategic Partnership of Cooperation," Xinhua, March 30, 2018.

26. "China, Oman Issue Join Statement on Establishment of Strategic Partnership," Xinhua, May 26, 2018.

27. "China Focus: China, Kuwait Agree to Establish Strategic Partnership," Xinhuanet, July 10, 2018.

and Turkey. Even within the Arab world, it maintains its strategic partnership with Qatar as other GCC members implement an embargo against it. As of 2020, China had established strategic partnerships with every significant economic, political, and military power in the Middle East except Israel. The only countries left out were Bahrain, Lebanon, Libya, Palestine, Syria, Tunisia, and Yemen.

In sub-Saharan Africa, China's fifteen strategic partnerships have also targeted the regional economic, political, and military powers. China has established strategic partnerships with the top six sub-Saharan African economies: Nigeria, South Africa, Angola, Ethiopia, Kenya, and Sudan. It also now has a strategic partnership with Djibouti that houses China's first overseas military base.

This chapter characterizes China's behavior of developing these strategic partnerships in the Middle East and sub-Saharan Africa as competitive with the United States and other Western powers in these regions. All of these partnerships were established after 1998 as China's economic interests in the Middle East and sub-Saharan Africa were increasing rapidly, and it was seeking access to resources and markets. Although China did establish some partnerships during the 2000s and early 2010s, under Xi Jinping's leadership, these partnerships proliferated. As part of its Belt and Road Initiative, China is increasingly attempting to establish spheres of influence in these regions, and building these strategic partnerships is one part of that effort. These partnerships support China's political interests of seeking support in the international arena from other great and regional powers. They also demonstrate the importance of these countries to China and provide China an opportunity to lay a foundation to balance against the United States and the rest of the West.

China uses these partnerships as a way to protect its sovereignty by soliciting support for its claims in the South China Sea. For example, when Oman signed its partnership agreement, it publicly stated, "Oman supports the Chinese government's position on issues concerning Taiwan, Tibet, and the South China Sea, which China supports Oman's efforts in safeguarding sovereignty, independence and territorial integrity, and national security and stability."[46] Press releases about the Gabon agreement stated, "Gabon will continue to firmly stick to the one-China policy, support China's great cause of reunification and safeguard China's legitimate rights and interests in China-related issues, such as the South China Sea issue."[47]

No specific international norms govern strategic partnerships, so this behavior is categorized as norm neutral. That said, it is very much in alignment with the practices of great powers to seek alliances and partnerships with other countries to pursue their political, economic, and security goals. Also, these formal agreements to establish official strategic partnerships with countries throughout these regions are an important element of the order China is building to govern its relations with the Middle East and sub-Saharan Africa.

Conclusion

China uses its political relations with countries in the Middle East and sub-Saharan Africa to pursue a broad range of interests. It promotes its domestic economic growth by linking bilateral political, economic, and security relations through strategic partnerships. It also desires stability in these regions for continued access to resources and markets. It attempts to promote stability by playing a constructive role in the Middle East peace process and protecting states in these regions from destabilizing foreign intervention and interference through its UNSC voting.

China fosters support in the international arena through its political relations. In particular, it advocates for the Five Principles and the rights of Palestinians to solicit support throughout the Middle East and Africa. China also uses its UNSC voting and strategic partnerships as a way to advocate for developing country causes and South-South cooperation. It leverages its status as a permanent member of the Security Council to protect its territorial integrity by fighting against foreign interventions and protecting the sovereignty of states with its votes. China even includes wording in some of its strategic partnerships to demonstrate support for its sovereignty claims, including in the South China Sea. This chapter analyzes specific political foreign policy tools China uses to achieve all of these interests.

To pursue its interests, China competes through UNSC voting and strategic partnerships in the Middle East and sub-Saharan Africa. In the UNSC, China votes to stand up to the United States and the West in defense of the Five Principles and to combat foreign intervention into the internal affairs of states. It also competes with the United States by voting against Israel's actions to demonstrate support for the Palestinians. This competition works toward China's goal of fostering support for itself in the international system. Often in the UNSC, China is cooperating with Russia against the Western permanent members (France, the United Kingdom, and United States). One particularly salient example of this cooperation with Russia and competition against the United States and the rest of the West is their ten double vetoes on Syria since 2011.

China's strategic partnerships are also competitive. China is using these instruments to improve bilateral relations as a way to build spheres of influence in these regions. In particular, during the Xi Jinping era and China's focus on Belt and Road, it is targeting regional powers for strategic partnerships. This tool allows China to create linkages between bilateral economic, political, and security cooperation with these countries.

China's voting in the UNSC on sovereignty and intervention is norm divergent from the liberal order. China advocates for a strict interpretation of Westphalian sovereignty in opposition to the liberal order's contemporary emphasis on responsibility to protect and regime change. Especially after NATO invaded Libya in 2011, China's views on sovereignty have hardened and diverged away from R2P and other foreign intervention and interference.

China's UNSC voting also differs from that of the United States on the Palestinian-Israeli conflict. In the Security Council, the United States serves as Israel's defender and China advocates for the rights of the Palestinians. In alignment with its pledges via cooperation forums and its special envoys, although China does have strong bilateral relations with Israel, it attempts to act as a balanced actor and to help ensure that Palestinian, Arab, and Israeli interests are all considered in pursuing peace in the Middle East. Although China's support for the Palestinians in the UNSC is competitive with the United States, it is also norm convergent because it votes to encourage other states to abide by UN resolutions on the Arab-Israeli conflict.

China's strategic partnerships are categorized as norm neutral. No explicit norms govern these activities, but China's behavior is in alignment with those of other great powers operating in these regions.

The political behavior examined in this chapter demonstrates that China's advocacy for the normative framework of the Five Principles guiding state-to-state relations is reinforced through its defense of state sovereignty and non-interference in the UNSC, as well as the formal texts establishing strategic partnerships. China's emphasis on the norm of South-South cooperation is also supported by its behavior in the UNSC and its cooperation with many developing countries through its strategic partnerships. China's bilateral strategic partnerships complement the cooperation forums it has established in these regions. Its contributions to Arab causes, such as supporting Palestinians in the Palestinian-Israeli conflict through UNSC voting, also align with its support for these causes in the CASCF as well as its special envoy for Middle East issues.

China uses all of the tools discussed in this chapter, together with its cooperation forums, special envoys, economic and military relations, and BRI, to build spheres of influence in these regions. It also uses political foreign policy tools to differentiate itself from other great powers. It claims to be a defender of state sovereignty that fights against foreign intervention and interference and demonstrates that it cares about the plight of the Palestinians and is willing to stand up to the United States on that issue. China's double vetoes and other overlapping votes with Russia in the UNSC also demonstrate that it is willing to cooperate with Russia in the Middle East due to shared interests and a desire to gain Russian support of China more broadly in the international system. China also pursues strategic partnerships with a wide range of countries in these regions regardless of regime type. Through its UNSC voting and strategic partnerships China portrays itself as a responsible member of the Security Council that stands up for developing countries and is attempting to establish positive political relations with all regional powers in the Middle East and sub-Saharan Africa.

CHAPTER 8

COOPERATING FOR PEACE AND SECURITY?

Military Relations

During the Mao era, China actively supported national liberation movements throughout the Middle East and sub-Saharan Africa. Since the 1970s, its military behavior in these areas has dramatically changed. During the post–Cold War era, in contrast with other functional areas of politics and economics, as China's power in the Middle East and sub-Saharan Africa expanded, its military behavior became increasingly cooperative with the United States, other great powers, and regional powers and convergent with liberal rules of the international system. Building on China's security relations in its cooperation forums and special envoys discussed in chapters 4 and 5, this chapter explores some other aspects of China's post–Cold War military ties with the Middle East and sub-Saharan Africa. It examines China's involvement in UN peacekeeping operations (UNPKO), sales of conventional arms, participation in antipiracy initiatives, and establishment of a base in Djibouti.

The primary questions driving this chapter and the rest of the book are: Is China cooperating or competing with the United States in the Middle East and sub-Saharan Africa? Is its behavior converging with or diverging from international norms? Is it building an alternative international order in these regions? If so, what are the characteristics of that order? Ultimately, what does China's behavior in the Middle East and sub-Saharan Africa indicate about its rise globally? Analyzing China's military relations with these regions through UNPKO, conventional arms sales, antipiracy activities, and its base in Djibouti in a comparative perspective over time generates important insights about how China is competing in these regions and diverging from or converging with international norms.[1] It shows how China is developing spheres of influence, approaching the rules of the system, and supporting the existing multilateral security order in these regions. It also provides insights into how China is portraying itself as a great power and how it conceptualizes the linkage of its security, economic, and political activities in these regions.

China pursues many of its interests discussed in chapter 3 through military behavior. It promotes its economic growth through stability in regions to ensure continued access to resources and markets by supporting UNPKO missions, antipiracy initiatives, and its base in Djibouti. Contributions to UNPKO and antipiracy, as well as limiting conventional arms sales, help China foster support for itself in these regions. Antipiracy activities and setting up the base in Djibouti work toward safeguarding China's citizens and businesses abroad.

The primary sources used in examining China's UNPKO, conventional arms sales, antipiracy, and Djibouti base in the Middle East and sub-Saharan Africa include documents and data from the United Nations; China's defense white papers; Stockholm International Peace Research Institute (SIPRI) data on arms transfers; media reports and government statements; and interviews with Chinese and regional government officials and scholars. The selected foreign policy tools provide data to analyze within and between regions as well as over time. Because Djibouti is China's first declared overseas military base, it is an important case study in understanding China's security role in these regions.

This chapter examines whether China's military behavior through UNPKO, conventional arms sales, antipiracy initiatives, and the Djibouti base diverges from or converges with norms governing these interactions and whether China competes or cooperates with the United States in its relations with these regions. This chapter in particular focuses on norms associated with the Western liberal security order. Together with chapters on China's cooperation forums and special envoys, this chapter examines military foreign policy tools over time and across regions to draw broad conclusions about China as a rising power in these regions.

Chapter 4 analyzed China's security behavior through cooperation forums: the Forum on China-Africa Cooperation (FOCAC), the China-Arab States Cooperation Forum (CASCF), and the Shanghai Cooperation Organization (SCO). A component of those cooperation forums is security relations.

As discussed in chapter 4, China's security behavior in the FOCAC and CASCF is mostly cooperative and norm convergent. It focuses on issues such as nuclear-free zones, peacekeeping through the UN and the AU, antipiracy activities in the Gulf of Aden and the Gulf of Guinea, and global terrorism. The forums stress security cooperation through regional multilateral organizations, especially the African Union, the United Nations, and multinational peacekeeping operations. Due to its heavy reliance on multilateral action, this behavior is also categorized as cooperative in Africa because Western states too are working through these multilateral mechanisms.

Through its special envoys, China's security cooperation is also norm convergent and cooperative. Concerning the liberal order, China's special envoy for Syria promotes the utilization of multilateral mediation mechanisms as well as humanitarian aid, reconstruction assistance, support for counterterrorism, and criticism on the use of chemical weapons. With its Africa special envoy, in alignment with the liberal international order, China is promoting multilateralism and seeking negotiated solutions to conflicts. When it aims to contribute to conflict resolution, it does so through international and regional organizations. Through these envoys, China tends to cooperate with the United States and the rest of the West on issues directly affecting peace and security by advocating for the use of multilateral dispute resolution mechanisms that involve international organizations in pursuing peace.

In alignment with the findings in other chapters about China's security behavior in the Middle East and sub-Saharan Africa, this chapter asserts that overall, China's behavior is cooperative and norm convergent in all of the foreign policy tools examined. One exception is China's establishment of a navy base in Djibouti. Similar to its cooperation forums and special envoys, China engages in issues of peace and security through multilateral mechanisms that are part of the liberal order. In those mechanisms, it cooperates with both the United States and other Western powers. It conducts the vast majority of its military activities in these regions through UNPKO and multilateral antipiracy operations. Its conventional arms sales have been minimal since the Iran-Iraq War. Sales have not increased as China's power in the region expanded or demand for weapons grew due to instability in the aftermath of the Arab awakening.

United Nations Peacekeeping Operations

China is a relative newcomer to UN peacekeeping operations.[2] Its first contribution to UNPKO troops anywhere in the world did not occur until 1991.[3] By 2019, China was the tenth largest contributor country to UN peacekeeping missions, and it was providing more troops, police, and military observers than any other UN Security Council permanent member.[4] In January 2021, China's worldwide UNPKO contribution of 2,465 personnel included troops (2,390), experts (27), police (7), and staff officers (41).[5] Table 8.1 provides an overview of China's UNPKO activities in the Middle East and sub-Saharan Africa since 1990. China's decision criteria in determining which UNPKO missions to support are its interests, UN personnel needs to support missions, local country agreement to allow UNPKO to operate within their borders, and the level of danger to China's participants.[6]

China's increases in UNPKO combat contributions over time directly correspond to escalating economic interests in the Middle East and sub-Saharan Africa, concerns over the need for stability in these regions to ensure economic security, a desire to protect its businesses and citizens abroad, and its need to foster support for itself in these regions by demonstrating it is a responsible power contributing to regional security by operating through well-respected international organizations. Starting in 2003, China's concern over hot spots in these regions became more pronounced as its economic interests in these regions skyrocketed. As discussed extensively in chapter 5 on special envoys, during the 2000s, China became particularly concerned about the Palestinian-Israeli conflict and Sudan as hot spots, which could cause instability and economic insecurity for China in these regions. After the beginning of the Arab awakening, China's concerns over stability in these regions substantially increased, and its contributions to peacekeeping escalated. Its deployments of peacekeeping troops to Lebanon, Sudan, Darfur, South Sudan, Mali, Syria, and the Democratic Republic of the Congo directly reflect concerns over the impact of these hot spots on regional stability and its own economic security.

China's rising UNPKO activity is cooperative and convergent toward the military rules of the international system. This behavior is conducted through the multilateral mechanism of the UN, the foundation of the liberal international order for issues of peace and security. Through this multilateral mechanism, China cooperates with the United States, the rest of the West, and regional powers to encourage stability in countries that request UNPKO support. Because China's interests in these regions are primarily economic

Table 8.1. China UN Peacekeeping Operation Contributions in the Middle East and Sub-Saharan Africa through January 2021

UN Peacekeeping Mission	*Acronym*	*Time Frame*	*Personnel*	*Region*
UN Transition Assistance Group for Namibia	UNTAG	April 1989–March 1990	20 (total contributions)[1]	Sub-Saharan Africa
UN Truce Supervision Organization	UNTSO[2]	April 1990–present	4 experts on mission[3]	Middle East
UN Iraq-Kuwait Observer Mission	UNIKOM	April 1991–October 2003	1 troop, 11 observers[4]	Middle East
UN Mission for Referendum in Western Sahara[5]	MINURSO	September 1991–present	11 experts on mission[6]	Sub-Saharan Africa
UN Operation in Mozambique	ONUMOZ	June 1993–December 1994	10 observers[7]	Sub-Saharan Africa
UN Observer Mission in Liberia	UNOMIL	November 1993–September 1997	5 observers[8]	Sub-Saharan Africa
UN Mission in Sierra Leone	UNAMSIL	August 1998–December 2005	3 observers[9]	Sub-Saharan Africa
UN Mission in Ethiopia and Eritrea	UNMEE	October 2000–August 2008	7 observers[10]	Sub-Saharan Africa
UN Mission in Democratic Republic of Congo (Kinshasa)	MONUC	April 2001–June 2010	204 contingent troops and 16 experts on missions[11]	Sub-Saharan Africa
UN Mission in Liberia	UNMIL	October 2003–March 2018	140 formed police units, 1 individual police, and 1 staff officer[12]	Sub-Saharan Africa
UN Operation in Cote d'Ivoire	UNOCI[13]	March 2004– June 30, 2017	3 experts on mission[14]	Sub-Saharan Africa
UN Action in Burundi	ONUB	June 2004–September 2006	3 observers[15]	Sub-Saharan Africa

Table 8.1. China UN Peacekeeping Operation Contributions in the Middle East and Sub-Saharan Africa through January 2021 (*continued*)

UN Peacekeeping Mission	*Acronym*	*Time Frame*	*Personnel*	*Region*
UN Mission in Sudan	UNMIS	April 2005–July 2011	435 contingent troops, 22 individual police and 12 experts on mission[16]	Sub-Saharan Africa
UN Interim Force in Lebanon	UNIFIL	Mar 2006–present	410 contingent troops and 9 staff officers[17]	Middle East
UN Integrated Office in Sierra Leone	UNIOSIL	February 2007–February 2008	1 (total contribution)[18]	Sub-Saharan Africa
AU-UN Hybrid Operation in Darfur	UNAMID	November 2007–2020	310 contingent troops[19]	Sub-Saharan Africa
UN Organization Stabilization Mission in the Democratic Republic of the Congo[20]	MONUSCO	July 2010–present	218 contingent troops and 9 staff officers[21]	Sub-Saharan Africa
UN Interim Security Force for Abyei (Sudan)	UNISFA	July 2011–October 2011	1 expert on mission[22]	Sub-Saharan Africa
UN Mission in the Republic of South Sudan	UNMISS	July 2011 to present	1,031 contingent troops and 18 staff officers[23]	Sub-Saharan Africa
UN Supervision Mission in Syria	UNSMIS	April 2012–August 2012	4 experts on mission[24]	Middle East
UN Multidimensional Integrated Stabilization Mission in Mali[25]	MINUSMA	April 2013–present	413 contingent troops and staff officers.[26]	Sub-Saharan Africa

Notes

1. "The Diversified Employment."

2. For more information on UNTSO, see http://www.un.org/en/peacekeeping/missions/untso/index.shtml and http://untso.unmissions.org/.

3. Troop and Police Contributors as of January 31, 2021. UNPKO Website. https://peacekeeping.un.org/en/troop-and-police-contributors.

4. Summary of Contributions to UN Peacekeeping by Country, Mission and Post as of December 31, 2002. UNPKO Website. www.un.org/en/peacekeeping/resources/statistics/contributors.shtml.

5. For more information on MINURSO, see http://www.un.org/en/peacekeeping/missions/minurso/index.shtml.

6. Troop and Police Contributors as of January 31, 2021. UNPKO Website. https://peacekeeping.un.org/en/troop-and-police.

7. Monthly Contribution of Troop Contributions to UN Peacekeeping Operations as of December 31, 1994. www.un.org/en/peacekeeping/resources/statistics/contributors.shtml

8. Monthly Summary of Troop Contributions Peacekeeping Operations as of December 31, 1996. www.un.org/en/peacekeeping/resources/statistics/contributors.shtml.

9. UN Missions Summary detailed by Country as of December 31, 2004. www.un.org/en/peacekeeping/resources/statistics/contributors.shtml.

10. UN Missions Summary detailed by Country as of December 31, 2007. www.un.org/en/peacekeeping/resources/statistics/contributors.shtml.

11. UN Mission Summary detailed by country as of December 31, 2009. www.un.org/en/peacekeeping/resources/statistics/contributors.shtml.

12. Summary of Contributions to UN Peacekeeping by Country, Mission and Post as of June 30, 2017. www.un.org/en/peacekeeping/resources/statistics/contributors.shtml. For information UNMIL UNPKO United Nations Mission in Liberia, see http://www.un.org/en/peacekeeping/.

13. For more information on UNOCI, see www.un.org/en/peacekeeping/missions/unoci/background.shtml.

14. UN Mission Summary detailed by country as of December 31, 2016. www.un.org/en/peacekeeping/resources/statistics/contributors.shtml, For information on UNOCI UNPKO United Nations Operation in Cote d'Ivoire, see http://www.un.org/en/peacekeeping/missions/unoci/.

15. UN Mission Summary detailed by country as of December 31, 2005. www.un.org/en/peacekeeping/resources/statistics/contributors.shtml.

16. UN Mission Summary detailed by country as of December 31, 2010. UNPKO Website. www.un.org/en/peacekeeping/resources/statistics/contributors.shtml.

17. Troop and Police Contributors as of January 31, 2021. UNPKO Website. https://peacekeeping.un.org/en/troop-and-police-contributors

18. UN Mission Summary detailed by country as of December 31, 2007. www.un.org/en/peacekeeping/resources/statistics/contributors.shtml.

19. Troop and Police Contributors as of January 31, 2021. UNPKO Website. https://peacekeeping.un.org/en/troop-and-police-contributors.

20. UN renamed MONUC the United Nations Organization Stabilization Mission in the Democratic Republic of the Congo (MONUSCO) to reflect the new phase reached in the country. See http://monusco.unmissions.org/.

21. Troop and Police Contributors as of January 31, 2021. UNPKO Website. https://peacekeeping.un.org/en/troop-and-police-contributors.

22. UN Mission Summary detailed by country as of September 30, 2011. www.un.org/en/peacekeeping/resources/statistics/contributors.shtml. For information on

and political, its military involvement is limited to actions that strive to ensure regional stability and protect China's economic interests. In light of these limited interests, UN peacekeeping operations provide China an opportunity to participate in resolving hot spot issues while maintaining an image as a responsible rising power. China frequently portrays its participation in UNPKO activities as responsible behavior for a great power. For example, its 2010 National Defense white paper states, "As a responsible major power, China has consistently supported and actively participated in the UN peacekeeping operations, making a positive contribution to world peace."[7]

Participation through the United Nations enables China to communicate to states in these regions that its military motives are benign. Also, due to China's desire not to challenge the United States in its sphere of influence (the Middle East),[8] UNPKO provide China a tool to maintain stability that is less likely to be perceived as hostile by the United States or states in the Middle East and sub-Saharan Africa. It differentiates itself as a great power in these regions by significantly contributing troops to UNPKO missions.

Conventional Arms Sales

During the Mao era, China provided arms to a number of national liberation movements in the Middle East and sub-Saharan Africa. Since 1978, China's behavior in conventional arms sales has been much more norm convergent. In the 1980s, its sales to the Middle East significantly increased while sales to sub-Saharan Africa were relatively limited (see figure 8.1). Elevated Middle Eastern sales were primarily driven by supplying both belligerents in the Iran-Iraq War.

In contrast, from 1990 to 2019, China was not a significant arms supplier to the developing world.[9] Globally, it was the fifth-largest supplier of major

---

UNISFA UNPKO United Nations Interim Security Force for Abyei (UNISFA), see http://www.un.org/en/peacekeeping/missions/unisfa/.

23. Troop and Police Contributors as of January 31, 2021. UNPKO Website. https://peacekeeping.un.org/en/troop-and-police-contributors.

24. UN Mission Summary detailed by country as of July 31, 2012. www.un.org/en/peacekeeping/resources/statistics/contributors.shtml.

25. For more information on MINUSMA, see www.un.org/en/peacekeeping/missions/minusma/.

26. Troop and Police Contributors as of January 31, 2021. UNPKO Website. https://peacekeeping.un.org/en/troop-and-police-contributors.

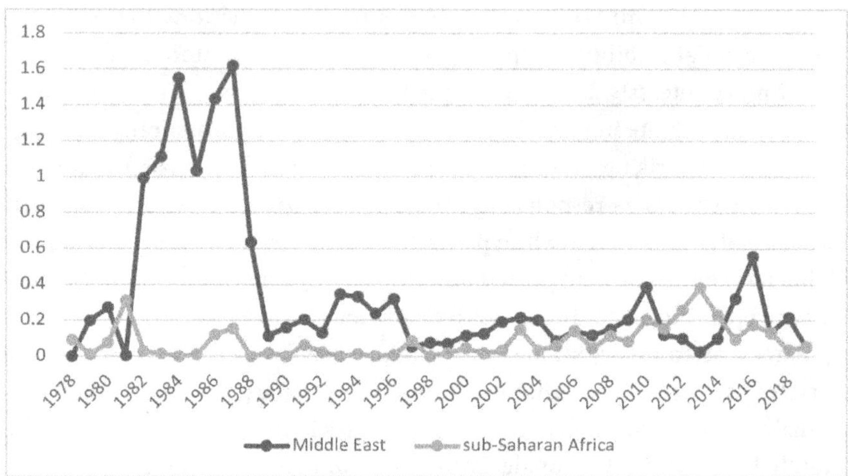

Figure 8.1. China's Conventional Arms Transfers to the Middle East and Sub-Saharan Africa, 1978–2019 (trend indicator values expressed in billions). Source: Data compiled and graph created by author from SIPRI Arms Transfers Database data, accessed June 12, 2017, November 14, 2019, and January 22, 2020, at http://www.sipri.org/databases/armstransfers.

conventional weapons to the developing world, after the United States, Russia, France, and the United Kingdom.[10] China is a provider of relatively low-quality arms, and in general, its developing country customers are poor countries that lack resources and cannot afford more advanced systems from other suppliers or countries that suffer from restricted access to global arms markets.[11]

Other than sales to Iran and Iraq in the 1980s, China's conventional arms sales to countries in these regions have been consistently limited. From 1978 to 1989, China's top conventional arms customers in the Middle East were Iraq, Egypt, Iran, and Saudi Arabia. In sub-Saharan Africa, they were Sudan, Somalia, Zimbabwe, Tanzania, the Democratic Republic of Congo, and Zambia. After the Iran-Iraq War, China's arms sales to the Middle East decreased: it no longer sold arms to Iraq, but Iran remained an important arms customer.

Between 1990 and 1999, China's top conventional arms customers in the Middle East were Iran, Egypt, Yemen, Algeria, and Tunisia. Iran was by far China's most important arms customer in the Middle East during this period. In contrast, arms sales to sub-Saharan African countries were limited at this time. Top customers were Sudan, Tanzania, Ethiopia, Zimbabwe, Kenya, and Mauritania.

Between 2000 and 2010, China's conventional arms exports to the Middle East and sub-Saharan Africa continued to be limited. Top customers in the Middle East were Iran, Egypt, Algeria, Kuwait, Syria, and Saudi Arabia. Iran continued to be the most significant regional customer, but sales volume to Iran decreased compared to the previous decade. sub-Saharan African sales also remained low. Top customers were Sudan, Nigeria, Namibia, Zambia, Tanzania, and Zimbabwe.

Finally, from 2011 to 2019, China's top customers in the Middle East were Algeria, Qatar, Saudi, UAE, and Iran. Algeria was by far the most significant customer in the region with a total of 864 million trend-indicator values (TIVs).[12] In sub-Saharan Africa, top customers were Tanzania, Sudan, Cameroon, Zambia, and Nigeria. From 1978 to 2019, the top customers in the Middle East were Iraq (4.3 billion TIV), Iran (4.25 billion), Egypt (2.842 billion), Algeria (1.114 billion), and Saudi Arabia (0.641 billion). In sub-Saharan Africa, they were Sudan (0.799), Tanzania (0.575 billion), Nigeria (0.271 billion), Namibia (0.252 billion), and Zimbabwe (0.225 billion).[13]

Since China's economic opening in the late 1970s, its behavior in the realm of arms sales has been cooperative and norm convergent. The primary liberal norm here is minimizing the proliferation of weapons. Other than sales during the Iran-Iraq War in the 1980s, China's sales of conventional weapons to these regions have been minimal. China is not a significant arms supplier in these regions. It sells low-quality arms to countries that do not have other options in the international arms market due to a lack of funds or restrictions to access due to sanctions.[14] China is pragmatically searching for profits selling limited volumes of low-quality arms to customers with no other options. In light of its advocacy for noninterference in the domestic politics of other countries, selling arms to countries regardless of the ruling regime is very much in alignment with China's overall normative stance. It can be argued that by limiting its conventional arms sales to these regions, China is contributing to regional stability and is attempting to foster support for itself in the international system by demonstrating that it is a responsible power in these regions.

Antipiracy Operations

China's involvement in antipiracy operations is another example of its cooperative and norm- convergent military behavior toward the liberal rules of the international system in the Middle East and sub-Saharan Africa. The free flow of goods through the Gulf of Aden is a significant national interest. China seeks to ensure its economic development through regional stability and needs to safeguard its businesses and citizens abroad. Protecting vessels carrying resources and goods to and from China is essential to attaining those goals. The Gulf of Aden leads to several African countries, Middle Eastern countries, and the Suez Canal, and it is the quickest sea route from China to Europe and many countries in the Americas. Much of those goods are oil and other natural resources essential for China's development. For example, ships from two of China's top oil suppliers, Iran and Angola, can avoid transiting through the Gulf of Aden. Still, other leading oil suppliers such as Saudi Arabia, Sudan, and Libya are highly reliant on shipments through this Gulf. Also, the Gulf of Aden provides access to the Suez Canal, which is strategically important for linking China with significant markets in Europe and North Africa.

In 2008, piracy increasingly threatened China's trade shipments through the Gulf of Aden when pirates hijacked numerous Chinese vessels.[15] In response to these threats to its vital interests, for the first time in modern history, China's navy (People's Liberation Navy, PLAN) deployed to engage in an operational mission, combating piracy off the Horn of Africa, outside its claimed territorial waters.[16] China first dispatched naval ships to conduct escort operations in the Gulf of Aden and the waters off Somalia on December 26, 2008.[17] The initial deployment included three of the PLAN's most advanced ships: the Lanzhou-class (Type 052C) guided-missile destroyer *Haikou*, the Guangzhou-class (Type 052B) destroyer *Wuhan*, and a Weishanhu supply ship.[18] The primary objectives of these operations were to protect Chinese vessels and personnel, guard ships delivering humanitarian supplies for international organizations, and, to the degree possible, shelter passing foreign vessels from pirate attacks.[19]

China's antipiracy operations in the Gulf of Aden have been cooperative with other nations, including the United States. It is categorized as norm convergent toward the military rules of the international system because it is in alignment with UN Security Council resolutions and actively involves cooperation with a wide range of other countries. In 2008, China announced its plans to deploy naval forces a few days after the passage of UN Security Council resolution 1851 that encouraged member states to assume a more active role in combating Somali piracy.[20]

From 2008 through the end of 2010, the Chinese navy established intelligence and information-sharing mechanisms with various countries and organizations. As of the end of December 2010, it had exchanged twenty-four boarding visits of commanders with fleets from the EU, NATO, Russia, the Republic of Korea, the Netherlands, and Japan. China conducted joint escort operations with the Russian fleet. It also participated in joint maritime exercises with Republic of Korea ships. The Chinese had exchanged officers for onboard observations with the Dutch fleet. In addition to these exercises, China had joined numerous international regimes associated with piracy in the Gulf of Aden, including the UN liaison groups that were meeting on Somali pirates and an international conference on intelligence sharing and conflict prevention in escort operations.[21]

As of the end of 2010, China had dispatched seven naval sorties with eighteen ships, sixteen helicopters, and 490 special operations forces (SOF) soldiers. Through area escort, area patrol, and onboard escort, the Chinese navy protected 3,139 ships sailing under Chinese and foreign flags, rescued 29 ships from pirate attacks, and recovered 9 ships released from captivity.[22]

Although China has cooperated with other nations and has participated in a multinational initiative, its involvement with antipiracy operations has been different from its other multilateral military behavior in the Middle East and sub-Saharan Africa. UNPKO operations are commanded by an international organization, the United Nations, and military officials from other countries often command Chinese troops. China conducts antipiracy initiatives in the Gulf of Aden in cooperation with other countries, but all Chinese naval forces remain under Chinese control in these operations. China's reluctance to join multinational taskforces formally is likely because Western governments or organizations that do not include China as a member lead the antipiracy task forces in the region. The primary task forces are the US 151 Combined Task Force (CTF), the NATO Operation Protector, and the EU Atalanta.[23] That said, over time, China's cooperation with these task forces has increased. For example, in November 2009, China hosted an international conference to coordinate antipiracy escorts. Representatives from Russia, Japan, India, the European Union, and NATO attended the meeting.[24] In November 2009, China also hosted Rear Admiral Scott E. Sanders, commander of the CTF and vice commander of the naval forces of the US Central Command, and his four-member party to visit the Chinese *Zhoushan* warship. They conducted briefings about the military strength and organization of each escort task force.[25] In January 2010, China agreed to increase its cooperative efforts, and the multinational Contact Group on Piracy off the Coast of Somalia announced that China would coordinate its operations with NATO- and EU-led task forces.[26]

As of the end of 2012, China dispatched 13 task groups, 34 warships, 28 helicopters, and 910 special forces soldiers to support the multilateral Gulf of Aden antipiracy activities. The Chinese task forces were mainly responsible for safeguarding Chinese ships and ships delivering World Food Programme supplies. They escorted almost 5,000 ships in 532 groups. Those ships included 1,150 from the Chinese mainland, 940 Hong Kong ships, 74 Taiwan ships, and 1 from Macau. While engaged in these activities, they rescued 2 Chinese ships from pirates who had boarded the vessels and 22 ships that were being chased by pirates.[27]

In 2011, Chinese vessels supporting antipiracy in the Gulf of Aden contributed to the evacuation of Chinese citizens from Libya.[28] The PLAN also played a role in evacuating Chinese citizens and other foreigners out of Yemen in 2015.[29] Supporting these types of evacuation missions, as well as fighting against piracy in the Gulf of Aden, are two important reasons why China chose to establish a military base in Djibouti.

In 2018, Xinhua News Agency noted that between 2010 and 2018, China contributed 26,000 officers and soldiers, escorted 6,595 ships, and rescued or aided 20 Chinese and foreign ships.[30] Although piracy has mostly been eradicated from the Gulf of Aden over the past several years, China continues to provide ships and personnel to support the effort. As of May 2021, the Chinese PLAN contingent included the guided-missile destroyer *Nanjing*, the missile frigate *Yangzhou*, and supply ship *Gaoyouhu*, as well as dozens of special operations soldiers and two helicopters.[31]

China's work on antipiracy is cooperative and norm convergent. It cooperates with the United States and the rest of the West through engaging in multilateral activities to combat this threat to global shipping and peace and stability in the Gulf of Aden. This type of multilateral activity to fight a security threat is very much in alignment with the liberal order, and this behavior is convergent with that order. Through antipiracy activities, China pursues its interests in ensuring its economic growth through continued access to resources and markets, and it protects its businesses and citizens abroad. Another reason China has chosen to participate in multinational antipiracy initiatives, as opposed to more unilateral action, is to demonstrate that it is a responsible great power and to improve its international image.[32] This behavior supports its interests in fostering support for China in the international arena. At the beginning of China's involvement in these operations, a Chinese scholar wrote, "China should demonstrate her soft power to the international community and show her positive image as a responsible big power, so China must also take part in the joint action of the major countries in fighting pirates."[33] China's participation in these multilateral antipiracy activities does appear to work toward building an image of a responsible great power. China shows the Middle East and sub-Saharan Africa that it is interested in resolving this hot spot issue and that the methods it uses to pursue that goal are conducted through well-respected multilateral mechanisms that are not threatening to countries in the region. China's desire to continue to contribute to these multilateral antipiracy initiatives is a significant driver for China establishing a base in Djibouti.

China's Base in Djibouti

In November 2015, China announced it was establishing an installation in Djibouti to resupply Chinese navy ships participating in the Gulf of Aden antipiracy missions[34] and signed a ten-year contract with the Djibouti government.[35] Apart from its buildup of military assets in the South China Sea before Djibouti, China's policy was to pursue no foreign basing. When the installation was initially announced, the Chinese government referred to it as a naval support facility.[36] Although the government was deeply uncomfortable with calling it a base,[37] Djibouti was a military base and is now referred to as one. Other bases in Djibouti include those of the United States, France, Italy, and Japan. Camp Lemonnier is the headquarters of the US Africa Command Joint Task Force for the Horn of Africa and houses four thousand US and allied personnel. France's Base Aerienne 188 is home to French as well as Spanish and German forces.[38]

China's military personnel first deployed to the Djibouti base in July 2017 and later that year conducted their first live-fire exercise.[39] According to the US Department of Defense, the base includes barracks, an underground facility, a tarmac, and eight hangars for helicopter and unmanned aerial vehicle (UAV) operations. It does not have a dedicated runway, but has recently completed a berthing space that can accommodate PLAN ships, including its carriers.[40] China's 2019 National Defense white paper states that the base has "provided equipment for the maintenance of four escort task groups, offered medical services for over 100 officers and sailors on board, conducted joint medical exercises with foreign militaries, and donated over 600 teaching aids to local schools."[41] It is reported that China's base will host thousands of troops, but as of September 2019, only 150 were stationed there.[42]

After its founding, the base quickly resulted in tensions between the United States and China. In May 2018, the United States issued a demarche to China over incidents of lasers pointed from the Chinese base at military aircraft that resulted in eye injuries to US pilots. China denied those allegations.[43] In 2019, the US Department of Defense again expressed concern that China had constrained international airspace by blocking American aircraft from flying over the Chinese base, fired lasers at American pilots, and flown drones to interfere with US missions. It also accused China of intrusion activity and attempts to gain access to Camp Lemonnier. In response, China has denied those allegations and complained that low-flying American aircraft have been conducting spy missions near its base.[44]

Why did China deviate from its no-foreign-basing policy and establish this base in Djibouti? Why did it choose Djibouti for its base? China pursues a number of its interests discussed in chapter 3 through this base.[45] It will, for example, enable China to protect its businesses and citizens abroad more effectively, and it supports its objective of promoting economic growth through continued access to resources and markets.

Chapter 3 discusses China's concerns about protecting its citizens and businesses in this region in detail. Together with several Chinese white papers and other government statements, China's 2015 National Security Law, clauses 28 and 30, calls for the protection of strategic energy supply channels and citizens abroad.[46] Based on its experience evacuating over 35,000 citizens from Libya in 2011 and over 600 from Yemen in 2015, China determined it needed a more permanent presence to facilitate future civilian evacuations from conflict zones in this region.[47] The Djibouti base contributes to that goal.

The location of Djibouti also provides China an opportunity to protect sea lanes of communication (SLOCs) in this region. According to Naval War College scholar Andrew Erickson, "China has likely chosen Djibouti because it provided the most secure and politically stable location near the largest number of key Chinese maritime and terrestrial interests in the region, including the supply routes for its oil imports."[48] The SLOCs are important to China's antipiracy activities. Its base in Djibouti will facilitate future support for China's PLAN participation in antipiracy activities and address other threats to the SLOCs as they occur. For years, the United States and other countries have encouraged China to stop free riding and contribute more global public goods. Positioning itself to protect these SLOCs could be China's way of providing those goods. This base also provides China the opportunity to defend its interests if the United States ceases its protection of these SLOCs or it or other powers threaten China's access to the SLOCs. According to the Chinese Ministry of Defense, Djibouti's location also ensures China can contribute to international peacekeeping and humanitarian assistance in the region[49]

In some ways, China may be attempting to demonstrate it is a responsible power by selecting Djibouti as a location for a base. Several other countries already have bases there, so China could have perceived this as a nonthreatening position for a base, especially in light of its experience with multilateral antipiracy activities in cooperation with the same countries that have bases in Djibouti.[50] Also, interview respondents indicated that one reason that China chose Djibouti was that establishing a base in an Arab country would be negatively perceived by Iran.[51]

Djibouti has economic and political significance too. China is engaged in a wide range of economic and political activities in Djibouti, including a special economic zone and a strategic partnership. It is involved as well in building Djibouti's commercial ports, infrastructure, railways, and telecommunications.[52] Ethiopia is a significant trading partner for China, and Djibouti serves as Ethiopia's only port.[53] Djibouti also encouraged China to provide a base in its country because bases generate much-needed government revenues.[54]

Unlike China's UNPKO, conventional arms sales, and multilateral antipiracy activities, the base in Djibouti is competitive behavior. China has unilaterally established a military base that provides it the opportunity to project power. Although China primarily claims a need to protect its businesses and citizens with the base, it also facilitates China's ability to build up its military capability in the Horn of Africa. Positioned next to the US base, China's Djibouti base could be interpreted as an attempt to build its military capability relative to the United States.

Although the behavior is competitive, it is also norm neutral. There is no relevant liberal norm governing basing. That said, it is common practice for great powers to establish military bases to support their foreign interests. Several powers, including the United States and France, already have bases in Djibouti, so China's establishment of its base converges with that behavior. Also, at this point, the base's purpose is to support the multilateral, norm-convergent behavior discussed earlier in the chapter, including supporting multilateral antipiracy activities in the Gulf of Aden, providing public goods, protecting SLOCs, participating in UNPKO, and evacuating Chinese citizens out of harm's way if violence erupts in countries in this region.

Establishing this base is yet another way China is developing influence in Africa and the Middle East. That said, it could be argued that China is portraying itself as a responsible great power that is setting up the base to support its participation in multilateral activities through international institutions, evacuate its citizens in case of emergency, and participating in humanitarian assistance. China is still differentiating itself from other great powers that possess a more robust military presence in this region, such as the United States and France.

Conclusion

China's military behavior in the Middle East and sub-Saharan Africa seeks to ensure its continued economic growth through access to resources and markets. It also strives to protect its businesses and citizens in these regions and to foster support for it in the international system.

In contrast with China's competitive political, economic, and foreign aid behavior in the Middle East and sub-Saharan Africa, most of its military behavior in this region is cooperative with the United States and the West. UNPKO and antipiracy activities are conducted jointly with the United States and other Western countries through international organizations and multilateral mechanisms. China works with Western countries to pursue the stabilization of conflict and reducing the risks of piracy. Also, over time, China's conventional arms sales to these regions compared to the past have been cooperative due to their minimal nature. One exception to China's cooperative behavior is its base in Djibouti. China unilaterally established this base, and it could provide it the capability to compete with the United States in this region. There have already been several incidents between this Chinese base and the US base in Djibouti.

Most of China's military behavior described in this chapter is norm convergent. In alignment with the liberal norm of nonproliferation, China's conventional arms sales to these regions have been minimal. UNPKO and antipiracy are in alignment with the Western liberal order because they emphasize collective security and using multilateral mechanisms to address security challenges.

China's base in Djibouti is norm neutral because there is no relevant liberal norm governing basing. Similar to many other great powers, China has established a base in Djibouti. So far, the use of this base supports China's other norm-convergent behavior described in this chapter.

At this point, China is not building an alternative military order in the Middle East and sub-Saharan Africa. Overall, it is relying on existing architecture such as UN and multilateral antipiracy activities. Its base in Djibouti is its first overseas base and does not constitute a new security order.

By operating primarily through international organizations and multilateral organizations, China portrays itself as a great power that cooperates with others in the realm of security in this region. Its deliberate use of multilateral mechanisms could be understood as a way it signals it does not have territorial aspirations or unilateral military goals in these regions and wants to cooperate with other countries in seeking security solutions to hot spot issues in these regions.

The previous chapters introduced China's post–Cold War economic, political, and military behavior in the Middle East and sub-Saharan Africa. The next chapter explores how China's Belt and Road integrates these instruments of power to pursue China's broader strategic objectives in these regions.

CHAPTER 9

BELT AND ROAD AND CHINA'S RELATIONS WITH THE MIDDLE EAST AND SUB-SAHARAN AFRICA

Since 2013, China's Belt and Road Initiative (BRI) has become a foreign policy priority for President Xi Jinping's administration.[1] Interpreted narrowly, BRI is a project encompassing a suite of investment and foreign aid tools to enhance China's economic interactions with almost 140 countries in Central Asia, Southeast Asia, South Asia, the Middle East, Africa, Europe, Latin America, and the Arctic.[2] In this vein, much current analysis examines BRI in economic terms focused on Chinese outbound investment and trade, the need to develop poor Western regions within China (especially Xinjiang), and a desire by the government to provide opportunities for struggling Chinese state-owned enterprises. In contrast, this chapter argues BRI is a strategic initiative building on decades of China's interactions with these regions that aims to facilitate China's growth as a Eurasian power across all domains (economic, political, military, and foreign aid).[3] Increasing Sino-American competition in Asia and globally fuels BRI's development. This chapter explores how the Belt and Road strategy interacts with China's overall approach toward the Middle East and sub-Saharan Africa discussed throughout this book.

The primary questions driving this chapter are: What is the Belt and Road in the Middle East and sub-Saharan Africa? Does China's BRI cooperate or compete with the United States in these regions? Does BRI converge with or diverge from international norms? Through Belt and Road, is China building an alternative international order in these regions? If so, what are the characteristics of that order? How does China portray and differentiate itself as a great power in these regions? How is it building spheres of influence? Ultimately, what does China's BRI behavior in the Middle East and sub-Saharan Africa indicate about its rise globally?

China uses the Belt and Road to pursue all of its interests in the Middle East and sub-Saharan Africa discussed in chapter 3: promoting domestic economic growth through access to both resources and markets, fostering support in the international arena in an era of emerging multipolarity or bipolarity, protecting domestic stability from Muslim separatists in Xinjiang and the radicalization of Muslims throughout China, advocating for developing country causes including a just and equitable new economic and political order, safeguarding its citizens and businesses abroad, and protecting its territorial integrity and sovereignty from the United States. Belt and Road integrates the foreign policy tools discussed in this book to achieve those goals.

Analyzing China's Belt and Road generates essential insights about how China is competing in these regions and diverging from or converging with international norms. Examining BRI shows how China is developing spheres of influence, approaching the rules of the system, and building a new political, economic, and foreign aid order in these regions. It also provides insights into how China is portraying itself as a great power and how it conceptualizes the linkage among its economic, political, foreign aid, and military activities in these regions.

This chapter differs from others in this book in some fundamental ways. Its purpose is to discuss how China is using Belt and Road as an overarching strategy that uses all of its instruments of power to achieve its objectives. Previous chapters provided a detailed analysis of the foreign policy tools in this chapter. This chapter discusses how China incorporates those specific tools into its strategy.

This chapter asserts that overall, China's behavior in the BRI is competitive with the United States in the economic, political, and foreign aid spheres. One significant purpose of Belt and Road is to establish positive economic and political relations with countries to its west as a contingency if ties with the United States or countries in Pacific Asia deteriorate. At this point, China's military behavior in support of BRI is limited and is primarily cooperative. Although China's economic, political, and foreign aid behavior is competitive, its behavior in those functional areas diverges from and converges with the liberal international order. One needs to consider the specific foreign policy tools to determine China's approach to the international order in these regions through BRI. This chapter explores those nuances.

Power Transition and China's Emerging Grand Strategy

The world is in the midst of a potential power transition between the United States and China. The United States now identifies a rising China as its top long-term national security threat.[4] Increasingly, it stresses that China is a competitor, rival, and revisionist across functional domains (military, political, and economic).[5] According to some scholars, a dissatisfied rising power will attempt to change the rules governing the international system, the division of spheres of influence, and the international distribution of territory.[6] Chapters 4 through 8 argue that as China's power grows, it is increasingly engaging in competitive and norm-divergent political, economic, and foreign aid behavior in the Middle East and sub-Saharan Africa as it seeks to challenge the rules of the international system and develop spheres of influence. That said, unlike its behavior in Asia, there is no indication that China is challenging the international distribution of territory in the Middle East and sub-Saharan Africa. Its military behavior in these regions remains primarily cooperative and norm convergent.

As it rises and competes with the United States globally, China's grand strategy is emerging to pursue its interests and ensure its security. One crucial component of that grand strategy is BRI. This chapter argues that Belt and Road is a Chinese strategy driven by economic requirements for resources and markets, political needs for support in the international system, and geostrategic desires to assert itself as a Eurasian power and develop strategic alternatives if relations with the United States and China's Asia-Pacific neighbors sour. It seeks to understand what BRI is and how China uses it to compete or cooperate with the United States and the rest of the West. It also explores how BRI converges with and diverges from the liberal international order.

What Is the Belt and Road?

BRI is China's new geopolitical strategy to become a Eurasian power and balance against the United States in an era of increasing tensions in Asia Pacific. China announced the first formal elements of what is now called Belt and Road in 2013. While holding talks with counterparts in Uzbekistan, Tajikistan, and Kyrgyzstan in September 2013, Xi Jinping started to promote the "Silk Road Economic Belt," which eventually became the land-based component of BRI.[7] In October, Xi encouraged maritime cooperation with Association of Southeast Asian Nations (ASEAN) while visiting Indonesia by introducing the concept of a "21st Century Maritime Silk Road" that became the maritime aspect of BRI with initial projects in Southeast Asia, East Africa, India, and the Middle East. China combined the maritime Silk Road and economic belt into one initiative in March 2015. At first, China referred to the initiative as One Belt One Road in English, but over time, the Chinese government started using the term *Belt and Road Initiative*. The Chinese name has stayed the same.

The National Development and Reform Commission (NDRC) of the PRC officially announced the Belt and Road in a report issued in March 2015" "The Belt and Road Initiative aims to promote the connectivity of Asian, European, and African continents and their adjacent seas, establish and strengthen partnerships with countries along the Belt and Road, set up all-dimensional, multi-tiered and composite connectivity networks and realize diversified, independent, balanced and sustainable development in these countries." The report stressed that BRI aligns with the purpose and principles of the United Nations Charter as well as China's Five Principles of Peaceful Coexistence. It also highlighted the inherently global nature of the BRI: "It is open for cooperation. It covers, but is not limited to, the area of the ancient Silk Road. It is open to all countries, and international and regional organizations for engagement, so that the results of the concerted efforts will benefit wider areas."[8]

The original 2015 NDRC report on BRI highlighted cooperation priorities in policy coordination, facilities connectivity, unimpeded trade, financial integration, and people-to-people interaction. It also stressed that BRI should enhance the role of existing multilateral cooperation mechanisms (e.g., Shanghai Cooperation Organization, China-Arab States Cooperation Forum, China-Gulf Cooperation Council Strategic Dialogue).

In May 2017, China held its first Belt and Road Forum.[9] In the keynote address, Xi Jinping noted that over one hundred countries and international organizations were involved in BRI, which was already making progress in the critical areas of policy, infrastructure, trade, financial, and people-to-people connectivity. He also stressed that BRI required a peaceful and stable environment and urged participant countries to work together to resolve hot spot issues through political means, increase counterterrorism efforts, and strive to "eradicate poverty, backwardness and social injustice."[10]

BRI has since become a key foreign policy priority of the Xi administration. His work report to the Chinese Communist Party's Nineteenth Party Congress in 2017 stressed the BRI.[11] During the party congress, the Chinese Communist Party enshrined the BRI in the party constitution.[12]

The BRI continues to expand globally. Although the original regions of emphasis were Southeast Asia, Central Asia, South Asia, the Middle East, Africa, and Europe, in early 2018, China invited the thirty-one members of the Community of Latin American and Caribbean States (CELAC) to join the BRI.[13] In January 2018, China also started to articulate its vision of the "Polar Silk Road" and the inclusion of the Arctic in the BRI.[14] China's Arctic policy white paper explicitly refers to the Arctic in the BRI.[15] During the COVID-19 pandemic, China even began to refer to a Health Silk Road. With the addition of these regions, BRI is now more than just a Eurasian initiative. Increasingly, BRI is a new vision for China's role in the world and highlights how it portrays itself as a responsible great power.

China held its second BRI forum in 2019. During his keynote speech, Xi Jinping noted that more than 150 countries and international organizations had signed agreements on Belt and Road cooperation with China.[16] The forum continued to stress multilateral cooperation with countries in scope for BRI as well as many specific initiatives synergizing development policy, infrastructure connectivity, and sustainable development.[17]

Is Belt and Road a Strategy in the Middle East and Sub-Saharan Africa?

For years, scholars have debated whether China has a strategy in the Middle East and sub-Saharan Africa. This chapter uses Hal Brands's definition of *strategy*: "Grand strategy is a purposeful and coherent set of ideas about what a nation seeks to accomplish in the world, and how it should go about doing so."[18] It is essentially the coordinated use of instruments of power (e.g., economic, political, and military) to achieve a state's objectives. Before Xi Jinping announced the Silk Road Economic Belt and the 21st Century Maritime Silk Road in 2013, analysts could convincingly argue that it was challenging to determine that China had a strategy in these regions. Analysts often characterized China's behavior as ad hoc or pragmatic with a lack of coordination.

The rise of Xi Jinping and the emergence of BRI has now answered that question in a much more definitive way: BRI is China's strategy toward the Middle East and sub-Saharan Africa. It coordinates and leverages China's political, economic, foreign aid, and military activities in these regions to meet China's objectives. As China is building an alternative international order and spheres of influence in the Middle East and sub-Saharan Africa, BRI is the conceptual umbrella encompassing that order. Many of the foreign policy tools that can now be considered part of BRI predate it. As seen in other chapters of this book, some of these foreign policy tools have been used since the 1950s, and most of them started long before BRI. The significance of BRI is that it provides a coherent and unified approach to the ways China leverages these preexisting foreign policy tools. Also, since China announced BRI, the use of some of these foreign policy tools is increasing to support the initiative's objectives.

The Chinese government vehemently denies that BRI is a strategy.[19] In March 2018, in an article pointedly titled "Govt: Wrong to Label Belt and Road Initiative a Geo-Strategic Tool," Xinhua reported, "It is a misinterpretation to regard the country's Belt and Road Initiative as China's geo-strategic tool as the initiative is aimed at pursuing shared benefit for all parties involved, a spokesman said during the opening news conference of the first session of the 13th National People's Congress."[20] Despite that denial, Belt and Road appears to be an emerging strategy to use all instruments of power to pursue China's interests and ensure its security.

What does China seek to accomplish in the Middle East and sub-Saharan Africa? What are its objectives? As discussed in detail in chapter 3, China's primary post–Cold War interests (objectives) in the Middle East and sub-Saharan Africa are to:

- Promote China's domestic economic growth through access to both resources and markets
- Foster support for China in the international arena in an era of emerging multipolarity or bipolarity
- Protect China's domestic stability from Muslim separatists in Xinjiang and the radicalization of Muslims throughout China
- Advocate for developing country causes including a just and equitable new economic and political order
- Safeguard China's citizens and businesses abroad
- Protect China's territorial integrity and sovereignty from the United States.

The BRI contains specific policy tools to address all of these interests.

China Marches West

BRI as a strategy to promote China's interests and balance against the United States emerged with the deterioration of US-China relations in the early 2010s. In response to the Obama-era Rebalance to Asia[21] and increasingly heated disputes in Pacific Asia, primarily related to the South China Sea, the East China Sea, and North Korea, China started to emphasize strengthening relations with countries to its west.[22] Both the Middle East and Africa are part of that westward push. Chinese scholarly writings, Chinese government documents, and interview data for this project provide evidence for this linkage.

The first significant public articulation of the need for China to start to look west in reaction to souring relations with the United States in Pacific Asia occurred in 2012. Scholar Wang Jisi's argued from 2011 to 2015 that China needed to "March West" in response to rising tensions in Pacific Asia. [23] The Chinese government appears to be pursuing that strategy.[24]

One of the primary manifestations of China's March West approach is the BRI.[25] The initiative primarily includes the Middle East and sub-Saharan Africa, as well as Central Asia, South Asia, Southeast Asia, Europe, Latin America, and the Arctic. Although Chinese government documents do not tend to articulate a direct linkage between the BRI's westward focus and rising tensions in Pacific Asia, the announcement of BRI in 2015 occurs in parallel with increasing Chinese rhetoric about rising tensions to its East.[26]

In recent years, interviewees for this project have started to stress that China's Belt and Road initiative, including its enhanced relations with the Middle East and sub-Saharan Africa, is a direct response to the US rebalance and that BRI is a significant part of China's global strategy to balance against the United States.[27] They emphasize that as the United States shifts east, China is going west to the Middle East and Africa to avoid future conflict with the United States.[28]

If Belt and Road is a strategy largely driven by concerns about competition with the United States in the Asia Pacific and globally, that dynamic is likely to intensify over time. Since the end of 2017, the United States has characterized Sino-American relations as more competitive from a US perspective. For example, the December 2017 National Security Strategy, the 2018 Summary of the National Defense Strategy, and the 2018 Nuclear Posture Review characterize China as a competitor, a rival, and a revisionist state.[29] Also, the United States increasingly portrays China as a competitor across military, political, and economic functional domains.[30] This competitive dynamic will only increase the strategic importance of BRI for China.

Foreign Policy Tools Encompassed by BRI in the Middle East and sub-Saharan Africa

This section highlights briefly some of the economic, foreign aid, political, and military foreign policy tools now encompassed under the strategy of Belt and Road in the Middle East and sub-Saharan Africa.

Cooperation Forums

China's Forum on China-Africa Cooperation (FOCAC) and the China-Arab States Cooperation Forum (CASCF) are its primary multilateral political, economic, foreign aid, and security coordination mechanisms with the Middle East and sub-Saharan Africa.

CASCF's focus on BRI began even before BRI was officially announced. The 2014 CACSF declaration and ten-year plan contain the first mention of the Silk Road Economic Belt and Maritime Silk Road:[31] "The Arab side welcomes China's initiative on the construction of the `Silk Road Economic Belt' and `21st Century Maritime Silk Road', the two sides are willing to further expand bilateral trade and mutual investment in Arab states, and focus on active cooperation in the following areas: to promote infrastructure construction, promote the development of industrial cooperation in Arab States, especially the deepening energy, finance, human resources cooperation."[32] The 2016 CASCF declaration and ten-year plan further expand the scope of BRI cooperation between China and Arab states to include nuclear energy, space satellites, new energy, and Arab capacity strengthening.[33] The 2018 and 2020 CASCF documents continued to stress the importance of BRI in cooperation between China and Arab states.

FOCAC documents started to stress BRI in 2015. The 2015 FOCAC declaration committed both sides to "actively explore the linkages between China's initiatives of building the Silk Road Economic Belt and 21st Century Maritime Silk Road and Africa's economic integration and sustainable development agenda, and seek more opportunities to promote common development and realize our common dreams."[34]

As of the 2018 meetings of FOCAC and CASCF, these cooperation forums are now framed as falling under the BRI. The 2018 FOCAC declaration states, "We recognize that the FOCAC mechanism is increasingly efficient and has become a leading player in international cooperation with Africa. We agree to uphold the existing mechanism and preserve its uniqueness and strengths to further advance China-Africa relations and cooperation in the new era. We also agree to make the Forum a major platform for China-Africa cooperation under the Belt and Road Initiative."[35] The 2018 CASCF even issued a separate declaration, specifically discussing Arab-China cooperation under the BRI.[36]

CASCF and FOCAC are China's primary multilateral coordination mechanisms under Belt and Road. Through these cooperation forums under BRI, China pursues all of its interests discussed in chapter 3. The forums promote and facilitate BRI's connectivity in policy coordination, connectivity, unimpeded trade, financial integration, and people-to-people interaction. China's behavior in these forums is mostly competitive and norm divergent in the functional areas of economics, political, and foreign aid. Its security behavior in these forums as a whole is limited.

Government Support for Chinese Companies

China's economic interests in the Middle East and sub-Saharan Africa or resources and markets dramatically increased from 1990. Its most prominent corporate actors are state-owned enterprises (SOEs), and the vast majority of on-the-ground Chinese company activity is in energy, mining, construction, telecommunications, and finance. Over the past two decades, the Chinese government has actively encouraged these enterprises to pursue opportunities in the Middle East and sub-Saharan Africa. In addition to the fact that these enterprises are ultimately owned and controlled by the Chinese state, the state guides the behavior of these enterprises through many initiatives. These companies receive direct and indirect government subsidies, favorable financing in the form of generous credit lines and low-interest loans from state-owned banks, preferential awarding of construction contracts tied to concessional loans, expedited mandatory approvals for large-scale overseas foreign direct investment (OFDI) activities, and political support, particularly via FOCAC and CASCF. These companies have been encouraged to pursue overseas opportunities in target industries and regions through the creation of national champions, going out/going global programs, and initiatives announced in the cooperation forums.

Since the announcement of BRI in 2015, all of this state support for Chinese companies should be considered part of BRI. This support facilitates the trade, facilities, investment, and financial connectivity encouraged through BRI. Chinese government support for companies helps China pursue its interests in promoting its domestic economic growth through access to resources and markets. China's state support for companies is competitive as well as norm divergent from the liberal economic norms of free-market economics and limited state involvement in the economy.

Financing for BRI Projects in the Middle East and Sub-Saharan Africa

Financing for BRI projects is primarily facilitated through bilateral funding mechanisms such as the Silk Road Fund, China Development Bank, and the Export-Import Bank of China. Other encouraged sources of funding include multilateral banks such as the China-initiated Asian Infrastructure and Investment Bank (AIIB),[37] the BRICS New Development Bank, and the World Bank.[38] (See chapter 4 for a discussion of China's financing of projects in the Middle East and sub-Saharan Africa through FOCAC and CASCF.) Financing BRI projects through these various mechanisms helps China promote its domestic economic growth through access to both resources and markets and, in some cases, advocate for developing country causes including a just and equitable new economic order.

The classification of these financing mechanisms depends on the characteristics of lending organizations. China's use of multilateral mechanisms such as the World Bank is cooperative and norm convergent with the liberal order. Its use of unilateral mechanisms that lack transparency and have a strong relationship with the Chinese state, such as the Silk Road Fund, China Development Bank, and Chexim bank, tend to be competitive and norm divergent from the liberal order. Organizations such as the AIIB and BRICS New Development bank fall somewhere in the middle. They are not necessarily cooperative with the United States, but they cooperate with many other great and regional powers and are, in many ways, providing financing in alignment with Western standards and liberal norms.

Foreign Aid for the Middle East and Sub-Saharan Africa

Although China often publicizes its foreign aid in cooperation forums, assistance tends to be provided on a bilateral basis by China's Ministry of Commerce. Aid is an important tool for BRI. Together with China's other BRI economic and political tools, foreign aid helps China build spheres of influence in these regions. (See chapter 4 for a discussion of foreign aid in China's cooperation forums and chapter 6 for discussion of the role of China's foreign aid in these regions to support trade, services, and investment, as well as building political support for China in these regions.)

China's foreign aid under BRI helps it to promote its domestic economic growth through access to resources and markets by providing funding for Chinese companies to engage in economic activity in developing countries; foster support for China in the international arena in an era of emerging multipolarity or bipolarity; and advocate for developing country causes, including a just and equitable new economic and political order.

China's foreign aid is competitive with the West and in some ways diverges from liberal international norms. China's provision of aid generally is in alignment with the international expectation that great powers will engage in assisting less developed countries. Chinese aid through concessional loans diverges from liberal international norms because it is allocated without consideration for local regime type and governance. The only political condition of Chinese aid is that the country must support the one-China principle.

One emerging criticism of China's foreign aid through the BRI is that it is engaging in debt-trap diplomacy.[39] This book does not explicitly explore those allegations, but China's special envoy for Africa actively speaks out against these sorts of accusations. Also, China's FOCAC meetings in 2018 explicitly attempted to alleviate cooperation forum members' concerns about debt-trap diplomacy, and documents from the 2020 China-AU-FOCAC COVID summit discuss debt relief for African countries.

Free Trade Agreements

Another economic foreign policy tool that supports BRI is free trade agreements. In the Middle East, China is negotiating free trade agreements with the GCC (Gulf Cooperation Council), Israel, and Palestine. In sub-Saharan Africa, it has signed a free trade agreement with Mauritius. (Chapter 6 provides a more detailed analysis of the FTAs China is pursuing in these regions.) In addition, China provides unilateral tariff-free trade benefits to all LDC countries in Africa and the Middle East. (That tariff treatment is discussed in more detail in chapter 4 on cooperation forums.)

These free trade agreements and tariff-free trade promote trade connectivity under BRI. They support China's interest in promoting its economic growth through access to resources and markets. This behavior is competitive but norm convergent because it promotes free trade and institutions to promote trade cooperation. Also, the WTO allows regional trade agreements, and the international community encourages tariff-free trade with less developed economies.

Special Economic Zones

Special economic zones (SEZs) are another important economic tool of BRI. China is establishing special economic zones in the Middle East and sub-Saharan Africa. Under BRI, these SEZs enable China to promote its domestic economic growth through access to both resources and markets, foster support for China in the international arena in an era of emerging multipolarity or bipolarity, and advocate for developing country causes, including a just and equitable new economic order.

The SEZs are competitive but norm neutral. They are competitive because they are building influence for China and are an important example of South-South cooperation. Their purpose is to share China's development with developing countries and encourage economic development in less developed economies. That said, they are norm neutral because there are no relevant liberal norms governing the formation of SEZs.

Between 1990 and 2018, China's companies launched eleven SEZs in sub-Saharan Africa and the Middle East. FOCAC highly publicizes these zones (see chapter 5). These SEZs are located in Algeria, Djibouti, Egypt, Ethiopia, Kenya, Mauritius, Mauritania, Nigeria (two), Oman, and Zambia. (For a detailed discussion of these zones, see chapter 6.)

Agricultural Technology Demonstration Centers

China first announced its plans to promote agricultural technology demonstration centers at the 2006 FOCAC meeting. Between 2006 and 2018, it launched centers in nineteen countries throughout Africa: Angola, Benin, Cameroon, Democratic Republic of Congo, Ethiopia, Gabon, Liberia, Mauritania, Mozambique, the Republic of Congo, Senegal, Rwanda, South Africa, Sudan, Tanzania, Togo, Uganda, Zambia, and Zimbabwe. Fourteen of nineteen of the demonstration centers have been established in LDCs. Most of the centers focus on a diverse set of agricultural needs, including rice, corn, soy, livestock, and fisheries. All of the centers are in sub-Saharan Africa. None are in the Middle East. Chinese agricultural companies run the centers (e.g., the China National Agricultural Corporation) or province-level agriculture institutes. (For an in-depth discussion of these agricultural technology demonstration centers, see chapter 6.) These centers help China promote its domestic economic growth through access to both resources and markets, foster support for China in the international arena in an era of emerging multipolarity or bipolarity, and advocate for developing country causes including a just and equitable new economic and political order.

Similar to its SEZs, China's behavior in agricultural technology demonstration centers is competitive but norm neutral. China uses these centers to compete for influence and gain support from South-South cooperation. Through these centers, China is sharing its agricultural development expertise with LDCs. They are norm neutral because there are no relevant liberal norms governing them. These SEZs are a highly publicized aspect of BRI that facilitates Chinese SMEs to enter into markets in the Middle East and sub-Saharan Africa.

Strategic Partnerships

Strategic partnerships are important political tools under BRI. China established a strategic partnership with Africa as a continent at the 2006 FOCAC Summit and with the League of Arab States via the CASCF in 2010. To date, China has initiated strategic partnerships with the following countries in the Middle East: Egypt (1999), Algeria (2004), Turkey (2010), the United Arab Emirates (2012), Qatar (2014), Jordan (2015), Iraq (2015), Iran (2016), Morocco (2016), Saudi Arabia (2016), Oman (2018), and Kuwait (2018). In sub-Saharan Africa, it has established strategic partnerships with South Africa (2000), Nigeria (2005), Angola (2010), Ethiopia (2014), Sudan (2015), Gabon (2015), Sierra Leone (2016), Republic of Congo (2016), Mozambique (2016), Guinea (2016), Senegal (2016), Kenya (2017), Djibouti (2017), Zimbabwe (2018), and Namibia (2018). Since China launched the BRI in 2015, China has strongly emphasized establishing strategic partnerships with countries in these regions.

In BRI, China uses strategic partnerships to foster support it in the international arena in an era of emerging multipolarity or bipolarity, advocate for developing country causes including a just and equitable new economic and political order by establishing partnerships with many developing countries, and protect China's territorial integrity and sovereignty from the United States by seeking explicit support for China's South China Sea claims in the declaration of these strategic partnerships. Strategic partnerships also contain economic elements, so they facilitate China's economic growth through access to resources and markets. Chapter 7 provides a detailed analysis of these strategic partnerships. They are competitive with the United States and the rest of the West by building political influence in these regions but norm neutral because there are no relevant norms governing them. That said, they are very much in alignment with the behavior of other great powers.

Antipiracy Operations

Even before China announced the BRI, the free flow of goods through the Gulf of Aden had become an important interest due to its desire to maintain access to resources and markets in this region and protect its businesses and citizens from harm. Trade connectivity is an important component of BRI. The Gulf of Aden leads to several African countries, Middle Eastern countries, and the Suez Canal and is the quickest sea route from China to Europe and many countries in the Americas.

In 2008, piracy increasingly threatened China's trade shipments through the Gulf of Aden, with pirates hijacking numerous Chinese vessels. In response to these threats to its economic interests, for the first time in modern history, China's navy (People's Liberation Navy, PLAN) deployed to engage in an operational mission outside East Asia and the Pacific. The primary objectives of these antipiracy operations were to protect Chinese ships and personnel, guard ships delivering humanitarian supplies for international organizations, and shelter passing foreign vessels from pirate attacks.

Although piracy in the Gulf of Aden has decreased significantly over the years, China's involvement in multilateral initiatives to protect the Gulf, as well as potential future activities in other emerging areas of piracy (e.g., the Gulf of Guinea), is an essential part of protecting its BRI connectivity with these regions. This engagement continues to this day. (Chapter 8 provides a discussion of China's role in fighting piracy in the Gulf of Aden.)

These antipiracy activities promote China's domestic economic growth through access to both resources and markets; foster support for China in the international arena in an era of emerging multipolarity or bipolarity by engaging in cooperative, multilateral security cooperation; and safeguard China's citizens and businesses abroad. This behavior is particularly important in protecting the maritime components of the BRI.

This antipiracy security behavior is cooperative. China is fighting piracy with a multilateral group of countries, including the United States and the rest of the West. This utilization of a multilateral mechanism to address this security concern is convergent with the liberal order.

China's Base in Djibouti

In 2015, China announced its first overseas base in Djibouti. The base opened in 2017. Very much in alignment with the BRI, China's justifications for establishing this base include the need to fight piracy, protect Chinese citizens abroad, and ensure freedom of navigation through sea lanes of communication. The base is not listed in official BRI documents. Nevertheless, a convincing case can be made that BRI engagement increasingly necessitates an overseas military presence in this region to protect China's economic and political interests. (Chapter 8 discusses this new base.)

The base supports China's interests by promoting its domestic economic growth through access to both resources and markets, safeguarding China's citizens and businesses abroad, and protecting China's territorial integrity and sovereignty from the United States.

China's base in Djibouti is competitive but norm neutral because there are no liberal norms governing the establishment of global bases. Many great powers have bases in Djibouti, so this behavior is in alignment with the behavior of other great powers. That said, the base is competitive because it does increase China's capacity to project power into the Gulf of Aden region.

Conclusion

BRI is a geopolitical strategy that aims to establish China as a Eurasian power and balance against the United States in an era of increasing tensions in the Pacific Asia. First announced in 2013 as a land belt and maritime road, the BRI is evolving into a grand strategy that is enshrined in the Chinese Party Constitution. BRI coordinates the utilization of a wide range of instruments of power to achieve China's goals.

In the Middle East and sub-Saharan Africa, China's objectives are to secure resources and markets to fuel its domestic economic growth, build political support in an increasingly multipolar or bipolar world, ensure its internal stability by preventing the spread of violence from the Middle East to Xinjiang by securing support for Arab states for its activities to suppress potential insurgency within China, advocate for developing country causes and build a just and equitable new political and economic order, protect

Chinese citizens and businesses, and balance against an increasingly threatening United States. BRI works to support all of those needs.

As we enter a potential power transition between the United States and China and an increasingly competitive dynamic in the relations between the two states, BRI is the way China is challenging the international system and building new spheres of influence. If relations between the United States and China sour and the current international order unravel, China is already building an institutional infrastructure to take its place. The content of BRI and the accompanying foreign policy tools discussed in this chapter provide initial glimpses into the content of that new order.

Broadly, BRI is a strategy for China to become a Eurasian power. To implement that strategy, in the Middle East and sub-Saharan Africa, it is using a wide range of foreign policy tools across instruments of power (economic, political, and military). Many of these tools predate BRI and have been used for decades. As BRI becomes China's grand strategy, China is increasingly using it as a way to tie together its disparate economic, political, foreign aid, and military activities in the Middle East and sub-Saharan Africa. The tools highlighted in this chapter include China's cooperation forums, government support for Chinese companies, financing for BRI projects, foreign aid, strategic partnerships, free trade agreements, special economic zones, agricultural technology demonstration centers, antipiracy activities, and a base in Djibouti.[40]

China competes with the United States through the BRI in the economic, political, and foreign aid spheres.[41] It is using the concept of the BRI and the tools encompassed within it to increase its influence in the Middle East and sub-Saharan Africa. It uses BRI to leverage connections between its economic, political, and military instruments of power. This integration provides China an opportunity to amplify its power. Although its economic, political, and foreign aid behavior is competitive, its military behavior within BRI in these regions has been mostly cooperative.

One primary driver of the development of BRI was increasing tension between the United States and China. The United States increasingly characterizes BRI as competitive behavior from China across instruments of power.[42] BRI allows China to march West and develop relationships with countries that may in the future balance against the United States. It also provides China with alternative political and economic opportunities to its West as its relations with the United States continue to deteriorate.

Although China's economic, political, and foreign aid behavior in BRI is primarily competitive, some of its behavior is norm divergent from the liberal order, some is norm convergent, and some norm neutral. China competes inside and outside the liberal order through BRI. Reflecting its own domestic political and economic system, most of the divergence with the international order is over issues of sovereignty and the relationship between state and economic activities. China's political behavior in its cooperation forum is norm divergent through its strong advocacy for the Five Principles. Its economic behavior in the forums and state support for Chinese companies are mostly norm divergent from liberal economic norms of free markets and limited state involvement in the economy. China's foreign aid provision diverges from norms of good governance in the Western order. That said, China's behavior in FTAs, antipiracy activities, and its base in Djibouti are norm convergent. Its SEZs, agricultural technology demonstration centers, and strategic partnerships are all norm neutral in relation to the liberal order. China's behavior with these tools is in alignment with other great powers, and much of its behavior is focused on sharing its development experiences with less developed countries.

Through Belt and Road, China is building alternative economic and political international orders in these regions. Its cooperation forums provide the foundation of those new orders, and the economic and political tools discussed in this chapter are components of those orders. That said, China is not building a new military order in these regions. Aside from its one base in Djibouti, its military activities to support BRI are all conducted through multilateral organizations that are aligned with the liberal order.

The normative foundations of the order China is building with BRI are connectivity (trade, infrastructure, investment, finance, policy, and people-to-people), the contribution of economic development to stability, a strict interpretation of Westphalian sovereignty through the Five Principles, substantial Chinese state support for economic activities of Chinese companies in these regions, South-South solidarity, support for Arab causes (especially the Palestinians), and the importance of providing aid and assistance to less developed countries and advocating for developing country causes. China built its cooperation forums and other foreign policy tools on those normative foundations. Through the BRI, China also encourages robust engagement with international and regional economic and political organizations.

In some ways, this order converges with the current international order, both Westphalian and liberal. In other ways, it diverges.

China uses BRI as a way to differentiate itself from other great powers. The initiative stresses China's support for development and building connectivity throughout the world. It provides an opportunity for China to articulate a positive image of its role in the world as a driver of economic development, trade, connectivity, and globalization while continuing to act as a champion of sovereignty and advocate for developing countries.

CHAPTER 10

CONCLUSION

In 1970, scholar Peter Van Ness described China's behavior during the early Cold War era:

> The Chinese apparently saw the Third World as the area of greatest political opportunity in the contemporary world scene. It was a world in flux, one in which old political orders and alliances were crumbling and new ones being formed—an area where new friends could be won, old balances of power upset, and powerful new alliances established. . . . The Peking government saw in the volatile conditions of Asia, Africa and Latin America, its best chance to influence world politics and to apply most fruitfully China's limited resources toward the attainment of foreign policy objectives.[1]

These words may equally apply to China's role in the Middle East and sub-Saharan Africa and the way it is approaching the Global South today.

The primary purpose of this book is to understand China's rise in these regions and globally better. It explores a number of questions: What are China's interests in the Middle East and sub-Saharan Africa? How and why have they changed over time? How and why is China cooperating or competing with the United States in these regions? How and why is China's behavior converging with or diverging from international norms in these regions? How and why does China's behavior vary across regions? How and why does China's behavior vary across functional areas in these regions? Since the beginning of the Arab awakening, how has China's behavior toward these regions changed? Is increasing competition between the United States and China in Pacific Asia affecting China's behavior in the Middle East and sub-Saharan Africa? Is China building an alternative international order in these regions? If yes, what are the characteristics of that order? How does China portray and differentiate itself as a great power in these regions? How is it building spheres of influence? Ultimately, what does China's behavior in the Middle East and sub-Saharan Africa indicate about its rise globally?

This book argues that although China does not seek to change the international distribution of territory in the Middle East and sub-Saharan Africa, as its power grows, it increasingly competes with the United States and the rest of the West, challenges the rules of the liberal international system, and builds spheres of influence in these regions. China is constructing an alternative international order to interact with these regions. If the current liberal international system unravels due to China's or US actions, this alternative order will serve as the foundation of China's economic, political, and military relations with the Middle East and sub-Saharan Africa, as well as much of the rest of the developing world. In an era of emerging great power competition, it is both theoretically and practically essential to understand the specific features of that order and how China competes and builds influence. This book explores the characteristics of that competition and emerging order. It also provides insights into how increasing Sino-American tensions, criticism, and backlash against BRI and China's response to COVID-19 may shape that competition in the future.

China's Interests

China's domestic economic and political system, as well as the international environment, shape its interests and perception of external threats in the Middle East and sub-Saharan Africa. During the Mao era, its interests in these regions were promoting revolution through national liberation movements, building support for China in the international system, balancing against the United States and the Soviet Union, and advocating for third world causes. After Mao's death in 1976 and the beginning of Deng Xiaoping's economic and political reforms, China turned inward to focus on its economic restructuring, attracting foreign direct investment into China, and developing an export-oriented industrialization strategy. Most of its economic, political, and military interests in the Middle East and Africa atrophied during the 1980s. Two exceptions to that trend were that it continued to encourage countries to switch recognition from Taiwan to it and supported select national liberation causes such as the fight against apartheid in South Africa and the rights of Palestinians.

Changes in China's internal needs and the international environment shape its post–Cold War interests and threat perceptions in the Middle East and sub-Saharan Africa. During the Mao era, China created turmoil in these regions. Now it wants to avoid it. China's post–Cold War interests in these regions are promoting its domestic economic growth through access to resource and markets, fostering support for it in the international system, ensuring its internal stability, advocating for developing country causes, safeguarding Chinese citizens and businesses abroad, and protecting its sovereignty and territorial integrity from the United States. China increasingly sees the United States as a great power threat.

Both the Middle East and sub-Saharan Africa are important sources of resources and markets for China. The Middle East provides energy resources primarily, while sub-Saharan Africa is a source of energy as well as industrial minerals and agricultural resources. In terms of markets, both regions are important for Chinese goods, services, and investment.

Compared to sub-Saharan Africa, China worries much more about turmoil and conflict in the Middle East that could affect its interests. That concern has significantly increased since the beginning of Arab awakening. The Middle East is also a much more important region for ensuring China's domestic stability. China sees it as a source of cross-broader terrorism and funding for potential Muslim insurgency in China. Sub-Saharan Africa is not seen as generating those same threats to China's domestic stability. China is concerned about threats to its citizens and businesses operating in sub-Saharan Africa, but it does not worry about those activities spilling over into China.

Both regions provide China opportunities to build support for itself in the international system. In the Middle East, China attempts to gain that support by emphasizing support for Arab causes, supporting the Palestinians, and standing up against foreign interference and intervention. In sub-Saharan Africa, it builds support by emphasizing South-South cooperation and various development initiatives. In contrast with the Middle East, sub-Saharan Africa is a more important region for China to pursue its interest in advocating for developing country causes.

Both regions pose threats to China's citizens and businesses abroad, but the Middle East is perceived to be more unstable and therefore a greater risk.

Finally, both regions are important for China to protect its sovereignty and territorial integrity from the United States. Both provide many states to support China's claims in the South China Sea and behavior in Hong Kong. That said, the prevalence of foreign intervention from the United States and the rest of the West in the Middle East is greater, so China appears to consider that region a more important battleground for standing up to the United States on issues of sovereignty.

How did the Arab awakening change China's interests in these regions? China has long-standing worries about instability in the Middle East, and the awakening heightened that concern. Domestic upheavals and the need for Chinese citizen evacuations out of Libya and Yemen increased China's concern about the safety and security of its citizens and businesses in these regions. Increased terrorist attacks and kidnappings of Chinese citizens in the Middle East and sub-Saharan Africa also heightened this concern. The Arab awakening and the rise of ISIS in Syria made China more worried about protecting its domestic stability from terrorist threats in Xinjiang and throughout the rest of China. Finally, foreign intervention in Libya, Syria, and Yemen after the Arab awakening increased China's need to protect its sovereignty and territorial integrity by standing up to the United States and the rest of the West from their armed foreign interventions in these conflicts.

How has increased competition with the United States, including the rebalance and characterization of China as a potential adversary, changed China's interests in the Middle East and sub-Saharan Africa? This competition has increased the importance of China's fostering support in the international system from countries in these regions. Before the rebalance, China did not characterize the Middle East and sub-Saharan Africa as regions of competition with other great powers. Partially because of the rebalance and increased competition with the United States, China launched BRI to increase its influence in these regions to balance against the United States. This increased competition has also led China to stand up more to the United States and the rest of the West about sovereignty issues globally. Going forward, as tensions between the United States and China grow, the Middle East and Africa become even more important for China in acquiring resources and markets, fostering support in the international system, and finding partners to side with it to protect its sovereignty and territorial integrity from the United States and others.

Due to the instability caused by the Arab awakening and China's expanding presence, there was a proliferation of hot spots after 2011 that worried China in these regions. Before 2011, hot spots in the Middle East were the Palestinian-Israeli conflict, the Iraq War, and Iran. After 2011, they expanded to include Tunisia, Egypt, Libya, Syria, Yemen, and ISIS. Hot spots before 2011 in sub-Saharan Africa were Darfur, Zimbabwe, and Somalia. Now they also include Sudan and South Sudan, Guinea Bissau, Mali, DRC, Central Africa Republic, Nigeria, Gulf of Guinea, and the spread of Ebola. There are now more actual hot spots in these regions, and China's concerns regarding them have increased.

China's Post–Cold War Behavior

This book analyzes a wide range of China's post–Cold War behavior in the Middle East and sub-Saharan Africa, including cooperation forums, special envoys, relations in specific functional areas (economic, political, and security), and Belt and Road. How and why is this behavior cooperating or competing with the United States in these regions? How and why is it converging with or diverging from liberal international norms?

Cooperation Forums

China's cooperation forums, CASCF and FOCAC, provide valuable insights into how China manages its relations with these regions. They are the primary multilateral mechanisms China uses to coordinate its economic, political, foreign aid, and security relations.

First, it is important to note that although there are many similarities in China's behavior in these forums, the characteristics of the regions themselves shape China's behavior. FOCAC members include many developing countries, democracies, and countries with concerns about neocolonialism due to a bitter history with past imperial powers. Most conflict in Africa is internal instability rather than interstate conflicts.

CASCF members are engaged in regional power competition among themselves as well as with regional powers of Israel and Iran. Many countries in the CASCF are relatively affluent Gulf countries. Members are anxious about the impact of foreign intervention on internal and regional stability. The region is a significant part of the US sphere of influence, and many transborder terrorist threats emanate from it.

The foundational political norms of both forums are the Five Principles of

Peaceful Coexistence and South-South cooperation. The CASCF also includes strong support for Arab causes, including the Palestinians and standing up for the sovereignty of Middle Eastern states. FOCAC stresses the normative imperative to support the development of less developed countries and create a just and equitable new international political and economic order. After the NATO invasion of Libya in 2011, China's stance on the Five Principles hardened further. In particular, China seeks to stand up against US and other Western intervention in the Middle East. Also, as tensions between the United States and China rise, China is increasingly seeking support for its stance on issues in the South China Sea and Hong Kong via these forums.

China's political behavior in the forums is competitive. It excludes the United States and encourages South-South cooperation in opposition to the developed world. China's advocacy for the Five Principles is competitive and diverges from the Western liberal political order. Its support for the Palestinians is also competitive with US support for Israel, and it is norm convergent with the liberal order because it encourages states to abide by UN resolutions and use multilateral mechanisms to pursue Middle East peace.

Economic behavior in the forums is also competitive. The forums exclude the United States and the West and facilitate significant Chinese state support for Chinese company activities in these regions. This behavior is norm divergent from the liberal order's emphasis on free markets and limited state intervention in the economy. There are areas of behavior that are norm convergent with the liberal order, including preferential trade with LDCs and the pursuit of FTAs. Still, most of China's overall investment and financing behavior via the forums is norm divergent and competitive.

China's foreign aid behavior in the forums contains elements of competition and divergence. It should be acknowledged that China's provision of aid to less developed countries through debt cancellation, development assistance, health care provision, education, concessional loans, and other types of aid converges with liberal norms of developed countries providing aid to less developed ones. That said, China uses its aid programs to build soft power and influence to compete with the United States and the West in these regions. Also, its foreign aid programs normatively diverge from the Western order due to the lack of political conditionality on good governance.

In contrast with China's competitive and norm-divergent political, economic, and foreign aid behavior via the forums, China's security actions overall tend to be cooperative and norm convergent with the liberal order. The forums emphasize creating nuclear-free zones in these regions, security assistance, UN peacekeeping operations, antipiracy activities, and combating terrorism. All of these activities are in alignment with the Western liberal order, and most are conducted multilaterally through international institutions.

How does China portray and differentiate itself as a great power via FOCAC and CASCF? In the cooperation forums, China portrays itself as a champion of sovereignty, nonintervention, and noninterference. It provides a significant level of state support for economic engagement with these regions compared to other great powers. China advocates for South-South cooperation and support for developing countries. It also highlights that although it wants to be seen as a balanced player in these regions, it strongly supports Arab causes via the CASCF.

Special Envoys

China created special envoys for the Middle East, Syria, and Africa to address what it perceives as hot spots and challenges to peace and security in these regions. When it was established, China's special envoy for Middle East issues focused on the Arab-Israeli conflict, including the Palestinian-Israeli conflict and Israel's territorial disputes with Syria and Lebanon. In a post–Arab awakening environment, the envoy's scope expanded to include the Syria war, Iran, Yemen, Libya, and BRI. Eventually China set up a separate envoy to address issues in Syria. In Africa, China's envoy initially focused on Darfur, but in recent years, it shifted attention to South Sudan and Sudan, Mali, the African Great Lakes region, economic engagement with Africa, a shared colonial history with the continent, and the spread of Ebola.

All three envoys articulate the need for economic development to promote long-term stability and peace. The envoys for Syria and Africa often stress China's aid to these regions.

There is considerable variation in China's behavior across these three envoys. The special envoy for Middle East issues and special envoy for Syria are both competitive with the United States and normatively mixed. China's special envoy for Africa is cooperative with the United States and norm convergent with the liberal order.

In the Middle East, China's special envoys compete with the United States and cooperate with Russia and Iran. They stand up against US and other Western intervention and regime change. They criticize the United States for its preferential treatment of Israel, picking sides in the Syrian civil war, and withdrawing from the nuclear agreement with Iran. In contrast, China's Africa envoy stresses a desire to cooperate with the United States and the rest of the West, as well as the African Union to resolve issues in Sudan and South Sudan.

Does China's special envoy behavior converge with or diverge from the liberal international order? China's behavior in the Middle East Special issues and Syria envoy are normatively mixed, but its Africa envoy's behavior converges with liberal international norms.

In China's special envoy for Middle East issues, China's support for the Arab and Palestinian stance on the Palestinian-Israeli conflict converges with the liberal order because it calls on states to abide by UN resolutions and use multilateral mechanisms for resolving disputes. On other hot spot issues in the region, the Middle East issues envoy diverges from the liberal order due to its strict interpretation of Westphalian sovereignty and its firm stance against foreign intervention and regime change by the United States and the rest of the West.

The Syria envoy's normative behavior is also mixed. Through its strong focus on sovereignty and nonintervention, it diverges from the liberal order. That said, it converges with the liberal order by promoting the utilization of multilateral mediation mechanisms as well as humanitarian aid, reconstruction assistance, support for counterterrorism, and criticism on the use of chemical weapons.

China's behavior through the Africa envoy also converges with liberal international norms. In alignment with the liberal international order, China is promoting multilateralism and seeking negotiated solutions to conflicts. When it aims to contribute to conflict resolution, it does so through international and regional organizations.

Through all of its special envoys, China portrays itself as a balanced actor and responsible power emphasizing that it never acted as a colonial power in these regions. It attempts to act as a mediator within and between countries with these envoys. When addressing threats to peace and security via these envoys, China promotes the role of the UN, regional organizations, and other multilateral mechanisms. It supports political solutions to disagreements but rarely offers its own solutions. China is not building a separate order with these envoys but is reinforcing the existing order. It usually supports proposals from other actors or multilateral institutions. As it seeks to address threats to peace and security, China is willing to work with all states and parties with a stake in the resolution of an issue.

Economic, Political, and Military Relations

All of the economic tools analyzed in chapter 6 (state support for Chinese companies, foreign aid, free trade agreements, special economic zones, and agricultural technology demonstration centers) are competitive with the United States. That said, sometimes that competition occurs within the liberal order and sometimes outside it. China's behavior sometimes converges with international norms, sometimes it diverges, and sometimes it is norm neutral.

Although China's level of investment in these regions is low compared with other areas of the world, it is heavily involved in trade, services, and aid provision. It uses its economic foreign policy tools to increase its influence and power in these regions, often in combination with political foreign policy tools. Its neomercantilist behavior is an external reflection of its domestic economic system and the strong role of the state in its state-led capitalism. China differentiates itself from the United States and other great powers by providing substantial state support for economic activity, distributing foreign aid without political conditions, sharing its development experience with other developing countries, and supporting broad economic development in these regions.

All of China's economic behavior is competitive with the United States, but sometimes China competes inside the liberal order, and sometimes it competes outside it. China's state support for companies is divergent with the liberal economic order that emphasizes the importance of free markets and limited state involvement in the economy. Its foreign aid approach is also divergent because it directly confronts the political and good governance conditionality of liberal aid. In contrast, China's free trade agreements (FTAs) are norm convergent. Regional FTAs are allowed under the WTO and further promote the liberal norms of free trade. Great powers frequently pursue FTAs to complement WTO commitments. SEZs and agricultural technology demonstration centers are both norm neutral in relation to the liberal order, but they are very much in alignment with international expectations of sharing development experience with less developed countries.

All of the foreign policy tools discussed in chapter 6 should be considered elements of the economic order China is building in these regions. They must be considered together with China's cooperation forums, special envoys, and Belt and Road to fully understand how China is managing its economic relations with these regions and the order China is constructing. China is advocating for norms of heavy state involvement in the economy that diverges from the liberal order's emphasis on free markets and limited state intervention. It is also providing its aid approach without political conditions as a model to challenge the liberal order's demands for good governance from recipients. Specific institutions China is building to facilitate its economic relations with these regions are free trade agreements, special economic zones, and agricultural technology demonstration centers.

All of the political behavior discussed in chapter 7 (United Nations Security Council voting and strategic partnerships) is competitive with the United States. Still, sometimes China is competing inside the international order and sometimes outside it. Through its political behavior, China differentiates itself from the United States and other Western great powers with its emphasis on South-South cooperation, defense of sovereignty against foreign intervention and interference, and focus on aid and sharing its experiences as a developing country.

China's normative behavior in the UN Security Council is mixed. Its voting on sovereignty issues diverges from the liberal order in its staunch defense of the Five Principles of Peaceful Coexistence. Its views on sovereignty only hardened after the 2011 NATO invasion of Libya. China's support for the Palestinians in Security Council voting is norm convergent because it encourages countries to abide by relevant UN resolutions and use multilateral mechanisms for resolving the Palestinian-Israeli conflict.

China's strategic partnerships are norm neutral because there are no applicable norms of the liberal order governing these behaviors, but they are in alignment with the behavior of all great powers. China uses both of these tools to build its spheres of influence and linkages between economic, political, and security objectives in these regions and to garner support from the regions for China's stance on issues outside these regions, such as the South China Sea.

Both politically and economically, China competes inside and outside the international order, but militarily its behavior is cooperating inside the Western liberal order. Chapter 8 examines its conventional arms sales, UN peacekeeping organizations, antipiracy activities, and its new base in Djibouti. China's military behavior is the most significant change from the Mao era.

During Mao's time, China actively supported national liberation movements aiming to overthrow local governments and the international system more broadly. This behavior was competitive and norm divergent. In contrast, China's security behavior in these regions today, including its behavior in its cooperation forums and special envoys, is mostly cooperative and norm convergent with the liberal order. China stresses the need to use multilateral mechanisms such as the UN to address hot spots and threats to peace and security. Its conventional arms sales to these regions are minimal. Although China's new base in Djibouti may be competitive, it is norm neutral because there is not a relevant liberal norm governing basing. Most of China's military behavior in these regions today conforms to the rules of the liberal order. In contrast with the Mao era, China is not attempting to create its own military rules.

In the security realm, China attempts to differentiate itself as a great power from the United States by conducting its security behavior through multilateral international and regionals organizations. It also stresses that it has never colonized these regions and that it is opposed to foreign intervention and interference in the Middle East and Africa.

Belt and Road

Overall, China's behavior through Belt and Road is competitive, but some elements are norm convergent and some norm divergent from the liberal order. China competes inside and outside the economic and political order with various foreign policy tools that support BRI (e.g., cooperation forums, state support for Chinese companies, aid, FTAs, SEZs, agricultural demonstration technology centers, strategic partnerships, antipiracy, UN peacekeeping operations, and China's new base in Djibouti). Through Belt and Road and the foreign policy tools used to support the initiative, China is building a new order that reflects its values.

China differentiates itself as a great power through BRI with its emphasis on connectivity. It is attempting to demonstrate that it plays a positive role as a great power. It portrays itself as a driver of connectivity, development, trade, and globalization as it defends sovereignty and advocates for developing country causes. The normative foundation of its great power behavior through BRI is a belief that economic development leads to stability, a strict interpretation of sovereignty through the Five Principles, strong state support for economic activity, substantial aid to developing countries without political strings attached, South-South cooperation, and support for Arab causes.

Table 10.1 summarizes China's foreign policy behavior through the tools discussed in this book.

In considering China's behavior across foreign policy tools, there are some common themes. The foundation of all of China's political behavior in these

Table 10.1. China's Post–Cold War Behavior in the Middle East and Sub-Saharan Africa

	Competitive with the US	*Cooperative with the US*
Divergent from Liberal Order	Cooperation Forums • Political * Five Principles of Peaceful Coexistence * Arab Causes: Sovereignty • Economic * Investment and Financing * Infrastructure * Economic Security • Foreign Aid Special Envoy: Syria • Non-intervention Government Support for Chinese Companies Foreign Aid UNSC Voting: Sovereignty (Political, Econ, and Aid)	(None)
Norm Neutral	• SEZs • Agricultural Technology Demonstration Centers • Strategic Partnerships • Djibouti Base	(None)
Convergent with Liberal Order	Cooperation Forums • Political * South South Cooperation * Arab Causes: Support for Palestinians • Economic * Trade with LDCs * FTAs * Multilateral development finance Special Envoy: Middle East Special Envoy: Syria • Multilateralism UNSC Voting-Palestinians FTAs (Mostly Political, Econ, and Aid)	Cooperation Forums • Security Cooperation Special Envoy: Africa UNPKO Antipiracy Conventional Arms Sales (Military/ Peace and Security)

regions is the Five Principles. China consistently calls for respect for sovereignty, nonintervention, and noninterference in its political interactions with these regions.

China expresses its past and current support for the Palestinians through the CASCF and its special envoy for the Middle East, its UNSC voting, and aid. Negotiations for an FTA with Palestine also demonstrate that support.

Another common theme is support for the developing world. China shows that support through promoting South-South cooperation, generous foreign aid provision, sharing its experience with less developed countries, and advocating for a just and equitable new political and economic order. Activities supporting development are seen in China's cooperation forums, special envoys, aid programs, SEZs, agricultural technology demonstration centers, and BRI.

The utilization of multilateral mechanisms to promote peace and stability is another common theme. That behavior is seen in China's coordination with the AU via the FOCAC. China's cooperation with multilateral organizations is also demonstrated through its special envoys as well as participation in UN peacekeeping operations and multilateral antipiracy activities.

Across its foreign policy tools, China desires to work with all states and actors in a region. It also actively cooperates with Russia in the Middle East. Two specific examples of that cooperation are China and Russia jointly leading the SCO, as well as interactions between the two countries via China's special envoy for Middle East issues and China's Syria envoy.

Regional Variation

How and why does China's behavior vary across regions? There is a great deal of consistency in China's approach to these regions. For the most part, China uses the same foreign policy tools and normative foundation to pursue its interests in both regions as well as much of the global South.

One difference in China's behavior in these regions is that it provides more aid and assistance to sub-Saharan African countries and emphasizes support for the developing world more strongly when it interacts with the region. Part of that difference is because of sub-Saharan Africa's level of economic development. That said, the Middle East also includes many developing countries, but China's approach to the region does not as strongly emphasize developing country causes.

Another difference is that China sees the Middle East as a region of instability in comparison to sub-Saharan Africa and worries about interstate war in the Middle East as opposed to intrastate war in sub-Saharan Africa. In the Middle East, China is particularly concerned about foreign intervention from the United States and the rest of the West causing instability. As a result, it acts as a defender of sovereignty in that region. In comparison, China does not appear to be as concerned about intervention and interference from the United States in sub-Saharan Africa. China is also particularly sensitive to the role of the United States in the Middle East and does not want to be seen as challenging the United States there.

Finally, before the Arab awakening, China was able to interact with a League of Arab States and the Gulf Cooperation Council that represented the unified views of their members. In the wake of the Arab awakening, the unity in both of those organizations frayed, but they are both still critical regional organizations for China to gauge the needs of states in the Middle East.

Variation across Functional Areas

How and why does China's behavior vary across functional areas in these regions? The main difference is that its political, economic, and foreign aid behavior tends to be competitive and its military behavior cooperative. For the most part, China conducts its military behavior through international, multilateral organizations. All of its military behavior examined in this book converges with liberal international norms.[2] Its economic, political, and foreign aid behavior sometimes converges with and sometimes diverges from the liberal order. China is competing inside and outside the liberal order with its political, economic, and foreign aid activities.

China's interests drive the differences between functional areas. In these regions, China seeks to secure resources and markets, build international support for itself, protect its domestic stability, advocate for developing country causes, protect its citizens and business, and defend its sovereignty against the United States. It pursues those interests by competing with political, economic, and foreign aid tools and building influence in these regions. When its interests align with existing norms and institutions of the liberal order, it uses those instruments. When its interests diverge from those aspects of the order, it builds its own political, economic, and foreign aid institutions.

Although it competes in the political, economic, and foreign aid realm to pursue its interests, its military behavior is cooperative and convergent because it wants to demonstrate to these regions and the rest of the world that it does not possess territorial aspirations in these regions. It does not want to become entangled in unilateral military action in these trouble-prone regions. It does not want to be seen as a foreign power that interferes and intervenes. As a result, it conducts its security behavior and attempts to pursue peace and stability through the UN, regional organizations, and other multilateral mechanisms. Even China's base in Djibouti is framed as necessary for its economic and political needs as opposed to security considerations.

Impact of the Arab Awakening

The effect of the Arab awakening on China's behavior is mostly seen in the Middle East. Ever since protests broke out in Tunisia and Egypt, China has expressed concern about turbulence and foreign intervention. NATO's invasion of Libya in 2011 hardened China's stance on sovereignty. As conflict broke out in Syria, China's behavior become more active through its double UN vetoes with Russia and establishing a Chinese special envoy for Syria. Splits within the Arab League and GCC have made it more difficult for China to achieve its goals in the Middle East. CASCF initiatives have slowed, and the GCC-China negotiations on FTA have stalled. Increasing tensions between regional powers in the wake of the Arab awakening (e.g., Saudi and UAE versus Qatar, Saudi versus Iran, and the Arab states versus Israel) make regional war more likely. China must now treat the region more carefully and stand up against Western intervention more. Because of the upheaval in the region, China needs to protect its citizens and businesses from war and terrorism. Even as its footprint across these regions expands, China suffers from an increased sense of vulnerability. This concern arguably motivated the opening of China's base in Djibouti. Instability in the Middle East and the rise of organizations such as ISIS caused China's fear over domestic terrorism in Xinjiang and throughout China to increase. Chaos in the Middle East also led to more Chinese cooperation with Russia on issues such as Syria and the Middle East peace process.

Increasing Sino-American Competition

Is rising competition between the United States and China in Pacific Asia affecting China's behavior in the Middle East and sub-Saharan Africa? Increasing competition between the United States and China in Pacific Asia was a significant cause of the BRI. It has increased the importance of the Middle East and sub-Saharan Africa for China, renewed China's interest in protecting sovereignty, and resulted in China's increasingly linking issues between Asia Pacific and regions discussed in this book.

The competitive dynamic in Sino-American relations contributed significantly to China's westward push of Belt and Road. BRI can be seen as a direct result of Sino-American competition. As discussed in chapters 3 and 9, China's March West, in many ways driven by a desire to ensure economic opportunities to China's west, provides it a strategic alternative if relations with its Pacific Asian neighbors deteriorate and reinvigorates China's role as a continental Eurasian power. As competition between the United States and China grows, BRI enables China to use all of its instruments of power in concert to pursue its goals. As competition in the economic, political, and foreign aid realms increases, the Middle East and sub-Saharan Africa become more important for accessing resources and markets, as well as building influence and support for China in the international system.

Tensions with the United States in Asia and globally also renewed China's interests in protecting its sovereignty and encouraged it to link issue areas across regions. China increasingly calls for the protection of sovereignty and nonintervention by foreign powers in the Middle East and sub-Saharan Africa. Part of the rationale for that stance is a desire for the United States not to interfere in China's domestic politics. China has even sought the support of many Middle Eastern and African countries for its approach in Xinjiang to help deflect criticism of China in international organizations by the West. For example, China secured the endorsement of its behavior in Xinjiang from some Middle Eastern and African countries. When Crown Prince Mohammed bin Salman of Saudi Arabia visited China in February 2019, he was quoted on Chinese state television saying, "China has the right to carry out anti-terrorism and de-extremization work for its national security."[3] In July 2019, after twenty-two countries formally condemned China for its mass detention of ethnic and religious minorities in China, thirty-seven states signed a letter praising China's "remarkable achievements in the field of human rights." This letter is the type of support China is seeking from the Middle East and sub-Saharan Africa. Signatories included several Muslim majority states, such as Algeria, Bahrain, Egypt, Kuwait, Oman, Qatar, Saudi Arabia, Syria, Sudan, and the UAE. Qatar later unsigned the letter. Sub-Saharan Africa signatories were Angola, Burkina Faso, Burundi, Cameroon, Comoros, DRC, Eritrea, Gabon, Nigeria, Republic of Congo, Somalia, South Sudan, Sudan, Togo, and Zimbabwe.[4] China has also included wording about countries supporting its stance on the jurisdiction of arbitration mechanisms about South China Sea disputes in its cooperation forums and strategic partnership with these regions. The latest CASCF and FOCAC documents specifically highlight Arab state support for China's approach to Hong Kong.

Another consequence of increasingly global competition between the United States and China is that countries in the Middle East and sub-Saharan Africa, especially US allies and partners, may feel more pressure to choose between the United States and China. Whether it is a decision to use China 5G technology or for China to participate in the building of infrastructure that could be dual use, countries in these regions are increasingly caught in struggles between the United States and China.

Alternative Order?

China is building an alternative international order in these regions in the functional areas of politics, economics, and foreign aid. Sometimes that order is based on the liberal order, and sometimes it is not. In general, the order that China is building excludes the United States and other great powers. The norms underlying China's order are the Five Principles, with their emphasis on sovereignty, nonintervention, and noninterference; a strong role for the state in economic activity; South-South cooperation; supporting various development activities; sharing China's development experience; and the benefits of connectivity.

BRI can be understood as an overarching initiative that encompasses aspects of China's emerging order: cooperation forums, free trade agreements, agricultural technology demonstration centers, foreign aid norms, and strategic partnerships. Some elements complement the current international order; some exist in parallel and could take its place if the liberal order collapses. At this point, the order China is building complements the existing international order of Westphalian sovereignty and the liberal economic order. In some ways, China is even presenting itself as a protector of the current liberal economic order.[5] If the current order breaks down, these institutions could replace that order to manage China's political, economic, and foreign aid relations with these regions.

The order China is building in the Middle East and Africa tends to encompass economic, political, and foreign aid institutions but not security organizations. One exception is the Shanghai Cooperation Organization, which includes Russia, India and Pakistan and is heavily focused on security issues.

Differentiating Itself as a Great Power

During the Mao era, China portrayed itself as a leader of the third world. His efforts promoted national liberation movements and advocated for a new approach to aid for developing countries. It differentiated itself from the imperialist and colonial United States and Soviet Union and fought for itself against these powers despite its history of colonization and victimization. China still promotes itself as a protector of sovereignty and advocate for development and developing countries. Although it no longer supports national liberation movements throughout the world, many normative elements of its Mao-era great power behavior endure to this day: its Five Principles, approach for foreign aid, support for the Palestinians, efforts to stand up for previously colonized countries, and efforts to establish economic and political institutions better representing the needs of the developing world. Memories of those legacies continue to shape China's relations with these regions to this day.

China now portrays itself as a defender of sovereignty and champion of development and South-South cooperation. It promotes connectivity and the utilization of multilateral institutions. It prides itself on being a balanced actor that does not take sides and is willing to talk to any parties in a political dispute. China actively highlights itself as different from the United States and the rest of the West, especially in its respect for sovereignty, promotion of development with no political strings attached, and lack of colonial history in the Middle East and Africa. The positive image China portrays gains traction with many states in the Middle East and sub-Saharan Africa due to their domestic political systems and historical experiences with the West. China's normative stance on the Five Principles and emphasis on economic over political issues also aligns with the views and values of many states in these regions, as well as regional organizations in the Middle East and sub-Saharan Africa.

Spheres of Influence

To build spheres of influence in these regions, China is linking its political, economic, foreign aid, and military behavior. Before 2015, those connections occurred mostly via its cooperation forums as well as bilateral relations with individual countries in these regions. Since 1990, China has become the top trade partner of most countries in these regions. Now that it is pursuing Belt and Road, its cooperation forums fall under that initiative and BRI is the overarching strategy China uses to leverage its instruments of power in unison to pursue its objectives in the Middle East and sub-Saharan Africa. China is primarily building spheres of influence with its economic tools, including aid. Still, increasingly political instruments such as its strategic partnerships and BRI are building goodwill for it in these regions. China's attempts to build influence tend to center on economic and political activities as opposed to the military.

Building Influence during COVID-19

One important emerging dynamic of great power competition is the impact of COVID-19 on China's relations with the Middle East and Africa. Health diplomacy is arguably building China's influence in these regions. It is too early to know the long-term impact of COVID on China as a great power, but so far its reaction to COVID in the developing world is starting to receive praise.

At the beginning of the outbreak, the Middle East was the hardest-hit region after China.[6] While China was still battling its own outbreak, Middle Eastern states such as Saudi Arabia, Qatar, the United Arab Emirates, and Israel delivered aid to China to assist in the effort.[7] During the early stages of the outbreak, the Chinese government discriminated against Africans living in its borders, targeting them for extraordinary quarantine and testing requirements. As a result, a number of African countries filed formal complaints with the Chinese government on behalf of their citizens.[8] This treatment initially caused alarm, but appears to be now overshadowed by more positive developments in China's behavior as the pandemic progressed.

Starting in late March 2020, a wide array of Chinese actors including the government, state-owned enterprises, private companies, and Chinese diaspora began donating medical supplies to African and Middle Eastern countries for fighting the pandemic, including face masks, testing kits, medical equipment, and drugs for treatment. Chinese embassies facilitated these donations. Prominent examples include assistance to South Africa, Zimbabwe,

Ghana, Nigeria, Ethiopia,[9] the Palestinian Authority, Lebanon, Egypt, Syria,[10] Turkey, Israel, and Oman.[11] Also, reporting by CGTN claims the Jack Ma Foundation "delivered over four hundred tons of medical supplies across Africa, including monthly deliveries of thirty million testing kits, ten thousand ventilators, and eight million surgical masks."[12] Although later allegations of corruption in the distribution of these supplies by local governments in Kenya and Tanzania tarnished the image of these activities,[13] Chinese donations of supplies in general appear to have cultivated a positive impression of China as a great power among many of the recipient countries.

To respond to the pandemic, China also sent medical teams to help fight the virus. For example, China sent medical teams with experience treating COVID to Algeria, Nigeria, and Zimbabwe.[14] The Chinese government claims it dispatched nearly two hundred medical experts across Africa[15] who provided assistance to the Africa Centers for Disease Control and Prevention headquarters.[16]

In order to respond to calls for financial relief for African countries during the pandemic, China has announced that it would cancel all interest-free loans that it gave to African states[17] and was delaying required payments for many others.[18] China claims it has suspended more debt service than any other G20 member. [19]

The Middle East and Africa are also important regions for China's vaccine development, testing, production, and distribution. China has four vaccines in various stages of development and often proclaims that these vaccines should be considered a global public good.[20] Across the Middle East, countries are using Chinese vaccines. The UAE, Bahrain, Egypt, Jordan,[21] and Morocco[22] all participated in China's vaccine trials. The UAE and Morocco plan to participate in production and distribution of the vaccine regionally.[23] In December 2020, the UAE became the first country in the world to approve a Chinese vaccine.[24] Examples of other countries in the Middle East now using them include Bahrain, Egypt, Turkey,[25] Morocco,[26] Iran, and the Palestinian Authority.[27] The ruler of Dubai, Sheikh Mohammed bin Rashid Al Maktoum; Turkey's president, Recep Tayyip Erdogan; and Bahrain's king, Hamad bin Isa Al Khalifa, all publicly received Chinese vaccines.[28]

In mid-2020, fifty African diplomats visited a Sinopharm facility in China to learn about China's vaccines.[29] Examples in sub-Saharan Africa of counties already distributing Chinese vaccines include Senegal and Zimbabwe.[30] Their leaders also publicly received the vaccine to promote its use by their populations.

China is also actively involved in multilateral efforts to provide vaccine access to the developing world. It joined the COVAX alliance in January 2021.[31] The United States also recently joined this WHO-supported effort.[32]

It is too early to know the ultimate impact of these efforts on China's image as a great power in these regions. That said, China's health diplomacy for COVID ties into decades of history of health cooperation with these regions. It demonstrates that China is focused on South-South cooperation and advocating for developing country causes at a time that most Western countries are preoccupied with handling outbreaks within their own borders. It is possible that China may be remembered after COVID as the great power in Africa and the Middle East that practiced what it preached and stood up for less developed countries that are structurally disadvantaged in their ability to acquire vaccines in short supply. Together with the foreign policy tools discussed in this book, China's COVID efforts may enable it to establish a sphere of influence in these regions that will contribute to its ability to continue to access resources and markets and build up support from countries in these regions in the international system.

China's Global Rise

Ultimately, what does China's behavior in the Middle East and sub-Saharan Africa indicate about its global rise? International relations scholars and China specialists provide varied predictions about China's behavior as a rising power. Offensive realists stress China will attempt to maximize power and prevent other great powers from maintaining hegemony in resource-rich regions. Liberal scholars tend to predict that China will be socialized into the international order and gain more than it loses by participating in the existing order. Power transition theorists, including Gilpin, highlight how a dissatisfied rising power will seek to gain territory, challenge the rules of the international system, and build spheres of influence.

This book contributes to the overall literature on China as a rising power by showing how China is challenging some rules of the liberal order, how it builds spheres of influence, and how it portrays itself as a great power. It also provides an opportunity to see how China has responded to upheaval in a region through the Arab awakening as well as a change in the US approach to its relationship. Increasingly, scholars are examining how China's current interactions with a wide range of international orders could be understood.[33] This book will contribute to those debates through its exploration of how China's behavior converges with and diverges from some aspects of the current liberal economic and political orders.

The Middle East and sub-Saharan Africa serve as important case studies in understanding China's rise. Unlike in Pacific Asia, China does not have territorial claims in these regions. Also, these regions share many characteristics with other developing regions, such as Latin America and Central Asia. As a result, examining China's relations with the Middle East and sub-Saharan Africa may provide significant insights into other regions of the world.

The findings of this book indicate that in the Middle East and sub-Saharan Africa, China is not attempting to maximize its power. Still, it is also not entirely socializing into the Western international order. China is competing with economic, political, and foreign aid foreign policy tools, but sometimes that competition occurs within the existing international and regional rules and sometimes outside. This book provides insights into the characteristics of that competition and the emerging order China is constructing.

China is building significant multilateral governance mechanisms in these regions, especially through cooperation forums. If the current liberal order crumbles, China has parallel structures to take its place. As discussed in chapter 4, China is building a similar order in Central Asia via the SCO, which focuses more on security issues and includes Russia, India, and Pakistan, other great and regional powers. It is likely an outlier in China's cooperation forums around the world. Most appear to prioritize economic and political relations similar to CASCF and FOCAC. China leverages cooperation forums and related foreign policy tools to manage its relationships with much of the developing world (e.g., the China-CELAC Forum with Latin America and the Caribbean, the 17+1 Central and Eastern Europe States Forum, and the Forum for Economic and Trade Co-operation between China and Portuguese-speaking countries). Although it is not establishing a cooperation forum in Southeast Asia, it is coordinating with the preexisting Association of Southeast Asian Nations to accomplish many of the same goals. One important area of further research is for analysts to conduct more detailed studies of China's cooperation forums across regions to better understand the parallel orders China is building.

The foreign policy tools discussed in this book also provide insight into China's behavior globally. Often these tools are not limited to the Middle East and sub-Saharan Africa. Most of the economic, political, and foreign tools examined in this book are or will be used in regions around the world, especially in the developing world. Around the world, in the economic realm, China leverages state support for Chinese companies, provides foreign aid to less developed countries, pursues free trade agreements, and establishes special economic zones and agricultural technology demonstration centers. Politically, it develops strategic partnerships to pursue its objectives and deploys special envoys to address hot spot issues. In the security realm, it participates in UN peacekeeping and antipiracy initiatives and sells conventional arms. BRI, which spans all of these functional areas, now includes all regions of the world except North America. As a result, this book's detailed case studies of these tools in the Middle East and sub-Saharan Africa could be used to understand China's global behavior better. In the future, these case studies should be compared and contrasted with case studies of similar foreign policy tools in other regions to tease out similarities and differences in China's rise across regions of the world. Also, this book explores the foreign policy tools China is using but does not necessarily measure the effectiveness and outcome of those tools, an essential area for further exploration.

This book discusses the degree to which China competes or cooperates with the United States in the Middle East and sub-Saharan Africa. Further research should explore this topic in more detail and examine the specific aspects of cooperation and competition between these two great powers in these regions and others.

In chapters 4 and 5, this book explores China's cooperation with Russia in these regions via the SCO and China's special envoys. In light of the increased emphasis on China and Russia as strategic competitors of the United States, more research needs to be conducted on China-Russia cooperation and competition around the world.

In the Middle East and sub-Saharan Africa, China's behavior varies across functional areas. Its economic, political, and foreign aid behavior tends to be competitive, but its security behavior is cooperative. This pattern may also apply to China's behavior in most of the world outside its territorial perimeter and its relations with the United States. If this is the case, it is essential for analysts and policymakers to understand better the ways claims about China's behavior on its periphery can or cannot be generalized to its global behavior. Based on findings in this book, outside its core territorial claims in Asia, China's competitive behavior may be limited to the economic and political realm and not extend to its security behavior. Analysts should be cautious when they attempt to extrapolate China's behavior along its territorial periphery and its relations with the United States to China's behavior in other regions. China's interests and behavior in other regions may be different.

China portrays itself in the Middle East and sub-Saharan Africa as a defender of sovereignty, advocate for development and South-South solidarity, and champion of connectivity. Promoting those values and not taking sides in disputes is how China demonstrates it is a responsible power in these regions. Reflective of its own domestic economic and political system, there is a heavy hand of the state in China's economic relations with these regions as well as a strong focus on protecting sovereignty and promoting development. Much of the research on China's rise considers the degree to which China is socialized into the Western liberal order. Based on how China is approaching the Middle East and sub-Saharan Africa, analysts should also examine its normative interactions with the Global South and better understand the degree to which norms of interaction are developing among those states through socialization with China. Further exploring China's relations with the Middle East and sub-Saharan Africa in comparison to the rest of the developing world should be a fruitful area of research.

This book focuses on how China's portrays itself in these regions and the views of China among government elites from these regions. Another important area for research would be to develop a much more comprehensive and nuanced understanding of how China is perceived within these regions as a rising power. Currently, the US government focuses on the negatives of BRI and accusing China of debt diplomacy and exporting authoritarianism.[34] Still, a more significant threat to the United States may be the positive image and legitimacy China is cultivating in the Middle East and sub-Saharan Africa, as well as the rest of the developing world. How the Middle East and Africa ultimately respond to COVID-19 may be an indication of how that image is evolving.

As China's perception of external threat and rivalry with the United States increases over time, its competitive economic and political behavior appears to be escalating both inside and outside the liberal order. That said, even with growing tensions between China and the United States, China's security behavior in the Middle East and sub-Saharan Africa remains mostly cooperative and norm convergent with the liberal order. Policymakers and scholars around the world should reflect on the implications of that finding for how China is perceived and treated as a great power. Misunderstanding China as a rising power could have dire consequences for global peace and security.

NOTES

CHAPTER 1

1. I use "potential" because there is much debate about the speed of China's rise relative to that of other great powers, the endurance of American power, and the probability of China's economic or political collapse.

2. "National Security Strategy of the United States of America" (Washington, DC: White House, 2017); "Summary of the National Defense Strategy of the United States of America Sharpening the American Military's Competitive Edge" (Washington, DC: Department of Defense, 2018); "Remarks by Vice President Pence on the Administration's Policy toward China" (Washington, DC: Hudson Institute, October 4, 2018); "Remarks by Vice President Pence at the Frederic V. Malek Memorial Lecture" (Washington, DC, October 24, 2019); and Michael Pompeo, "Communist China and the Free World's Future," Richard Nixon Presidential Library and Museum, Yorba Linda, CA, July 23, 2020.

3. "China's National Defense in the New Era," white paper (Beijing: Information Office of the State Council of the People's Republic of China, 2019).

4. This book is particularly inspired by Gilpin's arguments regarding power transitions. He argues that a dissatisfied rising power will attempt to change spheres of influence, the rules governing the international system, and the international distribution of territory. See Robert Gilpin, *War and Change in World Politics* (Cambridge: Cambridge University Press, 1981).

5. The current liberal international order could unravel in many ways. It could be due to the United States or other great powers abandoning the order or inherent tensions between the liberal order and other norms in the international order, as well as rising nationalism and backlash against globalization and Westernization. If the existing liberal order deteriorates, regardless of the root cause of its destruction, China has built an alternative order to take its place in relations with the Middle East and Africa.

6. I use the term *Palestine* here because the PRC and the League of Arab States recognize the State of Palestine.

7. For the purposes of this book, Turkey is included in the Middle East due to the strong emphasis of Chinese scholars on Turkey as an important Middle Eastern state. In general, China includes the Middle East as part of West Asia and tends to refer to all of Africa rather than North Africa and sub-Saharan Africa. I use the term *Middle East* because that is how the United States tends to frame the region in its own policy and

discourse. Some Chinese scholars use *Middle East* when writing for Western audiences, but most use the regions of West Asia and Africa.

8. For examples of analysis of China's increasing global impact, see Andrew J. Nathan and Andrew Scobell, *China's Search for Security* (New York: Columbia University Press, 2012); David Shambaugh, *China Goes Global: The Partial Power* (New York: Oxford University Press, 2013); Thomas J. Christensen, *The China Challenge: Shaping the Choices of a Rising Power* (New York: Norton, 2015); Graham Allison, *Destined for War: Can America and China Escape Thucydides's Trap?* (Boston: Houghton Mifflin Harcourt, 2017); and David Shambaugh, ed., *China and the World* (New York: Oxford University Press, 2020).

9. A limited number of book-length studies examine China's involvement with the Middle East as a region in the post–Cold War era. Some recent examples include Guy Burton, *China and Middle East Conflicts: Responding to War and Rivalry from the Cold War to the Present* (New York: Routledge, 2020), Robert Bianchi, *China and the Islamic World: How the New Silk Road Is Transforming Global Politics* (New York: Oxford University Press, 2019); Anoushivaran Ehteshami and Niv Horesh, *How China's Rise Is Changing the Middle East* (Abingdon: Routledge, 2020); Jonathan Fulton, *China's Relations with the Gulf Monarchies* (London: Routledge, 2019); James M. Dorsey, *China and the Middle East: Venturing into the Maelstrom* (Cham, Switzerland: Palgrave Macmillan, 2019); James Reardon-Anderson, ed., *The Red Star and the Crescent: China and the Middle East* (London: Hurst, 2018); Anoushrivan Ehteshami and Niv Horesh, *China's Presence in the Middle East: Implications of the One Belt, One Road Initiative* (London: Routledge, 2018); Jon B. Alterman, *The Other Side of the World: China, the United States and the Struggle for Middle East Security* (Washington, DC: Center for Strategic and International Studies, 2017); Niv Horesh, *Toward Well-Oiled Relations? China's Presence in the Middle East following the Arab Spring* (New York: Palgrave Macmillan, 2016); Andrew Scobell and Alireza Nader, "China in the Middle East: The Wary Dragon" (Santa Monica, CA: RAND, 2016); Muhamad S. Olimat, *China and North Africa: A Bilateral Approach* (Lanham, MD: Lexington Books, 2014); Muhamad S. Olimat, *China and the Middle East since World War II: A Bilateral Approach* (Lanham, MD: Lexington Books, 2014); and Muhamad S. Olimat, *China and the Middle East: From Silk Road to Arab Spring* (Milton Park: Routledge, 2013).

10. Some recent examples of in-depth studies of China-Africa post–Cold War relations include Chris Alden, Abiodun Alao, Zhang Chun, and Laura Barber, eds., *China and Africa: Building Peace and Security Cooperation on the Continent* (Cham, Switzerland: Palgrave Macmillan, 2018); Anja Lahtinen, *China's Diplomacy and Economic Activities in Africa : Relations on the Move* (Cham, Switzerland: Palgrave Macmillan, 2018); David Dollar, *China's Engagement with Africa: From Natural Resources to Human Resources* (Washington, DC: Brookings, 2016); Larry Hanauer and Lyle J. Morris, *Engagement in Africa: Drivers, Reactions, and Implications for U.S. Policy* (Santa Monica, CA: RAND Corporation, 2014); Li Xing and Abdulkadir Farah, eds., *China-Africa Relations in an Era of Great Transformations* (Burlington, VT: Ashgate, 2013); and David H. Shinn and Joshua Eisenman, *China and Africa: A Century of Engagement* (Philadelphia: University of Pennsylvania Press, 2012).

11. For example, see Shambaugh, *China and the World*; Christensen, *The China Challenge;* Shambaugh, *China Goes Global*; Nathan and Scobell, *China's Search for Security.*

12. The United States is rapidly heading toward energy independence due to shale oil and gas technology, but until that potential is realized, access to oil will remain a vital US interest. Even if the United States achieves energy independence, global oil prices will continue to affect it in many ways, including its own consumption and profitability for its producers.

13. Throughout the book, I use the acronym ISIS because that is the predominant term China uses for this group. That said, the United States often refers to it as the Islamic State of Iraq and the Levant (ISIL), and the Arabic name for the group is Daesh.

14. For an overview of current United States interests in the Middle East and sub-Saharan Africa, see "National Security Strategy," 2017.

15. For example, see "Remarks by National Security Advisor Ambassador John R. Bolton on the Trump Administration's New Africa Strategy," December 13, 2018.

16. Examples of book-length treatments of China's post–Cold War relations with the developing world as a whole include Joshua Eisenman and Eric Heginbotham, eds., *China Steps Out: Beijing's Major Power Engagement with the Developing World* (New York: Routledge, 2018); Andrew Scobell, Bonny Lin, Howard J. Shatz, Michael Johnson, Larry Hanauer, Michael S. Chase, Astrid Stuth Cevallos, et al. *At the Dawn of Belt and Road: China in the Developing World* (Santa Monica, CA: RAND Corporation, 2018), Lowell Dittmer and George T. Yu, eds., *China, the Developing World and the New Global Dynamic* (Boulder, CO: Lynne Rienner, 2010); and Joshua Eisenman, Eric Heginbotham, and Derek Mitchell, eds. *China and the Developing World (*Armonk, NY: M. E. Sharpe, 2007).

17. There are many foreign policy tools that China uses that I do not examine in this book—for example, the international division of the Chinese Communist Party and cyber-offensive operations. This study is not meant to cover all foreign policy tools that China uses in its relations with these regions.

18. For a discussion of the dangers of selecting on the dependent variable and ahistorical analysis of China's foreign policy behavior, see Alastair Iain Johnston. "How New and Assertive Is China's New Assertiveness?" *International Security* 37, no. 4 (2013): 7–48.

19. See Kupchan for a discussion of how norms informing hegemonic orders are often derived from the state's own domestic order and how hegemons replicate their own ordering norms throughout spheres of influence due to their material interests. Charles A. Kupchan, "Unpacking Hegemony: The Social Foundations of Hierarchical Order," in *Power, Order and Change in World Politics*, ed. G. John Ikenberry (Cambridge: Cambridge University Press, 2014), 25–26.

CHAPTER 2

1. Mearsheimer, *The Tragedy of Great Power Politics* (New York: Norton, 2001).

2. Mearsheimer, *Tragedy*, 22.

3. Mearsheimer, *Tragedy*, 144.

4. For example, see John J. Mearsheimer, "The Gathering Storm: China's Challenge to US Power in Asia," *Chinese Journal of International Politics* 3 (2010): 381–396, and John J. Mearsheimer, "China's Unpeaceful Rise" *Current History* (2006): 160–163.

5. Mearsheimer, *Tragedy*, 144.

6. Gilpin, *War and Change*. Gilpin wrote his seminal work on rising powers in 1981, long before it was apparent that China would grow to become a challenger of the United States. That said, his arguments apply to all rising great powers over time. For a discussion of how Gilpin's insights could apply to contemporary China, see G. John Ikenberry, ed., *Power, Order and Change in World Politics* (Cambridge: Cambridge University Press, 2014).

7. Gilpin, *War and Change*, 9.

8. Gilpin, *War and Change*, 23–24.

9. For example, see Allison, *Destined for War*; Michael Pillsbury, *The Hundred Year Marathon: China's Secret Strategy to Replace American as the Global Superpower* (New York: Holt, 2015); Aaron L. Friedberg, *A Contest for Supremacy: China, America, and the Struggle for Mastery in Asia* (New York: Norton, 2011); and Martin Jacques, *When China Rules the World: The End of the Western World and the Birth of a New Global Order* (New York: Penguin Press, 2009).

10. Naazneen Barma, Ely Ratner, and Steven Weber, "A World without the West," *National Interest* 90 (2007): 23–30 ; Azar Gat, "The Return of Authoritarian Great Powers," *Foreign Affairs* 86, no. 4 (2007): 59–69.

11. G. John Ikenberry, "Why the Liberal World Order Will Survive." *Ethics and International Affairs* 32, no. 1) (2018): 17–29; G. John Ikenberry, "The Rise of China, the United States and the Future of the Liberal International Order," in *Tangled Titans: The United States and China*, ed. David Shambaugh, 53–73 (Lanham, MD: Rowman & Littlefield, 2013); G. John Ikenberry, *Liberal Leviathan: The Origins, Crisis and Transformation of the American World Order* (Princeton: Princeton University Press, 2011); G. John Ikenberry, "The Rise of China and the Future of the West: Can the Liberal System Survive?" *Foreign Affairs* 87, no. 1 (2008): 23–37; and G. John Ikenberry, "The Rise of China: Power, Institutions, and the Western Order," in *China's Ascent: Power, Security, and the Future of International Politics*, ed. Robert S. Ross and Feng Zhu (Ithaca, NY: Cornell University Press, 2008).

12. Ikenberry, "Rise of China and the Future," 32, Ikenberry, "The Rise of China: Power."

13. Ikenberry, "Rise of China and the Future," 24.

14. For example, see his discussion of the AIIB in G. John Ikenberry and Darren Lim, "What China's Institutional Statecraft Could Mean for the International Order," *Brookings*, April 13, 2017.

15. Ikenberry, *Liberal Leviathan*.

16. John G. Ikenberry, "The Plot against American Foreign Policy: Can the Liberal Order Survive?" *Foreign Affairs* 96, no. 3 (May–June 2017).

17. Many authors examine the socialization of China into various international organizations and norms. Some prominent examples include Alastair Iain Johnston, "China

in a World of Orders: Rethinking Compliance and Challenge in Beijing's International Relations," *International Security* 44, no. 2 (2019): 9–60; Alastair Iain Johnston "How New and Assertive Is China's New Assertiveness?" *International Security* 37, no. 4 (2013); Rosemary Foot and Andrew Walter, *China, the United States and the Global Order* (New York: Cambridge University Press, 2011); Allen Carlson, "Moving beyond Sovereignty? A Brief Consideration of the Recent Changes in China's Approach to the International Order and the Emergence of the Tianxia Concept," *Journal of Contemporary China* 20, no. 68 (2011); Alastair Iain Johnston, *Social States: China in International Institutions, 1980–2000* (Princeton, NJ: Princeton University Press, 2008); Ann Kent, *Beyond Compliance: China, International Organizations, and Global Security* (Stanford, CA: Stanford University Press, 2007); Allen Carlson, *Unifying China, Integrating with the World: Securing Chinese Sovereignty in the Reform Era.* (Stanford, A: Stanford University Press, 2005), 34–96; Alastair Iain Johnston, "Beijing's Security Behavior in the Asia-Pacific: Is China a Dissatisfied Power?" in *Rethinking Security in East Asia: Identity, Power, and Efficiency*, ed. J. J. Suh, Peter J. Katzenstein, and , Alaistair Iain Johnston, "Is China a Status Quo Power?" *International Security* 27, no. 4 (2003): 5–56; and Samuel S. Kim, "Chinese Foreign Policy in Theory and Practice," in *China and the World: Chinese Foreign Policy Faces the New Millennium*, ed. Samuel S. Kim (Boulder, CO: Westview Press, 1998).

18. For example, see Johnston, "China in a World of Orders"; Charles L. Glaser. "A Flawed Framework: Why the Liberal International Order Concept Is Misguided." *International Security* 43, no. 4 (2019): 51–87; and John J. Mearsheimer. "Bound to Fail: The Rise and Fall of the Liberal International Order," *International Security* 43, no. 4 (2019): 7–50.

19. Johnston, "China in a World of Orders," 25–56.

20. Alexander Wendt, "Anarchy Is What States Make of It: The Social Construction of Power Politics," *International Organization* 46, no. 2 (1992); John Gerard Ruggie, "What Makes the World Hang Together? Neo-Utilitarianism and the Social Constructivist Challenge," *International Organization* 52, no. 4 (1998).

21. For a discussion of China's competing identities, see David Shambaugh, "Coping with a Conflicted China," *Washington Quarterly* 34, no. 1 (2011). For a discussion of China's identity as a developing country, see Lowell Dittmer, "China's Rise, Global Identity, and the Developing World," in *China, the Developing World, and the New Global Dynamic*, ed. Lowell Dittmer and George T. Yu (Boulder, CO: Lynne Rienner, 2010). For an example of non-Western states bonding together to create an alternative order based on their values, see Barma et al., "A World Without,"; Naazneen Barma, Ely Ratner, and Steven Weber, "The Mythical Liberal Order," *National Interest* 124 (2013); and Gat, "Return of Authoritarian."

22. The concept of sphere of influence has changed over time. This book defines a sphere of influence as a "determinate region with which a single external power exerts a predominant influence, which limits the independence or freedom of action of political entities within it." See Paul Keal, *Unspoken Rules and Superpower Dominance* (New York: St. Martin's Press, 1983), 15.

23. Another way to frame this is that China is setting up a parallel order of institu-

tions that it dominates. See Oliver Stuenkel, *Post-Western World: How Emerging Powers Are Remaking Global Order* (Cambridge: Polity Press, 2016).

24. Some of the foreign policy tools in this book draw on other sets of international norms (e.g., foreign aid). That said, most of these tools are evaluated in relation to the Westphalian order and the liberal political and economic order. For an excellent recent discussion of various ways to think about China's approach to international orders, see Alastair Iain Johnston, "China in a World of Orders: Rethinking Compliance and Challenge in Beijing's International Relations," *International Security* 44, no. 2 (2019).

25. G. John Ikenberry, "The Logic of Order: Westphalia, Liberalism, and the Evolution of International Order in the Modern Era," in *Power, Order and Change in World Politics*, ed. G. John Ikenberry (Cambridge: Cambridge University Press, 2014), 92.

26. For a detailed discussion of the composition of the international order, see Ikenberry, "Logic of Order"; Michael J. Mazarr, Miranda Priebe, Andrew Radin, and Astrid Stuth Cevallos, *Understanding the Current International Order* (Santa Monica, CA: RAND, 2016); and Stewart Patrick, "World Order: What, Exactly, Are the Rules?" *Washington Quarterly* 39 (1) (2016).

27. Barma et al., "Mythical Liberal Order," 56.

28. Barma et al., "Mythical Liberal Order," 57. In addition, Dai Xinyuan and Duu Renn, "China and International Order: The Limits of Integration," *Journal of Chinese Political Science* 22 (2016), find that China's engagement with the international order via multilateral agreements is weak compared to other countries.

29. For a discussion of power in international politics, see Carr, *The Twenty Year Crisis*, chap. 8, and Gilpin, *War and Change*, 13.

30. It should be noted that China's cooperation with one great power (e.g., Russia) could result in competitive behavior with another great power (e.g., the United States).

31. For example, see G. John Ikenberry and Amitai Etzioni, "Is China More Westphalian Than the West?" *Foreign Affairs* 90, no. 6 (2011). For an in-depth discussion of China's views on sovereignty and how China's interpretations of sovereignty have changed over time, see Allen Carlson, "Moving beyond Sovereignty? A Brief Consideration of the Recent Changes in China's Approach to the International Order and the Emergence of the Tianxia Concept," *Journal of Contemporary China* 20, no. 68 (2011), and Allen Carlson, *Unifying China, Integrating with the World: Securing Chinese Sovereignty in the Reform Era* (Stanford, CA: Stanford University Press, 2005). Thanks to Tom Christensen for his feedback that led me to shift my emphasis from status quo versus revisionist to competition versus cooperation and convergence versus divergence.

32. For an in-depth discussion of this issue, see Randall L. Schweller and Xiaoyu Pu, "After Unipolarity: China's Visions of International Order in an Era of U.S. Decline," *International Security* 36 , no. 1 (2011): 45.

33. There is a healthy debate in the theoretical literature regarding the current polarity of the international system and how rapidly shifts in the balance of power are occurring. Tunsjo argues the system is already bipolar. See Oystein Tunsjo, *The Return of Bipolarity in World Politics: China, the United States, and Geostructural Realism* (New York: Columbia University Press, 2018). In contrast, Beckley asserts the world is far

from bipolar and the United States will remain the most powerful state in the system for the foreseeable future. See Michael Beckley, *Unrivaled: Why America Will Remain the World's Sole Superpower* (Ithaca: Cornell University Press, 2018). Although these are important debates, this book operates under the assumption that we are moving from an era of US hegemony or unipolarity to a more multipolar or bipolar world. It also assumes we are experiencing a power shift from the United States to China. The current polarity of the system (bipolar versus multipolar) does not affect the overall findings of the book.

34. This book is the product of approximately two hundred interviews and research conducted from 2009 through 2019. While a visiting scholar at the Chinese Academy of Social Science, Institute of World Economics and Politics, in Beijing (September 2009 through May 2010), I interviewed Chinese scholars, government officials, and economic actors, as well as a number of Middle Eastern and African embassy officials (including Bahrain, Israel, Jordan, Palestine, South Africa, Tunisia and Turkey). As a visiting research fellow at the American University in Cairo, Egypt (September 2010 through December 2010), I interviewed relevant scholars and government officials in the Egyptian government, the League of Arab States, and the Africa Union. In May 2011, I conducted research in South Africa interviewing scholars and government officials. In 2013, I held follow-up interviews in Beijing regarding the impact of the Arab awakening on China's interests and behavior after 2010 (including formal interviews with those from Iraq, Israel, Oman, Palestine, and the United Arab Emirates as well as informal interactions with representatives of all member states of the Arab League). From 2015 to 2016, I conducted interviews in China, Washington, DC, Saudi Arabia, Qatar, the United Arab Emirates, Kuwait, Bahrain, and Oman on changes in China's approach to the Middle East and sub-Saharan Africa after the Arab awakening (also including government officials from Djibouti, Israel, and Palestine). In 2017 and 2018, I conducted interviews with government officials, intergovernmental organizations, and scholars about China's Belt and Road Initiative in Washington, DC, Belgium, France, the Netherlands, and the United Kingdom (including officials from the European Union and NATO). My last round of interviews for this project occurred in fall 2019 in the United Arab Emirates meeting with scholars studying China and government officials.

CHAPTER 3

1. Lin Biao, "Long Live the Victory of People's War! In Commemoration of the 20th Anniversary of Victory in the Chinese People's War of Resistance Against Japan" (Beijing, Foreign Language Press, September 3, 1965).

2. China's national defense white papers: "China's National Defense in the New Era," white paper (Beijing: Information Office of the State State Council of the People's Republic of China, 2019); "China's Military Strategy," white paper (Beijing: State Council Information Office of the People's Republic of China, 2015); "The Diversified Employment of China's Armed Forces" (Beijing: Infomation Office of the State Council of the People's Republic of China, 2013); "China's National Defense in 2010" (Beijing: Information Office of the State Council of the People's Republic of China, March 31, 2011);

"China's National Defense in 2008," white paper (Beijing: Information Office of the State Council of the People's Republic of China, January 20, 2009); "China's National Defense in 2006" (Beijing: Information Office of the State Council of the People's Republic of China, December 2006); "China's National Defense in 2004" (Beijing: Information Office of the State Council of the People's Republic of China, December 2004); "China's National Defense in 2002" (Beijing: Information Office of the State Council of the People's Republic of China, December 2002); "China's National Defense in 2000" (Beijing: Information Office of the State Council of the People's Republic of China, October 2000); and "China's National Defense" (Beijing: Information Office of the State Council of the People's Republic of China, July 1998).

3. Peaceful development white papers: "China's Peaceful Development" (Beijing: Information Office of the State Council of the People's Republic of China, September 6, 2011); "China's Peaceful Development Road" (Beijing: Information Office of the State Council of the People's Republic of China, December 12, 2005). "China and the World in the New Era" (Beijing: State Council Information Office of the People's Republic of China, September 2019) also discusses peaceful development in China's interactions with the world.

4. Middle East and Africa white papers: "Full Text of China's Arab Policy Paper," Xinhua, January 14, 2016; "Full Text: China's Second Africa Policy Paper," Xinhua, December 5, 2015; "China-Africa Economic and Trade Cooperation" (Beijing: Information Office of the State Council of the People's Republic of China, 2013); "China Africa Economic and Trade Cooperation" (Beijing: Information Office of the State Council of the People's Republic of China, December 23, 2010); and "China's African Policy" (Beijing: Information Office of the State Council of the People's Republic of China, January 12, 2006).

5. Energy white papers: "China's Energy Policy" (Beijing: Information Office of the State Council of the People's Republic of China, 2012); "China's Energy Conditions and Policies" (Beijing: Information Office of the State Council of the People's Republic of China, December 26, 2007).

6. Foreign trade white paper: "China's Foreign Trade" (Beijing: Information Office of the State Council of the People's Republic of China, 2011).

7. Foreign aid white papers: "China's Foreign Aid" (Beijing: Information Office of the State Council, People's Republic of China, 2014); "China's Foreign Aid" (Beijing: Information Office of the State Council of the People's Republic of China, April 21, 2011). Also see "Seeking Happiness for People: 70 Years of Progress in Human Rights" (Beijing: State Council Information Offices of the People's Republic of China, September 2019), which discusses China's foreign aid history as advancing the international cause of human rights.

8. Xinjiang white papers: "Vocational Education and Training in Xinjiang" (Beijing: State Council Information Office of the People's Republic of China, August 17, 2019); "Historical Matters Concerning Xinjiang" (Beijing: State Council Information Office of the People's Republic of China, July 2019); "The Fight against Terrorism and Extremism and Human Rights Protection in Xinjiang" (Beijing: State Council Information Office

of the People's Republic of China, March 2019); "Cultural Protecton and Developent in Xinjiang" (Beijing: State Council Information Office of the People's Republic of China, November 2018); "Human Rights in Xinjiang- Development and Progress" (Beijing: Information of the State Council of the People's Republic of China, 2017); "Historical Witness to Ethnic Equality, Unity and Development in Xinjiang" (Beijing: Information Office of the State Council of the People's Republic of China, 2016); "Freedom of Religious Belief in Xinjiang" (Beijing: Information Office of the State Council of the People's Republic of China, 2016); and "Development and Progress in Xinjiang" (Beijing: Information Office of the State Council of the People's Republic of China, 2009).

9. Editions of *China's Foreign Affairs* examined are from 2003 to 2018.

10. For full text of National Party Congress work reports since 1992, see Xi Jinping, "Secure a Decisive Victory in the Building of a Moderately Prosperous Society in All Respects and Strive for the Great Success of Socialism with Chinese Characteristics for a New Era," in *Work Report Delivered at the 19th National Congress of the Communist Party of China* (Beijing: Xinhua, 2017); Hu Jintao, "Firmly March on the Path of Socialism with Chinese Characteristics and Strive to Complete the Building of a Moderately Prosperous Society in All Respects," in *Work Report to the 18th National Congress of the Communist Party of China* (Beijing: Xinhua, 2012); Hu Jintao, "Hold High the Great Banner of Socialism with Chinese Characteristics and Strive for New Victories in Building a Moderately Prosperous Society," in *Work Report to the 17th National Congress of the Communist Party of China* (Beijing: Xinhua, 2007); Jiang Zemin, "Full Text of Jiang Zemin's Report at 16th Party Congress," in *Work Report to 16th Party Congress of the Communist Party of China* (Beijing: Xinhua, 2002); Jiang Zemin, "Hold High the Great Banner of Deng Xiaoping Theory for an All-round Advancement of the Cause of Building Socialism with Chinese Characteristics into the 21st Century," in *Work Report to the 15th Party Congress of the Communist Party of China* (Beijing: Xinhua, 1997); and Jiang Zemin, "Full Text of Jiang Zemin's Report at 14th Party Congress," in *Work Report to the 14th Party Congress of the Communist Party of China* (Beijing: Xinhua, 1992).

11. The purpose of this section is not to provide a thorough review of the literature about China's peaceful development rhetoric. The main objective is to introduce China's interests in its own development and peace required to support that development during this time period.

12. Deng Xiaoping "Peace and Development Are the Two Outstanding Issues in the World Today," March 4, 1985, excerpt from a talk with a delegation of the Japanese Chamber of Commerce and Industry, in Deng, *Selected Works of Deng Xiaoping (1982–1992)* (Beijing: Foreign Languages Press, 1994), 110–113.

13. For example, see "China's National Defense," 1998; "Full Text Jiang Zemin Speech at Cambridge," Xinhua, October 22, 1999; "China's National Defense in 2000"; "China's National Defense in 2002"; *China's Foreign Affairs: 2003*; "China's National Defense 2004"; "China's Peaceful Development Road," 2005; "China's National Defense in 2006"; "Full Text of Hu Jintao Speech to Nigerian National Assembly on 27 Apr," Xinhua Domestic Service, April 28, 2006; "Full text of Hu Jintao's Speech at South Africa's Pretoria University," Xinhua Domestic Service, February 10, 2007; "China's National Defense in

2008"; "China's National Defense in 2010"; "Full Text of Wen Jiabao's Speech at General Debate of 65th UNGA 23 Sep," Xinhua Domestic Service, September 24, 2010; "Full Text of Hu Jintao Speech at BRICS Leaders Meeting—Comparison," Xinhua Domestic Service, April 14, 2011; "Full Text of Wen Jiabao's Speech at China-Arab Ministerial Conference in Tianjin 13 May," Xinhua Domestic Service, May 15, 2010; "China's Peaceful Development 2011"; Hu, "Firmly March," 14; and Xi, "Secure a Decisive Victory," 52.

14. For example, Hu Jintao's work report to the 18th National Party Congress in 2012. See Hu, "Firmly March."

15. Xi, "Secure a Decisive Victory," 52.

16. "China and the World," 2019.

17. For an in-depth discussion of China's global quest for resources, see Elizabeth Economy and Michael Levi, *By All Means Necessary: How China's Resource Quest Is Changing the World* (New York: Oxford University Press, 2014).

18. For example, deteriorating economic relations with the United States could occur through an intensifying trade war or increased scrutiny of Chinese investments in the United States via its Committee on Foreign Investment in the United States.

19. "China's National Defense," 1998.

20. "China's National Defense," 1998; "China's National Defense in 2000"; "China's National Defense in 2002."

21. For example, see "China's National Defense in 2004"; *China's Foreign Affairs: 2005*, 6; *China's Foreign Affairs: 2006*, 4; "Full Text of Hu Jintao Speech at G-8, Developing Countries Dialogue Meeting," Xinhua Domestic Service, July 17, 2006; "China's National Defense 2006"; *China's Foreign Affairs: 2007*, 4–5, 33–35; "China's Energy Conditions and Policy"; "Full Text of Hu Jintao's Speech at BRIC Summit in Yekaterinburg on 16 June," Xinhua Domestic Service, June 17, 2009; "Full Speech of Hu Jintao at 64th Session of UN General Assembly," Xinhua Domestic Service, September 24, 2009; "Full Text of Wen Jiabao's Speech at China-Arab Ministerial Conference in Tianjin 13 May."

22. For example, see Sun Bigan, "Obama's New Middle East Policy and China's Energy Security," *Asia and Africa Review* 5 (2009): 17–20; Sun Xia and Guang Pan, "Energy Politics in the Middle East and China's Energy Security Strategy," *Arab World Studies* 4 (July 2009): 38–45; Qian Xuewen, "Energy Cooperation between China and the Middle East," *International Review* 1 (2008): 45–50; Shu Xianlin, "Analysis of Sino-US Relations in the Middle East Oil," *Arab World Studies* 5 (2009): 27–33; and Yang Hongxi, "Analysis of the Middle East Transformation of the International System," *Arab World Studies* 6 (2009): 11–17.

23. Sun and Pan, "Energy Politics."

24. Yang, "Analysis of the Middle East." Also see Qian, "Energy Cooperation"; "Obama's New Middle East Policy"; Shu, "Analysis of Sino-US Relations."

25. For example, see *China's Foreign Affairs: 2011*.

26. *China's Foreign Affairs: 2013*.

27. "The Diversified Employment," 2013 and "China's Military Strategy 2015."

28. For example, see "China's Energy Policy 2012"; "The Diversified Employment of

China's Armed Forces," and "China's Military Strategy in 2015;" "China's Foreign Affairs in 2015," and "China and the World in the New Era."

29. For example, see "Full Text of Hu Jintao Speech at Meeting of Five Developing Countries," Xinhua Domestic Service, July 9, 2008; "Full Text of Hu Jintao Speech at G8 Outreach Session 9 July in Toyko, Japan," Xinhua Domestic Service, July 10, 2008; "Hu Jintao's Speech at BRIC Summit"; "Full Speech of Hu Jintao at 65th Session of UN General Assembly."

30. "Hu Jintao at G8."

31. For example, see "The Diversified Employment"; "China's Military Strategy 2015"; *China's Foreign Affairs: 2015*. For a discussion of food security issues, see Economy and Levi, *By All Means Necessary*, 29–32. Although China mostly focused on self-sufficiency for food, its imports of food have grown over time and it is heavily dependent on imports for some products, such as soy. See Deborah Brautigam, *Will Africa Feed China?* (Oxford: Oxford University Press, 2015). Brautigam provides an in-depth analysis of China's food security need from Africa and argues that China imports much less food product than commonly believed.

32. "Comparison—Jiang's Speech in Israel," Xinhua Domestic Service, April 13, 2000.

33. For example, see *China's Foreign Affairs: 2003*, 6.

34. *China's Foreign Affairs: 2004*, 10.

35. *China's Foreign Affairs: 2004*, 10.

36. For example, see *China's Foreign Affairs 2004*, 2, 4–6, 42; "China's National Defense 2004"; *China's Foreign Affairs: 2005*, 8–10, 43; "China's Peaceful Development Road 2005"; *China's Foreign Affairs 2006*, 6; "China's National Defense in 2006"; "Full Text of Hu Jintao's Speech at Saudi Consultative Council on 23 Apr," Xinhua Domestic Service, April 24, 2006; *China's Foreign Affairs 2007*, 6–8; and *China's Foreign Affair 2009*, 6–9.

37. See An Weihua, "The Thirty Years of Inaugurating China: The Middle East Countries Relations," *West Asia and Africa* 11 (November 2008): 7; An Huihou, "The Hot Spot Issues in the Middle East and Big Power Relations," *Arab World Studies* 2 (2009): 3–4; Sun, "Obama's New Middle East Policy and China's Energy Security"; Sun and Pan, "Energy Politics in the Middle East and China's Energy Security Strategy."

38. *China's Foreign Affairs 2013*. For post–Arab awakening views of the Middle East, see also *China's Foreign Affairs 2014*; and *China's Foreign Affairs 2012*.

39. For example, see *China's Foreign Affairs 2014*, 4; *China's Foreign Affairs 2015*, 5; *China's Foreign Affairs 2016*, 2, 4; *China's Foreign Affairs 2017*, 4; *China's Foreign Affairs 2018*, 3; and "China's National Defense in the New Era," 2019.

40. Most frequently discussed in Chinese government documents and Chinese scholarly analysis. For government discourse, see "Jiang's Speech in Israel"; *China's Foreign Affairs 2003*, 1–2, 4–6, 10–12, 42; "China's National Defense 2004"; *China's Foreign Affairs 2005*, 8–10, 37; "China's Peaceful Development Road 2005"; *China's Foreign Affairs 2006*, 1–2, 6, 44–45; "China's National Defense 2006"; *China's Foreign Affairs 2007*, 6–8; *China's Foreign Affairs 2008*, 2–3, 5–7, 23–30; *China's Foreign Affairs 2009*, 4–5, 6–9, 40; "Comparison—Full Text of Wen Jiabao's Speech at the Arab League," Xinhua Domestic Service, November 9, 2009; and "Full Text of Wen Jiabao's Speech at UN Security

Council Summit 24 Sept, " Xinhua Domestic Service, September 28, 2010; and *China's Foreign Affairs 2011*. For examples of Chinese scholarly work, see Qian, "Energy Cooperation"; An Huihou, "The Middle East Hot Spot Issues and World Powers' Middle East Policies under New Circumstances," *Arab World Studies* 2 (2008): 3–10; An, "The Thirty Years of Inaugurating China"; "The Middle East: Seeking Stability and Development in Turbulence: On the Regional Situation from Scholars," *West Asia and Africa* (December 2008): 5–11; An, "The Hot Spot Issues in the Middle East and Big Power Relations"; Sun and Pan, "Energy Politics in the Middle East and China's Energy Security Strategy"; *China's Foreign Affairs 2014*.

41. See *China's Foreign Affairs 2003*, 1–2, 4–6, 10–12, 42; "China's National Defense 2004"; *China's Foreign Affairs 2005*, 8–10, 37; "China's Peaceful Development Road 2005"; *China's Foreign Affairs 2006*, 1–2, 6, 44–45; "China's National Defense 2006"; *China's Foreign Affairs 2007*, 6–8; *China's Foreign Affairs 2008*, 2–3, 5–7, 23–30; *China's Foreign Affairs 2009*, 4–5, 6–9, 40; *China's Foreign Affairs 2011*.

42. *China's Foreign Affairs 2009*, 4–5, 40.

43. *China's Foreign Affairs 2009*, 4–5.

44. *China's Foreign Affairs 2012*; *China's Foreign Affairs 2013*; and *China's Foreign Affairs 2014*, 4; *China's Foreign Affairs 2015*, 4; *China's Foreign Affairs 2016*, 4.

45. *China's Foreign Affairs 2016* and *China's Foreign Affairs 2017*, 2, 4; *China's Foreign Affairs 2018*, 4. Chapter 5 of this book on special envoys discusses China's concerns in Syria in much more detail. China is concerned not only about ISIS but also Uyghur-affiliated groups operating in Syria, such as TIP.

46. *China's Foreign Affairs 2013; China's Foreign Affairs 2014*; interview, Embassy of the State of Palestine, Beijing, China, January 30, 2013; *China's Foreign Affairs 2014*, 5–6; *China's Foreign Affairs 2015*, 6–7; *China's Foreign Affairs 2016*, 5–6; *China's Foreign Affairs 2017*, 5–6; and *China's Foreign Affairs* 2018, 4.

47. For examples of Chinese scholarly analysis of great power competition in the Middle East, see Qian, "Energy Cooperation"; Yang Hongxi, "The Big Power Factors Influencing the Middle East Situation," *Peace and Development* 4 (2008): 23–26; Li Weijian, "The Adjustment of the US Mideast Policy and Its Implications on Interactions among China, US and Arab Countries," *Arab World Studies* 2 (2008): 42–49; Li Yi, "China's Energy Diplomacy under the Security Situation of the Gulf," *West Asia and Africa* (July 2008): 46–51; Sun and Pan, "Energy Politics"; Yang, "Analysis of the Middle East"; An, "The Hot Spot Issues"; and Sun Degang, "International System Transformation and the Big Powers Quasi Alliance Diplomacy in the Middle East," *Arab World Studies* 6 (2009): 18–25.

48. For example, see Yang, "The Big Power Factors"; Qian, "Energy Cooperation" ; Li, "The Adjustment of the US"; Li, "China's Energy Diplomacy," 46–47; Sun, "Obama's New Middle East Policy"; Shu, "Analysis of Sino-US"; and Sun, "International System Transformation."

49. Li, "China's Energy Diplomacy," 46–47.

50. Chinese analysis of the Middle East heavily focuses on the role of the United States. For examples of analysis of the role of the United States in the Middle East, see

Yang, "The Big Power Factors"; Qian, "Energy Cooperation"; Li, "The Adjustment of the US"; An Huihou, "Middle Eastern Situation in the Change of International Configuration," *Arab World Studies* 6 (2009): 3–10; An Huihou, "President Obama's Middle East Policy Adjustment and Development of Hot Issues in the Region," *Asia and Africa Review* 3 (2009): 52–56; Sun, "Obama's New Middle East"; Sun and Pan, "Energy Politics"; Shu, "Analysis of Sino-US I"; and Sun, "International System Transformation."

51. For example, see *China's Foreign Affairs 2012* and *China's Foreign Affairs 2014*.

52. Discussed further in chapter 5 on China's special envoys.

53. *China's Foreign Affairs 2017*, 5.

54. *China's Foreign Affairs 2018*, 3.

55. Especially since the beginning of the embargo on Qatar in 2017.

56. For example, see *China's Foreign Affairs 2003*, 19; *China's Foreign Affairs 2004*, 12; *China's Foreign Affairs 2005*, 10–12; *China's Foreign Affairs 2006*, 7–9; *China's Foreign Affairs 2008*; and *China's Foreign Affairs 2009*, 9–10. Three exceptions are concerns over Darfur, Zimbabwe, and Somali piracy.

57. For example, see *China's Foreign Affairs 2003*, 5, 19 *China's Foreign Affairs 2004*, 12; *China's Foreign Affairs 2005*, 10–12; *China's Foreign Affairs 2006*, 7–9; and "China's African Policy."

58. For example, see *China's Foreign Affairs 2004*, 12; *China's Foreign Affairs 2005*, 10–12; *China's Foreign Affairs 2006*, 7–9; *China's Foreign Affairs 2007*, 9–10; *China's Foreign Affairs 2008*; *China's Foreign Affairs 2009*, 9–10; *China's Foreign Affairs 2011; China's Foreign Affairs 2012; China's Foreign Affairs 2013 ; China's Foreign Affairs 2014, 5–6; China's Foreign Affairs 2015, 7–8; China's Foreign Affairs 2016, 5–6; and China's Foreign Affairs 2018, 4–5.*

59. For example, see *China's Foreign Affairs 2012*; *China's Foreign Affairs 2013*; *China's Foreign Affairs 2014*.

60. *China's Foreign Affairs 2014*, 7; *China's Foreign Affairs 2015*, 8; *China's Foreign Affairs 2016*, 6–7; *China's Foreign Affairs 2018*, 8.

61. For example, see "Remarks by Bolton on Africa Strategy."

62. China in particular seeks support in international organizations such as the United Nations.

63. Deng Xiaoping, March 3, 1990, talk with leading members of the Central Committee: "The International Situation and Economic Problems" in Deng, *Selected Works of Deng Xiaoping, 1982–1992*, 341–343.

64. For example, see Sutter, *Chinese Foreign Relations*, chap. 3.

65. "China's National Defense 1998."

66. For example, see "China's National Defense 2000"; "Jiang's Speech in Israel; "China's National Defense 2002"; "China's National Defense 2004"; *China's Foreign Affairs 2005*, 1; "China's National Defense 2006"; "Text of Hu Jintao's Speech at Opening Ceremony of China-Africa Summit 4 Nov," Xinhua Domestic Service, November 6, 2006; "Full Text of Hu Jintao's Speech at Saudi Consultative Council on 23 April"; "Full Text of Hu Jintao's Speech at South Africa's Pretoria University"; and *China's Foreign Affairs 2008*, 1.

67. *China's Foreign Affairs 2004*, 35–36.

68. "China's National Defense 2008."

69. For example, see *China's Foreign Affairs 2008*, 1–2; "Full Text of Hu Jintao Speech at Meeting of Five Developing Countries"; and *China's Foreign Affairs 2009*, 1–3. For additional discussion of multipolarity in the late 2000s, see "Full Speech of Hu Jintao at 64th Session of UN General Assembly"; "Full Text of Wen Jiabao's Speech at China-Arab Ministerial Conference in Tianjin 13 May"; "Full Text of Wen Jiabao's Speech at UN Security Council Summit 24 Sep"; and "Full Text of Hu Jintao Speech at BRICS Leaders Meeting—Comparison," Xinhua Domestic Service, April 14, 2011. For a scholarly discussion of the shifting multipolarity in the Middle East, see Li, "The Adjustment of the US."

70. For example, see "China's National Defense 2010." *China's Foreign Affairs 2011* makes a similar argument.

71. For example, see *China's Foreign Affairs 2005*, 2–3, 36; "China's Peaceful Development Road 2005"; *China's Foreign Affairs 2006*, 37; "China's National Defense 2006"; "Text of Hu Jintao's Speech at Opening Ceremony of China-Africa Summit 4 Nov"; *China's Foreign Affairs 2007*, 40–41; *China's Foreign Affairs 2008*, 36; "Full Text of Hu Jintao Speech at Meeting of Five Developing Countries"; *China's Foreign Affairs 2009*, 39–40; "Comparison—Full Text of Wen Jiabao's Speech at the Arab League"; "Full Text of Hu Jintao's Speech at BRIC Summit in Yekaterinburg on 16 June"; "China Africa Economic and Trade Cooperation"; and "China's Peaceful Development 2011"; *China's Foreign Affairs 2014*, 1–2; and "China's Military Strategy 2015"; *China's Foreign Affairs 2015*, 2; *China's Foreign Affairs 2016*, 2; *China's Foreign Affairs 2017*, 1–2; *China's Foreign Affairs 2018*, 1–2; and "China's National Defense," 2019.

72. "China and the World," 2019.

73. For example, see Yan Xuetong. "China Needs to Purchase Friendships," *Nikkei Asian Review*, March 2, 2015. Yan also argues that this bipolar competition in the international order will not be over strategic hot spots but about the rules of the world order. In addition to some Chinese scholars, for a Western scholar who asserts the world is already bipolar see Tunsjo, *Bipolarity*.

74. Yan, "Purchase Friendships."

75. There is broad consensus among China scholars that China's two most important interests are maintaining the power of the Chinese Communist Party and protecting China's territorial integrity and sovereignty. For a detailed discussion of those interests, see Nathan and Scobell, *China's Search for Security*.

76. US Commission on International Religious Freedom, "China," in *Annual Report 2017* (Washington, DC: USCIRF, June 2017).

77. Although I believe that the threat to the CCP from Uyghurs is exaggerated, a number of Uyghur- orchestrated terrorist attacks have occurred within the PRC. I label these as terrorist attacks because they have targeted civilians in pursuit of a political objective.

78. "China's National Defense 2002."

79. For a discussion of China and international terrorism, see Dawn Murphy, "Chi-

na's Approach to International Terrorism," Peace Brief, United States Institute of Peace, September 2017.

80. For example, see "China's National Defense in 2004"; "China's National Defense in 2008"; Qian, "Energy Cooperation."

81. Edward Wong, "China Raises Death Toll in Ethnic Clashes to 184," *New York Times*, July 10, 2009.

82. "China's National Defense 2010."

83. Interview with Middle East analyst, Chinese Institute of International Studies (CIIS), March 22, 2011, Beijing.

84. Interview with Middle East scholar, Beijing University. April 14, 2010. Beijing.

85. Interview with Middle East analyst, Chinese Institute of Contemporary International Relations (CICIR), January 13, 2010, Beijing.

86. Interview, scholar, Beijing University, August 9, 2015; interview, Middle East Analyst, Institute of West Asian and African Studies (IWAAS), Chinese Academy of Social Sciences (CASS), Beijing, August 11, 2015.

87. Interview with embassy official, Embassy of the Hashemite Kingdom of Jordan, March 24, 2010, Beijing.

88. Interview with former Egyptian ambassador to China, October 21, 2010, Cairo.

89. Interview with former Arab League ambassador to China, October 26, 2010, Cairo. Some scholars did suggest that after the beginning of the Arab awakening, concerns about external support for Xinjiang decreased in importance. For example, interview, Beijing University, January 22, 2013. That said, since the rise of ISIS and China's crackdown in Xinjiang in recent years, my perception is that those concerns are again a major emphasis.

90. Murray Scot Tanner with James Bellacqua. "China's Response to Terrorism," CNA, June 2016.

91. "Historical Witness to Ethinic Equality." See also "Freedom of Religious Belief," and "Development and Progress." Also see "China's Military Strategy in 2015."

92. National Security Law of the PRC, National People's Congress, July 1, 2015.

93. Counter-Terrorism Law of the PRC, National People's Congress, December 27, 2015.

94. "China," U.S. Commission on International Religious Freedom Annual Report 2017. Over the past several years, the Chinese government has produced a number of white papers to present its own view of the situation in Xinjiang. See "Cultural Protection and Development"; "The Fight against Terrorism and Extremism"; "Historical Matters Concerning Xinjiang"; "Vocational Education and Training"; and "Seeking Happiness for People."

95. This book does not seek to provide an in-depth discussion of the situation in Xinjiang. Its purpose is to describe the links between China's concerns about stability in Xinjiang and relations with states in the Middle East and sub-Saharan Africa. For a brief overview of developments in Xinjiang, see James Millward, "Reeducating' Xinjiang's Muslims," *New York Review of Books*, February 7, 2019; James Millward and Dahlia Peterson, "China's System of Oppression in Xinjiang: How It Developed and How to Curb It," *Brookings Report*, September 2020.

96. Footnote of Deng Xiaoping's December 28, 1977, "Speech at a Plenary Meeting of the Military Commission of the Central Committee of the CPC," in Deng, *Selected Works of Deng Xiaoping, 1975–1982*, 403.

97. For an in-depth discussion of China's relations with the Third World over time, see George T. Yu, "China and the Third World," *Asian Survey* 17, no. 11 (1977): 1036–1048.

98. For more information on the New International Economic Order, see "Declaration on the Establishment of a New International Economic Order," United Nations General Assembly Resolution, Vol. RES/3201, May 1, 1974; "Programme of Action on the Establishment of a New International Economic Order," United Nations General Assembly Resolution, Vol. RES/3202, May 1, 1974; "Charter of Economic Rights and Duties of States," United Nations General Assembly Resolution, Vol. A/RES/3281, New York, December 12, 1974 .

99. Deng, "Speech by Chairman of the Delegation of the People's Republic of China, Teng Hsiao-Ping, at the Special Session of the U.N. General Assembly."

100. Deng Xiaoping, "We Must Safeguard World Peace and Ensure Domestic Development," May 29, 1984, in Deng, *Selected Works of Deng Xiaoping, 1982–1992*, 66–67.

101. For example, see "Full Text of Hu Jintao's Speech at South Africa's Pretoria University."

102. For example, see "Text of Jiang Zemin's Speech at Banquet in South Africa," Xinhua Domestic Service, April 26, 2000.

103. "China's National Defense in 2002"; "Comparison—Text of Wen Jiabao's Speech at China-African Cooperation Forum," Xinhua Domestic Service, December 15, 2003; "China's National Defense 2004"; "Comparison—'Full Text' of Hu Jintao's Speech at Opening of G-20 Meeting," Xinhua Domestic Service, April 16, 2005; "Full Text of Hu Jintao Speech at Asia-Africa Summit in Jakarta 22 Apr," Xinhua Domestic Service, May 5, 2005; "China's African Policy"; "Full Text of Hu Jintao Speech to Nigerian National Assembly on 27 Apr"; "Text of Hu Jintao's Speech at Opening Ceremony of China-Africa Summit 4 Nov"; "Full Text of Hu Jintao Speech at Dialogue Between G-8, Developing-Countries," Xinhua Domestic Service, June 9, 2007; "Full Text of Hu Jintao's Speech at South Africa's Pretoria University," Xinhua Domestic Service, February 10, 2007; "China's Energy Conditions and Policies"; "Xinhua Carries Apparent 'Full Text' of Wen Jiabao's Speech at Summer Davos," Xinhua, September 6, 2007; "Full Text of Wen Jiabao Speech at UN High-Level Meeting on MDGs," Xinhua Domestic Service, September 26, 2008; "Full Speech of Hu Jintao at 64th Session of UN General Assembly"; "Full Text of Wen Jiabao's Speech at General Debate of 65th UNGA 23 Sep," Xinhua Domestic Service, September 24, 2010; "China Africa Economic and Trade Cooperation," *White Paper*; "Full Text of Hu Jintao's Speech at BRIC Summit in Brazil 15 Apr," Xinhua Domestic Service, April 17, 2010; "China's Foreign Aid," 2011.

104. For example, see "Text of Jiang Zemin's Speech at Banquet in South Africa"; "Comparison—Text of Wen Jiabao's Speech at China-African Cooperation Forum"; "Comparison—Full Text of Hu Jintao's Speech at Opening of G-20 Meeting"; "China's African Policy," white paper; "Text of Hu Jintao's Speech at Opening Ceremony of China-Africa Summit 4 Nov"; "Full Text of Hu Jintao Speech at Dialogue Between

G-8, Developing-Countries"; "Full Text of Hu Jintao's Speech at South Africa's Pretoria University"; "China's Energy Conditions and Policies," white paper; "Comparison—Full Text of Wen Jiabao's Speech at the Arab League"; "China Africa Economic and Trade Cooperation"; "Full Text of Hu Jintao's Speech at BRIC Summit in Brazil 15 Apr"; and "China's Foreign Aid," 2011.

105. See "Comparison—PRC: Xinhua Text of Speech by Premier Wen Jiabao at Cambridge," Xinhua Domestic Service, February 5, 2009.

106. Xi, "Secure a Decisive," 10

107. For example, see "China and the World," 2019. China's discourse in its cooperation forums also often refers to China as a developing country. See chapter 4. Scholars also note the ways in which China sees itself as a developing country and how that affects its foreign policy behavior. For example, see Pu Xiaoyu, *Rebranding China: Contested Status Signaling in Changing Global Order* (Stanford, CA: Stanford University Press, 2019); Courtney J. Fung, *China and Intervention at the UN Security Council: Reconciling Status* (Oxford: Oxford University Press, 2019).

108. https://data.worldbank.org/indicator/NY.GDP.PCAP.CD?view=map.

109. "Speech by Chairman of the Delegation of the People's Republic of China, Teng Hsiao-Ping, at the Special Session of the U.N. General Assembly."

110. For example, see Deng Xiaoping, "Promote the Friendship between China and India," October 22, 1982, in Deng, *Selected Works of Deng Xiaoping, 1982–1992*, 29–30. In 1984 Deng also emphasized the dramatic differences between rich and poor countries. See Deng Xiaoping, "We Must Safeguard World Peace and Ensure Domestic Development," May 29, 1984, in Deng, *Selected Works of Deng Xiaoping*, 1982–1992, 66–67.

111. Deng Xiaoping "A New International Order Should Be Established with the Five Principles of Peaceful Coexistence as Norms," December 21, 1988, in Deng, *Selected Works of Deng Xiaoping*, 1982–1992, 275–276.

112. "China's National Defense," 1998.

113. For example, see "Full Text of Jiang Zemin Speech at Cambridge"; "China's National Defense in 2000," white paper; "Text of Jiang Zemin's Speech at Banquet in South Africa," Xinhua Domestic Service, April 26, 2000, and "China's National Defense in 2002," white paper.

114. For example, see "China's National Defense 2002"; *China's Foreign Affairs 2003*, 1, 6; "Comparison—Text of Wen Jiabao's Speech at China-African Cooperation Forum"; "Full Text of Hu Jintao Speech at North-South Leaders' Dialogue Meeting," Xinhua Domestic Service, June 1, 2003; *China's Foreign Affairs 2004*, 1, 7–8, 35–36; "Wen Jiabao Delivers Speech Marking Five Principles of Peaceful Coexistence Anniversary," Xinhua Domestic Service, June 28, 2004; "China's National Defense in 2004"; *"China's Peaceful Development Road 2005*"; "Full Text of Hu Jintao's Speech at UN Summit 15 September," Xinhua Domestic Service, September 16, 2005; "Full Text of Hu Jintao Speech at Asia-Africa Summit in Jakarta 22 Apr"; "Full Text of Hu Jintao's Speech at Asian-African Business Summit Reception," Xinhua, April 21, 2005; "Comparison—'Full Text' of Hu Jintao's Speech at Opening of G-20 Meeting"; *China's Foreign Affairs: 2006 Edition*, 3–4, 6, 38; "Full Text of Hu Jintao Speech to Nigerian National Assembly on 27 Apr"; "Text

of Hu Jintao's Speech at Opening Ceremony of China-Africa Summit 4 Nov"; "China's National Defense in 2006"; "Full Text of Hu Jintao Speech at Dialogue Between G-8, Developing-Countries"; *China's Foreign Affairs: 2007 Edition*, 4–5; "Full Text of Hu Jintao's Speech at South Africa's Pretoria University"; "Full Text of Hu Jintao Speech at G8 Outreach Session 9 July in Toyko, Japan"; and "China's Peaceful Development 2011."

115. For example, see "Comparison—PRC: Xinhua Text of Speech by Premier Wen Jiabao at Cambridge"; "Full Text of Hu Jintao's speech at Second G20 Financial Summit in London," Xinhua Domestic Service, April 4, 2009; "Full Text of Hu Jintao's Speech at BRIC Summit in Yekaterinburg on 16 June"; "Full Speech of Hu Jintao at 64th Session of UN General Assembly"; "Full Text of Wen Jiabao's Speech at Opening of FOCAC Ministerial Conference," Xinhua Domestic Service, November 10, 2009; "Full Text of Hu Jintao's Speech at G-20 Third Financial Summit in Pittsburgh," Xinhua Domestic Service, September 26, 2009; "China's National Defense in 2010"; "China Africa Economic and Trade Cooperation"; "Full Text of Hu Jintao's Speech at Fourth Summit of G-20 Leaders in Toronto," Xinhua Domestic Service, June 29, 2010; "Full Text of Hu Jintao's Speech at BRIC Summit in Brazil 15 Apr"; "Full Text of Hu Jintao Speech at BRICS Leaders Meeting—Comparison"; "Full Text of Wen Jiabao's Speech at General Debate of 65th UNGA 23 Sep"; and "Full Text of Wen Jiabao's Speech at China-Arab Ministerial Conference in Tianjin 13 May."

116. For example, see *China's Foreign Affairs 2009, 4–5.*

117. Hu, "Firmly March," 43.

118. "China's Arab Policy Paper."

119. "China's Arab Policy Paper."

120. For a more detailed description of this argument, see Wang Jisi, "China in the Middle," *American Interest* 10 , no. 4 (2015).

121. Over time, China does tend to refer to the need for this new just and equitable economic order more often when the audience is developing states.

122. Li Zhongfa and Xueyi Xu, "Xi Jinping Chairs and Delivers an Important Speech at the Ninth BRICS Leaders' Meeting: Stresses Comprehensive Deepening of BRICS Partnershio to Open Up a Brighter Future," Xinhua Domestic, September 4, 2017. China's renewed focus on this new just and equitable international and economic order may be partially a response to former president Trump's approach to the world economic order.

123. Xi, "Secure a Decisive Victory," 54

124. Xi, "Secure a Decisive Victory," 9. In recent years, Chinese government officials have vigorously denied that there was a China model for other countries to follow. That makes the content of this speech an interesting deviation from official rhetoric and may signal that China will take a more active role in providing models.

125. "China and the World," 2019.

126. For an in-depth discussion of China's emerging needs to protect its citizens and businesses abroad, see Mathieu Duchatel, Oliver Brauner, and Hang Zhou, "Protecting China's Overseas Interests: The Slow Shift Away from Non-Interference," SIPRI policy paper (Stockholm: Stockholm International Peace Research Institute, 2014). Also see

Ely Ratner, "The Emergent Security Threats Reshaping China," *Washington Quarterly* 31, no. 1 (2011): 29–44. For a discussion of China and international terrorism, see Murphy, "China's Approach to International Terrorism."

127. Interview, Chinese Academic of Socials Science, Institute of West Asian and African Studies, January 25, 2017; interview, Beijing University, January 22, 2013.

128. "The Diversified Employment," 2013.

129. "China's Military Strategy," 2015.

130. "China's National Defense," 2019.

131. Duchatel et al., "Protecting China's Overseas Interests" 46, 48–51.

132. Duchatel et al., "Protecting China's Overseas Interests," 46.

133. Mordechai Chaziza. "China's Middle East Foreign Policy and the Yemen Crisis: Challenges and Implications." *Middle East Review of International Affairs* 19, no. 2 (2015): 21.

134. Interview, Beijing University, January 22, 2013; interview, Chinese Academy of Social Sciences, Institute of World Economics and Politics, January 28, 2013.

135. Interview, Chinese Academy of Social Sciences, Institute of World Economics and Politics, January 28, 2013.

136. See Li Xiaojun and Zeng Ka, "Beijing Is Counting On Its Massive Belt and Road Initiative. But Are Chinese Firms On Board?" *Washington Post*, May 14, 2019; Li, Xiaojun and Zeng Ka, "To Join or Not to Join? State Ownership, Commercial Interests, and China's Belt and Road Initiative," *Pacific Affairs* 92, no. 1 2019).

137. "ISIL Video Threatens China with 'Rivers of Bloodshed,'" *Al Jazeera*, March 1, 2017.

138. Matthieu Duchatel, "Terror Overseas: Understanding China's Evolving Counter-Terror Strategy," policy brief, European Council on Foreign Relations. October 2016.

139. Michael Clark, "Executions in Pakistan: Is ISIS Targeting China?" *CNN*, June 16, 2017.

140. Idrissa Sangare, Adama Diarre, and Lizzie Deardon, "Al-Qaeda Claims Responsibility for Terror Attack That Killed at Least Five People at Luxury Resort in Mali," *Independent*, June 20, 2017.

141. "Chinese UN Peacekeeper Killed in Mali attack by Al-Qaeda Brach," *South China Morning Post*, June 1, 2016.

142. Tom Phillips, "Suicide Bomber Attacks Chinese Embassy in Kyrgyzstan," *Guardian*, August 20, 2016.

143. Merrit Kennedy and Camila Domonoske, "The Victims of the Brussels Attack: What We Know," *NPR*, March 31, 2016.

144. Interview, scholar, King Faisal Center for Research, Riyhad, Saudi Arabia, August 8, 2016, and interview, journalist, *Al Riyhad* Newspaper, Riyhad, Saudi Arabia, August 2016.

145. Larry Hanauer and Lyle J. Morris, *Engagement in Africa: Drivers, Reactions, and Implications for U.S. Policy* (Santa Monica, CA: RAND, 2014), 86. The fallout of the Sudan kidnappings is discussed in chapter 5 about China's special envoy for Africa.

146. See allafrica.com/stories/202105300064.html; news.cgtn.com/news/2021-

06-08/Two-Chinese-mining-employees-kidnapped-in-western-Niger-report-10V6GXPIGe4/index.html; www.thecitizen.co.tz/tanzania/news/africa/two-chinese-mine-workers-kidnapped-in-southwest-nigeria-3352236; and saharareporters.com/2021/06/16/gunmen-abduct-four-chinese-railway-workers-kill-policeman-ogun.

147. *China's Foreign Affairs 2014*.

148. Interview, Embassy of the Republic of Djibouti, Beijing, China, August 12, 2015; "China's Energy Policy 2012."

149. James Chen, *The Emergence of China in the Middle East* (Washington, DC: Institute for National Strategic Studies, National Defense University, 2011), 4–5.

150. "Zambian Miners Kill Chinese Manager during Pay Protest," *BBC News*, August 5, 2012.

151. "The Colony: China in West Africa," Witness, *Al Jazeera*, September 7, 2010. https://www.aljazeera.com/program/witness/2010/9/7/the-colony-china-in-west-africa/

152. Freeman Sipila, "3 Chinese Nationals Killed in CAR Attack," *Voice of America*, October 5, 2018.

153. Interview, Chinese Academy of Social Sciences, Institute of West Asia and African Studies, January 25, 2013.

154. The year 2012 was not the first time Wang Jisi wrote about the need for China to start to look west. In a 2011 *Foreign Affairs* piece, he discussed China's new Western outlook and said it "may reshape China's geostrategic vision as well as the Eurasian landscape." Wang Jisi, "China's Search for a Grand Strategy," *Foreign Affairs* 90, no. 2 (2011).

155. Wang Jisi, "March West: China Geostrategic Rebalancing," *Global Times*, October 2012. For an excellent discussion of Wang's March West piece, see Sun Yun. "March West: China's Response to the U.S. Rebalancing," *Brookings* (blog), January 31, 2013.

156. Wang, "March West."

157. Wang Jisi, "China in the Middle," *American Interest* 10, no. 4 (2015).

158. Wang, "China in the Middle."

159. Wang, "China in the Middle."

160. Yan Xuetong, "China Must Not Overplay Its Strategic Hand," *Global Times*, August 9, 2017.

161. "China's Military Strategy 2015."

162. Interview, Embassy of Palestine, August 6, 2015; interview, Embassy of the Sultanate of Oman, August 10, 2015.

163. Interview, Embassy of the Sultanate of Oman, August 10, 2015.

164. For example, interview, Beijing University, August 9, 2015; interview, China Foreign Affairs University, August 13, 2015.

165. Interview, Beijing University, August 9, 2015.

166. Interview, Beijing University, August 9, 2015.

167. Interview, scholar, Institute of West Asia and African Studies, Chinese Academy of Social Sciences, Beijing, China, January 25, 2013.

168. Interview, Embassy of Palestine, January 30, 2013.

169. Interview, Beijing University, August 9, 2015.

170. Interview, Chinese Academy of Social Sciences, Institute of West Asian and African Studies, August 10, 2015.

171. Interview, scholar, Institute of World Economic and Politics, Chinese Academy of Social Sciences, Beijing, China, August, 13, 2015.

172. Interview, journalist, *Al Riyadh* Newspaper, Riyadh, Saudi Arabia, August 8, 2016.

173. Interview, US. Department of Defense, Washington, DC, July 8, 2015.

174. Interview, Middle East Analysts, China Institute for International Studies, August 12, 2015.

175. Andrew Scobell and Scott W. Harold, "An `Assertive' China? Insights from Interviews," *Asian Security* 9, no. 2, (2013).

176. Michael D. Swaine, "Chinese Views and Commentary on the 'One Belt, One Road' Initiative," *China Leadership Monitor* 47 (2015): 7; Michael D. Swaine, "Chinese Views and Commentary on Peripheral Diplomacy," *China Leadership Monitor* 44 (2014): 19.

177. Jon B. Alterman, *China's Balancing Act in the Gulf*, Gulf analysis paper (Washington, DC: Center for Strategic and International Studies), 2013.

178. Andrew Scobell and Alireza Nader, "China in the Middle East: The Wary Dragon" (Santa Monica, CA: RAND, 2016).

179. Scobell and Nader, "China in the Middle East."

180. Interview, scholar, Near East and South Asia Center for Strategic Studies, US National Defense University, Washington, DC, July 8, 2015; interview, US Embassy in Kuwait, August 2016.

181. Interview, Embassy of the State of Palestine, Beijing, China, August 6, 2015. US China scholars have also started to notice this linkage between East China Sea and South China Sea and March West. For example, see Swaine, "Chinese Views and Commentary on Peripheral Diplomacy," 8. China's relations with the Middle East can be seen as part of its broader peripheral diplomacy push that Swaine described.

182. *China's Foreign Affairs 2014*. Section on China's relations with sub-Saharan African countries

183. "China-Arab Cooperation Forum Ministerial Conference of the Seventh Doha Declaration," section 6. My translation.

184. See chapter 4 on cooperation forums for a further discussion of this issue.

185. Interview, Embassy of the Sultanate of Oman in Beijing, January 29, 2013; interview, Beijing University, January 22, 2013. Also see Xu Yixiang. "Evolving Sino-Russian Cooperation in Syria." United States Institute of Peace brief, 2017.

186. Interview, Beijing University, January 22, 2013; interview, Embassy of the State of Palestine, Beijing, January 30, 2013; interview, Institute of World Economics and Politics, Chinese Academy of Social Sciences, Beijing, January 24, 2013; interview, Institute of World Economics and Politics, Chinese Academy of Social Sciences (CASS), Beijing, January 17, 2013.

187. Interview, Beijing University, January 22, 2013.

188. Interview, Chinese Academy of Social Sciences, Institute of World Econom-

ics and Politics, January 17, 2013; interview, scholar, China Foreign Affairs University, August 14, 2015.

189. Interview, Chinese Academic of Social Sciences, January 24, 2013. The NATO Libya intervention was a turning point in Chinese thinking about Western interventionism. China does not want to set that precedent going forward and is now explicitly taking a stand against this type of interventionism. Also see interview, Chinese Academy of Social Sciences, Institute of West Asian and African Studies, January 25, 2013. The interviewee stressed that China's interests in Syria are not material but more of a philosophical stance against a trend toward Western interference in the internal affairs of other countries, especially in the Middle East in a post–Arab awakening environment.

190. Interview, Beijing University, January 22, 2013.

191. Interview, Chinese Academy of Social Sciences, Institute of World Economics and Politics, January 24, 2013; interview, Beijing University, August 9, 2015.

192. *China's Foreign Affairs 2012.*

193. *China's Foreign Affairs 2013*, 6.

194. One exception was the growing role of Africa in global food security after the global financial crisis in 2008.

CHAPTER 4

1. For more information on these other cooperation forums, see SCO at eng.sectsco.org; Forum of China and Community of Latin American and Caribbean States (China-CELAC) at www.chinacelacforum.org/eng; Central and Eastern European countries (17+1) at www.china-ceec.org/eng,;and Forum for Economic and Trade Cooperation between China and Portuguese Speaking Countries (Forum Macao) at www.forumchinaplp.org.mo.

2. One exception is Southeast Asia. In that region, China interfaces with the Association of Southeast Asian Nations (ASEAN). Since the early 2000s, China's activities with ASEAN have been very similar to the agreements formed through cooperation forums. See asean.org/asean/external-relations/china

3. Most academic work on China's cooperation forums in these regions analyzes them in isolation, but some articles do compare cooperation forums across regions. For an in-depth analysis of FOCAC, see Ambrose Du Plessis, "The Forum on China-Africa Cooperation, Ideas, and Aid: National Interest(s) or Strategic Partnership?" *Insight on Africa* 6, no. 2 (2014); Sithara Fernando, "China-Africa Relations: An Analysis of Forum on China-Africa Cooperation (FOCAC) Documents Using Shinn and Eisenman's Optimist-Pessimist Dual Framework," *Insights on Africa* 6, no. 2 (2014); Garth Shelton, April Yazini, April Funeka, and Li Anshan, eds., *FOCAC 2015: A New Beginning of China-Africa Relations* (Pretoria, South Africa: African Institute of South Africa, 2015); Ian Taylor, *The Forum on China-Africa Cooperation (FOCAC)* (London: Routledge, 2011). For an in-depth case study on CASCF, see Yao Kuangyi, "China-Arab State Cooperation Forums in the Last Decade," *Journal of Middle Eastern and Islamic Studies (in Asia)* 8, no. 4 (2014). Recent articles examining the forums in comparative perspective include Jakub Jakóbowski, "Chinese-Led Regional Multilateralism in Central and Eastern Europe, Af-

rica and Latin America: 16 + 1, FOCAC, and CCF," *Journal of Contemporary China* 27 (2018); and Nicola Contessi, "Experiments in Soft Balancing: China-Led Multilateralism in the Arab World," *Caucasian Review of International Affairs* 3, no. 4 (2009). Contessi's piece is the only one that compares FOCAC and CASCF. It was published in 2009. His work does highlight the similarities between the two forums and speculates that they may be a model for China's foreign policy or an emerging grand strategy.

4. FOCAC documents in Chinese, English, and French are available at www.focac.org. CASCF documents are available in Arabic and Chinese at www.cascf.org . Quotations from these documents in this chapter are from the English version of FOCAC documents and my translation from Chinese for CASCF documents.

5. Swaziland changed its name to eSwatini in 2018. eSwatini recognizes Taiwan as opposed to the PRC, so it is not eligible for membership in FOCAC.

6. Interview, Embassy of South Africa official, April 16, 2010, Beijing; interview, CASS, IWAAS, April 2010, Beijing; interview, Chinese Academy of Social Sciences (CASS), Institute of West Asia and Africa Studies (IWAAS), April 2010, Beijing; interview, Beijing University, January 22, 2013, Beijing.

7. See www.dirco.gov.za/docs/2020/au_focac0617.htm.

8. Interview, CASS, IWAAS, April 27, 2010, Beijing; interview, Embassy of South Africa, April 16, 2010, Beijing; interview, Stellenbosch University's Center for Chinese Studies, May 30, 2011, Stellenbosch, South Africa.

9. Interview, CASS, IWAAS, April 27, 2010, Beijing.

10. Interview, SOAS scholar from South Africa, January 12, 2010, Beijing; interview, government official, Department of International Relations and Co-operation, June 15, 2011, South Africa (interview conducted via phone). For more information on TICAD, see www.mofa.go.jp/region/africa/ticad/index.html

11. Interview, CASS, IWAAS, April 27, 2010, Beijing.

12. Interview, CASS, IWAAS, April 27, 2010, Beijing; interview, former African Union official, November 9, 2010, Cairo, Egypt; interview, Embassy of the Republic of Turkey, March 30, 2010, Beijing. The India-Africa and Turkey-Africa cooperation forums were established in 2008.

13. Interview, CASS, IWAAS, January 27, 2010, Beijing; interview, Beijing University Scholar, April 14, 2010, Beijing; interview, CIIS, March 30, 2010, Beijing; interview, Embassy of the Kingdom of Bahrain, April 20, 2010, Beijing; interview, Kuwait University Scholar, November 17, 2010, Cairo, Egypt.

14. The State of Palestine is a member of the League of Arab States.

15. Interview, Embassy of the Hashemite Kingdom of Jordan, May 24, 2010, Beijing; interview, former League of Arab States official, October 26, 2010, Cairo.

16. Interview, Embassy of the Republic of Iraq, January 24, 2013, Beijing.

17. For more information about the Summit of South American-Arab Countries, see merip.org/2018/04/south-south-solidarity-and-the-summit-%E2%80%A8of-south-american-arab-countries/.

18. For background the Turkish-Arab Cooperation Forum, see www.mfa.gov.tr/guam_.en.mfa.

19. Japan-Arab Economic Forum: see www.jccme.or.jp/english/jaef_outline.html.

20. Russian-Arab Cooperation Forum: see www.rusemb.org.uk/foreignpolicy/718.

21. Arab-India cooperation forum: see mea.gov.in/outoging-visit-detail.htm?26292/Manama%B1Declaration%B1of%B1the%B1First%B1Ministerial%B1Meeting%B1of%B1the%B1ArabIndia%B1Cooperation%B1Forum%B1January%B124%B12016.

22. Interview, League of Arab States, November 30, 2010, Cairo.

23. Another political norm for the forums is that all members recognize the one-China principle.

24. The Five Principles of Peaceful Coexistence were developed by China in the early 1950s. See http://www.fmprc.gov.cn/eng/ziliao/3602/3604/t18053.htm.

25. The Five Principles were originally called Panchsheel. See Kimche, *Afro-Asian Movement*, 48, and Alan Lawrence, *China's Foreign Relations since 1949* (London: Routledge, 1975), 160. The term was first formally incorporated into a treaty between China and India in 1954. The Five Principles share many norms with the Westphalian system.

26. Interview, Embassy of the Republic of Tunisia, May 24, 2010, Beijing; interview, Chinese Academy of Social Sciences (CASS), Institute of World Economics and Politics (IWEP), January 28, 2010, Beijing; interview, Egyptian Ministry of Foreign Affairs, December 1, 2010, Cairo; interview, Embassy of the State of Palestine, May 28, 2010, Beijing; interview, Embassy of the Republic of Djibouti, August 12, 2015, Beijing.

27. Interview, Egyptian Ministry of Foreign Affairs, November 24, 2010, Cairo.

28. Interview, CASS, IWEP, January 14, 2010, Beijing; interview, Embassy of the Kingdom of Bahrain, April 20, 2010, Beijing; interview, Beijing University Scholar, April 14, 2010.

29. Interview, CIIS, March 30, 2010, Beijing; interview, CASS IWAAS, January 27, 2010, Beijing.

30. "China-Arab Cooperation Forum Fifth Ministerial Meeting Declaration," 2012; "China-Arab Cooperation Forum Ministerial Conference of the Seventh Doha Declaration," 2016.

31. In this book, Sudan and Somalia are classified as sub-Saharan African countries. That said, they are members of the China-Arab States Cooperation Forum (CASCF), and political issues related to these countries are directly addressed in this cooperation forum.

32. Khalili, *Communist China's Interaction*, 11; Nasser-Eddine, *Arab-Chinese Relations*, 85.

33. See Nasser-Eddine, *Arab-Chinese Relations*, 85."Formosa" is the Portuguese term for Taiwan.

34. See Harris, *China's Foreign Policy*, 21, 54, 76, and Behbehani, *China's Foreign Policy*, 84.

35. Interview, CASS IWAAS, January 27, 2010, Beijing.

36. My translation from the Chinese. See "China-Arab States Cooperation Forum Declaration," September 14, 2004.

37. My translation from Chinese text. See Political Cooperation section of "China-Arab States Cooperation Forum Action Plan," September 14, 2004. Also, documents

from the Second Ministerial Meeting in 2006 contain similar wording. See "China-Arab States Cooperation Forum Second Ministerial Meeting Communique," June 1, 2006.

38. My translation from Chinese text. See "China-Arab States Cooperation Forum Third Ministerial Meeting Communique," May 21, 2008.

39. My translation from Chinese text. See "China-Arab States Cooperation Forum Fourth Ministerial Meeting Communique," May 13, 2010.

40. Interview, Embassy of the State of Palestine, May 28, 2010, Beijing.

41. Interview, Embassy of the State of Palestine, May 28, 2010, Beijing.

42. Interview, Kuwait University Scholar, November 17, 2010, Cairo, Egypt.

43. Interview, Embassy of Palestine, January 30, 2013, Beijing.

44. CASCF, "Fifth Ministerial Meeting Declaration," section 4.

45. "China-Arab Cooperation Forum Beijing Declaration of the Sixth Ministerial Conference," 2014.

46. CASCF, "Seventh Doha Declaration," 2016, Section 7.

47. http://www.un.org/webcast/pdfs/SRES2334–2016.pdf,

48. "Beijing Declaration of the Eighth Ministerial Conference of the China-Arab Cooperation Forum," 2018, section 6. My translation.

49. CASCF, "Beijing Declaration of the Eighth Ministerial," section 6.

50. "Amman Declaration of the Ninth Ministerial Conference of the China-Arab Cooperation Forum," July 2020.

51. CASCF, "Third Ministerial Meeting Communique," and CASCF, "Fourth Ministerial Meeting Communique."

52. CASCF, "Third Ministerial Meeting Communique."

53. CASCF, "Fourth Ministerial Meeting Communique."

54. CASCF, "Fifth Ministerial Meeting Declaration," section 6; CASCF "Sixth Ministerial Conference"; CASCF, "Seventh Doha Declaration," section 9; CASCF "Eighth Ministerial Conference," section 8; CASCF, "Amman Declaration."

55. CASCF "Fifth Ministerial Meeting Declaration"; CASCF, "Sixth Ministerial Conference"; CASCF, "Seventh Doha Declaration"; CASCF, "Eighth Ministerial Conference"; CASCF, "Amman Declaration."

56. China established formal diplomatic relations with Israel in 1992.

57. Interview, former African Union official, November 9, 2010, Cairo.

58. Interview, Embassy of the State of Palestine, May 28, 2010, Beijing

59. My translation from Chinese text. See CASCF, "Second Ministerial Meeting Communique," 2006.

60. CASCF, " Third Ministerial Meeting Communique"; CASCF, "Fourth Ministerial Meeting Communique"; CASCF, "Fifth Ministerial Meeting Declaration"; CASCF, "Sixth Ministerial Conference"; CASCF, "Seventh Doha Declaration"; CASCF, "Eighth Ministerial Conference"; CASCF, "Amman."

61. CASCF, " Second Ministerial Meeting Communique"; CASCF, " Third Ministerial Meeting Communique"; CASCF, " Fourth Ministerial Meeting Communique"; CASCF, "Fifth Ministerial Meeting Declaration" ; CASCF, "Sixth Ministerial Conference" ; CASCF, "Seventh Doha Declaration"; and CASCF, "Eighth Ministerial Conference."

62. CASCF, "Fifth Ministerial Meeting Declaration," section 7.

63. CASCF, "Fifth Ministerial Meeting Declaration," sections 14–15; CASCF "Sixth Ministerial Conference."

64. Interview, Embassy of the Sultanate of Oman, January 29, 2013, Beijing.

65. Interview, Beijing University, August 9, 2015, Beijing.

66. Interview, Embassy of the United Arab Emirates, January 21, 2013, Beijing; interview, Chinese Academy of Social Sciences, Institute of West Asian and African Studies. January 25, 2013. Beijing; interview, Beijing University, January 22, 2013.

67. Interview, Embassy of the State of Palestine, August 6, 2015, Beijing.

68. Interview, Beijing University, August 6, 2015, Beijing.

69. CASCF, "Seventh Doha Declaration," section 8.

70. CASCF, "Seventh Doha Declaration."

71. CASCF, "Eighth Ministerial Conference."

72. CASCF, "Seventh Doha Declaration," sections 14–15.

73. CASCF, "Eighth Ministerial Conference," section 14; CASCF, "Amman Declaration."

74. My translation from Chinese text. See CASCF, "Fourth Ministerial Meeting Communiqué."

75. Interview, former African Union official, November 9, 2010, Cairo, Egypt; interview, Kuwait University scholar, November 17, 2010, Cairo; interview, Egyptian Council for Foreign Affairs, November 10, 2010, Cairo. According to these interviewees, in 2010, the Organization of Islamic Cooperation (OIC) was much more concerned about insurgency activities in Afghanistan and the Taliban than about the situation in Xinjiang. Those views likely shifted with recent events in Xinjiang.

76. CASCF, "Fifth Ministerial Meeting Declaration," section 18; CASCF, "Sixth Ministerial Conference"; CASCF, "Seventh Doha Declaration," sections 5, 23; and CASCF, "Eighth Ministerial Conference," sections 4, 18, 19.

77. CASCF, "Eighth Ministerial Conference," section 4.

78. CASCF, "Amman Declaration," sections 12, 13. My translation.

79. Interview, Embassy of the United Arab Emirates, August 5, 2015, Beijing.

80. Interview, Chinese Academy of Social Sciences, Institute of West Asian and African Studies. August 11, 2015, Beijing.

81. Interview, Embassy of the State of Palestine, August 6, 2015, Beijing.

82. "Beijing Declaration of the Forum on China-Africa Cooperation," October 12, 2000.

83. "Programme for China-Africa Cooperation in Economic and Social Development," 2000, sections 1.2, 19.1.1, 19.1.2, 19.2.

84. "Declaration of the Beijing Summit of the Forum on China-Africa Cooperation," November 5, 2006.

85. "Forum on China-Africa Cooperation Sharm El Sheikh Action Plan (2010–2012)," November 12, 2009.

86. "Declaration of Sharm El Sheikh of the Forum on China-Africa Cooperation," November 12, 2009. The international financial order would include the Bretton Woods organizations of the International Monetary Fund and the World Bank.

87. "Beijing Declaration of the Fifth Minsterial Conference of the Forum on China-Africa Cooperation," 2012, sections 5, 7, 8, 9, 11, 12; "Implementation of the Follow-up Actions of the Fourth Ministerial Conference of the Forum on China-Africa Cooperation," 2012; "Declaration of the Johannesburg Summit of the Forum on China-Africa Cooperation," 2015, sections 11, 13, 15, 16, 17, 18.

88. "Beijing Declaration: Toward an Even Stronger China-Africa Community with a Shared Future," 2018.

89. Interview, CASS, Institute of West Asian and African Studies (IWAAS), February 1, 2010, Beijing; interview, CICIR, January 13, 2010, Beijing.

90. Interview, CASS, IWEP, January 14, 2010, Beijing; interview, CIIS, March 24, 2010, Beijing

91. Interview, SOAS scholar from South Africa, January 12, 2010, Beijing.

92. Interview, South African scholar, Stellenbosch Centre for Chinese Studies, May 30, 2011, Stellenbosch, South Africa.

93. Interview, CASS, IWEP, January 14, 2010, Beijing.

94. Interview, SOAS scholar from South Africa, January 12, 2010, Beijing.

95. Chinese scholars also highlighted this emerging focus on South-South cooperation in CASCF. Interview, Chinese scholar, CIIS, March 22, 2010, Beijing.

96. See CASCF, "Fourth Ministerial Meeting Communiqué."

97. CASCF, "Fifth Ministerial Meeting Declaration," section 21.

98. CASCF, "Fifth Ministerial Meeting Declaration," section 20.

99. CASCF, "Sixth Ministerial Conference"; CASCF, "Seventh Doha Declaration." The Palestinianissue is mentioned in section 3.

100. CASCF, "Eighth Ministerial Conference," sections 1, 2, 3, 27 "China-Arab Cooperation Forum 2018 to 2020 Action Plan," July 10, 2018, article 5; "Declaration of Action on China-Arab States Cooperation under the Belt and Road Initiative," July 2018, section 6.

101. CASCF, "Belt and Road Initiative," section 6.

102. CASCF, "Seventh Doha Declaration," section 6. My translation.

103. "Xinhua: Interview: Arab States Praiseworthy for Stance on South China Sea Issue—Chinese envoy," Xinhua in English, May 14, 2016.

104. CASCF, "Eighth Ministerial Conference," section 5; CASCF, "Amman Declaration." UNCLOS and South China Sea are not explicitly mentioned in FOCAC documents.

105. CASCF, "Amman," section 11. My translation.

106. "Joint Statement of the Extraordinary China-Africa Summit on Solidarity against COVID-19," June 2020.

107. "Beijing Declaration: Toward an Even Stronger China-Africa Community with a Shared Future," September 12, 2018, section 5.2.

108. "Declaration of Action on China-Arab States Cooperation under the Belt and Road Initiative."

109. CASCF, "Amman Declaration."

110. A full list of LDCs is available at https://www.un.org/development/desa/dpad/least-developed-country-category.html.

111. See section 4.4.1 of "Programme for China-Africa Cooperation in Economic and Social Development," 2000.

112. See section 4.3.4 of the "Forum on China-Africa Cooperation Addis Ababa Action Plan (2004–2006)," 2003.

113. "Follow-up Actions of the Second Ministerial Conference," 2005.

114. See the trade section of "Forum on China-Africa Cooperation Beijing Action Plan (2007–2009)," November 16, 2006.

115. "Implementation of the Follow-up Actions of the Beijing Summit of the Forum on China-Africa Cooperation," November 10, 2009.

116. See section 4.4.3 of FOCAC, "Sharm El Sheikh Action Plan (2010–2012)."

117. See section 4.4.5 of the 2012 FOCAC Plan at "The Fifth Ministerial Conference of the Forum on China-Africa Cooperation Beijing Action Plan."

118. "The Forum on China-Africa Cooperation Johannesburg Action Plan (2016–2018)," sections 3.8.3, 3.8.4, 3.8.5.

119. Stephan Klasen, Inmaculada Martinez-Zarzoso, Felicitas Nowak-Lehmann, and Matthias Bruckner, "Trade Preferences for LDCs. Are They Effective? Preliminary Econometric Evidence," United National Committee for Development Policy (October 2016).

120. "Beijing Declaration: Toward an Even Stronger China-Africa Community with a Shared Future," section 13.2; "The Forum on China-Africa Cooperation Johannesburg Action Plan (2016–2018)," sections 2.4.5, 3.8.2; and "Joint Statement on the Extraordinary China-Africa Summit on Solidarity against COVID-19."

121. See section 5.2 of "Programme for China-Africa Cooperation in Economic and Social Development"; FOCAC, "Addis Ababa Action Plan (2004–2006)."

122. FOCAC, " Addis Ababa Action Plan (2004–2006)."

123. See section 3.2.5 of FOCAC, "Beijing Action Plan (2007–2009),"

124. "Implementation of the Follow-up Actions of the Beijing Summit of the Forum on China-Africa Cooperation."

125. See section 4.2.3 of FOCAC, "Sharm El Sheikh Action Plan (2010–2012)."

126. FOCAC, "Johannesburg Action Plan (2016–2018)," section 3.9.5.

127. See section 4.5.3 of FOCAC, "Sharm El Sheikh Action Plan (2010–2012)."

128. FOCAC, "Johannesburg Action Plan (2016–2018)," section 3.2.5; "Forum on China-Africa Cooperation Beijing Action Plan (2019–2021)," section 3.2.2.

129. "The Forum on China-Africa Cooperation Johannesburg Action Plan (2016–2018)," section 3.7.1.

130. FOCAC, "Johannesburg Action Plan (2016–2018)," section 3.9.6; FOCAC. "Beijing Action Plan (2019–2021)," Section 3.2.2.

131. FOCAC. "Beijing Action Plan (2019–2021)," section 3.7.2.

132. China's three policy banks are the Agricultural Development Bank of China (ADBC), the China Development Bank (CDB), and the Export-Import Bank of China (Chexim).

133. FOCAC, "Beijing Action Plan (2019–2021)," section 3.2.2.

134. See section 3.4.2 of FOCAC, "Beijing Action Plan (2007–2009)."

135. FOCAC, "Beijing Action Plan (2019–2021)," section 3.9.6

136. "Programme for China-Africa Cooperation in Economic and Social Development"; FOCAC, "Beijing Action Plan (2019–2021)," section 3.9.5.

137. CASCF, "Action Plan (2008–2010)," 2008.

138. CASCF, "Action Plan (2018–2020)," section 3.1.15.

139. CASCF, "2018 to 2020 Action Plan," 2018, section 3.1.14.

140. CASCF, "2018 to 2020 Action Plan," section 16.

141. "Declaration of Action on the China-Arab States Cooperation under the Belt and Road Initiative," 2018.

142. See section 5.3 of FOCAC, "Addis Ababa Action Plan (2004–2006)."

143. See section 3.2.6 of FOCAC, "Beijing Action Plan (2007–2009)."

144. "Implementation of the Follow-up Actions of the Beijing Summit of the Forum on China-Africa Cooperation." See also section 4.2.4 of FOCAC, "Sharm El Sheikh Action Plan (2010–2012)." Some of these SEZs are in the very early stages of development.

145. CASCF "Action Plan (2014–2016)," Egypt's SEZ was announced under FOCAC, not CASCF. For the purposes of this book, Mauritania is categorized as sub-Saharan Africa, not the Middle East.

146. "China Africa Economic and Trade Cooperation," 2010.

147. See section 4.2.1 of "Forum on China-Africa Cooperation Addis Ababa Action Plan (2004–2006)," 2003.

148. "Programme for China-Africa Cooperation in Economic and Social Development."

149. See section 4.2.2 of FOCAC, " Addis Ababa Action Plan (2004–2006)."

150. See sections 3.5.2 and 3.5.3 of FOCAC, "Beijing Action Plan (2007–2009)."

151. See sections 4.3.2 and 4.3.3 of FOCAC, "Sharm El Sheikh Action Plan (2010–2012)."

152. FOCAC, "The Fifth Ministerial Conference of the Forum on China-Africa Cooperation Beijing Action Plan"; FOCAC, "Johannesburg Action Plan (2016–2018)."

153. See section 3.3 in the FOCAC, "Johannesburg Action Plan (2016–2018)."

154. See section 3.9.1 FOCAC, "Johannesburg Action Plan (2016–2018)."

155. CASCF, "China-Arab States Cooperation Forum Action Plan."

156. My translation from Chinese text. See "China-Arab States Cooperation Forum Action Plan."

157. CASCF, "Sixth Ministerial Conference"; CASCF "Action Plan (2014–2016)"; CASCF, "Action Plan (2016–2018)."

158. See section 3.5 of CASCF, "2018 to 2020 Action Plan."

159. "Declaration of Action on China-Arab States Cooperation Under the Belt and Road Iniative 2018."

160. "China-Arab Cooperation Forum Action Plan 2020–2022," July 2020.

161. "China-Arab States Cooperation Forum Action Plan (2004)."

162. "China-Arab States Cooperation Forum Action Plan (2006–2008)," 2006.

163. For example, see action plan CASCF, "Action Plan (2012–2014)"; CASCF, "Action Plan (2014–2016)"; CASCF, "Action Plan (2016–2018)"; CASCF, "Eighth Ministerial

Conference"; CASCF, "2018 to 2020 Action Plan," section 4; CASCF, "Action Plan for 2020–2022."

164. FOCAC, "Beijing Action Plan (2019–2021)," sections 3.4.1–3.3.4.

165. "Programme for China-Africa Cooperation in Economic and Social Development." See also FOCAC, " Addis Ababa Action Plan (2004–2006)."

166. "Programme for China-Africa Cooperation in Economic and Social Development," and FOCAC, "Addis Ababa Action Plan (2004–2006)."

167. Agricultural technology demonstration centers are discussed in more detail in chapter 6 on economic relations.

168. FOCAC, "Beijing Action Plan (2007–2009)."

169. FOCAC, "Sharm El Sheikh Action Plan (2010–2012)."

170. "Implementation of the Follow-up Actions of the Fourth Ministerial Conference of the Forum on China-Africa Cooperation," section 5; FOCAC, "Johanessburg Action Plan (2016–2018)," section 4.1; FOCAC, "Johannesburg Action Plan (2016–2018)," section 3.1; interview, Embassy of the Republic of Djibouti, August 12, 2015, Beijing.

171. Section 3.5.2 of FOCAC, "Johannesburg Action Plan (2016–2018)."

172. Section 3.1.3 of FOCAC "Beijing Action Plan (2019–2021)."

173. Section 3.1.7. and 3.1.8 of FOCAC, "Beijing Action Plan (2019–2021)."

174. Section 3.5 of FOCAC, "Beijing Action Plan (2019–2021)."

175. CASCF, "Action Plan (2010–2012)."

176. Article VII of CASCF, "Action Plan (2012–2014)," Article VII of CASCF, "Action Plan (2014–2016)," and Article VII of CASCF, "Action Plan (2016–2018)."

177. CASCF, "2018 to 2020 Action Plan," article 6.

178. CASCF, "2018 to 2020 Action Plan," article 6.6. Also see CASCF, "Eighth Ministerial Conference," 2018, #33.

179. CASCF, "Sixth Ministerial Conference"; CASCF, "China-Arab Cooperation Forum Development Plan (2014–2024)"; CASCF, "Action Plan (2014–2016)."

180. FOCAC, "Declaration of the Johannesburg Summit."

181. CASCF, "Action Plan (2016–2018)"; CASCF, "Seventh Doha Declaration."

182. "Declaration of Action on China-Arab States Cooperation under the Belt and Road Initiative"; FOCAC, "Beijing Action Plan (2019–2021)"

183. Many interview respondents indicated that foreign aid was out of CASCF's scope due to the more advanced level of economic development in the Arab world compared to Africa. For example, interview, CIIS, March 22, 2010, Beijing; interview, Chinese Ministry of Commerce, March 26, 2010, Beijing.

184. Interview, Chinese Ministry of Commerce, March 26, 2010, Beijing.

185. See chapter 6 for a more detailed discussion of China's foreign aid approach.

186. Except for recognition of the PRC.

187. FOCAC, "Beijing Declaration," 2000.

188. Interview, Democratic Republic of Congo Scholar at Beijing University, February 8, 2010, Beijing.

189. Interview, Ethiopian representative, Young Africans Professional Society, May 6, 2010, Beijing.

190. Interview, Gabonese scholar at Stellenbosch University's Centre for Chinese Studies, May 30, 2011, Stellenbosch, South Africa

191. Interview, SOAS scholar, January 12, 2010, Beijing

192. Interview, Stellenbosch University's Centre for Chinese Studies, May 30, 2011, Stellenbosch, South Africa.

193. Interview, Beijing University, School of International Studies, January 22, 2013, Beijing.

194. This chapter does not provide a detailed analysis of China's foreign aid activities. It describes the broad activities that are pledged via FOCAC. For a detailed analysis of China's aid to Africa, see Brautigam, *Dragon's Gift;* John Franklin Copper, *China's Foreign Aid and Investment Diplomacy* (New York: Palgrave Macmillan, 2016); Zhang Denghua and Graeme Smith, "China's Foreign Aid System: Structure, Agencies, and Identities," *Third World Quarterly* 38, no. 10 (2017). Also see chapter 6 in this book for a further discussion of China's aid.

195. For a list of HIPC, see www.worldbank.org/en/topic/debt/brief/hipc

196. "Programme for China-Africa Cooperation in Economic and Social Development."

197. See section 4.6.1 of FOCAC, "Addis Ababa Action Plan (2004–2006)."

198. FOCAC, " Beijing Action Plan (2007–2009)."

199. See section 5.1.3 of FOCAC, "Sharm El Sheikh Action Plan (2010–2012)."

200. "Implementation of the Follow-up Actions of the Fourth Ministerial Conference of the Forum on China-Africa Cooperation."

201. FOCAC, "Johannesburg Action Plan (2016–2018)."

202. FOCAC, "Beijing Action Plan (2019–2021)," section 4.1.4.

203. Yun Sun, "China's Debt Relief for Africa: Emerging Deliberation," June 9, 2020; "As Africa Faces COVID-19, Chinese Debt Relief Is a Welcome Development," Council on Foreign Relations, June 30, 2020.

204. "Programme for China-Africa Cooperation in Economic and Social Development," 2000.

205. See section 4.7.2 of FOCAC, "Addis Ababa Action Plan (2004–2006)." Although political conditions of this aid are limited, Chinese aid often includes economic conditions such as utilizing Chinese firms for the provision of services.

206. See section 5.1.2 of FOCAC, " Beijing Action Plan (2007–2009)."

207. "Implementation of the Follow-up Actions of the Fourth Ministerial Conference of the Forum on China-Africa Cooperation."

208. FOCAC, "Johannesburg Action Plan (2016–2018)," section 3.9.1.

209. FOCAC, "Beijing Action Plan (2019–2021)," section 4.1.4.

210. CASCF, "Action Plan (2006–2008)."Also see CASCF action plans for 2012 to 2020.

211. "The Implementation of the Follow-up Actions of the First Ministerial Conference of FOCAC," December 16, 2003.

212. See section 5.5.3 of FOCAC, "Beijing Action Plan (2007–2009)."

213. "Implementation of the Follow-up Actions of the Beijing Summit of the Forum on China-Africa Cooperation," 2009.

214. FOCAC, "Sharm El Sheikh Action Plan (2010–2012)."

215. 2012 FOCAC Action Plan, section 5.5.7

216. "The Fifth Ministerial Conference of the Forum on China-Africa Cooperation Beijing Action Plan," 2012, section 4.2.3.

217. FOCAC, "Johannesburg Action Plan (2016–2018)," section 4.2.7.

218. FOCAC, "Beijing Action Plan (2019–2021)," section 4.2.3.

219. FOCAC, "Beijing Action Plan (2007–2009)."

220. See section 5.4.4 of FOCAC, "Beijing Action Plan (2007–2009)."

221. FOCAC, "Sharm El Sheikh Action Plan (2010–2012)."

222. FOCAC, "Sharm El Sheikh Action Plan (2010–2012)."

223. "The Fifth Ministerial Conference of the Forum on China-Africa Cooperation Beijing Action Plan," section 6.2.3.

224. "The Fifth Ministerial Conference of the Forum on China-Africa Cooperation Beijing Action Plan," section 6.2.4.

225. FOCAC, "Johannesburg Action Plan (2016–2018)," section 4.

226. FOCAC, "Beijing Action Plan (2019–2021)," section 4.

227. "China-Arab States Cooperation Forum Declaration," and "Beijing Declaration of the Forum on China-Africa Cooperation."

228. CASCF, " Forum Fourth Ministerial Meeting Communiqué"; CASCF, "Fifth Ministerial Meeting Declaration," #17; CASCF, "Sixth Ministerial Conference"; CASCF, "Seventh Doha Declaration," #24; and CASCF, "Eighth Ministerial Conference," #20.

229. FOCAC, "Addis Ababa Action Plan (2004–2006)"; FOCAC "Addis Ababa Action Plan (2004–2006)." The 2016 CASCF Arab Declaration also expresses support for China's participation in UNPKO activities. See CASCF "Seventh Doha Declaration," #4.

230. "Implementation of the Follow-up Actions of the Beijing Summit of the Forum on China-Africa Cooperation," 2009, and FOCAC, "Sharm El Sheikh Action Plan (2010–2012)"; FOCAC, "Fifth Ministerial Conference," 2012, section 2.6.6.

231. FOCAC, "Beijing Action Plan (2019–2021)," section 6.1.8.

232. "The Fifth Ministerial Conference of the Forum on China-Africa Cooperation Beijing Action Plan," 2012, section 2.6.3. Also see FOCAC, "Declaration of the Johannesburg Summit," section 25.4.

233. FOCAC, "Beijing Action Plan (2019–2021)," section 6.1.3.

234. FOCAC, "Beijing Action Plan (2019–2021)," sections 6.1.4, 6.1.7.

235. FOCAC, "Beijing Action Plan (2019–2021)," sections 6.1.9, 6.1.1.

236. CASCF, "Action Plan (2006–2008)"; CASCF, " Third Ministerial Meeting Communiqué"; CASCF, "Fourth Minsterial Meeting Communique"; CASCF, "Fifth Ministerial Meeting Declaration," CASCF, "Sixth Ministerial Conference"; CASCF "Seventh Doha Declaration," 2016, #23; CASCF, "Eighth Ministerial Conference," 2018, #18.

237. "Forum on China-Africa Cooperation Addis Ababa Action Plan (2004–2006)," 2003, and CASCF "Action Plan (2006–2008)"; "The Fifth Ministerial Conference of the Forum on China-Africa Cooperation Beijing Action Plan," 2012, 3.9.

238. FOCAC, "Action Plan (2019–2021)," section 6.1.6.

239. See "Charter of the Shanghai Cooperation Organization," 2001, for a full description of the organization.

240. SCO, "Charter," article 15.

241. Refer to the Charter of the Shanghai Cooperation Organization for the organizational structure of the organization. SCO meets once per year while the FOCAC meets every three years and CASCF every two. SCO "Charter," article 15.

242. For the founding principles of the SCO, see SCO, "Charter," article 2.

243. SCO, "Charter," article 3, Areas of Cooperation.

244. SCO, "Charter," article 10.

245. "Qingdao Declaration of the Council of Heads of States of Shanghai Cooperation Organisation," 2018.

246. "Bishkek Declaration of the Shanghai Cooperation Organization's Heads of State Council," 2019.

247. "The Moscow Declaration of the Council of Heads of State of the Shanghai Cooperation Organization," 2020.

248. "Qingdao Declaration"; "Bishkek Declaration"; "Moscow Declaration."

249. "Qingdao Declaration"; "Bishkek Declaration"; "Moscow Declaration."

250. "Joint Communiqué of the Heads of State of the Shanghai Cooperation Organization on Simplifying Trade Procedures," 2018.

251. "Charter of the Shanghai Cooperation Organization."

252. "Qingdao Declaration"; "Bishkek Declaration"; "Moscow Declaration."

253. At the April 2019 SCO Finance Ministers' meeting, India was the only SCO member country that did not endorse China's Belt and Road Initiative.

CHAPTER 5

1. Tan Jingjing "Chinese Special Envoys Travel All Around World," Xinhua Domestic Service, October 2, 2009.

2. Statements and media reporting analyzed from 2002 to September 2018.

3. "China: Qian Qichen Outlines PRC Stand on Mideast Peace Process," Beijing Xinhua in English, December 25, 1997.

4. Many interview respondents cited Arab expectations as the main reason for formation of the envoy. Some examples include interview, Beijing University Scholar, April 14, 2010, Beijing; interviews, CIIS, March 30, 2010, Beijing; interview, Embassy of the Sultanate of Oman, March 31, 2010, Beijing; interview, former Arab League official, October 26, 2010, Beijing; and interview, former African Union official, November 9, 2010, Cairo. See also "Xinhua: Egypt Welcomes China's Active Role in Mideast Peace Process," Beijing Xinhua in English, November 7, 2002; "Syrian Vice President Discusses Mideast Situation with Visiting PRC Envoy 10 Nov," Xinhua Hong Kong Service, November 10, 2002; "Jordan's King Welcomes China's Role In Mideast Peace Process," Beijing Xinhua in English, November 11, 2002.

5. Interview, Beijing University Scholar, April 14, 2010, Beijing; interview, Embassy of the State of Palestine, May 28, 2010, Beijing. For more information about the Quartet, see https://unsco.unmissions.org/mideast-quartet.

6. Interview, Embassy of the Hashemite Kingdom of Jordan, May 24, 2010, Beijing.

7. Interview, Beijing University scholar, April 14, 2010, Beijing; interview, CIIS, March 30, 2010, Beijing; interview, Embassy of the Sultanate of Oman, March 31, 2010, Beijing; interview, Embassy of the State of Palestine, May 28, 2010, Beijing.

8. Interview, Embassy of the State of Israel, May 18, 2010, Beijing.

9. "Xinhua: Egypt Welcomes China's Active Role in Mideast Peace Process."

10. "Xinhua: Jordanian FM Hails China's Decision to Send Middle East envoy," Beijing Xinhua in English, November 11, 2002.

11. "Chinese Ambassadors to Bahrain," Embassy of the People's Republic of China in the Kingdom of Bahrain, November 15, 2000, http://bh.china-embassy.org/chn/dsxx/lrds/

12. "Chinese Ambassadors to Jordan," China Foreign Ministry Website, September 20, 2006. www.fmprc.gov.cn.

13. "Chinese Ambassadors to Iran," China Foreign Ministry Website, November 15, 2000, www.fmprc.gov.cn.

14. "Syrian Vice President Discusses Mideast Situation With Visiting PRC envoy 10 Nov."

15. "Visiting PRC envoy Stresses Need to Resolve Middle East Issue through Peace Talks," Beijing Xinhua Domestic Service in Chinese, November 11, 2002.

16. "Syrian Vice President Discusses Mideast Situation With Visiting PRC envoy 10 Nov."

17. "Envoy Wang Shijie Says China Determined to Push Forward Mideast Peace Process," Beijing Xinhua in English, November 7, 2002.

18. "Four sides" refers to the Quartet.

19. "PRC Middle East Special Envoy Elaborates 5-Point Proposal on Middle East Issues," Beijing Xinhua Domestic Service in Chinese, May 28, 2003.

20. "Chinese Envoy Says PRC May Set Forth Mideast Peace Proposals at 'Convenient Time,'" Beijing Xinhua in English, June 16, 2004.

21. "Chinese Special Envoy on the Middle East Issue Wang Shijie Talks about His Middle East Tour," China Foreign Ministry Website, April 19, 2005, https://www.fmprc.gov.cn/web/.

22. "Chinese Special Envoy on the Middle East Issue Wang Shijie Talks about His Visit to the Middle East."

23. "Chinese Special Envoy on the Middle East Issue Wang Shijie Talks about His Visit to the Middle East."

24. "China's Outgoing and Succeeding Special Envoys on the Middle East Question Meet Press," Chinese Foreign Ministry, March 29, 2006, http://www.fmprc.gov.cn/eng/zxxx/t243235.htm.

25. "Chinese Ambassadors to Iran."

26. "Foreign Ministry Spokesman Kong Quan's Statement on the Release of 7 Kidnapped Chinese Citizens," Embassy of the People's Republic of China in the United States of America, April 13, 2004, http://www.china-embassy.org/eng/fyrth/t84326.htm.

27. "PRC Premier Wen Jiabao Discusses Middle East Issues in Cairo News Conference," Xinhua Domestic Service, June 19, 2006.

28. Wang Bo, "PRC Deputy Representative to UN Urges Lebanon, Israel to Solve Crisis Peacefully," Xinhua Domestic Service, July 14, 2006.

29. Gu Kang and Li Teng, "China's Middle East Special Envoy Calls for Unconditional Ceasefire, Xinhua Domestic Service, August 8, 2006.

30. Ma Shijun, "PRC Special Envoy Exchanges Views with Lebanese PM on UN Resolution," Xinhua Domestic Service, September 1, 2006.

31. See Pu Ning, "China's Participation in International Relief, Peace-Keeping Missions," *Jiefangjun Bao*, October 1, 2006.

32. See "Ambassador to Jordan Luo Xingwu Reiterates China's Call for Ceasefire in Lebanon," Xinhua Saturday, August 5, 2006. Also, Chinese UNPKO to Lebanon in chapter 8 on military relations.

33. Wang Hao and Huang Min, "PRC Middle East Special Envoy, Rafiq Husseini Discuss Palestine-Israel Issue," Xinhua Domestic Service, August 12, 2006.

34. This statement was made during the Gaza conflict, 2008–2009. For more information, see Jim Zanotti, Carol Migdalovitz, Jeremy M. Sharp, Casey L. Addis, Christopher M. Blanchard, and Rhoda Margesson, "Israel and Hamas: Conflict in Gaza (2008–2009)," Congressional Research Service Report for Congress, February 19, 2009, https://fas.org/sgp/crs/mideast/R40101.pdf

35. 2009 UNSCR "Stresses the Urgency of and Calls for an Immediate, Durable and Fully Respected Ceasefire, Leading to the Full Withdrawal of Israeli Forces from Gaza."

36. "Xinhua: 1st LD: Chinese Special Envoy Calls for an Immediate Ceasefire in Gaza," Xinhua, January 12, 2009.

37. Zhai Xiangdong, "Wu Sike: A Special Envoy's Job Is By No Means Easy," *Liaowang Dongfang Zhoukan*, May 20, 2009.

38. See Liu Yuehua, "The Mideast Peace Process Needs to Be Pushed Forward In Confidence: Chinese envoy," Xinhua, June 29, 2009.

39. See Su Xiaobo, "2010 Is a Year Full of Expectations for the Middle East Peace Process: Interview with Wu Sike, Special envoy to the Middle East," Xinhua Domestic Service, March 12, 2010.

40. Hao Fangjia and Yuan Zhenyu: "Chinese Special Envoy on the Middle East Issue Meets Israeli Foreign Minister Lieberman," Xinhua Domestic Service, June 7, 2010.

41. Interview, CIIS, March 30, 2010, Beijing.

42. "Iran Restates Support for China's Efforts to Safeguard Unification," Xinhua, August 2, 2009; Zhou Zhaojun, "Wu Sike Says China Actively Promotes Solution to Iranian Nuclear Issue Through Dialogue," *Zhongguo Xinwen She*, August 11, 2009; Mehdi Bagheri, "Iran Accuses West of Cheating World, Vows to Pursue Nuclear Program," Xinhua, June 10, 2010; and "China Seeks Peaceful Solution to Iran Nuclear Issue: Special Envoy," Xinhua, June 10, 2010.

43. "Chinese Envoy: Urumqi Riot Not to Affect Ties with Islamic Countries," Xinhua, August 11, 2009; "Special Envoy for Middle East: '5 July Incident' Will Not Adversely Affect China's Relations with Islamic Countries," Xinhua Asia-Pacific Service, August 11, 2009.

44. "China to Support Mideast Peace Process Despite Situations Change," Xinhua in English, March 30, 2011.

45. "Palestinian Reconciliation a Key Step toward Peace Talks with Israel: Chinese Envoy," Xinhua in English, May 5, 2011; "Israel Should Accept Palestinian Unity Bid: China's Mideast Envoy," Xinhua in English, February 20, 2012.

46. "PRC Envoy Says Palestinian UN Membership Drive Aims to Revive Peace Talks," Xinhua Domestic Service, September 9, 2011. The PLO announced in June 2011 that it would ask the UN to recognize the State of Palestine based on the borders before the 1967 war with East Jerusalem as its capital, grant Palestine UN membership, and recognize its right to self-government pursuant to the United Nations Charter.

47. "PRC Envoy Says Palestinian UN Membership Drive Aims to Revive Peace Talks."

48. "China's Special Envoy Calls for Halting Violence in Syria," Xinhua in English, October 27, 2011.

49. "China Maintains Contact with Syrian Parties: FM Spokesperson," Xinhua in English, February 14, 2012.

50. "Xinhua Year-End Report in PRC's Diplomatic Endeavors, Practice in 2012," Xinhua Domestic Service, December 30, 2012.

51. "China Raises Six-Point Statement for Resolving Syria Issue," Embassy of the People's Republic of China in the Republic of Zimbabwe, March 4, 2012.

52. "China Urges Swift Political Solution to Syrian Crisis: Envoy," Xinhua in English, December 7, 2012.

53. See chapter 7 for a full discussion of China's veto behavior in the UN Security Council.

54. "Envoy Says Communication Helps Gulf States Understand PRC Stance on Syria," Xinhua Domestic Service, April 10, 2013.

55. "Envoy Says Communication Helps Gulf States Understand PRC Stance on Syria."

56. "China's Envoy Slams End of EU Arms Embargo to Syrian Rebels," Xinhua in English, May 29, 2013.

57. "Moving toward Each Other, Key to Palestinian Israeli Issue: Chinese Envoy," Xinhua in English, July 30, 2013.

58. "Envoy Says Communication Helps Gulf States Understand PRC Stance on Syria," Xinhua Domestic Service, April 10, 2013.

59. "Xinhua News Analysis View Favorably on Palestine-Israel Peace Talks in Beijing," Xinhua Domestic Service, May 5, 2013. Also see "Commentary: China's Renewed Effort to Restart Mideast Peace Talks," Xinhua in English, June 19, 2013; "China Committed to Boosting Mideast Peace Process: Envoy," Xinhua in English, June 19, 2013.

60. "Chinese President Makes Four-Point Proposal for Settlement of Palestinian Question," Xinhua, May 6, 2013.

61. "Xinhua: Roundup: FMs Visit Shows China's Willingness to Wield Greater Clout in the Middle East," Xinhua in English, December 27, 2013.

62. "China's Mideast Envoy Visits Palestinian Territory over Peace Process," Xinhua in English, April 27, 2013.

63. "China Urges Israelis, Palestinians to Strive for Substantial Progress," Xinhua in English, March 9, 2014.

64. "Chinese Envoy Urges Israeli Palestinian Ceasefire," Xinhua in English, July 13, 2014.

65. "Vice FM Meets Separately with Palestinian, Israeli Envoys, Urges to Achieve Immediate Ceasefire," Xinhua Domestic Service, July 15, 2014.

66. "China Calls for Ceasefire to Stop Civilians' Losses in Gaza," Xinhua in English. July 20, 2014.

67. "Chinese Envoy Urges Israel Palestine Ceasefire," Xinhua in English, July 25, 2014.

68. "FM Spokesperson: China's Efforts in Settling Syrian Issue," Xinhua in English, December 27, 2013.

69. "Chinese Envoy on Middle East Affairs Wu Sike Arrives in Turkey, Discusses Iraq and Syria," Xinhua Asia-Pacific Service, July 10, 2014.

70. "China Mideast Envoy Urges Negotiations over Regional Issues," Xinhua in English, February 19, 2012.

71. "International Conference Pledges Support to Libya, Calls for Stability," Xinhua in English, March 7, 2014.

72. "Chinese Envoy to Attend Meeting for Lebanese Forces," Xinhua in English, June 13, 2014.

73. "China Supports Iraq to Maintain Sovereignty, Calls for Inclusive Government: Envoy," Xinhua in English, July 7, 2014.

74. "Transcript of PRC FM Spokesman News Conference," September 3, 2014.

75. This chapter does not analyze the tenure of the newest special envoy appointed in September 2019, Zhai Jun.

76. "Envoy to Middle East Covers a Lot of Ground," *China Daily Online in English*, April 11, 2016.

77. "China Appoints New Middle East Envoy," Xinhua General News Service, September 3, 2014.

78. "Xinhua Middle East News Summary at 2200 GMT, Sept 18," Xinhua General News Service, September 18, 2014.

79. "China Strongly Supports Palestinian People, Peace Process: Middle East Envoy," Xinhua English, January 31, 2016.

80. "China Strongly Supports Palestinian People."

81. "China Supports Palestine Peace Process—Envoy," BBC Monitoring Asia Pacific–Political, February 1, 2016.

82. "PRC MOFA: Chinese Special Envoy to the Middle East Issue Gives Joint Interview on Syrian, Other Issues," Ministry of Foreign Affairs of the People's Republic of China, Beijing, November 11, 2015.

83. "Italy Seeks More Chinese Help in Fight against Terror: Chinese Aid 'Can Help Mediterranean,'" *South China Morning Post*, January 10, 2016.

84. "Iran, China Stress Peaceful Resolution of Yemen Crisis," *Trend Daily News (Azerbaijan)*, April 8, 2015.

85. "Foreign Minister Meets Austrian Counterpart," Jordan News Agency, May 23, 2015.

86. "China Says Syrians Themselves Should Decide Their Future," *Iranian Government News*, November 28, 2015.

87. "PRC MOFA: Special Envoy on Middle East Issue Gong Xiaosheng Gives Interview to Chinese Media," Ministry of Foreign Affairs of the People's Republic of China, Beijing, April 6, 2016.

88. Wang Xu, "China Wins International Praise for Yemen Peace Efforts," *China Daily European Edition*, April 7, 2016.

89. "China, Morocco Hold Convergent Views on Regional Issues: Chinese Envoy," Xinhua General News Service, May 26, 2015.

90. "PRC MOFA: China's Special Envoy on Middle East Issues Attends Ministerial Meeting on Libyan Issue," Ministry of Foreign Affairs of the People's Republic of China, Beijing, December 14, 2015.

91. "Italy Seeks More Chinese Help in Fight against Terror China Aid 'Can Help Mediterranean,'" *South China Morning Post*, January 19, 2016.

92. Nida Ibrahim, "News Analysis: Palestinians Press for Ending Israeli Occupation," Xinhua General News Service, April 17, 2015.

93. "China Strongly Supports Palestinian People, Peace Process: Mideast Envoy," Xinhua General News Service, January 31, 2016.

94. "China Strongly Supports Palestinian People."

95. "China Strongly Supports Palestinian People."

96. "China Strongly Supports Palestinian People."

97. "China Strongly Supports Palestinian People."

98. "Full Text of China's Arab Policy Paper," Xinhua, January, 14, 2016.

99. "China Strongly Supports Palestinian People."

100. "Envoy to Middle East Covers a Lot of Ground," *China Daily–US Edition*, April 11, 2016; "Xinhua Middle East News Summary at 2200 GMT, May 11," Xinhua General News Service, May 12, 2018.

101. Chapter 9 discusses BRI in the Middle East more broadly. "Interview: Arab States Praiseworthy for Stance on South China Sea Issue—Chinese Envoy," Xinhua in English, May 14, 2016; "Interview: Chinese Envoy Says Belt and Road Initiative to Promote Middle East Peace Process," Xinhua General News Service, April 15, 2017.

102. "Interview: Chinese Envoy Says Belt and Road."

103. "Interview: Chinese Envoy Says Belt and Road."

104. "Interview: Chinese Envoy Says Belt and Road."

105. "Statement by Ambassador LIU Jieyi at the Security Council Open Debate on the Middle East," Permanent Mission of the People's Republic of China to the UN website July 25, 2017, http://chnun.chinamission.org.cn/eng/hyyfy/t1481733.htm.

106. "China: US Needs UN Permit before Military Moves against Syria," *Tehran Times*, May 8, 2018.

107. "China Says It Regrets US Decision to Pull Out of Iran Nuclear Deal," *China Daily Hong Kong Edition*, May 9, 2018.

108. "China: US Needs."

109. "Chinese Special Envoy Urges Upholding Iran Nuclear Deal," *BBC Monitoring Asia Pacific*, May 9, 2018.

110. "China: US Needs."

111. "Europe Vows to Keep Iran Nuclear Deal Alive," *Times*, May 9, 2018.

112. "China Strongly Supports JCPOA, Says 'A Deal Is Better Than No Deal at All,'" Mehr News Agency, May 9, 2018.

113. "China Supports Holistic Approach to Mideast Hot Issues: Special Envoy," Xinhua General News Service, May 12, 2018.

114. "Press Release on Deputy Foreign Minister Mikhail Bogdanov's Meeting with China's Special Envoy on Middle East Issue Gong Xiaosheng," States News Service, April 11, 2017; "Russian Deputy Foreign Minister Discusses Middle East with Special Envoy Ministry," Sputnik News Service, March 16, 2018; "Russia Deputy Foreign Minister, Chinese Special Envoy Discuss Syrian Settlement–Moscow," Sputnik News Service, June 21, 2018.

115. "Russian, Chinese Diplomats Discuss Situation in Syria, Iraq–Foreign Ministry," ITAR-TASS Russian News Agency, November 12, 2014.

116. "Press Release on the BRICS Consultative Meeting on the Middle East and North Africa," Russia Government News, June 22, 2018.

117. Interview, Egyptian Council for Foreign Affairs, November 10, 2010, Cairo, Egypt; interview, Embassy of the State of Palestine, May 28, 2010, Beijing.

118. "Foreign Ministry Spokesperson Hong Lei's Regular Press Conference on March 29, 2016," PRC Ministry of Foreign Affairs, March 29, 2016.

119. "Envoy Looks to Objective Mideast Role," *China Daily Online in English*, April 11, 2016.

120. "Envoy Looks to Objective Mideast Role."

121. For example, see "Chinese Envoy Advises Against 'Regime Change' in Syria," Xinhua General News Service, April 26, 2017.

122. "Foreign Ministry Spokesperson Hong Lei's Regular Press Conference on March 29, 2016," PRC Ministry of Foreign Affairs, March 29, 2016; "Special Envoy of the Chinese Government on Syrian Issue Xie Xiaoyan Introduced China' Principles and Stance on 08 April 16," Ministry of Foreign Affairs of the People's Republic of China, April 8, 2016.

123. "China Appoints Special Envoy to Syria," *Paris AFP in English*, March 29. 2016; Javier C. Hernandez, "Chinese Citizen Held by ISIS Poses Test for Beijing," *New York Times*, September 10, 2015; Shannon Tiezzi, "ISIS: Chinese Hostage 'Executed,'" *Diplomat*, November 19, 2015.

124. "Jordan, China Share Views on Syria Solution," *BBC Monitoring Asia Pacific*, August 24, 2016; "Chinese Envoy for Syria: Political Dialogue Is the Only Solution in Syria, No Double Standards in Fighting Terrorism," *Syrian Arab News Agency*, December 8, 2016. For an in-depth examination of China's approach to nonintervention in Syria in the UN, see Courtney J. Fung, *China and Intervention at the UN Security Council: Reconciling Status* (Oxford: Oxford University Press, 2019)

125. "Jordan, China Share."

126. "Spotlight: Syrian Crisis at Crucial Junction as Aleppo May Change Hands," Xinhua General News Service, December 9, 2016. Liu Jieyi is China's permanent representative to the UN.

127. "Chinese FM: Fighting Terrorism, Dialogue, and Reconstruction Form Pillars of Ending Crisis in Syria," Syrian Arab News Agency, November 24, 2017.

128. "Envoy: Syria Solution Lies in Common Ground," *China Daily*, May 16, 2018.

129. ""China-Syria' Special Envoy of the Chinese Government on the Syrian Issue Xie Xiaoyan Attends International Symposium on the Syria Issue," Thai News Service, May 17, 2018.

130. "`China-Syria' Special Envoy."

131. "Envoy Proposes Political Settlement and Terror Fight in Parallel," *China Daily*, April 8, 2016. See also "Chinese Syria Envoy: Terrorists Crackdown a Must for Durable Ceasefire," *Iranian Government News*, March 3, 2017.

132. "Hariri Discusses with Chinese Envoy Situation in Syria," *National News Agency in Syria*, December 5, 2016. See also "Al-Moallem Underlines Need for Concerted International Efforts to Fight Terrorism," Syrian Arab News Agency, December 7, 2016.

133. "Al-Moallem Underlines Need for Concerted International Efforts to Fight Terrorism," Syrian Arab News Agency, December 7, 2016.

134. "Jordan, China Support Efforts to Reach a Political Solution in Syria," Jordan News Agency, August 24, 2016.

135. "China's Special Envoy to Syria Urges for Fight against Terrorism in Country to Continue," *Ria Novosti*, April 18, 2016.

136. "China's New Syria Envoy Praises Russian Military Mission," *Channel News Asia*, April 8, 2016.

137. "China to Purse Peace Talks to Promote Settlement of Syria Conflict: Envoy," Xinhua General News Service, June 17, 2017; "Chinese Official: International Communities Must Join to Combat Terrorism," *Jerusalem Post*, June 17, 2017; "China to Pursue Peace Talks to Promote Settlement of Syria Conflict: Envoy," *People's Daily Online–English*, June 18, 2017.

138. Uran Botobekov, "Silk Diplomacy of Celestial Empire against Turkistan Islamic Party," *Eurasia Review*, December 3, 2017. See chapter 3 for an in-depth discussion of China's concerns about links between international terrorism and Xinjiang.

139. Botobekov, "Silk Diplomacy"; Mehdi Jedina and Sirwan Kajjo, "Analysts: Uighur Jihadis in Syria Could Pose Threat," December 15, 2018.

140. Botobekov, "Silk Diplomacy."

141. "China Envoy Says No Accurate Figure on Uighurs Fighting in Syria," *Channel News Asia*, August 20, 2018.

142. Botobekov, "Silk Diplomacy."

143. Mehdi Jedina and Sirwan Kajjo, "Analysts: Uighur Jihadis in Syria Could Pose Threat."

144. Liu Zhen, "China's Military to Give Aid to Syria: Training Also Part of Agreement Reached on the Weekend as Beijing Gradually Steps Up Its Direct Involvement

in the Middle East," *South China Morning Post*, August 17, 2016; Harvey Morris, "China Pursues Active Role in Syrian Solution," *China Daily European Edition*, October 21, 2016.

145. "No Chinese Military Presence in Syria, Says Envoy," *ITAR-TASS*, August 20, 2018; "Beijing Denies Military Presence in Syria," *China Daily*, August 21, 2018.

146. "Syria Issue Must Be Resolved to Promote Fight against Terrorism–Chinese Envoy," ITAR-TASS, January 20, 2018. See also Zheng Jianhua, "Fighting against Terrorism Needs to Continue in Parallel with Pushing for Ceasefire in Syria: Chinese Envoy," Xinhua General News Service, April 25, 2018; and "China: Syria Counterterrorism Efforts as Important as Truce," *China Daily, Hong Kong Edition*, April 26, 2018, https://www.chinadailyasia.com/articles/111/71/24/1524709705824.html.

147. "Syria Issue Must Be Resolved to Promote Fight Against Terrorism—Chinese Envoy"; interview, scholar at RUSI, London, 2018. For a more in-depth discussion of TIP, see Andrew Small's work. For example, Andrew Small, "The Xinjiangistan Connection," *Foreign Policy*, July 30, 3014.

148. "Spotlight: Chinese Envoy Stresses 'Confidence' for Pushing Forward," Xinhua General News Service, April 18, 2016.

149. "Jordan, China Share Common Views on Resolving Syrian Crisis: Envoy," Xinhua General News Service, August 23, 2016.

150. "China to Continue Consultations with Lebanon over Syria Crisis: envoy." Xinhua General News Service, December 5, 2016.

151. "Hariri Discusses with Chinese Envoy Situation in Syria," National News Agency in Syria, December 5,2016; An Baijie and Mo Jingxi, "Xi Says More Help on Way for Syria Refugees," *China Daily*, January 20, 2017; "China to Pursue Peace Talks to Promote Settlement of Syria Conflict: Envoy," *China Daily–Africa Weekly*, June 18, 2017.

152. "Special Envoy: China Ready to Reconstruct Syria," FARS News Agency, July 25, 2017.

153. "Reconstruction of Syria Needs All Int'l Community's Help: Chinese Envoy," Xinhua General News Service, December 1, 2017; "Chinese, Syrian Diplomats Hold 'In-Depth' Talks," Mehr News Agency, July 28, 2018.

154. "Reconstruction of Syria Needs"; and "Chinese Envoy Urges Political Solution to Syrian Issue," *People's Daily Online–English*, April 2018.

155. "Financial Hurdles Hamper China's Involvement in Rebuilding Syria–China-Arab Association," Sputnik News Service, January 31, 2018.

156. "China Urges U.S., Russia to Avoid Clashes on Syria," Xinhua General News Service, April 13, 2017.

157. "Chinese Envoy Says Peace Talks Only Way to Solve Syrian Crisis," Xinhua General News Service, April 23, 2017.

158. "Political Settlement Only Way Out of Syrian Crisis: Chinese Envoy," Xinhua General News Service, April 22, 2018.

159. "Moscow, Beijing Opposed Staging Chemical Weapons Provocations Aimed at Using Force Against Syria-Russia Foreign Ministry," Russia and CIS General Newswire, April 27, 2018.

160. "Russia, China Condemn Staging of Chemical Attack in Syria," *Iran Daily*, April

28, 2018; "Press Release on Deputy Foreign Minister Mikhail Bogdanov's Meeting with Special Envoy of the Chinese Government on the Syria Issue Xie Xiaoyan," Russian Government News, April 30, 2018.

161. "Russia, China Condemn Staging."

162. "The Chinese Government Special Envoy on the Question of Syria Explains China's Position on Syria," Xinhua Domestic, April 21, 2016.

163. "Chinese Envoy to Visit Syria," Xinhua General News Service, April 19, 2016; "Hmeimin Group Says Discusses Creation of Unified Syria Opposition with China Envoy," *Ria Novasti*, April 19, 2016; "Presence of Syrian Parties in Geneva without Preconditions Is Significant: China's Envoy," Xinhua General News Service, December 1, 2017; "Report: China Move In to Help Resolve Syrian Crisis," FARS News Agency, December 13, 2016; "Chinese Diplomat Highlights Role of UN in Political Solutions for Syria," *China Daily*, February 23, 2017; "China/ Russia/ Syria: Special Envoy: China, Russia Have Potential to Expand Cooperation Regarding Syrian Crisis," Thai News Service, May 14, 2018.

164. "Don't Expect 'Quick Fix' in Syria, China Tells EU," *EU Observer*, April 26, 2017. For an in-depth examination of China's approach to nonintervention in Syria in the UN, see Courtney J. Fung, *China and Intervention at the UN Security Council: Reconciling Status* (Oxford: Oxford University Press, 2019).

165. "Chinese Envoy Advises against 'Regime Change' in Syria," Xinhua General News Service, April 26, 2017.

166. "Special Envoy: China Ready to Reconstruct Syria," FARS News Agency, July 25, 2017.

167. "Chinese Special Envoy Urges 'Facts' on Syria," *People's Daily Online English*, April 23, 2018.

168. "Chinese Special Envoy Urges 'Facts' on Syria."

169. For a summary of various rounds of Syria peace talks, see "Syria Diplomatic Talks: A Timeline," *Al Jazeera*, September 17, 2017.

170. For background on Geneva I, see https://www.un.org/News/dh/infocus/Syria/FinalCommuniqueActionGroupforSyria.pdf.

171. For background on Geneva II, see Shannon Tiezzi, "China at Geneva II: Beijing's Interests in Syria," *Diplomat*, January 22, 2014.

172. "Foreign Ministry Spokesperson Hua Chunying's Regular Press Conference on April 19, 2016," Ministry of Foreign Affairs of the People's Republic of China, April 19, 2016.

173. "China's Syrian Issue Envoy to Travel Abroad to Work on Political Solution," Xinhua General News Service, January 4, 2017; "China's Special Envoy to Hold Discussions with Russia on Settling Syrian Conflict," *ITAR-TASS*, January 4, 2017.

174. "The Latest: China Envoy Hails Syria Peace Talks 'Momentum,'" Associated Press International, March 22, 2017.

175. "Chinese Envoy for Syria Hope Constitutional Commission to Be Set Up by Late September," Sputnik News Service, August 20, 2018.

176. See https://www.un.org/undpa/en/Speeches-statements/14112015/syria for the

initial declaration from the first meeting in Vienna. See https://www.un.org/sg/en/content/sg/note-correspondents/2016-05-17/note-correspondents-statement-international-syria-support for a list of the members of the ISSG.

177. "International Meeting on Syria Focuses on Better Implementation of Cease Fire Deal," Xinhua in English, May 18, 2016.

178. "Interview: China Hopes Astana Talks Will Bear Fruit for Syria's Political Process: Chinese Envoy," Xinhua General News Agency, January 6, 2017.

179. "China: Geneva, Astana Platforms 'Mutually Supportive,'" *Tehran Times*, July 23, 2017.

180. "Syrian Army Says Fighting Has Halted Near Damascus," *China Daily*, July 24, 2017.

181. "China Ready to Consider Proposal to Become Observer at Astana Talks—Envoy for Syria," Russia and CIS News Service, September 21, 2017.

182. "China Ready to Regularly Coordinate with Russia on Syrian Settlement—Special Envoy," *Rian Novosti*, April 29, 2016.

183. "China Values Russian Role in Fighting Terror, Promoting Syrian Talks—Envoy," *Ria Novisti*, April 29, 2016.

184. "Chinese Envoy Says Presidents Assad's Fate Depends 'Entirely' on Syrian People," *Ria Novosti*, April 29, 2016.

185. "Russian, Chinese Diplomats Coordinate Stances on Syria Settlement," Russia and CIS General Newswire, January 13, 2017.

186. "Russia, China Speak Out for All Parties Concerned Implementing UNSC Resolutions on Syria- Russia Foreign Ministry," Russian and CIS General Newswire, April 28, 2017; "China to Keep Pushing for Political Settlement of Syrian Conflict," Xinhua General News Service, September 21, 2017; "China Ready to Consider Proposal to Become Observer at Astana Talks (Part 2)," Russia and CIS News Service, September 21, 2017.

187. "Russian, Chinese Foreign Ministers to Discuss Preparation for Putin's Visit," ITAR-TASS, April 5, 2018. See chapter 8 for a more in-depth discussion of China and Russia shared interests regarding Syria in UNSC voting.

188. "Moscow, Beijing against Provocative Fake News Episodes with Use of Chemical Weapons in Syria," ITAR-TASS, April 27, 2018. See chapter 5 for a discussion of China-Russia cooperation in the Shanghai Cooperation Organization.

189. For example, in June 2016 "Iran, China Stress Expansion of Bilateral Ties," FARS News Agency, June 3, 2016; February 2017 "Iran, China Enjoy Similar Views in Syria: Senior Diplomat," *Iranian Government News*, February 18, 2017, and July 2017; "Iranian, Chinese Diplomats Discuss Syrian Crisis," *Iran News*, July 24, 2017.

190. "Iran, China Stress Serious Campaign against Terrorism, Sending Humanitarian Aid to Syria," FARS News Agency, April 26, 2016; and "Iran, China Stress Serious Campaign Against Terrorism, Sending Humanitarian Aid to Syria," Thai News Service, April 28, 2016.

191. "Iran, China Warn against Foreign Intervention in Syria," *Press TV*, April 27, 2016.

192. "Special Envoy: China Strongly Opposed to Disintegration of Syria," FARS News Agency, July 22, 2017.

193. "Chinese Envoy to Syrian Visits Hezbollah's Moussawi," National News Agency Lebanon, December 7, 2016.

194. "Report: China Move In to Help Resolve Syrian Crisis," FARS News Agency, December 13, 2016.

195. Xie visited Egypt in 2016 and 2018. See "China Ready to Play Greater Role for Syria Crisis: Envoy," Xinhua General News Service, June 6, 2016; and "China: Special Envoy of the Chinese Government on the Syrian Issue Xie Xiaoyan Visits Egypt," Thai News Service, April 30, 2018.

196. "Arab-League Chief Meets Chinese Envoy," *Bahrain News Gazette*, June 6, 2016.

197. "Syrian Opposition Calls for Greater Gulf Role," *Gulf Daily News*, December 12, 2016.

198. "China's Special Envoy to Syria Confirms Kingdom's and China's Views on Syrian Crisis Are Identical," Saudi Press Agency, September 28, 2017; and "Saudi Arabia, China Hold Identical Views on Syrian Issue, Combatting Terrorism," *Arab News*, September 29, 2017.

199. "China's Syrian Envoy to 'Post': Netanyahu and Rouhani Should Meet," *Jerusalem Post*, July 30, 2018.

200. For example, see "Chinese Envoy Advises against 'Regime Change' in Syria," Xinhua General News Service, April 26, 2017.

201. "Sudan Welcomes China's Decision to Appoint Special Envoy for Africa," Xinhua, May 13, 2007.

202. "Sudanese President Meets with the Special Representative of the Chinese Government on Darfur," Chinese Ministry of Foreign Affairs Website, June 24, 2007, https://www.fmprc.gov.cn/mfa_eng/wjb_663304/zzjg_663340/fzs_663828/xwlb_663830/t333830.shtml. For an in-depth examination of China's stance on intervention in Darfur in the UN, see Courtney J. Fung, *China and Intervention at the UN Security Council: Reconciling Status* (Oxford: Oxford University Press, 2019).

203. Tan, "Chinese Special Envoys Travel All Around World." See also *China-Africa Confidential*, accessed December 11, 2011, at http://www.africa-confidential.com/whos-who-profile/id/3076.

204. AU is the African Union. LAS is the League of Arab States.

205. "The Chinese Government's Special Representative on the Darfur Issue Holds a Briefing to Chinese and Foreign Journalists," Embassy of the People's Republic of China in the United Kingdom of Great Britain and Northern Ireland website, July 24, 2007, https://www.fmprc.gov.cn/ce/ceuk/eng/zywl/2007/t344137.htm.

206. "The Chinese Government's Special Representative."

207. *China-Africa Confidential*, accessed January 29, 2012, at http://www.africa-confidential.com/whos-who-profile/id/3076,.

208. "Foreign Ministry Spokesperson Liu Jianchao's Regular Press Conference on February 28, 2008," Chinese Ministry of Foreign Affairs Website, February 29, 2008.

209. See "The Chinese Government's Special Representative on the Darfur Issue Holds a Briefing to Chinese and Foreign Journalists." See also "Premier Wen Jiabao

Holds Telephone Conversation with British Prime Minister Brown," *Chinese Ministry of Foreign Affairs Website*, February 19, 2008.

210. See "Highlights: Zimbabwe Online Media Roundup 03 Jul 08, " Zimbabwe, OSC Summary, July 4, 2008,.

211. For a time line of events in South Sudan, see "South Sudan Profile–Timeline," *BBC News*, August 6, 2018.

212. World Economic Forum, accessed on December 18, 2018, at https://www.weforum.org/people/zhong-jianhua.

213. Government of South Sudan (Juba), "South Sudan: RSS Media Team Meets Chinese Special Envoy on African Affairs," *Africa News*, April 9, 2012.

214. Government of South Sudan (Juba), "South Sudan"; "Sudanese President Meets China's Special Envoy," *Sudan Tribune*, June 20, 2013.

215. Susan Athiei Mangar, "China to Only Help in Nations' Dispute if Asked," *Citizen (Dar es Salaam)*, April 12, 2012.

216. "Xinhua China News Digest at 11:00 GMT, April 25," Xinhua General News Service Domestic News, April 25, 2012; "Foreign Ministry Spokesperson Liu Weimin's Regular Press Conference on April 25, 2012," States News Service, April 26, 2012; "China Reiterates Commitment to Support Negotiated Solution to Sudans' Disputes," *Sudan Tribune*, August 25, 2012.

217. "South Sudan: China Non-Committal on Financing Nation Pipeline as Kiir Cuts Short His Visit," *Africa News*, April 25, 2012.

218. "China Non-Committal on Financing South Sudan Pipeline as Kiir Cuts Short His Visit," *Sudan Tribune*, April 26, 2012.

219. Jane Perlez, "South Sudan to Get Aid from China: No Oil Deal," *New York Times*, April 26, 2012; Ulf Laessing and Sui-Lee Wee, "Kidnapped Chinese Workers Freed in Sudan Oil State," Reuters, February 7, 2012.

220. "Beijing Can Broker Sudan Peace," *South China Morning Post*, May 15, 2012.

221. "Chinese Envoy Urge Peaceful Settlement of Sudan's Disputes," *Sudan Tribune*, May 2012.

222. "Chinese Envoy Urge"; "China Reiterates Commitment to Support Negotiated Solution to Sudans' Disputes."

223. Thomas Kenneth, "H. E. Kiir Meets China's Presidential Envoy," Government of South Sudan, May 2012.

224. "China to Send Envoy to Sudans, Says Working with US," *DefenseWeb*, April 25, 2012. See also Jane Perlez, "South Sudan to Get Aid from China: No Oil Deal," *The New York Times*, April 26, 2012.

225. "The Forum on China-Africa Cooperation (FOCAC) and the Prospects for 'Trilateral' Development," States News Service, July 17, 2012.

226. "Beijing Envoy in Khartoum Amid Sudan-South Tension," AFP, May 13, 2012; "China Denies Promising South Sudan an US $8 Billion Development Deal," *Sudan Tribune*, March 15, 2013; "Chinese Envoy Meets Sudanese Officials on Ties, Darfur," Xinhua General News Service, April 22, 2013; "China Steps in to Seek Solution to Sudan's Oil Shutdown Crisis," *Sudan Tribune*, June 16, 2013.

227. "China Denies Promising South Sudan an US $8 Billion Development Deal," *Sudan Tribune*, March 15, 2013; "Chinese Envoy Meets Sudanese Officials on Ties, Darfur," Xinhua General News Service, April 22, 2013; "China Steps in to Seek Solution to Sudan's Oil Shutdown Crisis," *Sudan Tribune*, June 16, 2013; "Mbeki Seeks to Hold an Urgent Summit between Al-Bashir and Salva Kiir," Qatar News Agency, July 22, 2013.

228. Tesfa-Alem Tekle, "Sudan Postpones Deadline to Shutdown Oil Pipeline, Says Ethiopia," *Sudan Tribune*, June 26, 2013.

229. "Sudan Agrees to China-AU Pleas for Postponement of Oil Shutdown," *Sudan Tribune*, July 26, 2013; Ahmed Soliman, "Democratization by Dismissal?" Chatham House, July 29, 2013.

230. "Sudan Extends Oil Shutdown Deadline Again," *Sudan Tribune*, August 12, 2013.

231. Isma'il Kushkush, "President Says a Coup Failed in South Sudan," *New York Times*, December 16, 2013. For an in-depth discussion of China and Nonintervention in South Sudan, see "China's Foreign Policy Experiment in South Sudan," International Crisis Group, July 10, 2017.

232. "Chinese Government's Special Representative on African Affairs Zhong Jianhua Holds a Telephone Conversation with South Sudanese Foreign Minister on the Situation in South Sudan," States News Service, December 25, 2013.

233. "China Voices Concerns about South Sudan Humanitarian Situation," Xinhua Economic News Service, December 27, 2013; Hend Kortam, "Egyptian Envoy to South Sudan Meets with Salva Kiir," *Daily News Egypt*, December 28, 2013.

234. "China's Foreign Policy Experiment in South Sudan," International Crisis Group, July 10, 2017.

235. "China Appreciates IGAD Mediation in South Sudan," Xinhua General News Service, December 31, 2013; "China Appreciates IGAD Mediation in South Sudan," Qatar News Agency, January 1, 2014.

236. "Ethiopia Promises Continued Support to South Sudan's Unity Gov't," Ethiopian News Agency, May 7, 2016; "Chinese Official to Visit Africa for South Sudan Talks," Xinhua General News Service, July 20, 2016.

237. "China Continues to Support All Peaceful Efforts Towards Resolving Crisis in South Sudan," *China Daily*, January 3, 2014.

238. Zhou Wa, "China to Step Up Efforts to Find Peace in S Sudan," *China Daily*, January 18, 2014.

239. "South Sudan Marks New Foreign Policy Chapter for China," *Defense Web*, February 12, 2014.

240. "China Moves into South Sudan," *Sunday Tribune (South Africa)*, November 2, 2014.

241. China's Foreign Policy Experiment in South Sudan," International Crisis Group, July 10, 2017; "Xi Jinping's Africa Policy: The First Year," States News Service, April 14, 2014; Tim Steinecke, "Bad News for Beijing as Machar Attacks Oil Fields," *African Arguments*, April 16, 2014.

242. Marthe Van Der Worlf, "China's FM Calls for End of Violence in South Sudan," *Voice of America*, January 6, 2014.

243. Nichola Kotch, "Prospects for a Peaceful Birth of a Nation Were Never Auspicous," *Business Daily (South Africa)*, January 9, 2014.

244. "China Take More Assertive Line in South Sudan Diplomacy," *DefenceWeb*, June 5, 2014. Chapter 9 discusses China's UN peacekeeping activities in more detail.

245. "China Moves into South Sudan," *Sunday Tribune (South Africa)*, November 2, 2014.

246. "China's Mediation of South Sudan Issue Not for Beijing's Self-Interest- Minister," *BBC Monitoring Asia Pacific—Political*, January 12, 2015; Mo Jingxi, "FM Defends Mediation Efforts in South Sudan," *China Daily European Edition*, January 13, 2015.

247. "China's Mediation."

248. See https://microsites-live-backend.cfr.org/global-conflict-tracker/conflict/destabilization-mali.

249. Elissa Jobson, "Countries Pledge $455m for Mali Support at AU Conference," *Business Day (South Africa)*, January 30, 2013.

250. Jobson, "Countries Pledge $455m."

251. "Chinese Envoy to Attend Mali Conference," Xinhua Economic News Service, January 29, 2013.

252. Qin Zhongwei, "African Service Sector an Opportunity for Companies," *China Daily European Edition*, February 28, 2013.

253. "Kenya Urges Warring Burundi Leaders to Embrace Dialogue," Xinhua General News Service, November 18, 2015. See also "China Leader to Make 'Monumental Announcement' at China-Africa Summit," *BBC Monitoring Africa—Political*, December 4, 2015.

254. "Rwanda: China Proposed Strategy to Resolve Burundian Crisis," Pan African News Agency, November 24, 2015.

255. "Africa; Help Africa Solve Conflicts–Lungu," *Times of Zambia*. January 7, 2016.

256. Ma Shukun and Mu Dong, "Interview: Chinese Special Envoy Says Good Time to Invest in Africa," Xinhua Economic News Service, May 11, 2012.

257. "Remark by Special Representative for the Government on Africa Affairs Zhong Jianhua in National University of Rwanda," Forum on China-Africa Cooperation, March 26, 2013.

258. Frank Ching, "Criticism of China by Africans Grows," *EJ Insights (Hong Kong)*, April 2, 2013.

259. Ed Cropley and Michael Martina, "In Africa's Warm Heart, A Cold Welcome for Chinese Merchants; In Malawi and Elsewhere, Businesses Say They're Being Undercut with Prices They Can't Match," *Vancouver Sun (British Columbia)*, September 21, 2012.

260. "Special Representative for then Government of China on African Affairs Zhong Jianhua Exchanges with Students from National University of Rwanda [interview]," Forum on China-Africa Cooperation, March 28, 2013.

261. "China's $60bn Africa Vow," *Herald (Glasgow)*, December 5, 2015.

262. Susan Athiei Mangar, "China to Only Help in Nations' Dispute if Asked," *Citizen (Dar es Salaam)*, April 12, 2012.

263. "Chinese New President's Africa Visit Critical to Development: Chinese Envoy," Philippines News Agency, January 19, 2013.

264. "China's Xi Arrives in Africa with Focus on Trade Ties," *Sydney Morning Herald (Australia)*, March 25, 2013.

265. "China Moves to Reassure Africa over Relationship," *Irish Times*, March 26, 2013.

266. "Remark by Special Representative for the Government on Africa Affairs Zhong Jianhua in National University of Rwanda," Forum on China-Africa Cooperation, March 26, 2013.

267. The quote of US $200 was an exaggeration since market prices as the time were close to US $120, but his point was that China was buying African oil at market prices.

268. "Regional Integration Essential to Africa's Growth and Development, Says Carl Bildt," States News Service, May 10, 2013.

269. "Special Representative for Then Government of China on African Affairs Zhong Jianhua Exchanges with Students from National University of Rwanda [Interview]," Forum on China-Africa Cooperation, March 28, 2013.

270. "Africa Will Be China's Next Economic Competitor Says Beijing's Top Diplomat Zhong Jianhua [interview]," Africa Research Institute, August 7, 2013.

271. Qin Zhongwei, "China Hopes for Prosperous Africa," *China Daily European Edition*, March 30, 2013.

272. Qin, "China Hopes for Prosperous Africa."

273. "China to Play Bigger Role in Restoring Peace in Africa: Envoy," Xinhua General News Service, October 16, 2014.

274. "ISS: Beijing's Peacemaking Efforts in South Sudan," *DefenceWeb*, November 6, 2014.

275. "Remarks by H. E. Ambassador Liu Xianfa at the Ceremony of the Seminar on China-Africa Peace and Security Cooperation," States News Service, October 26, 2014.

276. Jonisayi Maromo, "No Special Treatment," *Independent on Saturday (South Africa)*, December 5, 2015.

277. Teddy Ng, "China Pulled towards Action in South Sudan; Beijing' Preference for Hands-Off Approach in Political Affairs in Africa Tested by Civil War That Threatens Its Energy Interests, Experts Say," *South China Morning Post*, February 3, 2014.

278. George Okore, "Keeping the Pirates at Bay: China Plays a Major Role on Combatting Maritime Crime," *Chinafrica*, May 1, 2014.

279. Zhao Shengnan and Chi Jun, "China to Help Africa Tackle Root Cause of Ebola," *China Daily European Edition*, September 26, 2014.

280. Liu Sha, "Into the Outbreak," *Global Times*, October 16, 2014.

281. This analysis examines 2016 to 2018. Xu is still the special envoy.

282. "Foreign Ministry Spokesperson Hua Chunying's Remarks on Ambassador Xi Jinghu's Appointment as Special Representative of Chinese Government on African Affairs," States News Service, August 4, 2016.

283. "Envoy Says China to Strengthen Ties with Uganda," BBC Monitoring Africa—Political, March 16, 2017; "China Special Rep for Africa in Uganda for Talks with President Museveni," *Africa Newswire*, March 17, 2017.

284. "Musevini in New Push for Peace in Jubal," *East African*, March 212017.

285. "China: Special Representative of the Chinese Government on African Affairs Xu Jinghu Attends the High Level Revitalization Forum on South Sudan Peace Agreement," Thai News Service, January 3, 2018.

286. "High Level Revitalization Forum on South Sudan Peace Agreement."

287. "China: Special Representative of the Chinese Government on African Affairs Xu Jinghu Attends the Fourth Dakar International Forum on Peace and Security in Africa," Thai News Service, November 23, 2017.

288. "China: Special Representative of the Chinese Government on African Affairs Xu Jinghu Attends the Oslo Forum," Thai News Service, July 3, 2018.

289. Luci Morangi, "The Road to Africa's Industrial Future," *China Daily European Edition*, August 10, 2018.

290. "China, Africa Continue to Enhance Cooperation on Peace, Security," *People's Daily Online English*, September 4, 2018.

291. "China-Mauritius to Explore New Strategic Partnership," Government of Mauritius, April 21, 2017.

292. "Special Representative of the Chinese Government on African Affairs Xu Jinghu Visits Seychelles," Forum on China-Africa Cooperation, June 23. 2017.

293. "China Willing to Implement Consensus Reached by Heads of State of China and Rwanda: Envoy," Xinhua General News Service, June 26, 2017.

294. "Special Representative of the Chinese Government on African Affairs Xu Jinghu Attends African Union Extraordinary Summit on Maritime Security and Safety and Development in Africa: During the summit, Xu Jinghu respectively met with President Faure Essozimna Gnassingbé and Foreign Minister Robert Dussey of Togo," Ministry of Foreign Affairs of the People's Republic of China, October 20, 2016; and "China, Africa Continue to Enhance Cooperation on Peace, Security," *People's Daily Online English*, September 4, 2018.

295. Andrew Moody, "The Road Ahead," *China Daily European Edition*, September 7, 2018.

296. Benjamin Haas," China Defends Plans to Spend $60bn in Africa over Three Years; Beijing's Investments in the Developing World Are Coming Under Increasing Scrutiny," *Guardian*, September 4, 2018.

CHAPTER 6

1. See chapter 3 for a detailed description of China's post–Cold War interests and ties to China's domestic economic and political system.

2. Of course, China engages in a number of international organizations and multilateral financing institutions to facilitate economic interactions with these regions, such as the WTO, G-20, Asian Infrastructure Investment Bank, and the World Bank. Those institutions are not the focus of this chapter.

3. International Monetary Fund Direction of Trade Statistics, accessed January 29, 2021, at www.imfstatistics.org.

4. US data compiled by author from United States International Trade Administration, tse.export.gov, accessed on February 5, 2021.

5. China's resource needs are not the only reason for the steep increase in imports starting in 2000. Other factors include China's entry into the WTO in 2001, China's broader go out/go global strategy encouraging Chinese business to engage with the global marketplace, and China's level of development increasingly generating a demand for a wide range of foreign imports.

6. US Energy Information Administration, *Country Analysis Briefs: China,* May 14, 2015.

7. US Energy Information Administration, *Today in Energy*, February 5, 2018.

8. US Energy Information Administration, "China's Crude Oil Imports Surpassed 10 Million Barrels per Day in 2019," *Today in Energy,* March 23, 2020.

9. Data compiled by author from "Imports of Major Commodities by Countries (Regions) of Origin, 2000–2001," in *China External Economic Statistical Yearbook* (Beijing: China Statistics Press, 2002), 112–113.

10. Calculated by author from data in United Nations Comtrade Database on February 5, 2021, at https://comtrade.un.org/labs/data-explore. Part of this decrease is due to China's diversification to other suppliers outside these regions, such as Russia and the United States. That said, with the current US-China trade war, China's imports of US energy resources plummeted.

11. United Nations Comtrade database.

12. Data from United Nations Comtrade.

13. United Nations Comtrade.

14. US data compiled by author from United States International Trade Administration on February 5, 2021*tse.export.gov*, accessed.

15. World Bank, accessed October 13, 2018, at https://wits.worldbank.org/CountryProfile/en/Country/CHN/Year/2016/TradeFlow/Export/Partner/MEA/Product/all-groups.

16. The UAE is a regional hub in the Middle East, and many companies re-export to other regional countries through free trade zones. Part of this trade is destined for Iran and the rest of the Middle East. As a relatively high-income economy, the UAE also consumes many Chinese goods.

17. International Monetary Fund, *Direction of Trade Statistics Database.*

18. IMF, *Direction of Trade.*

19. According to *China's Statistical Yearbooks*, contract services include "(1) overseas civil engineering construction projects financed by foreign investors; (2) overseas projects financed by the Chinese government through its foreign aid programs; (3) construction projects of Chinese diplomatic missions, trade offices and other institutions stationed abroad; (4) construction projects in China financed by foreign investment; (5) sub-contracted projects to be taken by Chinese contractors through a joint umbrella project with foreign contractor(s); (6) housing development projects." Also, "the business income from international contracted projects is the work volume of contracted projects completed during the reference period, expressed in monetary terms, including completed work on projects signed in previous years."

20. Data compiled by author from *China Statistical Yearbooks*, 2000–2020, Turnover of Economic Cooperation sections. See figure 6.7 sources for detailed citations.

21. Data compiled by author from *China Statistical Yearbooks*, 2000–2020, Turnover of Economic Cooperation sections. See figure 6.7 sources for detailed citations.

22. "11–22 Economic Cooperation by Country (Region) (2019)," in *China Statistical Yearbook 2020*.

23. Chinese government sources systematically understate China's OFDI. There is no comprehensive source for more accurate information on Chinese OFDI. Although it likely underreports some FDI, these are the best data available by country over the years examined and provide deep insights into the comparative magnitude of OFDI across countries and over time.

24. OECD's definition of FDI is "an incorporated or unincorporated enterprise in which a foreign investor owns 10 per cent or more." More definition information is available at http://stats.oecd.org/Index.aspx?DataSetCode=FDI_FLOW_PARTNER.

25. FDI flows are the amount of FDI entering a country in a given year. FDI stocks are the accumulated FDI in a country over a certain timeframe.

26. Almost $5 billion of South Africa's total for this time period is due to ICBC's 20 percent acquisition of South African Standard Bank in 2008.

27. China world net FDI flows obtained from 2019 *Statistical Bulletin of China's Outward Foreign Direct Investment*, 146–151.

28. Data from *2019 Statistical Bulletin of China's Outward Foreign Direct Investment* (China Ministry of Commerce, 2020), 146–149. For a discussion of these changes, see Thilo Hanneman and Daniel H. Rosen, "Chinese FDI in the US in 2017: A Double Policy Punch," Rhodium Group (January 2018), rhg.com/research/chinese-fdi-us-2017-double-policy-punch/, and Alan Rappeport, "Chinese Money in the US Dries Up as Trade War Drags On," *New York Times*, July 21, 2019.

29. For a discussion of investment shifting to Israel, see Julie Zhu and Tova Cohen, "Chinese Tech Money Heads for Israel as US Welcome Wanes," *Reuters*, May 10, 2017.

30. 2019 *Statistical Bulletin*, 119. Data include all countries in North Africa as well as sub-Saharan Africa.

31. For a discussion of China's economic statecraft, see William Norris, *Chinese Economic Statecraft: Commercial Actors, Grand Strategy, and State Control* (Ithaca: Cornell University Press, 2016).

32. For a detailed list of projects identified by company, see Dawn C. Murphy, "Operations of Select Chinese Companies," www.chinariseglobalsouth.com.

33. The vast majority of the dollar value of Chinese economic activity in these regions is conducted by state-owned enterprises. That said, most Chinese companies operating in these regions are small and medium-sized enterprises (SMEs). Many of those SMEs are privately owned.

34. Yang Dexin, *China's Offshore Investments: A Network Approach* (Cheltenham: Edward Elgar, 2005), 20.

35. Frederich Wu, "Corporate China Goes Global," in *Handbook of Research on Asian Business*, ed. Henry Wai-Chung Yeung (Cheltenham: Edward Elgar, 2007), 445.

36. Jiang, "Full Text of Jiang Zemin's Report at 14th Party Congress."

37. Yang Xiaohua and Clyde Stoltenberg,"Growth of Made in China Multinationals: An Institutional and Historical Perspective," in *Globalization of Chinese Enterprises*, ed. IIan Alon and John R. McIntyre (New York: Palgrave Macmillan, 2008), 64.

38. "Corporate China Goes Global," 445.

39. Interview, Chinese Academy of Social Sciences (CASS), Institute of World Economics and Politics (IWEP), March 10, 2010, Beijing.

40. Interview, Chinese Academy of Social Sciences (CASS), IWEP, March 10, 2010, Beijing. For an in-depth discussion of China's economic statecraft and National Champions, see William Norris, *Chinese Economic Statecraft: Commercial Actors, Grand Strategy, and State Control* (Ithaca: Cornell University Press, 2016).

41. Matthew Forney, "China's Going-Out Party: Beijing Is Pushing Chinese Firms to Establish a Global Presence—Despite the Many Risks That Involves," *Time International*, January 24, 2005: 29; Henry Wai-Chung Yeung and Liu Wedong, "Globalizing China: The Rise of Mainland Firms in a Global Economy," *Eurasian Geography and Economics* 49, no. 1 (2008): 64.

42. Zhao Hong, "China-US Oil Rivalry in Africa," Copenhagen Discussion Papers 2007–24, ed. Michael Jacobsen (Frederiksberg: Asian Research Center, CBS, 2007), 1–43.

43. *Statistical Bulletin of China's Outward Foreign Direct Investment* (Beijing: China Ministry of Commerce, 2015), 111.

44. Interview, University of International Business and Economics, March 24, 2010, Beijing.

45. Interview, Department of Asian and African Studies, Chinese Academy of International Trade and Economic Cooperation, China Ministry of Commerce, March 26, 2010, Beijing.

46. Interview, CASS, IWEP, Beijing, January 2013.

47. See Murphy, "Operations of Select Chinese Companies," for sources for operations, CNPC, 1991–2017, www.chinariseglobalsouth.com. See also www.cnpc.com.cn.

48. See Murphy, "Operations of Select Chinese Companies," for sources for operations, SINOPEC, 1991–2017.

49. See Murphy, "Operations of Select Chinese Companies." See also www.cnoocltd.com.

50. Syria stopped oil operations with civil war.

51. See Murphy, "Operations of Select Chinese Companies," for sources for operations of Sinochem, 1991–2017.

52. Foreign aid is discussed later in this chapter and in chapter 4 on cooperation forums.

53. See Murphy, "Operations of Select Chinese Companies,"for a detailed list of SINOHYDRO projects, 1991–2017. Also refer to eng.sinohydro.com.

54. See Murphy, "Operations of Select Chinese Companies," for a detailed list of CRCC projects, 1991–2017. See also english.crcc.cn.

55. See Murphy, "Operations of Select Chinese Companies," for a detailed list of

CRBC projects, 1991–2017. See also www.crbc.com.China Aid Data is a another great source of information for CRBC projects: https://china.aiddata.org/.

56. See Murphy, "Operations of Select Chinese Companies,"for a detailed list of CSCEC projects, 1991–2017. Also see China Aid Data, https://china.aiddata.org/.

57. See Murphy, "Operations of Select Chinese Companies," for a detailed list of NORINCO projects, 1991–2017.

58. Interview, South African bank, December 23, 2009, Beijing.

59. See Murphy, "Operations of Select Chinese Companies,"for a breakdown of Huawei's activities, 1991–2017. Also see http://e.huawei.com/en/branch-office.

60. See Murphy, "Operations of Select Chinese Companies," for a breakdown of Huawei's activities, 1991–2017. Also see http://pr.huawei.com/en/media-kit/fact-sheet/index.htm.

61. See Murphy, "Operations of Select Chinese Companies," for a breakdown of Huawei's activities, 1991–2017.

62. See Murphy, "Operations of Select Chinese Companies," for a breakdown of Huawei's activities, 1991–2017. Also see http://e.huawei.com/en/branch-office

63. See Murphy, "Operations of Select Chinese Companies," for a breakdown of Huawei's activities, 1991–2017. Also see http://pr.huawei.com/en/media-kit/fact-sheet/index.htm.

64. See Murphy, "Operations of Select Chinese Companies," for a breakdown of Huawei's activities, 1991–2017. Also see http://pr.huawei.com/en/media-kit/fact-sheet/index.htm.

65. Interview, South African bank, December 23, 2009, Beijing.

66. See Murphy, "Operations of Select Chinese Companies," for a breakdown of ICBC activities, 1991–2017. See also ICBC 2016 annual report, p. 43.

67. See Murphy, "Operations of Select Chinese Companies,"for a breakdown of Bank of China's activities 1991–2017. Also see http://www.boc.cn/en/aboutboc/ab6/.

68. See Murphy, "Operations of Select Chinese Companies," for a breakdown of Agricultural Bank of China's activities, 1991–2017. See also ABC 2016 Annual Report, p. 69.

69. See Murphy, "Operations of Select Chinese Companies," for a breakdown of China Construction Bank's activities, 1991–2017. See also China Construction Bank Annual Report 2016.

70. See Murphy, "Operations of Select Chinese Companies," for a breakdown of Chery's activities, 1991–2017.

71. See Murphy, "Operations of Select Chinese Companies," for a breakdown of Haier's activities, 1991–2017.

72. Dawn C. Murphy, "Irreversible Pathway? Examining the Trump Administration's Economic Competition with China," *Journal of War and Peace Studies* 2 (2020).

73. This chapter focuses on China's bilateral aid to states in the Middle East and sub-Saharan Africa, not trilateral aid initiatives. For a discussion of China's trilateral aid cooperation with the United States, see Zhang Denghua, "Why Cooperate with Others? Demystifying China's Trilateral Aid Cooperation," *Pacific Review* 30, no. 5 (2017); Zhang

Denghua, "A Tango by Two Superpowers: China-US Cooperation in Trilateral Aid and Implications for Their Bilateral Relations," *Asian Journal of Political Science* 26, 2 (2018).

74. Copper, *China's Foreign Aid*; John Franklin Copper, *China's Foreign Aid and Investment Diplomacy* (New York: Palgrave Macmillan, 2016).

75. Bartke, *China's Economic Aid*, 25; Hutchison, *China's African Revolution*, 220–222; Behbehani, *China's Foreign Policy*, 16; Snow, *Star Raft*, 146–157.

76. Copper, *China's Foreign Aid*, xii; Snow, *Star Raft*, 145.

77. Copper, *China's Foreign Aid*, xii.

78. Copper, *China's Foreign Aid*, 69–71; Armstrong, *Revolutionary Diplomacy*, 216.

79. Hutchison, *China's African Revolution*, 56; Snow, *Star Raft*, 145.

80. Part of this is explained by the fact that a major driver of China's foreign aid program was to develop influence with these countries.

81. "China's Foreign Aid," White Paper Beijing (Beijing: Information Office of the State Council of the People's Republic of China, April 21, 2011), appendix I.

82. Hutchison, *China's African Revolution*, 51–52.

83. Bartke, *China's Economic Aid*, 9.

84. Hutchison, *China's African Revolution*, 49.

85. Bartke, *China's Economic Aid*, 12.

86. Axel Dreher, Andreas Fuchs, Bradley Parks, Austin M. Strange, and Michael J. Tierney, "Aid, China, and Growth: Evidence from a New Global Development Finance Dataset," AidData working paper 46 (Williamsburg, VA: AidData, 2017).

87. For an in-depth discussion of China's foreign aid, see "China's Foreign Aid," 2014; "China's Foreign Aid," 2011; Brautigam, *Dragon's Gift*.

88. Zhang Denghua and Graeme Smith, "China's Foreign Aid System: Structure, Agencies, and Identities," *Third World Quarterly* 38, no. 10 (2017).

89. See Lo Kinling, "China Launches Mega Aid Agency in Big Shift from Recipient to Donor," *South China Morning Post*, March 13, 2018; Sun Yun, "One Year On, the Role of the China International Development Cooperation Administration Remains Cloudy," *Africa in Focus*, Brookings, April 30, 2019.

90. Charles Wolf Jr., Wang Xiao, and Eric Warner, "China's Foreign Aid and Government-Sponsored Investment Activities: Scale, Content, Destinations, and Implications" (Santa Monica, CA: RAND, 2013).

91. That said, global norms of foreign aid may be starting to reconverge with China's approach as aid providers and intergovernmental organizations start to reconsider infrastructure projects.

92. See Austin Strange, "China's Foreign Aid Beyond the Headlines," blog, February 12, 2018.

93. Axel Dreher and Andreas Fuchs, "Rogue Aid? An Empirical Analysis of China's Aid Allocation," *Canadian Journal of Economics* 48, no. 3 (2015).

94. Pang Xun and Wang Shuai, "The International Political Significance of Chinese and US Foreign Aid: As Seen in United Nations General Assembly Voting," *Social Sciences in China* 39, no. 1 (2018).

95. Xun and Shui, "International Political Significance," argue that this effect is

driven by China's pursuing its economic interests rather than a purposeful strategic use of aid for this result.

96. The likely purpose of the FTA with Palestine is to balance the China-Israel FTA. China is concerned about perceptions of Arab states and wants to be seen as a balanced player between Israel and Palestine.

97. For more information on China's FTA negotiations, refer to the Chinese Ministry of Commerce website: http://fta.mofcom.gov.cn/english/. China also provides tariff-free trade benefits to all LDCs in SSA and ME (discussed more in chapter 4 on cooperation forums).

98. Information on all US FTAs available at https://ustr.gov/trade-agreements/free-trade-agreements.

99. For more information on AGOA, see https://www.trade.gov/agoa/eligibility/.

100. fta.mofcom.gov.cn/english/.

101. ustr.gov/trade-agreements/free-trade-agreements.

102. See "Forum on China-Africa Cooperation Beijing Action Plan (2019–2021)," September 12, 2018, section 2.4.5, https://focacsummit.mfa.gov.cn/eng/hyqk_1/t1594297.htm.

103. For more information on the Gulf Cooperation Council (GCC), see www.gcc-sg.org/eng/indexc64c.html?action=GCC.

104. "The Joint Press Communiqué between the People's Republic of China and The Cooperation Council for the Arab States of the Gulf (GCC)," Embassy of the People's Republic of China in New Zealand, July 7, 2004. http://nz.china-embassy.org/eng/xw/t142542.htm.

105. PRC Ministry of Commerce, China FTA Network, accessed January 12, 2012, at fta.mofcom.gov.cn/topic/engcc.shtml and May 24, 2018, at fta.mofcom.gov.cn/english/. Some interviewees noted that this FTA is more symbolic than substantive. For example, interview, United States Embassy in Abu Dhabi, UAE, August 2016.

106. PRC Ministry of Commerce, *China FTA Network (China-GCC FTA Page)*, http://fta.mofcom.gov.cn/english/index.shtml.

107. "Facts, Figures about Chinese President Hu Jintao's Foreign Tour," Xinhua, February 12, 2009.

108. PRC Ministry of Commerce, *China FTA Network (China-GCC FTA Page)*.

109. PRC Ministry of Commerce, *China FTA Network (China-GCC FTA Page)*.

110. Interview, Department of Asian and African Studies, Chinese Academy of International Trade and Economic Cooperation, Ministry of Commerce, March 26, 2010, Beijing.

111. Interview, Beijing University, Beijing, January 2013.

112. Interview, Beijing University, Beijing, January 2013.

113. Interview, Embassy of the Sultanate of Oman, Beijing, August 2015.

114. "China-Arab Cooperation Forum Action Plan (2016–2018)," and "China-Arab Cooperation Forum Action Plan, 2020-2022."

115. Interview, United States Embassy in Riyhad, Saudi Arabia, August 2016.

116. "Arab States; Rift with Qatar Clouds China's Plans for Gulf Free-Trade Deal,"

South China Morning Post, June 6, 2017; "Why Qatar Matters to China, In Spite of Gulf Isolation." *South China Morning* Post, June 12, 2017.

117. http://fta.mofcom.gov.cn/english/.

118. http://fta.mofcom.gov.cn/english/.

119. http://fta.mofcom.gov.cn/english/.

120. Zeng Ka, "China's Free Trade Diplomacy," *Chinese Journal of International Politics* 9, no. 3 (2016).

121. For a detailed discussion of these SEZs, see Deborah Brautigam and Tang Xiaoyang, "African Shenzhen: China's Special Economic Zones in Africa," *Journal of Modern African Studies* 49, no. I (2011): 27–54. Also see Tang Xiaoyang, "How Do Chinese 'Special Economic Zones' Support Economic Transformation in Africa," ODI's Supporting Economic Transformation, July 10, 2015.

122. Brautigam and Tang, "African Shenzhen," 30–31.

123. Brautigam and Tang, "African Shenzhen."

124. Brautigam and Tang, "African Shenzhen," 31.

125. Deborah Brautigam and Tang Xiaoyang, "'Going Global in Groups'": Structural Transformation and China Special Economic Zones Overseas," *World Development* 63 (2014).

126. "China Africa Economic and Trade Cooperation," 2010.

127. Brautigam and Tang, "African Shenzhen," 34.

128. Brautigam and Tang, "African Shenzhen."

129. "China Helps Africa Build over 142 Agricultural Projects by End of 2009," Xinhua, December 23, 2010.

130. "China Helps Africa Build over 142 Agricultural Projects."

131. "An Interpretation of New Measures on Economic and Trade Cooperation from 4th Ministerial Conference," May 24, 2010.

132. "Forum on China-Africa Cooperation Sharm El Sheikh Action Plan (2010–2012)."

133. "Forum on China-Africa Cooperation Johannesburg Action Plan (2016–2018)."

134. "Forum on China-Africa Cooperation Beijing Action Plan (2019–2021)."

135. "China-Arab Cooperation Forum Action Plan (2016–2018)" and "China-Arab Cooperation Forum 2018 to 2020 Action Plan."

136. This book does not explicitly discuss accusations of China's involvement in land grabs in Africa. For discussion of this issue, see Brautigam, *Will Africa Feed China?*

137. Hou Liqiang and Zhou Wa, "Agriculture Ties Grow Stronger," *China Daily Africa*, January 11, 2016.

138. Brautigam, *Dragon's Gift*, 249.

139. Brautigam, *Dragon's Gift*, 234.

140. Brautigam, *Dragon's Gift*, 246. See also Chen, "New Impetus to China-Africa Agricultural Cooperation" and "*China Africa Economic and Trade Cooperation*" and Xu, et al, "Science, Technology."

141. Brautigam and Tang, "China's Engagement," 694.

CHAPTER 7

1. See chapter 4 for a more in-depth discussion of the Five Principles.

2. This book examines China's political behavior toward these regions only through cooperation forums, special envoys, UNSC voting, strategic partnerships, and BRI. There are a number of other institutions and tools that could be examined (e.g., BRICS, Non-Aligned Movement, UN General Assembly and other UN organizations, and the African Union).

3. See chapter 3 for a detailed description of China's post–Cold War interests and ties to China's domestic economic and political system.

4. For a detailed analysis of China's historical voting in the United Nations Security Council, see Joel Wuthnow, *Chinese Diplomacy and the UN Security Council* (New York: Routledge, 2013).

5. Between joining the United Nations in 1971 and 2012, China exercised its Security Council veto only nine times. See Medeiros, *China's International Behavior*, 190, for a detailed list of vetoes from 1971 to 2010. In 1972, its veto was used to support the Palestinian PLO. Also see Wuthnow, *Chinese Diplomacy.*

6. China also voted no on a resolution regarding Iran in 2020, but I am not classifying it as a veto because the resolution did not have enough yes votes to pass. For a detailed discussion of voting behavior on Syria, see Courtney Fung, "Separating Intervention from Regime Change: China's Diplomatic Innovations at the UN Security Council Regarding the Syria Crisis'" *China Quarterly* 235 (2018): 693–712.

7. Those resolutions were S/RES/1696 (2006), S/RES/1737 (2006), S/RES/1747 (2007), S/RES/1803 (2008), S/RES/1835 (2008), S/RES/1929 (2010) and S/RES/2231 (2015).

8. Interview, Egyptian Council for Foreign Affairs, November 10, 2010, Cairo,.

9. Courtney J. Fung, "Global South Solidarity? China, Regional Organizations, and Intervention in the Libyan and Syrian Civil Wars," *Third World Quarterly* 37, no. 1 (2016).

10. See chapter 5 for a detailed discussion of China's role in Darfur and the establishment of a special envoy for Africa issues established in 2007.

11. For an excellent discussion of the role of the League of Arab States influencing China's voting, see Fung, "Global South Solidarity?"

12. Interview, Embassy of the State of Palestine, Beijing, January 2013; interview, Embassy of the State of Israel, Beijing, January 2013.

13. Interview, CASS, IWEP, Beijing, January 2013.

14. Interview, Beijing University, Beijing, January 2013; interview, Embassy of the Sultanate of Oman, Beijing, January 2013; interview, CASS, IWEP, January 2013.

15. Interview, Embassy of the State of Palestine, Beijing, January 2013; interview, Embassy of the Republic of Iraq, Beijing, January 2013; interview, CASS, IWAAS, Beijing, January 2013; interview, Beijing University, Beijing, August 2015; interview, China Foreign Affairs University, Beijing, August 2015.

16. Interview, Embassy of the State of Palestine, Beijing, August 2015.

17. Interview, Beijing University, Beijing, August 2015.

18. Interview, Embassy of the State of Palestine, Beijing, January 2013; interview,

CASS, IWAAS, Beijing, January 2013; interview, Beijing University, Beijing, January 2013.

19. Interview, Embassy of the Sultanate of Oman, Beijing, January 2013.

20. Interview, Beijing University, Beijing, January 2013.

21. Interview, *Al Riyahd* newspaper, Riyahd, August 2016.

22. Interview, Beijing University, Beijing, January 2013; interview, CASS, IWEP, January 2013; interview, CIIS, Beijing, August 2015.

23. Interview, *Al Rihyad* newspaper, Riyadh, August 2016.

24. See the detailed discussion in chapters 4 and 5.

25. Interview, Embassy of the Republic of Tunisia, May 24, 2010, Beijing; interview, CASS, IWAAS, January 27, 2010, Beijing

26. Interview, Embassy of the State of Palestine, May 28, 2010, Beijing.

27. Interview, Embassy of the State of Palestine, Beijing, January 2013; interview, Embassy of the State of Israel, Beijing, January 2013; interview, Embassy of the Republic of Iraq, Beijing, January 2013; interview CASS, IWAAS, Beijing, January 2013; interview, Embassy of the State of Palestine, Beijing, August 2015. See a fuller discussion of this issue in chapter 5 on special envoys.

28. Interview, Embassy of the Republic of Iraq, Beijing, January 2013.

29. "Declaration of the Beijing Summit of the Forum on China-Africa Cooperation," 2006,; "Beijing Declaration of the Fifth Minsterial Conference of the Forum on China-Africa Cooperation."

30. See "Strategic Partnership Heralds New Era in China, Arab States Ties: FM," Xinhua, July 10, 2018, http://www.xinhuanet.com/english/2018-07/10/c_137315150.htm.

31. For an argument that China should be establishing military alliances around the world, see Yan Xuetong, "Inside the China-US Competition for Strategic Partners." *Huffington Post,* November 2, 2015.

32. For a detailed discussion of China's strategic partnerships globally, see Medeiros, *China's International Behavior*, 82–89, and Feng Zhongping and Huang Jing, "China's Strategic Partnership Diplomacy: Engaging with a Changing World," working paper 8, European Strategic Partnership Observatory, June 2014. For a discussion of China's strategic partnerships with Middle Eastern countries, see Jonathan Fulton, "China's Changing Role in the Middle East" (Washington, DC: Atlantic Council, 2019).

33. "PRC's Wang Gang Heads Delegation to Egypt on Friendship, Bilateral Ties" and "Chinese Magazine Lauds Development of Egyptian-Chinese Relations."

34. "President Mubarak Speaks Highly of Egypt-PRC Friendly Relations," *Renmin Ribao,* June 6, 2001.

35. "Egypt, China Sign Strategic Cooperation Accord," *MENA,* June 17, 2006. See also Wang Jinglie, "Review and Thoughts over the Relationship between China and the Middle East," *Journal of Middle Eastern and Islamic Studies (in Asia)* 4, no. 1 (2010): 25.

36. "China, Egypt Vow to Enhance Strategic Cooperation," Xinhua, June 16, 2009.

37. Interview, Egyptian Ministry of Foreign Affairs, November 24, 2010, Cairo, Egypt.

38. Interview, Egyptian Ministry of Foreign Affairs, November 24, 2010, Cairo, Egypt.

39. "Xi Jinping's Speech at Opening of Seminar on 10th Anniv of China-Africa Forum," Xinhua Domestic Service, November 20, 2010; interview, Embassy of South Africa, April 16, 2010, Beijing.

40. "Beijing Declaration on the People's Republic of China and the Republic of South Africa Establishing a Comprehensive Strategic Partnership."

41. "Chinese Vice President Arrives in South Africa for Visit," Xinhua, November 16, 2010. See also "Ambassador Zhong Jianhua Talks on President Zuma's Visit to China and China-South Africa Relationship," Chinese Ministry of Foreign Affairs, September 10, 2010.

42. For the full text of the 2010 agreement, see "Beijing Declaration on the People's Republic of China and the Republic of South Africa Establishing a Comprehensive Strategic Partnership."

43. Interviews, Stellenbosch University, May 24, 25, 2011, Stellenbosch, South Africa; interview, interview, Stellenbosch University, May 27, 2011, Stellenbosch, South Africa.

44. Interview, Embassy of South Africa, April 16, 2010, Beijing; interviews, Stellenbosch University, May 24, 25, 27, 30, 2011, Stellenbosch, South Africa; ; interview, Stellenbosch University, May 30, 2011, Stellenbosch, South Africa; and interview, South African Department of International Relations and Co-operation, June 15, 2011.

45. Interviews, Stellenbosch University, May 24, 25, 27, 2011, Stellenbosch, South Africa; interview, South African Department of International Relations & Co-operation, June 15, 2011.

46. "China, Oman Issue Joint Statement on Establishment of Strategic Partnership," Xinhua May 26, 2018.

47. "Wang Yi meets with President Ali Bongo Ondimba of Gabon." Embassy the People's Republic of China in the Republic of South Africa website, June 15, 2018. http://za.chineseembassy.org/eng/zfgxss/t1529104.htm

CHAPTER 8

1. Of course, China is engaged in other military activity such as military exchanges, port visits, the sale of unmanned aerial vehicles and satellites, and potentially information sharing for counterterrorism activities. China also engages with the African Union on conflict resolution and peacekeeping and interacts with states in these regions through the Conference on Interaction and Confidence Building Measures in Asia (CICA). Foreign policy tools were selected for this chapter because they represent the major aspects of China's military relations with these regions, and country-level data over time are available to examine China's behavior.

2. For a detailed analysis of China's global historical UNPKO involvement, see Bates Gill, Chin-hao Huang, and J. Stephen Morrison, *China's Expanding Role in Africa: Implications for the United States,* (Washington, DC: CSIS, 2007). Also see Courtney J. Fung, "Explaining China's Deployment to UN Peacekeeping Operations," *International Relations of the Asia-Pacific* 16, no. 3 (2016); Courtney J. Richardson, "A Responsible Power? China and the UN Peacekeeping Regime," *International Peacekeeping* 18, no. 3 (2011): 288—299.

3. China's first UNPKO troops were deployed to Cambodia in 1991.

4. See https://peacekeeping.un.org/en/troop-and-police-contributors.

5. Accessed March 13, 2021, at https://peacekeeping.un.org/en/troop-and-police-contributors.

6. Interview, CASS, IWEP, Beijing, January 2013.

7. "China's National Defense in 2010."

8. Discussed in detail in chapter 3.

9. Due to a lack of high-quality data availability, this chapter does not include small arms and light weapons. If they were included, Chinese arms sales to these regions would be higher, but it would not significantly influence the findings of this chapter.

10. "Conventional Arms Transfers to Developing Nations, 2008–2015," Congressional Research Service, December 19, 2016, 23. For more discussion of China's arms sales to the developing world over the time frame considered in this book, also see Grimmett, *Conventional Arms Transfers to Developing Nations, 1992–1999*, 8, 20; and Grimmett, *Conventional Arms Transfers Developing Nations, 2003–2010*, 26.

11. Medeiros, *China's International Behavior*, 91–92; Richard F. Grimmett, *Conventional Arms Transfers to Developing Nations, 2000–2007* (Washington, DC: Congressional Research Service, 2008), 11; and Grimmett, *Conventional Arms Transfers Developing Nations, 2003–2010*, 10.

12. SIPRI calculates TIV "based on the known unit production costs of a core set of weapons and . . . intended to represent the transfer of military resources rather than the financial value of the transfer." For a more in-depth discussion of this methodology, see https://www.sipri.org/databases/armstransfers/background.

13. Data compiled by author from SIPRI Arms Transfers database, accessed June 12, 2017, November 14, 2019, and January 22, 2021, at http://www.sipri.org/databases/armstransfers online on 1.

14. One deviation from this pattern has been the sale of missile technology to Iran, but that behavior appears to be the exception rather than the rule. See Grimmett, *Conventional Arms Transfers to Developing Nations, 1992–1999*, 8; Grimmett, *Conventional Arms Transfers to Developing Nations, 2000–2007*, 11.

15. Peng and Wu, "China's Piracy Fight to Boost US Ties."

16. Alison A. Kaufman, *China's Participation in Anti-Piracy Operations off the Horn of Africa* (Arlington, VA: Center for Naval Analyses, July 2009),) 1. This chapter provides only a brief overview of China's antipiracy activities. For a wealth of information on this topic, see Andrew Erickson's work at www.andrewerickson.com.

17. "China's National Defense in 2010."

18. Erik Lin-Greenberg, "Dragon Boats: Assessing China's Anti-Piracy Operations in the Gulf of Aden," *Defense and Security Analysis* 26, no. 2 (2010): 215, "Xinhua Reviews Brief History of PLA Navy," Xinhua, October 2, 2009. See also Andrew S. Erickson and Justin D. Mikolay, "Welcome China to the Fight against Pirates," *US Naval Institute Proceedings* (March 2009): 34–41.

19. "China's National Defense in 2010."

20. See Lin-Greenberg, "Dragon Boats," 219.

21. "China's National Defense in 2010."

22. "China's National Defense in 2010."

23. See Lin-Greenberg, "Dragon Boats," 220.

24. "China to Host International Conference on Anti-Piracy in the Gulf of Aden," Xinhua, November 5, 2009.

25. Zhu Da and Zifu Yu, "Commander of USCTF 151 Visits 'Zhoushan' Warship," *Jiefangjun Bao Online*, November 4, 2009.

26. Lin-Greenberg, "Dragon Boats," 214.

27. "The Diversified Employment."

28. "The Diversified Employment."

29. Ankit Panda, "China Dispatches New Naval Fleet for Gulf of Aden Escort Mission," *Diplomat*, December 11, 2018.

30. Panda, "China Dispatches."

31. "China's New Naval Fleet Embarks on Escort Mission," *China Daily*, May 15, 2021, http://www.chinadaily.com.cn/a/202105/15/WS609f842fa31024ad0babe172.html.

32. Kaufman, *China's Participation;* Lin-Greenberg, "Dragon Boats"; Jonathan Hogslag, "Embracing China's Global Security Ambitions," *Washington Quarterly* 32, no. 3 (2009): 105–118; Erickson and Mikolay, "Welcome China to the Fight against Pirates."

33. Song Jie, "The Mission of Combatting Pirates Will Test China's Wisdom in Diplomacy," *Wen Wei Po Online*, February 16, 2009.

34. Jane Perlez and Chris Buckley, "China Retools Its Military with a First Overseas Outpost in Djibouti," *New York Times*, November 27, 2015.

35. Perlez and Buckley, "China Retools Its Military."

36. Jeremey Page, "China to Build Naval Hub in Djibouti," *Wall Street Journal*, November 26, 2015.

37. Perlez and Buckley, "China Retools."

38. Dietmar Pieper, "How Djibouti Became China's Gateway to Africa," *Spiegel Online*, February 8, 2019.

39. "China's Engagement in Djibouti," *In Focus*, Congressional Research Service, September 4, 2019.

40. "China's Engagement in Djibouti," *In Focus*, Congressional Research Service, September 4, 2019.

41. "China's National Defense in the New Era," 2019.

42. "China's Engagement in Djibouti."

43. "China Denies Using Lasers on US Aircraft in Djibouti," Associated Press, May 6, 2018.

44. David Brennan, "US Commander Says China Tried to Sneak into American Military Base in Africa," *Newsweek*, June 18, 2019.

45. For a discussion of the Djibouti base, see Hend Elmahly and Sun Degang, "China's Military Diplomacy towards Arab Countries in Africa's Peace and Security: The Case of Djibouti," *Contemporary Arab Affairs* 11, no. 4 (2018).

46. Gabriel B. Collins and Andrew S. Erickson, "Djibouti Likely to Become China's First Indian Ocean Outpost," *China Signpost*, July 11, 2015.

47. Shannon Tiezzi, "US General: China Has 10 Year Contract for First Overseas Military Base," *Diplomat,* November 26, 2015. The Libya evacuation was the PLA's most extensive overseas evacuation since the founding of the PRC. For more detailed discussion of this evacuation, see "The Diversified Employment," 2013. For a discussion of the Yemen evacuation, see "China's National Defense in the New Era," 2019.

48. Page, "China to Build."

49. Page, "China to Build."

50. Interview, scholar, CASS, IWAAS, Beijing, August 11, 2015; interview, scholar, King Faisal Center for Research, Riyadh, Saudi Arabia, August 6, 2016.

51. Interview, scholar, Beijing University, Beijing, August 9, 2015.

52. Interview with embassy official, Embassy of the Republic of Djibouti, Beijing, August 12, 2015.

53. Interview with embassy official, Embassy of the Republic of Djibouti, Beijing, August 12, 2015.

54. Interview with embassy official, Embassy of the Republic of Djibouti, Beijing, August 12, 2015.

CHAPTER 9

1. For an introduction to Belt and Road, see Bruno Macaes, *Belt and Road: A Chinese World Order* (Oxford: Oxford University Press, 2019); Li Xing, ed., *Mapping China's "One Belt One Road" Initiative* (Cham, Switzerland: Palgrave Macmillan, 2019); Anoushiravan Ehteshami and Niv Horesh, *China's Presence in the Middle East: The Implications of the One Belt, One Road Initiative* (London: Routledge, 2018); Rolland Nadege, *China's Eurasian Century? Political and Strategic Implications of the Belt and Road Initiative* (Seattle, WA: National Bureau of Asian Research, 2017). For a discussion of BRI in the Middle East, see Jonathan Fulton, *China's Changing Role in the Middle East* (Washington, DC: Atlantic Council, 2019); Liana M. Petranek, "Paving a Concrete Path to Globalization with China's Belt and Road Initiative through the Middle East," *Arab Studies Quarterly* 41, no. 1 (2019). For a discussion of BRI in Africa, see Thokozani Simelane , and Lavhelesani Managa, eds., *Belt and Road Initiative: Alternative Development Path for Africa* (Pretoria, South Africa: Africa Institute of South Africa, 2018). For Xi Jinping speeches about BRI, see "Full Text of President Xi's Speech at Opening of Belt and Road Forum," Xinhua, May 14, 2017; and Xi Jinping, "Working Together to Deliver a Brighter Future For Belt and Road Cooperation," keynote speech at the Second Belt and Road Forum for International Cooperation, Beijing, April 26, 2019.

2. As of June 2019, there were 137 countries profiled on the Chinese government's official Belt and Road website. This number includes countries along the Belt and Road and countries that have signed cooperation agreements with China on Belt and Road. See https://eng.yidaiyilu.gov.cn/info/iList.jsp?cat_id=10076&tm_id=80&cur_page=1. Xi Jinping's April 2019 speech from the Second BRI forum claims that 150 countries and international organization have signed agreements on BRI with China. Xi, "Working Together to Deliver a Brighter Future for Belt and Road Cooperation," http://beltandroadforum.org/english/n100/2019/0426/c22-1266.html

3. One of the most important goals of BRI is connecting China with Europe and supporting China's growth as a Eurasian power. This chapter focuses on BRI in the Middle East and Africa, but the comments on the Eurasian aspect of BRI are informed by my interviews about Belt and Road with scholars and intergovernmental organizations as well and US and European government officials in the United Kingdom, Netherlands, Belgium, and France in 2017 and 2018.

4. "National Security Strategy" 2017 and "Summary of the National Defense Strategy," 2018.

5. See Pence, "Policy toward China," and Pence, "Frederic V. Malek Memorial Lecture."

6. Gilpin, *War and Change*. See chapter 2 for a discussion of the theoretical literature about rising powers.

7. "China Pledges 40 Bln USD for Silk Road Fund," Xinhua in English, May 11, 2015.

8. "Vision and Actions on Jointly Building Silk Road Economic Belt and 21st Century Maritime Silk Road" (Beijing: National Development and Reform Commission, 2015).

9. Belt and Road Forum documents are available at www.beltandroadforum.org. For example, see "Joint Communique of the Leaders' Roundtable of the 2nd Belt and Road Forum for International Cooperation," Beijing, April 27, 2019; "List of Deliverables of the Second Belt and Road Forum for International Cooperation," Beijing, April 27, 2019.

10. "Full Text of President Xi's Speech at Opening of Belt and Road Forum," Xinhua, May 14, 2017.

11. See Xi Jinping's work report from the Nineteenth National Party Congress. Xi, "Secure a Decisive Victory in the Building of a Moderately Prosperous Society in All Respects and Strive for the Great Success of Socialism with Chinese Characteristics for a New Era," 2017.

12. "'Belt and Road' Incorporated into CPC Constitution," Xinhua, October 24, 2017.

13. F. Cambero and D. Sherwood, "China Invites Latin America to Take Part in One Belt, One Road," *Reuters Business News*, January 22, 2018; C. Gao, "China Says Latin America 'Eager' to Join Belt and Road," *Diplomat*, January 24, 2018.

14. "China Unveils Vision for 'Polar Silk Road' across Arctic," *Reuters Business News*, January 26, 2018; A. Wong, "China: We Are a 'Near-Arctic State' and We Want a 'Polar Silk Road,'" *CNBC News*, February 14, 2018.

15. *China's Arctic Policy* (Beijing: State Council Information Office of the People's Republic of China, 2018).

16. Xi Jinping, "Working Together to Deliver a Brighter Future for Belt and Road Cooperation," keynote speech by H. E. Xi Jinping at the Second Belt and Road Forum for International Cooperation, Beijing, April 26, 2019.

17. "Belt and Road Cooperation: Shaping a Brighter Shared Future." Joint Communiqué of the Leaders' Roundtable of the Second Belt and Road Forum for International Cooperation, April 27, 2019.

18. Hal Brands, *What Good Is Grand Strategy? Power and Purpose in American Statecraft from Harry S. Truman to George W. Bush* (Ithaca, NY: Cornell University Press, 2014), 3.

19. X. Ren and Y. Zheng, "Govt: Wrong to Label Belt and Road Initiative a Geo-Strategic Tool," *China Daily*, March 3, 2018.

20. Ren and Zheng, "Govt: Wrong to Label."

21. Although the United States no longer explicitly refers to the Obama era rebalance to the Pacific, all of the major components of the approach (political, military, and economic) remain in place except for the TPP.

22. It is important to note that much of China's Belt and Road activity is driven by economic interests and its desire for economic development to stabilize Xinjiang.

23. See chapter 3 for detailed discussion of Wang's arguments. The year 2012 was not the first time Wang Jisi wrote about the need for China to start to look west. In a 2011 *Foreign Affairs* piece, he discussed China's new Western outlook and said it "may reshape China's geostrategic vision as well as the Eurasian landscape." See Wang Jisi, "China's Search for a Grand Strategy," *Foreign Affairs* 90, no. 2 (2011. For Wang's writings on this topic since 2012, see Wang Jisi, "March West: China Geostrategic Rebalancing," *Global Times* (October 2012), and Wang Jisi, "China in the Middle," *American Interest* 10, no. (2015).

24. As discussed in chapter 3, it is hard to know whether Wang's thinking influenced top leaders in China or his writing merely reflected options that they were considering. Other Chinese scholars contest the wisdom of Wang Jisi's views and China's focus on its West. For example, another prominent Chinese international relations scholar, Yan Xuetong, has stressed that China should continue to focus on its immediate periphery rather than look west. See Yan Xuetong, "China Must Not Overplay Its Strategic Hand," *Global Times*, August 9, 2017, and chapter 3 in this book. This is a counterpoint to the BRI and the go west strategy. It says China should focus on Asia Pacific, not the West.

25. The first formal articulation of the BRI was "Vision and Actions."

26. For example, China's 2015 military strategy highlights PRC concerns with the increasingly competitive dynamic within Asia and on China's borders. See "China's Military Strategy," 2015.

27. Interview, Embassy of Palestine, August 2015; interview, Embassy of the Sultanate of Oman, August 2015.

28. Interview, Embassy of the Sultanate of Oman, August 2015.

29. "National Security Strategy," 2017; "Summary of the National Defense Strategy," 2018; "Nuclear Posture Review" (Washington, DC: Department of Defense, 2018).

30. Pence, "Policy toward China"; Pence, "Frederic V. Malek Memorial Lecture."

31. CASCF, "Declaration of the Sixth Ministerial Conference"; CASCF, "Development Plan (2014–2024)."

32. CASCF, "Declaration of the Sixth Ministerial Conference"; CASCF, "Development Plan (2014–2024)." My translation.

33. CASCF, "Seventh Doha Declaration"; CASCF "Action Plan (2016–2018)."

34. FOCAC, "Declaration of the Johannesburg Summit."

35. "Beijing Declaration: Toward an Even Stronger China-Africa Community with a Shared Future" (2018), 5.2.

36. "Declaration of Action on China-Arab States Cooperation under the Belt and Road Initiative," 2018.

37. For an introduction to AIIB, see https://www.aiib.org/en/about-aiib/governance/members-of-bank/index.html.

38. "Full Text of President Xi's Speech at Opening of Belt and Road Forum."

39. For a nuanced discussion of debt in China's international financing, see Chris Alden and Lu Jiang, "Brave New World: Debt, Industrialization and Security in China-Africa Relations," *International Affairs* 95, no. 3 (2019): 641–657; Deborah Brautigam and Meg Rithmire, "The Chinese 'Debt Trap' Is a Myth," *Atlantic*, February 6, 2021.

40. This chapter does not discuss other tools from chapters 4 to 8, such as special envoys, UNSC votes, UNPKO, and conventional arms sales. It could be argued that these tools also support BRI.

41. Although China competes with the United States with BRI, it cooperates with many other Western countries and Russia through this initiative.

42. For example, see Pence, "Frederic V. Malek Memorial Lecture."

CHAPTER 10

1. Peter Van Ness, *Revolution and Chinese Foreign Policy: Peking's Support for Wars of National Liberation* (Berkeley: University of California Press, 1970), 15–16.

2. This work does not cover all possible military behavior in these regions. For example, China's cyberactivity could be classified as norm divergent.

3. Cristina Maza, "Saudi Arabia's Mohammed bin Salman Defends China's Use of Concentration Camps for Muslims during Visit to Beijing," *Newsweek*, February 22, 2019.

4. Joshua Berlinger, "North Korea, Syria and Myanmar among Countries Defending China's Actions in Xinjiang," *CNN*, July 15, 2019.

5. See Xi Jinping, "Secure a Decisive Victory in the Building of a Moderately Prosperous Society in All Respects and Strive for the Great Success of Socialism with Chinese Characteristics for a New Era," in *Work Report Delivered at the 19th National Congress of the Communist Party of China, Beijing*,"Xinhua, 2017, 53–54

6. Mordechai Chaziza, "Coronavirus, China, and the Middle East," research report (Ramat Gan, Israel: Begin-Sadat Center for Strategic Studies, June 1, 2020).

7. Chaziza, "Coronavirus, China."

8. "China: Covid-19 Discrimination against Africans," *Human Rights Watch*, May 5, 2020.

9. R. Maxwell Bone and Ferdinando Cinotto, "China's Multifaceted COVID-19 Diplomacy across Africa," *Diplomat*, November 2, 2020.

10. Bone and Cinotto, "China's Multifaceted COVID-19."

11. Adam Hoffman, Roie Yellinek, "The Middle East and China: Trust in the Time of COVID-19," Middle East Institute, May 12, 2020.

12. Neil Edwards, "Vaccine Diplomacy: China and SinoPharm in Africa," *Council on Foreign Relations* (blog), January 6, 2021.

13. Neil Edwards, "Vaccine Diplomacy."

14. Bone and Cinotto, "China's Multifaceted COVID-19."

15. Neil Edwards, "Vaccine Diplomacy."

16. "China-Africa Friendship Emerges Still Stronger from COVID-19 Test, Says Chinese FM," Ministry of Foreign Affairs of the People's Republic of China, January 2, 2021.

17. Bone and Cinotto, "China's Multifaceted COVID-19."

18. "China-Africa Friendship Emerges."

19. "China-Africa Friendship Emerges."

20. Bone and Cinotto, "China's Multifaceted COVID-19."

21. Austin Bodetti, "China's Vaccine Diplomacy in the Middle East," *Diplomat*, January 16, 2021.

22. Bone and Cinotto, "China's Multifaceted COVID-19."

23. Bone and Cinotto, "China's Multifaceted COVID-19"; Areeb Ullah, "Why the UAE Adopted China's Covid-19 Vaccine," *Middle East Eye*, February 1, 2021.

24. Bodetti, "China's Vaccine Diplomacy."

25. Anchal Vohra, "Russia, China Expanding Middle East Sway with COVID-19 Vaccines," *Aljazeera*, February 9, 2021.

26. Bone and Cinotto, "China's Multifaceted COVID-19."

27. Anchal Vohra, "Russia, China Expanding."

28. Anchal Vohra, "Russia, China Expanding"; Bodetti, "China's Vaccine Diplomacy."

29. Bone and Cinotto, "China's Multifaceted COVID-19."

30. Mariama Diallo, "Africa Kicks Off Inoculation Campaign with Chinese COVID-19 Vaccine," *Voice of America*, February 25, 2021.

31. Bone and Cinotto, "China's Multifaceted COVID-19."

32. The Editorial Board, "The Era of Vaccine Diplomacy Is Here," *New York Times*, February 28, 2021.

33. For example, Johnston, "China in a World of Orders"; Glaser, "A Flawed Framework"; Mearsheimer, "Bound to Fail."

34. For a critique of that approach, see Brautigam and Rithmire, "The Chinese 'Debt Trap.'"

SELECTED BIBLIOGRAPHY

Cooperation Forum Documents

"Amman Declaration of the Ninth Ministerial Conference of the China-Arab Cooperation Forum." July 2020. www.chinaarabcf.org.

"Beijing Declaration of the Eighth Ministerial Conference of the China-Arab Cooperation Forum." 2018. http://www.chinaarabcf.org/chn/lthyjwx/bzjhywj/dbjbzjhy/t1577002.htm.

"Beijing Declaration of the Fifth Minsterial Conference of the Forum on China-Africa Cooperation." 2012. www.focac.org.

"Beijing Declaration of the Forum on China-Africa Cooperation." October 12, 2000. www.focac.org.

"Beijing Declaration: Toward an Even Stronger China-Africa Community with a Shared Future." September 12, 2018. www.focac.org.

"Bishkek Declaration of the Shanghai Cooperation Organization's Heads of State Council." 2019. eng.sectsco.org.

"Charter of the Shanghai Cooperation Organization." 2001.

"China-Africa Trade and Economic Relationship Annual Report 2010." China Ministry of Foreign Affairs. June 22, 2011. http://www.focac.org/eng/zfgx_4/jmhz/t832788.htm.

"China-Arab Cooperation Forum 2018 to 2020 Action Plan." July 10, 2018. www.chinaarabcf.org.

"China-Arab Cooperation Forum Action Plan (2012–2014)." 2012. www.cascf.org.

"China-Arab Cooperation Forum Action Plan (2014–2016)." 2014. www.cascf.org.

"China-Arab Cooperation Forum Action Plan (2016–2018)." 2016. www.cascf.org.

"China-Arab Cooperation Forum Action Plan 2020–2022." July 2020. www.chinaarabcf.org.

"China-Arab Cooperation Forum Beijing Declaration of the Sixth Ministerial Conference." 2014. www.cascf.org.

"China-Arab Cooperation Forum Development Plan (2014–2024)." 2014. www.cascf.org.

"China-Arab Cooperation Forum Fifth Ministerial Meeting Declaration." 2012. www.cascf.org.

"China-Arab Cooperation Forum Ministerial Conference of the Seventh Doha Declaration." 2016. www.cascf.org.

"China-Arab States Cooperation Forum Action Plan (2006–2008)." June 1, 2006. www.cascf.org.

"China-Arab States Cooperation Forum Action Plan (2008–2010)." May 21, 2008. www.cascf.org.

"China-Arab States Cooperation Forum Action Plan (2010–2012)." May 14, 2010. www.cascf.org.

"China-Arab States Cooperation Forum Action Plan." September 14, 2004. www.cascf.org.

"China-Arab States Cooperation Forum Declaration." September 14, 2004. www.cascf.org.

"China-Arab States Cooperation Forum Fourth Ministerial Meeting Communiqué." May 13, 2010. www.cascf.org.

"China-Arab States Cooperation Forum Second Ministerial Meeting Communiqué." June 1, 2006. www.cascf.org.

"China-Arab States Cooperation Forum Third Ministerial Meeting Communiqué." May 21, 2008. www.cascf.org.

"China-Arab States Cooperation under the Belt and Road Initiative." July 2018, www.chinaarabcf.org/chn/lthyjwx/bzjhywj/dbjbzjhy/.

"Declaration of the Beijing Summit of the Forum on China-Africa Cooperation." November 5, 2006. www.focac.org.

"Declaration of the Johannesburg Summit of the Forum on China-Africa Cooperation." 2015. www.focac.org.

"Declaration of Sharm El Sheikh of the Forum on China-Africa Cooperation." November 12, 2009. www.focac.org.

"Development Strategy of the Shanghai Cooperation Organization until 2025." 2014.

"The Fifth Ministerial Conference of the Forum on China-Africa Cooperation Beijing Action Plan." 2012. www.focac.org.

"Follow-Up Actions of the Second Ministerial Conference." 2005. www.focac.org.

"Forum on China-Africa Cooperation Addis Ababa Action Plan (2004–2006)." December 16, 2003. www.focac.org.

"Forum on China-Africa Cooperation Beijing Action Plan (2007–2009)." November 16, 2006. www.focac.org.

"Forum on China-Africa Cooperation Beijing Action Plan (2019–2021)." September 12, 2018. https://focacsummit.mfa.gov.cn/eng/hyqk_1/t1594297.htm

"Forum on China-Africa Cooperation Sharm El Sheikh Action Plan (2010–2012)." November 12, 2009. www.focac.org.

"Forum on China-Africa Cooperation Johannesburg Action Plan (2016–2018)." 2015. www.focac.org.

"Implementation of the Follow-Up Actions of the Beijing Summit of the Forum on China-Africa Cooperation." November 10, 2009. www.focac.org.

"The Implementation of the Follow-up Actions of the First Ministerial Conference of FOCAC." December 16, 2003. www.focac.org.

"Implementation of the Follow-up Actions of the Fourth Ministerial Conference of the Forum on China-Africa Cooperation." 2012. www.focac.org.

"An Interpretation of New Measures on Economic and Trade Cooperation from 4th Ministerial Conference." May 24, 2010. www.focac.org.

"Joint Communiqué of the Heads of State of the Shanghai Cooperation Organization on Simplifying Trade Procedures." 2018.

"Joint Statement between China and Arab Countries to Fight COVID 19 Epidemic." July 2020. www.chinaarabcf.org.

"Joint Statement of the Extraordinary China-Africa Summit on Solidarity against COVID-19." June 2020. www.fmprc.gov.cn/mfa_eng.

"List of Documents Introduced for Signing at the Meeting of the Council of Heads of State of the Shanghai Cooperation Organization." June 2018.

"The Member States of the Shanghai Cooperation Organization (SCO) Measures Taken in the Field of Healthcare to Counter the Spread of the Novel Coronavirus (COVID-19)." July 2020. eng.sectsco.org

"Joint Communiqué on Environmental Cooperation between the League of Arab States and the PRC Government, Implementation Plan (2008–2009)." May 21, 2008. www.cascf.org.

"The Moscow Declaration of the Council of Heads of State of the Shanghai Cooperation Organization." November 2020. eng.sectsco.org.

"Qingdao Declaration of the Council of Heads of States of Shanghai Cooperation Organisation." 2018.

"Programme for China-Africa Cooperation in Economic and Social Development." October 12, 2000. www.focac.org.

Belt and Road Forum Documents

"Belt and Road Cooperation: Shaping a Brighter Shared Future." Joint Communiqué of the Leaders' Roundtable of the Second Belt and Road Forum for International Cooperation, April 27, 2019. http://beltandroadforum.org/english/

"Joint Communiqué of the Leaders' Roundtable of the 2nd Belt and Road Forum for International Cooperation," Beijing, China, April 27, 2019. www.beltandroadforum.org

"List of Deliverables of the Second Belt and Road Forum for International Cooperation." Beijing, China, April 27, 2019. www.beltandroadforum.org

PRC Government Publications

"11–22 Economic Cooperation by Country (Region) (2019)." In *China Statistical Yearbook 2020.*

"11–22 Economic Cooperation with Foreign Countries or Regions (2017)." In *China Statistical Yearbook 2018.*

"11–22 Economic Cooperation with Foreign Countries or Regions (2018)." In *China Statistical Yearbook 2019.*

"China Africa Economic and Trade Cooperation." White paper. Beijing: Information Office of the State Council of the People's Republic of China, December 23, 2010. http://www.china.org.cn/government/whitepaper/node_7107834.htm.

"China-Africa Economic and Trade Cooperation." White paper. Beijing: Information Office of the State Council of the People's Republic of China, 2013.

"China's African Policy." White paper. Beijing, China: China Ministry of Foreign Affairs, January 12, 2006. http://english.people.com.cn/200601/12/eng20060112_234894.html.

"China's Arab Policy Paper." White paper. Beijing: State Council Information Office of the People's Republic of China, 2016.

"China's Energy Conditions and Policies." White paper. Beijing: Information Office of the State Council of the People's Republic of China, 2007. http://www.china.org.cn/english/whitepaper/energy/237089.htm.

"China's Energy Policy." White paper. Beijing: Information Office of the State Council of the People's Republic of China, 2012.

"China's Foreign Aid." White paper. Beijing: Information Office of the State Council of the People's Republic of China, 2011. http://www.china.org.cn/government/whitepaper/node_7116362.htm.

"China's Foreign Aid." White paper. Beijing: Information Office of the State Council, People's Republic of China, 2014.

"China's Foreign Trade." White paper. Beijing: Information Office of the State Council of the People's Republic of China, 2011.

"China's Military Strategy." White paper, Beijing: State Council Information Office of the People's Republic of China, 2015.

"China's National Defense." White paper. Beijing: Information Office of the State Council of the People's Republic of China, 1998. http://www.china.org.cn/e-white/5/index.htm.

"China's National Defense in 2000." White paper, Beijing: Information Office of the State Council of the People's Republic of China, 2000. http://www.china.org.cn/e-white/2000/index.htm.

"China's National Defense in 2002." White paper, Beijing: Information Office of the State Council of the People's Republic of China, 2002. http://www.china.org.cn/e-white/20021209/index.htm.

"China's National Defense in 2004." White paper. Beijing: Information Office of the State Council of the People's Republic of China, 2004. http://www.china.org.cn/e-white/20041227/index.htm.

"China's National Defense in 2006." White paper. Beijing: Information Office of the State Council of the People's Republic of China, 2006. http://www.china.org.cn/english/features/book/194421.htm.

"China's National Defense in 2008." White paper. Beijing: Information Office of the State Council of the People's Republic of China, 2009. http://www.china.org.cn/government/whitepaper/node_7060059.htm.

"China's National Defense in 2010." White paper. Beijing: Information Office of the State Council of the People's Republic of China, 2011. www.china.org.cn/government/whitepaper/node_7114675.htm.

"China's National Defense in the New Era." White paper. Beijing: Information Office of the State Council of the People's Republic of China, 2019.

"China's Peaceful Development." White paper. Beijing: Information Office of the State Council of the People's Republic of China, September 6, 2011. http://www.china.org.cn/government/whitepaper/node_7126562.htm.

"China's Peaceful Development Road." White paper. Beijing: Information Office of the State Council of the People's Republic of China, 2005. http://www.china.org.cn/english/features/book/152684.htm.

"China and the World in the New Era." White paper. Beijing: State Council Information Office of the People's Republic of China, September 2019. http://english.www.gov.cn/archive/whitepaper/.

"Cultural Protecton and Development in Xinjiang." White Paper. Beijing: The State Council Information Office of the People's Republic of China, November 2018. http://english.www.gov.cn/archive/whitepaper/

"Development and Progress in Xinjiang." White paper. Beijing: Information Office of the State Council of the People's Republic of China, 2009.

"Economic Cooperation with Foreign Countries or Regions (2012) Section 6–21." In *China Statistical Yearbook 2013*. Beijing: China National Bureau of Statistics, 2013.

"Economic Cooperation with Foreign Countries or Regions 2010 Section 6–22." In *China Statistical Yearbook 2011*. Beijing: China National Bureau of Statistics, 2012.

"Economic Cooperation with Foreign Countries or Regions 2011 Section 6–22." In *China Statistical Yearbook 2012*. Beijing: China National Bureau of Statistics, 2013.

"Economic Cooperation with Foreign Countries or Regions 2013 Section 11–22." In *China Statistical Yearbook 2014*. Beijing: China National Bureau of Statistics, 2014.

"Economic Cooperation with Foreign Countries or Regions 2014 Section 11–22." In *China Statistical Yearbook 2015*. Beijing: China National Bureau of Statistics, 2015.

"Economic Cooperation with Foreign Countries or Regions 2015 Section 11–22,." In *China Statistical Yearbook 2016*. Beijing: China National Bureau of Statistics, 2016.

"Economic Cooperation with Foreign Countries or Regions 2016 Section 11–22." In *China Statistical Yearbook 2017*. Beijing: China National Bureau of Statistics, 2017.

"Final Communiqué of the Asian-African Conference." Bandung, Indonesia, 1955.

"The Fight against Terrorism and Extremism and Human Rights Protection in Xinjiang." White paper. Beijing: State Council Information Office of the People's Republic of China, March 2019. http://english.www.gov.cn/archive/whitepaper/

"Freedom of Religious Belief in Xinjiang." White paper. Beijing: Information Office of the State Council of the People's Republic of China, 2016. english.www.gov.cn/archive/publications/2016/01/13/content_281475271412746.htm

"Full Text: China's Second Africa Policy Paper." White paper. Xinhua, December 5, 2015.

"Historical Matters Concerning Xinjiang." White paper. Beijing: The State Council Information Office of the People's Republic of China, July 2019. http://english.www.gov.cn/archive/whitepaper/

"Historical Witness to Ethnic Equality, Unity and Development in Xinjiang." White paper. Beijing: Information Office of the State Council of the People's Republic of China, 2016.

"Human Rights in Xinjiang: Development and Progress." White paper. Beijing: Information of the State Council of the People's Republic of China, 2017.

"Imports of Major Commodities by Countries (Regions) of Origin, 2000–2001." In *China External Economic Statistical Yearbook*, 112–113. Beijing: China Statistics Press, 2002. http://chinadataonline.org./member/yearbooksp/ybListDetail.asp?YBID=EXE2002001#.

"Imports of Major Commodities by Country or Region of Origin, 2003–2004." In *China External Economic Statistical Yearbook*, 117–118. Beijing: China Statistics Press, 2005. http://chinadataonline.org./member/yearbooksp/ybListDetail.asp?YBID=EXE2005001#.

"National Security Law of the PRC." National People's Congress, July 1, 2015. http://www.chinadaily.com.cn/hqcj/zgjj/2015-07-01/content_13912103.html.

"Seeking Happiness for People: 70 Years of Progress in Human Rights." White paper. Beijing: State Council Information Offices of the People's Republic of China, September 2019. http://english.www.gov.cn/archive/whitepaper/

"Turnover of Economic Cooperation with Foreign Countries or Regions 2002–2003 Section 18–22." In *China Statistical Yearbook 2004*. China National Bureau of Statistics, 2004.

"Turnover of Economic Cooperation with Foreign Countries or Regions 2003–2004 Section 18–22." In *China Statistical Yearbook 2005*. Beijing: China National Bureau of Statistics, 2005.

"Turnover of Economic Cooperation with Foreign Countries or Regions 2004–2005 Section 18–23." In *China Statistical Yearbook 2006*. Beijing: China National Bureau of Statistics, 2006.

"Turnover of Economic Cooperation with Foreign Countries or Regions 2005–2006 Section 18–23." In *China Statistical Yearbook 2007*. Beijing: China National Bureau of Statistics, 2007.

"Turnover of Economic Cooperation with Foreign Countries or Regions Section 2006–2007 Section 17–23." In *China Statistical Yearbook 2008*. Beijing: China National Bureau of Statistics, 2008.

"Turnover of Economic Cooperation with Foreign Countries or Regions 2007–2008 Section 17–23." In *China Statistical Yearbook 2009*. Beijing: China National Bureau of Statistics, 2009.

"Turnover of Economic Cooperation with Foreign Countries or Regions 2008–2009 Section 6–22." In *China Statistical Yearbook*. Beijing: China National Bureau of Statistics, 2010.

"Turnover of Economic Cooperation with Foreign Countries or Territories 1998–1999 Section 17–22," in *China Statistical Yearbook 2000*. Beijing: China National Bureau of Statistics, 2000.

"Turnover of Economic Cooperation with Foreign Countries or Territories 1999–2000 Section 17–22," in *China Statistical Yearbook 2001*. Beijing: China National Bureau of Statistics, 2001.

"Turnover of Economic Cooperation with Foreign Countries or Territories 2000–2001 Section 17–22," in *China Statistical Yearbook 2002*. Beijing: China National Bureau of Statistics, 2002.

"Turnover of Economic Cooperation with Foreign Countries or Territories 2001–2002 Section 17–22," in *China Statistical Yearbook 2003*. Beijing: China National Bureau of Statistics, 2003.

"Vision and Actions on Jointly Building Silk Road Economic Belt and 21st Century Maritime Silk Road." Beijing: National Development and Reform Commission People's Republic of China, 2015.

"China Africa Economic and Trade Cooperation," *White* paper. Beijing, China: State Counil Information Office of the People's Republic of China, December 23, 2010

China Statistical Yearbook 2001. Beijing: China National Bureau of Statistics, 2001.

China Statistical Yearbook 2002. Beijing: China National Bureau of Statistics, 2002.

China Statistical Yearbook 2003. Beijing: China National Bureau of Statistics, 2003.

China Statistical Yearbook 2004. Beijing: China National Bureau of Statistics, 2004.

China Statistical Yearbook 2005. Beijing: China National Bureau of Statistics, 2005.

China Statistical Yearbook 2006. Beijing: China National Bureau of Statistics, 2006.

China Statistical Yearbook 2007. Beijing: China National Bureau of Statistics, 2007.

China Statistical Yearbook 2008. Beijing: China National Bureau of Statistics, 2008.

China Statistical Yearbook 2009. Beijing: China National Bureau of Statistics, 2009.

China Statistical Yearbook 2010. Beijing: China National Bureau of Statistics, 2010.

China Statistical Yearbook 2011. Beijing: China National Bureau of Statistics, 2012.

China Statistical Yearbook 2012. Beijing: China National Bureau of Statistics, 2013.

China Statistical Yearbook 2013. Beijing: China National Bureau of Statistics, 2014.

China Statistical Yearbook 2014. Beijing: China National Bureau of Statistics, 2015.

China Statistical Yearbook 2015. Beijing: China National Bureau of Statistics, 2016.

China Statistical Yearbook 2016. Beijing: China National Bureau of Statistics, 2017.

China Statistical Yearbook 2017. Beijing: China National Bureau of Statistics, 2018.

China's Foreign Affairs: 2004 Edition. Beijing: Department of Policy Planning, Ministry of Foreign Affairs, People's Republic of China, World Affairs Press, 2004.

China's Foreign Affairs: 2005 Edition. Beijing: Department of Policy Planning, Ministry of Foreign Affairs, People's Republic of China, World Affairs Press, 2005.

China's Foreign Affairs: 2006 Edition. Beijing: Department of Policy Planning, Ministry of Foreign Affairs, People's Republic of China, World Affairs Press, 2006.

China's Foreign Affairs: 2007 Edition. Beijing: Department of Policy Planning, Ministry of Foreign Affairs, People's Republic of China, World Affairs Press, 2007.

China's Foreign Affairs: 2008 Edition. Beijing: Department of Policy Planning, Ministry of Foreign Affairs, People's Republic of China, World Affairs Press, 2008.

China's Foreign Affairs: 2009 Edition. Beijing: Department of Policy Planning, Ministry of Foreign Affairs, People's Republic of China, World Affairs Press, 2009.

China's Foreign Affairs: 2010 Edition. Beijing: Department of Policy Planning, Ministry of Foreign Affairs, People's Republic of China, World Affairs Press, 2010.

China's Foreign Affairs: 2011 Edition. Beijing: Department of Policy Planning, Ministry of Foreign Affairs, People's Republic of China, World Affairs Press, 2011.

China's Foreign Affairs: 2012 Edition. Beijing: Department of Policy Planning, Ministry of Foreign Affairs, People's Republic of China, World Affairs Press, 2012.

China's Foreign Affairs: 2013 Edition. Beijing: Department of Policy Planning, Ministry of Foreign Affairs, People's Republic of China, World Affairs Press, 2013.

China's Foreign Affairs: 2014 Edition. Beijing: Department of Policy Planning, Ministry of Foreign Affairs, People's Republic of China, World Affairs Press, 2014.

China's Foreign Affairs: 2015 Edition. Beijing: Department of Policy Planning, Ministry of Foreign Affairs, People's Republic of China, World Affairs Press, 2015.

China's Foreign Affairs: 2016 Edition. Beijing: Department of Policy Planning, Ministry of Foreign Affairs, People's Republic of China, World Affairs Press, 2016.

China's Foreign Affairs: 2017 Edition. Beijing: Department of Policy Planning, Ministry of Foreign Affairs, People's Republic of China, World Affairs Press, 2017.

China's Foreign Affairs: 2018 Edition. Beijing: Department of Policy Planning, Ministry of Foreign Affairs, People's Republic of China, World Affairs Press, 2018.

Ministry of Commerce. People's Republic of China. "China FTA Network." fta.mofcom.gov.cn/topic/engcc.shtml.

Ministry of Commerce. People's Republic of China. *Statistical Bulletin of China's Outward Foreign Direct Investment*. (2009): 78–83.

Ministry of Commerce. People's Republic of China., *Statistical Bulletin of China's Outward Foreign Direct Investment*. (2011): 82–84.

Ministry of Commerce. People's Republic of China. *Statistical Bulletin of China's Outward Foreign Direct Investment*. (2015):133–135.

Ministry of Commerce. People's Republic of China. *Statistical Bulletin of China's Outward Foreign Direct Investment*. (2016): p. 86–90.

Ministry of Commerce. People's Republic of China. *Statistical Bulletin of China's Outward Foreign Direct Investment in 2019*. (2020): 146–149.

United States Government Publications

"National Security Strategy of the United States of America." Washington, DC: White House, 2017.

"Nuclear Posture Review." Washington, DC: Department of Defense, 2018.

"Summary of the National Defense Strategy of the United States of America Sharpening the American Military's Competitive Edge." Washington, DC: Department of Defense, 2018.

US Commission on International Religious Freedom. "China." In *Annual Report 2017*. Washington, DC: USCIRF, June 2017.

United Nations Documents

"Charter of Economic Rights and Duties of States." United Nations General Assembly Resolution. Vol. A/RES/3281. New York, December 12, 1974 .

"Declaration on the Establishment of a New International Economic Order." United Nations General Assembly Resolution. Vol. RES/3201. May 1, 1974.

"Programme of Action on the Establishment of a New International Economic Order." United Nations General Assembly Resolution. Vol. RES/3202. May 1, 1974.

"Restoration of the Lawful Rights of the People's Republic of China in the United Nations." UNGA Resolution 2758. New York: United Nations General Assembly, 1971.

United Nation Peacekeeping Operations. Troop and Police Contributors. https://peacekeeping.un.org/en/troop-and-police-contributors

United Nations Comtrade Database. https://comtrade.un.org/data/.

United Nations, Security Council Meetings. http://research.un.org/en/docs/sc/quick/meetings/.

United Nations, *United Nations Documentation Research Guide, UNSC Resolutions*. https://www.un.org/securitycouncil/content/resolutions.

Full Text Speeches

"The Complete Text of President Xi Jinping's Speech at the Belt and Road Forum for International Cooperation 2019." Embassy of China, April 26, 2019. www.cpecinfo.com/news

"Full Text of President Xi's Speech at Opening of Belt and Road Forum." Xinhua, May 14, 2017. http://news.xinhuanet.com/english/2017-05/14/c136282982.htm.

"Remarks by National Security Advisor Ambassador John R. Bolton on the Trump Administration's New Africa Strategy." December 13, 2018.

"Remarks by Vice President Pence on the Administration's Policy Toward China" Washington, DC: Hudson Institute, October 4, 2018.

Deng Xiaoping. "Speech by Chairman of the Delegation of the People's Republic of China, Teng Hsiao-Ping, at the Special Session of the U.N. General Assembly." Beijing: Foreign Languages Press, 1974.

———. *Selected Works of Deng Xiaoping, 1975–1982.* Translated by Bureau for the Compilation and Translation of Works of Marx, Engels, and Stalin under the Central Committee of the Communist Party of China. Beijing: Foreign Languages Press, 1984.

———. *Selected Works of Deng Xiaoping. (1982–1992),* vol. 3. Translated by Bureau for the Compilation and Translation of Works of Marx, Engels, Lenin, and Stalin under the Central Committee of the Communist Party of China. Beijing: Foreign Languages Press, 1994.

Hu, Jintao. "Hold High the Great Banner of Socialism with Chinese Characteristics and Strive for New Victories in Building a Moderately Prosperous Society." Work Report to the 17th National Congress of the Communist Party of China. Beijing: Xinhua, 2007.

———. "Firmly March on the Path of Socialism with Chinese Characteristics and Strive to Complete the Building of a Moderately Prosperous Society in All Respects." Work Report to the 18th National Congress of the Communist Party of China. Beijing: Xinhua, 2012.

Jiang, Zemin. "Full Text of Jiang Zemin's Report at 14th Party Congress." In *Work Report Delivered at the 14th Party Congress of the Communist Party of China.* Beijing: Xinhua, 1992.

———. "Hold High the Great Banner of Deng Xiaoping Theory for an All-Round Advancement of the Cause of Builidng Socialism with Chinese Characteristics into the 21st Century." In *Work Report to the 15th Party Congress of the Communist Party of China.* Beijing: Xinhua, 1997.

———. "Full Text of Jiang Zemin's Report at 16th Party Congress." In *Work Report to 16th Party Congress of the Communist Party of China.* Beijing: Xinhua, 2002.

Pence, Michael. "Remarks by Vice President Pence at the Frederic V. Malek Memorial Lecture." Washington, DC, October 24, 2019.

Pompeo, Michael. "Communist China and the Free World's Future," Richard Nixon Presidential Library and Museum, Yorba Linda, CA, July 23, 2020.

Xi, Jinping. *The Governance of China*. Beijing: Foreign Languages Press, 2014.

———. "Full Text of President Xi's Speech at Opening of Belt and Road Forum." Xinhua. Beijing, May 14, 2017. http://news.xinhuanet.com/english/2017-05/14/c_136282982.htm.

———. "Full Text of Xi Jinping Keynote at the World Economic Forum." America CGTN. Davos, Switzerland, January 17, 2017. https://america.cgtn.com/2017/01/17/full-text-of-xi-jinping-keynote-at-the-world-economic-forum.

———. "Secure a Decisive Victory in the Building of a Moderately Prosperous Society in All Respects and Strive for the Great Success of Socialism with Chinese Characteristics for a New Era." In *Work Report Delivered at the 19th National Congress of the Communist Party of China*. Beijing: Xinhua, 2017.

———. "Working Together to Deliver a Brighter Future for Belt and Road Cooperation," Keynote Speech by H. E. Xi Jinping at the Opening Ceremony of the Second Belt and Road Forum for International Cooperation, Beijing, China, April 26, 2019. www.fmprc.gov.cn/mfa_eng/zxxx_662805/t1658424.shtml.

Secondary Sources

"China: COVID-19 Discrimination against Africans." Human Rights Watch, May 5, 2020.

"Conventional Arms Transfers to Developing Nations, 2008–2015" Congressional Research Service, December 19, 2016.

"The Middle East and the Rising Asian Powers: Imagining Alternative Futures: Section 2: Gulf-China Relations." Scenario prepared by the East Asia and Southwest Asia Programs at the Henry L. Stimson Center for the National Intelligence Council's 2020 Project, 2004.

"The Middle East: Seeking Stability and Development in Turbulence- On the Regional Situation from Scholars." *West Asia and Africa* (December 2008): 5–11.

Abedajo, Adekeyem "From Bandung to Durban: Whither the Afro-Asian Coalition?" In *Bandung Revisited: The Legacy of the 1955 Asian-African Conference for International Order*, edited by See Seng Tan and Amitov Acharya, 105–131. Singapore: National University of Singapore Press, 2008.

Acharya, Amitav. *Constructing a Security Community in Southeast Asia: ASEAN and the Problem of Regional Order*. New York: Routledge, 2001.

Afro-Asian Solidarity against Imperialism: A Collection of Documents, Speeches, and Press Interviews from the Visits of Chinese Leaders to Thirteen African and Asian Countries. Beijing: Foreign Language Press, 1964.

Alden, Chris. *China in Africa*. London: Palgrave Macmillan, 2007.

Alden, Chris, Abiodun Alao, Zhang Chun, and Laura Barber, eds. *China and Africa: Building Peace and Security Cooperation on the Continent*. Cham, Switzerland: Palgrave Macmillan, 2018.

Alden, Chris, and Lu Jiang. "Brave New World: Debt, Industrialization and Security in China-Africa Relations." *International Affairs* 95, no. 3 (2019): 641–657.

Alden, Chris, Daniel Large, and Ricardo Soares de Oliveira. *China Returns to Africa: A Rising Power and a Continent Embrace*. London: Hurst, 2008.

Aldie, W. A. C. "Chinese Policy toward Africa." In *The Soviet Bloc, China and Africa*, edited by Sven Hamrell and Carl Gesta Widstrand, 43–63. Uppsala: Scandinavian Institute of African Studies, 1964.

———. "Chou En-lai on Safari." *China Quarterly* 18 (1964): 174–194.

Allen, Robert Loring. *Middle East Economic Relations with the Soviet Union, Eastern Europe, and Mainland China*. Charlottesville: University of Virginia Press, 1958.

Allison, Graham. "China versus America: Managing the Next Clash of Civilizations." *Foreign Affairs* 96, no. 5 (2017): 80–89.

———.*Destined for War: Can America and China Escape Thucydides's Trap?* Boston: Houghton Mifflin Harcourt, 2017.

Alterman, Jon B. *China's Balancing Act in the Gulf*. Gulf Analysis Paper. Washington, DC: Center for Strategic and International Studies, 2013.

———. *The Other Side of the World: China, the United States and the Struggle for Middle East Security*. Washington, DC: Center for Strategic and International Studies, 2017.

Alterman, Jon B., and John W. Garver. *The Vital Triangle: China, the United States, and the Middle East*. Washington, DC: CSIS Press, 2008.

Alves, Philip. *Engaging China's Biggest Tiger: Exploring the Contours of a SACU-China Trade Deal*. Trade Policy Report. South African Institute of International Affairs, 2006.

Ampiah, Kweku, and Sanusha Naidu, eds. *Crouching Tiger, Hidden Dragon? Africa and China*. Scottsville, South Africa: University of KwaZulu-Natal Press, 2008.

An, Huihou. "President Obama's Middle East Policy Adjustment and Development of Hot Issues in the Region." *Asia and Africa Review* 3 (2009): 52–56.

———."Middle Eastern Situation in the Change of International Configuration." *Arab World Studies* 6 (2009): 3–10.

———."The Hot Spot Issues in the Middle East and Big Power Relations." *Arab World Studies* 2 (2009): 3–9.

———."The Middle East Hot Spot Issues and World Powers' Middle East Policies onder New Circumstances." *Arab World Studies* 2 (2008): 3–10.

———."The Thirty Years of Inaugurating China" The Middle East Countries Relations." *West Asia and Africa* 7 (2008): 5–12.

An, Weihua. "The Thirty Years of Inaugurating China: The Middle East Countries Relations." *West Asia and Africa* 11 (2008).

Armstrong, J. D. *Revolutionary Diplomacy: Chinese Foreign Policy and the United Front Doctrine.* Berkeley: University of California Press, 1977.

Barma, Naazneen, Ely Ratner, and Steven Weber. "A World without the West." *National Interest* 90 (2007): 23–30.

———. "The Mythical Liberal Order." *National Interest* 124 (2013): 56–67.

Bartke, Wolfgang. *China's Economic Aid.* London: Hurst, 1975.

Beckley, Michael. *Unrivaled: Why America Will Remain the World's Sole Superpower.* Ithaca, NY: Cornell University Press, 2018.

Behbehani, Hashim S. H. *China's Foreign Policy in the Arab World, 1955–75: Three Case Studies.* London: Kegan Paul International, 1981.

Bernstein, Richard, and Ross H. Munro. "The Coming Conflict with America." *Foreign Affairs* 76, no. 2 (1997): 18–32.

Bianchi, Robert R. 2013. "China–Middle East Relations in Light of Obama's Pivot to the Pacific." *China Report* 49, no. 1 (2013): 103–118.

———. *China and the Islamic World: How the New Silk Road Is Transforming Global Politics.* Oxford: Oxford University Press, 2019.

bin Huwaidin, Mohamed. *China's Relations with Arabia and the Gulf 1949–1999.* London: RoutledgeCurzon, 2002.

Bisley, Nick. *Great Powers in the Changing International Order.* Boulder, CO: Lynne Rienner, 2012.

Blumenthal, Dan. "China and the Middle East: Providing Arms." *Middle East Quarterly* 12, no. 2 (2005): 11–19.

Bodetti, Austin. "China's Vaccine Diplomacy in the Middle East." *Diplomat*, January 16, 2021.

Bone, R. Maxwell, and Ferdinando Cinotto, "China's Multifaceted COVID-19 Diplomacy across Africa." *Diplomat*, November 2, 2020.

Brands, Hal. *What Good Is Grand Strategy? Power and Purpose in American Statecraft from Harry S. Truman to George W. Bush.* Ithaca, NY: Cornell University Press, 2014.

Brautigam, Deborah. *The Dragon's Gift: The Real Story of China in Africa.* Oxford: Oxford University Press, 2009.

———. *Will Africa Feed China?* Oxford: Oxford University Press, 2015.

Brautigam, Deborah, and Meg Rithmire. "The Chinese 'Debt Trap' Is a Myth." *Atlantic*, February 6, 2021.

Brautigam, Deborah, and Tang Xiaoyang. "'Going Global in Groups': Structural Transformation and China Special Economic Zones Overseas." *World Development* 63 (2014): 78–91.

———. "African Shenzhen: China's Special Economic Zones in Africa." *Journal of Modern African Studies* 49, no. 1 (2011): 27–54.

———. "China's Engagement in African Agriculture: 'Down to the Countryside.'" *China Quarterly*, no. 199 (2009): 686–706.

Breslin, Shaun. "China's Emerging Global Role: Dissatisfied Responsible Great Power." *Politics* 30, no. S1 (2010): 52–62.

Broadman, Harry G. "China and India Go to Africa." *Foreign Affairs* 87, no. 2 (2008): 95–109.

———. *Africa's Silk Road: China and India's New Economic Frontier.* Washington, DC: World Bank, 2007.

Brooks, Stephen G., G. John Ikenberry, and William C. Wohlforth. "Don't Come Home America: The Case against Retrenchment." *International Security* 37, no. 3 (2012/13), 7–51.

Brown, David. *Hidden Dragon, Crouching Lion: How China's Advance in Africa Is Underestimated and Africa's Potential Underappreciated.* Carlisle, PA: Strategic Studies Institute, US Army War College, 2012.

Brown, Michael E., Sean M. Lynn-Jones, and Steven E. Miller, eds. *The Perils of Anarchy: Contemporary Realism and International Security.* Cambridge, MA: MIT Press, 1995.

Bull, Hedley. *The Anarchical Society: The Study of Order in World Politics.* New York: Columbia University Press, 1997.

Burton, Guy. *China and Middle East Conflicts: Responding to War and Rivalry from the Cold War to the Present.* New York: Routledge, 2020.

Cabestan, Jean Pierre. "China's Involvement in Africa's Security: The Case of China's Participation in the UN Mission to Stabilize Mali." *China Quarterly* 235 (2018): 713–734.

Carlson, Allen. *Unifying China, Integrating with the World: Securing Chinese Sovereignty in the Reform Era.* Stanford, CA: Stanford University Press, 2005.

———. "Moving beyond Sovereignty? A Brief Consideration of the Recent Changes in China's Approach to the International Order and the Emergence of the Tianxia Concept." *Journal of Contemporary China* 20, no. 68 (2011): 89–102.

Carlson, Allen, and J. J. Suh, "The Value of Rethinking East Asian Security: Denaturalizing and Explaining a Complex Security Dynamic." In *Rethinking security in East Asia: Identity, Power, and Efficiency*, edited by J. J Suh, Peter J. Katzenstein, and Allen Carlson, 209–234. Stanford, CA: Stanford University Press, 2004.

Carr, E. H. *The Twenty Years Crisis, 1919–1939: An Introduction to the Study of International Relations.* New York: Palgrave, 2001.

Carter, Hannah, and Anoushiravan Ehteshami, eds. *The Middle East's Relations with Asia and Russia.* New York: RoutledgeCurzon, 2004.

Chan, Steve. *China, the US, and the Power Transition Theory.* New York: Routledge, 2008.

Charvet, John, and Elisa Kaczynska-Nay. *The Liberal Project and Human Rights: The Theory and Practice of a New World Order.* Cambridge: Cambridge University Press, 2008.

Chau, Donovan C. *Political Warfare in Sub-Saharan Africa: U.S. Capabilities and Chinese Operations in Ethiopia, Kenya, Nigeria, and South Africa.* Carlisle, PA: Strategic Studies Institute, U.S. Army War College, 2007.

Chaziza, Mordechai. "China's Middle East Foreign Policy and the Yemen Crisis: Challenges and Implications." *Middle East Review of International Affairs* 19, no. 2 (2015): 18–25.

Chen, James. *The Emergence of China in the Middle East.* Washington, DC: Institute for National Strategic Studies, National Defense University, 2011.

Chen, Jian. "China and the Bandung Conference: Changing Perceptions and Representations." In *Bandung Revisited: The Legacy of the 1955 Asian-African Conference on International Order*, edited by See Seng Tan and Amitav Acharya, 132–159. Singapore: National University of Singapore Press, 2008.

Chin, Gregory, and Eric Helleiner. "China as a Creditor: A Rising Financial Power?" *Journal of International Affairs* 62, no. 1 (2008): 87–102.

China's Growing Role in the Middle East: Implications for the Region and Beyond. Washington, DC: The Nixon Center, 2010.

Christensen, Thomas J. "Pride, Pressure and Politics: The Roots of China's World View." In *In the Eyes of the Dragon: China Views the World*, edited by Yong Deng and Fei-Ling Wang, 239–256. Lanham, MD: Rowman & Littlefield, 1999.

———. "The Advantages of an Assertive China." *Foreign Affairs* 90, no. 2 (2011): 54–67.

———. *The China Challenge: Shaping the Choices of a Rising Power*. New York: Norton, 2015.

Clark, Ian. *Legitimacy in International Society.* Oxford: Oxford University Press, 2005.

Cohen, William. "China's Rise in Historical Perspective." *Journal of Strategic Studies* 30 (2007): 683–704.

Contessi, Nicola. "Experiments in Soft Balancing: China-Led Multilateralism in the Arab World." *Caucasian Review of International Affairs* 3, no. 4 (2009): 404–434.

Cooley, John K., ed. *East Wind over Africa: Red China's African Offensive.* New York: Walker, 1965.

Copper, John Franklin. *China's Foreign Aid: An Instrument of Peking's Foreign Policy.* Lexington, MA: Lexington Books, 1976.

———. *China's Foreign Aid and Investment Diplomacy*. New York: Palgrave Macmillan, 2016.

Corea, Gamani. "UNCTAD and the New International Order." *International Affairs* 53, no. 2 (1977): 177–187.

Craig, Campbell. "American Realism versus American Imperialism." *World Politics* 57 (2004): 143–171.

Dai, Xinyuan, and Duu Renn. 2016. "China and International Order: The Limits of Integration." *Journal of Chinese Political Science* 22 (2016): 177–197.

Davidson, Christopher. *The Persian Gulf and Pacific Asia: From Indifference to Interdependence.* New York: Columbia University Press, 2010.

Deng, Yong. "Conception of National Interests: Realpolitik, Liberal Dilemma, and the Possibility of Change." In *In the Eyes of the Dragon: China Views the World*, edited by Yong Deng and Fei-Ling Wang, 47–72. Lanham, MD: Rowman & Littlefield, 1999.

Deng, Yong, and Fei-Ling Wang. "Introduction: Toward an Understanding of China's World View." In *In the Eyes of the Dragon: China Views the World*, edited by Yong Deng and Fei-Ling Wang, 1–19. Lanham, MD: Rowman & Littlefield, 1999.

———., eds. *In the Eyes of the Dragon: China Views the World.* Lanham, MD: Rowman & Littlefield, 1999.

DiCicco, Jonathan M., and Jack S. Levy. "Power Shifts and Problem Shifts: The Evolution of the Power Transition Research Program." *Journal of Conflict Resolution* 43, no. 6 (1999): 675–704.

Dickson, Bruce J. "No 'Jasmine' for China." *Current History* 110, no. 737 (2011): 211–216.

Dillon, Michael. "The Middle East and China." In *The Middle East's Relations with Asia and Russia*, edited by Hannah Carter and Anoushiravan Ehteshami, 42–60. New York: RoutledgeCurzon, 2004.

Dittmer, Lowell. "China's Rise, Global Identity, and the Developing World." In *China, the Developing World, and the New Global Dynamic*, edited by Lowell Dittmer and George T. Yu. Boulder, CO: Lynne Rienner, 2010.

Dittmer, Lowell, and George T. Yu, eds. *China, the Developing World and the New Global Dynamic.* Boulder, CO: Lynne Rienner, 2010.

Dollar, David. *China's Engagement with Africa: From Natural Resources to Human Resources.* Washington, DC: Brookings, 2016.

Doran, Charles F. *Systems in Crisis: New Imperatives of High Politics at Century's End.* Cambridge: Cambridge University Press, 1991.

Dorsey, James M. *China and the Middle East: Venturing into the Maelstrom.* Cham, Switzerland: Palgrave Macmillan, 2019.

Douglas, John Keefer, Matthew B. Nelson, and Kevin Schwartz. *Fueling the Dragon's Flame: How China's Energy Demands Affect Its Relationships in the Middle East.* Washington, DC: U.S.-China Economic and Security Review Commission, 2006.

Dreher, Axel, and Andreas Fuchs. "Rogue Aid? An Empirical Analysis of China's Aid Allocation." *Canadian Journal of Economics* 48, no. 3 (2015): 988–1023.

Dreher, Axel, Andreas Fuchs, Bradley Parks, Austin M. Strange, and Michael J. Tierney. "Aid, China, and Growth: Evidence from a New Global Development Finance Dataset." AidData Working Paper 46. Williamsburg, VA: AidData, 2017.

Du Plessis, Ambrose. "The Forum on China-Africa Cooperation, Ideas, and Aid: National Interest(s) or Strategic Partnership?" *Insight on Africa* 6, no. 2 (2014): 113–130.

Duchatel, Matthiew. "Terror Overseas: Understanding China's Evolving Counter-Terror Strategy." Policy Brief. European Council on Foreign Relations. October 2016.

Duchatel, Mathieu, Oliver Brauner, and Hang Zhou. "Protecting China's Overseas Interests: The Slow Shift Away from Non-Interference." SIPRI Policy Paper. Stockholm, Sweden: Stockholm International Peace Research Institute, 2014.

Economy, Elizabeth C. *The Third Revolution: Xi Jinping and the New Chinese State*. New York: Oxford University Press, 2018.

Economy, Elizabeth, and Michael Levi. *By All Means Necessary: How China's Resource Quest Is Changing the World*. New York: Oxford University Press, 2014.

Edwards, Neil. "Vaccine Diplomacy: China and SinoPharm in Africa." *Council on Foreign Relations* (blog), January 6, 2021.

Ehteshami, Anoushiravan. "Asian Geostrategic Realities and Their Impact on Middle East-Asia Relations." In *The Middle East's Relations with Asia and Russia*, edited by Hannah Carter and Anoushiravan Ehteshami, 1–21. New York: RoutledgeCurzon, 2004.

Ehteshami, Anoushiravan, and Niv Horesh. *China's Presence in the Middle East: The Implications of the One Belt, One Road Initiative*. London: Routledge, 2018.

———. *How China's Rise Is Changing the Middle East*. Abingdon: Routledge, 2020.

Eisenman, Joshua. "China's Post–Cold War Strategy in Africa: Examining Beijing's Methods and Objectives." In *China and the Developing World*, edited by Joshua Eisenman, Eric Heginbotham, and Derek Mitchell, 29–59. Armonk, NY: M. E. Sharpe, 2007.

Eisenman, Joshua, and Eric Heginbotham, eds. *China Steps Out: Beijing's Major Power Engagement with the Developing World*. New York: Routledge, 2018.

Eisenman, Joshua, Eric Heginbotham, and Derek Mitchell, eds. *China and the Developing World*. Armonk, NY: M. E. Sharpe, 2007.

———. "Introduction." In *China and the Developing World*, edited by Joshua Eisenman, Eric Heginbotham, and Derek Mitchell, xiii–xxiii. Armonk, NY: M. E. Sharpe, 2007.

Eisenman, Joshua, and David Shinn. "China's Strategy in Africa." In *China Steps Out: Beijing's Major Power Engagement with the Developing World*, edited by Joshua Eisenman and Eric Heginbotham, 134–169. New York: Routledge, 2018.

Erickson, Andrew S., and Justin D. Mikolay. "Welcome China to the Fight against Pirates." *Proceedings*. U.S. Naval Institute 135(March 2009), 34–41.

Eurasia Group. "China's Overseas Investments in Oil and Gas Production." Report prepared for the US China Economic and Security Review Commission, 2006. http://www.uscc.gov/researchpapers/2006/oil_gas.pdf.

Fandy, Mamoun. "Energy Security: Implications for U.S.-China-Middle East Relations: China versus US: A View from the Arab World." Prepared in conjunction with an energy conference sponsored by the Shanghai Institute for International Studies and the James A. Baker III Institute for Public Policy, Rice University, 2005.

Fardella, Enrico. "China's Debate in the Middle East and North Africa: A Critical Review." *Mediterranean Quarterly* 26, no. 1.

Feng, Haiyun, and Kai He. "China's Institutional Challenges to the International Order." *Strategic Studies Quarterly* 11, no. 4 (2017), 23–49.

Fernando, Sithara. "China-Africa Relations: An Analysis of Forum on China-Africa Cooperation (FOCAC) Documents Using Shinn and Eisenman's Optimist-Pessimist Dual Framework." *Insights on Africa* 6, no. 2 (2014): 145–160.

Finnemore, Martha. *National Interests in International Society.* Ithaca, NY: Cornell University Press, 1996.

Fontaine, Richard, and Mira Rapp-Hooper. "How China Sees World Order." *National Interest* (2016).

Foot, Rosemary, and Andrew Walter. *China, the United States and the Global Order.* New York: Cambridge University Press, 2011.

French, Howard W. *Everything under the Heavens: How the Past Helps Shape China's Push for Global Power.* New York: Knopf, 2017.

Foster, Vivien, William Butterfield, Chuan Chen, and Nataliya Pushak. *Building Bridges: China's Growing Role as Infrastructure Financier for Sub-Saharan Africa.* Washington, DC: World Bank, 2009.

Friedberg, Aaron L. *A Contest for Supremacy: China, America, and the Struggle for Mastery in Asia.* New York: Norton, 2011.

Friedberg, Aaron L., and Robert S. Ross. "Here Be Dragons." *National Interest* 103 (2009): 19–34.

Fulton, Jonathan. *China's Changing Role in the Middle East.* Washington, DC: Atlantic Council, 2019.

———. *China's Relations with the Gulf Monarchies.* Abingdon: Routledge, 2019.

Fung, Courtney J. "Explaining China's Deployment to UN Peacekeeping Operations." *International Relations of the Asia-Pacific* 16, no. 3 (2016) : 409–441.

———. "Global South Solidarity? China, Regional Organizations, and Intervention in the Libyan and Syrian Civil Wars." *Third World Quarterly* 37, no. 1 (2016): 33–50.

———. "Separating Intervention from Regime Change: China's Diplomatic Innovations at the UN Security Council Regarding the Syria Crisis." *China Quarterly* 235 (2018): 693–712.

———. *China and Intervention at the UN Security Council: Reconciling Status.* Oxford: Oxford University Press, 2019.

Gallagher, Kevin P. *The China Triangle: Latin America's China Boom and the Fate of the Washington Consensus.* Oxford: Oxford University Press, 2016.

Garver, John W. *China and Iran: Ancient Partners in a Post-Imperial World.* Seattle: University of Washington Press, 2006.

———. "Is China Playing a Dual Game in Iran?" *Washington Quarterly* 34, no. 1 (2011): 75–78.

Gat, Azar. "The Return of Authoritarian Great Powers." *Foreign Affairs* 86, no. 4 (2007): 59–69.

Gee, John. "Middle East–Chinese Trade Ties Renew Old Links." *Washington Report on Middle Eastern Affairs* 26, no. 5 (2007): 25.

Gill, Bates. *Rising Star: China's New Security Diplomacy.* Washington, DC: Brookings Institution Press, 2007.

Gill, Bates, Chin-hao Huang, and J. Stephen Morrison. *China's Expanding Role in Africa: Implications for the United States.* Washington, DC: CSIS, 2007.

Gill, Bates, and James Reilly. "The Tenuous Hold of China Inc." *Washington Quarterly* 30, no. 3 (2007): 37–52.

Gilley, Bruce, and Andrew O'Neil, eds. *Middle Powers and the Rise of China.* Washington, DC: Georgetown University Press, 2014.

Gilpin, Robert. *War and Change in World Politics.* Cambridge: Cambridge University Press, 1981.

Glaser, Charles L. "A Flawed Framework: Why the Liberal International Order Concept Is Misguided." *International Security* 43, no. 4 (2019): 51–87.

Goldstein, Avery. *Rising to the Challenge: China's Grand Strategy and International Security.* Stanford, CA: Stanford University Press, 2005.

———. "Power Transitions, Institutions, and China's Rise in East Asia: Theoretical Expectations and Evidence." *Journal of Strategic Studies* (2007): 639–682.

Goldstein, Lyle. *Meeting China Halfway: How to Defuse the Emerging US-China Rivalry.* Washington, DC: Georgetown University Press, 2019.

Golub, Philip. "From the New International Economic Order to the G20: How the 'Global South' Is Restructuring World Capitalism from Within." *Third World Quarterly* 34, no. 6 (2013): 1000–1015.

Grimmett, Richard F. *Conventional Arms Transfers to Developing Nations, 1992–1999.* Washington, DC: Congressional Research Service, 2000.

———. *Conventional Arms Transfers to Developing Nations, 2000–2007.* Washington, DC: Congressional Research Service, 2008.

———. *Conventional Arms Transfers Developing Nations, 2003–2010.* Washington, DC: Congressional Research Service, 2011.

Guang, Pan. "China's Sucess in the Middle East." *Middle East Quarterly* 4, no. 4 (1997) 35–40.

Guang, Yang, ed. *China-Middle East Relations: Review and Analysis.* Reading, UK: Paths International, 2012.

Hall, John A. *International Orders.* Cambridge: Polity Press, 1996.

Hamrell, Sven, and Carl Gesta Widstrand, eds. *The Soviet Bloc: China and Africa.* Uppsala: Scandinavian Institute of African Studies, 1964.

Hanauer, Larry, and Lyle J. Morris. *Engagement in Africa: Drivers, Reactions, and Implications for U.S. Policy.* Santa Monica, CA: RAND Corporation, 2014.

Hanneman, Thilo, and Daniel H. Rosen, "Chinese FDI in the US in 2017: A Double Policy Punch." Rhodium Group, January 2018.

Harneit-Sievers, Axel, Stephen Marks, and Sanusha Naidu. *Chinese and African Perspectives on China in Africa.* Cape Town, South Africa: Pambazuka Press, 2010.

Harnisch, Sebastian, Sebastian Bersick, and Jorm-Carsten Gottwald, eds. *China's International Roles: Challenging or Supporting International Order?* New York: Routledge, 2016.

Harris, Lillian Craig. *China's Foreign Policy toward the Third World.* New York: Praeger, 1985.

Harris, Lillian Craig, and Robert L. Worden, eds. *China and the Third World: Champion or Challenger?* Dover, MA: Auburn House, 1986.

Heginbotham, Eric. "Evaluating China's Strategy Toward the Developing World." In *China and the Developing World,* edited by Joshua Eisenman, Eric Heginbotham, and Derek Mitchell, 189–216. Armonk, NY: M. E. Sharpe, 2007.

Heikal, Mohamed Hassanein. *The Cairo Documents: The Inside Story of Nasser and His Relationship with World Leaders, Rebels, and Statesmen.* Garden City, NY: Doubleday, 1973.

Hemmer, Christopher, and Peter Katzenstein. "Why Is There No NATO in Asia? Collective Identity, Regionalism, and the Origins of Multilateralism." *International Organization* 56, no. 3 (2002): 575–607.

Hend, Elmahly, and Sun Degang. "China's Military Diplomacy toward Arab Countries in Africa's Peace and Security: The Case of Djibouti, "*Contemporary Arab Affair* 11, no. 4 (2018): 111–134.

Hinton, Harold C. *Communist China in World Politics.* New York: Houghton Mifflin, 1966.

———. *China's Turbulent Quest: An Analysis of China's Foreign Relations since 1949.* Bloomington: Indiana University Press, 1972.

Hirsch, Fred. "Is There a New International Economic Order?" *International Organization* 30. no. 3 (1976): 521–531.

Hoffman, Adam, and Roie Yellinek, "The Middle East and China: Trust in the Time of COVID-19." Middle East Institute, May 12, 2020.

Holslag, Jonathan. "China's New Mercantilism in Central Africa." *African and Asian Studies* 5, no. 2 (2006): 133–169.

———. "The New Scramble for Africa." *New Presence: The Prague Journal of Central European Affairs* 9, no. 2 (2007): 23–25.

———.. "Embracing China's Global Security Ambitions." *Washington Quarterly* 32, no. 3 (July 2009): 105–118.

Hong, Eunsuk, and Sun Laixing. "Dynamics of Internationalization and Outward Investment: Chinese Corporations and Strategies." *China Quarterly* 187 (2006): 610–634.

Hongyi, Harry Lai. "China's Oil Diplomacy: Is it a Global Security Threat?" *Third World Quarterly* 28, no. 3 (2007): 519–537.

Horesh, Niv. *Toward Well-Oiled Relations? China's Presence in the Middle East following the Arab Spring.* New York: Palgrave Macmillan, 2016.

Hufbauer, Gary C., Jeffrey J. Schott, and Kimberly Ann Elliott. *Economic Sanctions Reconsidered,* 3rd ed. Washington, DC: Peterson Institute for International Economics, 2007.

Hutchison, Alan. *China's African Revolution.* Boulder, CO: Westview Press, 1975.

Ikenberry, G. John. "The Rise of China: Power, Institutions, and the Western Order." In *China's Ascent: Power, Security, and the Future of International Politics,* edited by Robert S. Ross and Feng Zhu. Ithaca, NY: Cornell University Press, 2008.

———. "The Rise of China and the Future of the West: Can the Liberal System Survive?" *Foreign Affairs* 87, no. 1 (2008): 23–37.

———. *Liberal Leviathan: The Origins, Crisis and Transformation of the American World Order.* Princeton: Princeton University Press, 2011.

———. "The Rise of China, the United States and the Future of the Liberal International Order." In *Tangled Titans: The United States and China* edited by David Shambaugh, 53–73. Lanham, MD: Rowman & Littlefield, 2013.

———. "The Logic of Order: Westphalia, Liberalism, and the Evolution of International Order in the Modern Era." In *Power, Order and Change in World Politics,* edited by G. John Ikenberry, 83–106. Cambridge: Cambridge University Press, 2014.

———. ed. *Power, Order and Change in World Politics.* Cambridge: Cambridge University Press, 2014.

———. "The Future of Liberal World Order." *Japanese Journal of Political Science* 16, no. 3 (2015): 450–455.

———. "The Future of Multilateralism" Governing the World in a Post-Hegemonic Era." *Japanese Journal of Political Science* 16, no. 3 (2015): 399–413.

———. "The Plot against American Foreign Policy: Can the Liberal Order Survive?" *Foreign Affairs* 93, no. 3 (May–June 2017).

———. "Why the Liberal World Order Will Survive." *Ethics and International Affairs* 32 (1) (2018): 17–29.

Ikenberry, G. John, and Amitai Etzioni. "Is China More Westphalian Than the West?" *Foreign Affairs* 90, no. 6 (2011): 172–176.

Ikenberry, G. John, and Darren Lim, "What China's Institutional Statecraft Could Mean for the International Order." *Brookings,* April 13, 2017.

International Monetary Fund (IMF). Direction of Trade Statistics Database. www.imf-statistics.

Jacobson, Harold K., Dusan Sidjanski, Jeffrey Rodamar, and Hougassian-Rudovich. "Revolutionaries or Bargainers? Negotiators for a New International Economic Order." *World Politics* 35, no. 3 (1983): 335–367.

Jacques, Martin. *When China Rules the World: The End of the Western World and the Birth of a New Global Order.* New York: Penguin Press, 2009.

Jakóbowski, Jakub. "Chinese-Led Regional Multilateralism in Central and Eastern Europe, Africa and Latin America: 16 + 1, FOCAC, and CCF." *Journal of Contemporary China* 27, no. 113 (2018): 659–673.

Jensen, Hans Grinstead, and Ron Sandrey. *A Possible SACU/ China Free Trade Agreement (FTA): Implications for the South African Manufacturing Sector.* TRALAC Working Paper, July 2006, 1–25. www.tralac.org

Jervis, Robert. "The Remaking of a Unipolar World." *Washington Quarterly* 29, no. 3 (2006): 7–19.

Jin, Liangxiang. "Sino Arab Relations: New Developments and Trends." *Middle East Policy* 11, no. 4 (2004): 113–121.

———. "Energy First: China and the Middle East." *Middle East Quarterly* 12, no. 2 (2005): 3–10.

Johnston, Alastair Iain. *Cultural Realism: Strategic Culture and Grand Strategy in Chinese History.* Princeton, NJ: Princeton University Press, 1995.

———. "International Structures and Chinese Foreign Policy." In *Chinese Foreign Policy Faces the New Millennium*, edited by Samuel S. Kim, 55–87. Boulder, CO: Westview Press, 1998.

———. "Is China a Status Quo Power?" *International Security* 27, no. 4 (2003): 5–56.

———. "Beijing's Security Behavior in the Asia-Pacific: Is China a Dissatisfied Power?" In *Rethinking Security in East Asia: Identity, Power, and Efficiency*, edited by J. J. Suh, Peter J. Katzenstein, and Allen Carlson, 34–96. Stanford, CA: Stanford University Press, 2004.

———. "How New and Assertive Is China's New Assertiveness?" *International Security* 37, no. 4 (2013): 7–48.

———. "China in a World of Orders: Rethinking Compliance and Challenge in Beijing's International Relations." *International Security* 44, no. 2 (2019): 9–60.

———. *Social States: China in International Institutions, 1980–2000.* Princeton, NJ: Princeton University Press, 2008.

———. "How New and Assertive Is China's New Assertiveness?" *International Security* 37, no. 4 (2013): 7–48.

Johnston, Alastair Iain, and Robert Ross, eds. *New Directions in the Study of China's Foreign Policy.* Stanford, CA: Stanford University Press, 2006.

Kagan, Robert. "What China Knows That We Don't: The Case for a New Strategy of Containment." *Weekly Standard*, January 20, 1997.

———. "The Illusion of 'Managing' China." *Washington Post*, March 15, 2005.

Kaiser-Cross, Sarah, and Mao Yufeng. "China's Strategy in the Middle East and the Arab World." In *China Steps Out: Beijing's Major Power Engagement with the Develop-*

ing World, edited by Joshua Eisenman and Eric Heginbotham, 170–192. New York: Routledge, 2018.

Kang, David C. "Getting Asia Wrong: The Need for New Analytical Frameworks." *International Security* 27, no. 4 (2003): 57–85.

———. *China Rising: Peace, Power, and Order in East Asia.* New York: Columbia University Press, 2007.

Kastner, Scott L., and Phillip C. Saunders. "Is China a Status Quo or Revisionist State? Leadership Travel as an Empirical Indicator of Foreign Policy Priorities." *International Studies Quarterly* 56, no. 1 (2011): 1–15.

Katzenstein, Peter J., and Rudra Sill. "Rethinking Asian Security: A Case for Analytic Eclecticism." in *Rethinking Security in East Asia: Identity, Power, and Efficiency*, edited by J. J. Suh, Peter J. Katzenstein and Allen Carlson. Stanford, CA: Stanford University Press, 2004.

Kaufman, Alison A. *China's Participation in Anti-Piracy Operations off the Horn of Africa.* Arlington, VA: Center for Naval Analyses, July 2009.

Kaufman, Stuart, Richard Little, and William C. Wohlforth, eds. *The Balance of Power in World History.* New York: Palgrave Macmillan, 2007.

Keal, Paul. *Unspoken Rules and Superpower Dominance.* New York: St. Martin's Press, 1983.

Kemp, Geoffrey. *The East Moves West: India, China and Asia's Growing Presence in the Middle East.* Washington, DC: Brookings Institution Press, 2010.

Kent, Ann. *Beyond Compliance: China, International Organizations, and Global Security.* Stanford, CA: Stanford University Press, 2007.

Khalili, Joseph E. *Communist China's Interaction with the Arab Nationalists since the Bandung Conference.* New York: Exposition Press, 1970.

Kim, Samuel S. "Chinese Foreign Policy in Theory and Practice." In *China and the World: Chinese Foreign Policy Faces the New Millennium*, edited by Samuel S. Kim, 3–33. Boulder, CO: Westview Press, 1998.

———. ed. *China and the World: Chinese Foreign Policy Faces the New Millennium.* Boulder, CO: Westview Press, 1998.

Kimche, David. *The Afro-Asian Movement: Ideology and Foreign Policy of the Third World.* Jerusalem: Israel Universities Press, 1973.

Kissinger, Henry. *World Order.* New York: Penguin Press, 2014.

Klasen, Stephan, Inmaculada Martinez-Zarzoso, Felicitas Nowak-Lehmann, and Matthias Bruckner, "Trade Preferences for Least Developed Countries. Are They Effective? Preliminary Econometric Evidence," United Nations Committee for Development Policy, October 2016.

Kugler, Jacek, and Douglas Lemke, eds. *Parity and Wars: Evaluations and Extension of "The War Ledger."* Ann Arbor: University of Michigan Press, 1996.

Kumaraswamy, P. R. "Israel-China Relations and the Phalcon Controversy." *Middle East Policy* 12, no. 2 (2005): 93–103.

———. "At What Cost Israel-China Ties." *Middle East Quarterly* 13, no. 2 (2006): 37–44.

Kupchan, Charles A. "Unpacking Hegemony: The Social Foundations of Hierarchical Order." In *Power, Order and Change in World Politics*, edited by G. John Ikenberry, 19–60. Cambridge: Cambridge University Press, 2014.

Lahtinen, Anja. *China's Diplomacy and Economic Activities in Africa: Relations on the Move.* Cham, Switzerland: Palgrave Macmillan, 2018.

Lake, Anthony, and Christine Todd Whitman, eds. "More Than Humanitarianism : A Strategic U.S. Approach toward Africa: Report of an Independent Task Force." Independent Task Force Report 56. New York: Council on Foreign Relations, 2006.

Lampton, David M. *The Three Faces of Chinese Power: Might, Money, and Minds.* Berkeley: University of California Press, 2008.

Lanteigne, Marc. "China's UN Peacekeeping in Mali and Comprehensive Diplomacy." *China Quarterly* 239 (2019): 1–21.

Larkin, Bruce D. *China and Africa, 1949–1970: The Foreign Policy of the People's Republic of China.* Berkeley: University of California Press, 1971.

Lawrence, Alan. *China's Foreign Relations since 1949.* London: Routledge, 1975.

Lee, Christopher J. *Making a World after Empire: The Bandung Movement and Its Political Afterlives.* Athens: Ohio University Press, 2010.

Lee, Pak K. "China's Quest for Oil Security: Oil (Wars) in the Pipeline?" *Pacific Review* 18, no. 2 (2005): 265–301 .

Legro, Jeffrey W. *Rethinking the World: Great Power Strategies and International Order.* Ithaca, NY: Cornell University Press, 2005.

———. "What China Will Want: The Future Intentions of a Rising Power." *Perspectives on Politics* 5, no. 3 (2007): 515–534.

———. "Purpose Transitions: China's Rise and the American Response." In *China's Ascent: Power, Security, and the Future of International Politics*, edited by Robert S. Ross and Feng Zhu. Ithaca, NY: Cornell University Press, 2008.

Lemke, Douglas. *Regions of War and Peace.* Cambridge: Cambridge University Press, 2002.

Leonard, Mark. "Why Convergence Breeds Conflict: Growing More Similar Will Push China and the United States Apart." *Foreign Affairs* 92, no. 5 (2013): 125–135.

Leverett, Flynt, and Jeffrey Bader. "Managing China-U.S. Energy Competition in the Middle East." *Washington Quarterly* 29, no. 1 (2005–2006): 187–201.

Levy, Jack S. "Power Transition Theory and the Rise of China." In *China's Ascent: Power, Security, and the Future of International Politics*, edited by Robert S. Ross and Feng Zhu, 11–33. Ithaca, New York: Cornell University Press, 2008.

Lewin, Pauline. *The Foreign Trade of Communist China: Its Impact on the Free World.* New York: Praeger, 1964.

Li, Weijian. "The Adjustment of the US Mideast Policy and Its Implications on Interactions among China, US and Arab Countries." *Arab World Studies* 2 (2008).

Li, Xiaojun, and Zeng Ka. "To Join or Not to Join? State Ownership, Commercial Interests, and China's Belt and Road Initiative." *Pacific Affairs* 92, no. 1 (2019): 5–26.

———. "Beijing Is Counting on Its Massive Belt and Road Initiative. But Are Chinese Firms on Board?" *Washington Post*, May 14, 2019.

Li, Xing, and Abdulkadir Farah, eds. *China-Africa Relations in an Era of Great Transformations*. Burlington, VT: Ashgate, 2013.

Li, Xing, ed. *Mapping China's "One Belt One Road" Initiative*. Cham, Switzerland: Palgrave Macmillan, 2019.

Li, Yi. "China's Energy Diplomacy under the Security Situation of the Gulf." *West Asia and Africa* 7 (July 2008): 46–51.

Liff, Adam P., and G. John Ikenberry. "Racing toward Tragedy? China's Rise, Military Competition, and the Security Dilemma." *International Security* 39, no. (2014): 52–91.

Lim, Yves-Heng. "How (Dis)Satisfied Is China? A Power Transition Theory Perspective." *Journal of Contemporary China* 24, no. 92 (2015): 280–297.

Lin , Biao. "Long Live the Victory of People's War! In Commemoration of the 20th Anniversary of Victory in the Chinese People's War of Resistance against Japan." Beijing: Foreign Language Press, September 3, 1965.

Lin, Christina. "China's Strategic Shift toward the Region of the Four Seas: The Middle Kingdom Arrives in the Middle East." *Middle East Review of International Affairs* 1, no. 1 (2013).

Lin, Kun Chin. "Macroeconomic Disequilibria and Enterprise Reform: Restructuring the Chinese Oil and Petrochemical Industries in the 1990s." *China Journal*, no. 60 (2008): 49–80.

Lin-Greenberg, Erik. "Dragon Boats: Assessing China's Anti-Piracy Operations in the Gulf of Aden." *Defense and Security Analysis* 26, no. 2 (2010): 213–230.

Liu, Haifang. "China-Africa Relations through the Prism of Culture: The Dynamics of China's Cultural Diplomacy with Africa." *Journal of Current Chinese Affairs* 37, no. 3 (2008): 9–44.

Liu, Mingfu. *The China Dream: Great Power Think and Strategic Posture in the Post-American Era*. New York: CN Times Books, 2015.

Lowenthal, Richard. "The Sino-Soviet Split and Its Repercussions in Africa." In *The Soviet Bloc, China and Africa*, 131–145. Uppsala: Scandinavian Institute of Africa Studies, 1964.

Lyman, Princeton N. "China Ups the Ante in Africa." in *Beyond Humanitarianism: What You Need to Know about Africa and Why It Matters*, edited by Princeton N. Lyman and Patricia Dorff, 19–22. New York: Council on Foreign Relations/Foreign Affairs, 2007.

Lyman, Princeton N., and Patricia Dorff, eds. *Beyond Humanitarianism: What You Need to Know about Africa and Why It Matters.* New York: Council on Foreign Relations/Foreign Affairs, 2007.

Macaes, Bruno. *Belt and Road: A Chinese World Order.* Oxford: Oxford University Press, 2019.

Manji, Firoze, and Stephen Marks, eds. *African Perspectives on China in Africa.* Cape Town: Fahamu, 2007.

Mao, Yufeng. "China's Interests and Strategy in the Middle East and the Arab World." In *China and the Developing World,* edited by Joshua Eisenman, Eric Heginbotham, and Derek Mitchell, 113–132. Armonk, NY: M. E. Sharpe, 2007.

Markey, Daniel Seth. *China's Western Horizon: Beijing and the New Geopolitics of Eurasia.* New York: Oxford University Press, 2020.

Mazarr, Michael J., Miranda Priebe, Andrew Radin, and Astrid Stuth Cevallos. *Understanding the Current International Order.* Santa Monica, CA: RAND, 2016.

Mearsheimer, John J. *The Tragedy of Great Power Politics.* New York: Norton, 2001.

———. "China's Unpeaceful Rise." *Current History* 105, no. 690 (2006): 160–163.

———. "The Gathering Storm: China's Challenge to US Power in Asia." *Chinese Journal of International Politics* 3 (2010): 381–396.

———. "Bound to Fail: The Rise and Fall of the Liberal International Order." *International Security* 43, no. 4 (2019): 7–50.

Medeiros, Evan S. *China's International Behavior: Activism, Opportunism, and Diversification.* Santa Monica, CA: RAND, 2009.

Michel, Serge. "When China Met Africa Foreign Policy." *Foreign Policy,* no. 166 (2008): 38–46.

Michel, Serge, and Michel Beuret. *China Safari: On the Trail of Beijing's Expansion in Africa.* New York: Nation Books, 2009.

Millward, James. "'Reeducating' Xinjiang's Muslims." *New York Review of Books,* February 7, 2019.

Millward, James, and Dahlia Peterson, "China's System of Oppression in Xinjiang: How It Developed and How to Curb It." *Brookings Report,* September 2020.

Modelski, George. *Long Cycles in Word Politics.* Seattle: University of Washington Press, 1987.

Modelksi, George, and William R Thompson. *Leading Sectors and World Powers: The Coevolution of Global Politics and Economics.* Columbia: University of South Carolina Press, 1996.

Monson, Jamie. *Africa's Freedom Railway: How a Chinese Development Project Changed Lives and Livelihoods in Tanzania.* Bloomington: Indiana University Press, 2011.

Mordechai Chaziza, "Coronavirus, China, and the Middle East." Ramat Ban, Israel: Begin-Sadat Center for Strategic Studies, June 1, 2020.

Morgenthau, Hans J. *Politics among Nations: The Struggle for Power and Peace*. New York: McGraw-Hill, 2006.

Muekalia, Domingos Jardo. "Africa and China's Strategic Partnership." *African Security Review* 13, no. 1 (2004): 5–11.

Muller, Kurt. "Soviet and Chinese Programmes of Technical Aid to African Countries." In *The Soviet Bloc, China and Africa*, edited by Sven Hamrell and Carl Gosta Widstrand, 101–130. Uppsala: Scandinavian Institute of African Studies, 1964.

Murphy, Dawn C. "China and the Middle East." Testimony before the U.S.-China Economic and Security Review Commission. June 6, 2013. https://www.uscc.gov/Hearings/hearing-china-and-middle-east-webcast

———. "China's Approach to International Terrorism." Washington, DC: US Institute of Peace. September 2017.

———. "Irreversible Pathway? Examining the Trump Administration's Economic Competition with China." *Journal of War and Peace Studies* 2 (2020).

Narayan, John, and Leon Sealey-Huggins. 2017. "Whatever Happened to the Idea of Imperialism?" *Third World Quarterly* 38, no. 11 (2017): 2387–2395.

Nasser-Eddine, Mon'im. *Arab-Chinese Relations 1950–1971*. Beirut: Arab Institute for Research and Publishing, 1972.

Nathan, Andrew J., and Andrew Scobell. *China's Search for Security*. New York: Columbia University Press, 2012.

Neuhauser, Charles. *Third World Politics; China and the Afro-Asian People's Solidarity Organization, 1957–1967*. Cambridge, MA: Harvard University Press, 1968.

Nolke, Andreas. "Second Image Revisited: The Domestic Sources of China's Foreign Economic Policies." *International Politics* 52, no. 6 (2015): 657–665.

Norris, William. *Chinese Economic Statecraft: Commercial Actors, Grand Strategy, and State Control*. Ithaca, NY: Cornell University Press, 2016.

Ogunsanwo, Alaba. *China's Policy in Africa 1958–1971*. Oxford: Cambridge University Press, 1974.

Olimat, Muhamad S. *China and the Middle East: From Silk Road to Arab Spring*. Abingdon: Routledge, 2013.

———. *China and North Africa: A Bilateral Approach*. Lanham, MD: Lexington Books, 2014.

———. *China and the Middle East Since World War II: A Bilateral Approach*. Lanham, MD: Lexington Books, 2014.

Organski, A. F. K. *World Politics*, 2nd ed. New York: Knopf, 1968.

Organski, A. F. K., and Jacek Kugler. *The War Ledger*. Chicago: University of Chicago Press, 1980.

Ottaway, Marina, and David Ottaway. *Afro-Communism*, 2nd ed. New York: Africana Publishing Company, 1986.

Panda, Ankit. "China Dispatches New Naval Fleet for Gulf of Aden Escort Mission." *Diplomat*, December 11, 2018.

Pang, Xun, and Wang Shuai. "The International Political Significance of Chinese and US Foreign Aid: As Seen in United Nations General Assembly Voting." *Social Sciences in China* 39, no. 1 (2018): 5–33.

Pant, Harsh V. "Saudi Arabia Woos China and India." *Middle East Quarterly* 13, no. 4 (2006): 45–52.

Paradise, James F. "China and International Harmony: The Role of Confucius Institutes in Bolstering Beijing's Soft Power." *Asian Survey* 49 (2009): 647–669.

Passin, Herbert. *China's Cultural Diplomacy.* New York: Praeger, 1962.

Patrick, Stewart. "World Order: What, Exactly, Are the Rules?" *Washington Quarterly* 39, no. 1 (2016): 7–27.

Paul, T. V. *Restraining Great Powers: Soft Balancing from Empires to the Global Era.* New Haven, CT: Yale University Press, 2018.

Paus, Eva, Penelope B. Prime, and Jon Western, eds. *Global Giant: Is China Challenging the Rules of the Game?* New York: Palgrave Macmillan, 2009.

Petranek, Liana M. "Paving a Concrete Path to Globalization with China's Belt and Road Initiative through the Middle East." *Arab Studies Quarterly* 41, no. 1 (2019): 7–32.

Pham, Peter J. "China's African Strategy and Its Implications for U.S. Interests." *American Foreign Policy Interests* 28, no. 3 (2006): 239–253.

Pigato, Miria. *Strengthening China's and India's Trade and Investment Ties to the Middle East and North Africa.* Washington, DC: World Bank, 2009.

Pillsbury, Michael. *China Debates the Future Security Environment.* Washington, DC: National Defense University Press, 2000.

———. *The Hundred Year Marathon: China's Secret Strategy to Replace American as the Global Superpower.* New York: Holt, 2015.

Pu, Xiaoyu. "Socialization as a Two-Way Process: Emerging Power and the Diffusion of International Norms." *Chinese Journal of International Politics* 5, no. 4 (2012): 1–27.

———. *Rebranding China: Contested Status Signaling in Changing Global Order.* Stanford, CA: Stanford University Press, 2019.

Qian, Xuewen. "Energy Cooperation between China and the Middle East." *International Review* 1 (2008): 45–50.

Radtke, Kurt W. "China and the Greater Middle East: Globalization No Longer Equals Westernization." *Perspective in Global Development and Technology* 6, no. 1 (2007): 389–416.

Ratner, Ely. "The Emergent Security Threats Reshaping China." *Washington Quarterly* 34, no. 1 (2011): 29–44.

Reardon-Anderson, James, ed. *The Red Star and the Crescent: China and the Middle East.* New York: Oxford University Press, 2018.

Reddy, Laroushka. "A China-SACU FTA: What's In It for SA." *South African Foreign Policy Monitor* (August/September 2004). http://us-cdn.creamermedia.co.za/assets/articles/attachments/01356_fpm.pdf.

Ren, Xiaojin, and Yiran Zheng. "Govt: Wrong to Label Belt and Road Intiative a Geo-Strategic Tool." *China Daily*, March 4, 2018.

Richardson, Courtney J. "A Responsible Power? China and the UN Peacekeeping Regime," *International Peacekeeping* 18, no. 3 (2011): 288—299.

Rogers, Philippe D. "China and the United Nations Peacekeeping Operations in Africa." *Naval War College Review* 60, no. 2 (2007): 73–93.

Rolland, Nadege. *China's Eurasian Century? Political and Strategic Implications of the Belt and Road Initiative.* Seattle, WA: National Bureau of Asian Research, 2017.

Ross, Robert S., and Feng Zhu, eds. *China's Ascent: Power, Security and the Future of International Politics.* Ithaca, NY: Cornell University Press, 2008.

Ross, Robert. "The Problem with the Pivot: Obama's New Policy Is Unnecessary and Counterproductive." *Foreign Affairs* 91, no. 6 (2012): 70–82.

Ross, Robert S. "The Rise of Chinese Power and Implications for the Regional Security Order." *Orbis* 54, no. 4 (2010): 525–545.

Rotberg, Robert I., ed. *China into Africa: Trade, Aid, and Influence.* Washington, DC: Brookings Institution Press, 2008.

Ruggie, John Gerard. "What Makes the World Hang Together? Neo-Utilitarianism and the Social Constructivist Challenge." *International Organization* 52, no. 4 (1998): 855–885.

Russell, James A. "Saudi Arabia in the 21st Century: A New Security Dilemma." *Middle East Policy* 12, no. 3 (2005): 64–78.

Rynning, Sten, and Jens Ringmose. "Why Are Revisionist States Revisionist? Reviving Classical Realism as an Approach to Understanding International Change." *International Politics* 45 (2008): 19–39.

Saab, Bilal Y. *After Hub-and-Spoke: US Hegemony in a New Gulf Security Order*. Washington, DC: Atlantic Council, 2016.

Salidjanova, Nargiza. *Going Out: An Overview of China's Foreign Direct Investment.* Washington, DC: U.S.-China Economic and Security Review Commission, 2011.

Saunders, Phillip C. *China's Global Activism: Strategies, Drivers and Tools.* Institute for National Strategic Studies. Occasional Paper 4. Washington, DC: National Defense University Press, October 2006. http://www.ndu.edu/inss/Occasional_Papers/OCP4.pdf.

Sautman, Barry, and Hairong Yan. "Friends and Interests: China's Distinctive Links with Africa." *African Studies Review* 50, no. 3 (2007): 75–114.

Schuman, Frederick L. "The Ethics and Politics of International Peace." *International Journal of Ethics* 42, no. 2 (1932): 148–162.

Schweller, Randall L. "Bandwagoning for Profit: Bringing the Revisionist State Back In." In *The Perils of Anarchy: Contemporary Realism and International Security*, edited by Michael E. Brown, Sean M. Lynn-Jones, and Steven E. Miller, 249–261. Cambridge, MA: MIT Press, 1995.

Schweller, Randall L., and Xiaoyu Pu. "After Unipolarity: China's Visions of International Order in an Era of U.S. Decline." *International Security* 36, no. 1 (2011): 41–72.

Scobell, Andrew, and Scott W. Harold. "An `Assertive' China? Insights from Interviews." *Asian Security* 9, no. 2 (2013): 111–131.

Scobell, Andrew, Bonny Lin, Howard J. Shatz, Michael Johnson, Larry Hanauer, Michael S. Chase, Astrid Stuth Cevallos, et al. *At the Dawn of Belt and Road: China in the Developing World.* Santa Monica, CA: RAND Corporation, 2018.

Scobell, Andrew, and Alireza Nader. *China in the Middle East: The Wary Dragon.* Santa Monica, CA: RAND, 2016.

Shambaugh, David, ed. *Power Shift: China and Asia's New Dynamics.* Berkeley: University of California Press, 2005.

———. "Coping with a Conflicted China." *Washington Quarterly* 34, no. 1 (2011): 7–27.

———. *China Goes Global: The Partial Power.* New York: Oxford University Press, 2013.

———. *China and the World.* Oxford: Oxford University Press, 2020.

Shambaugh, David, and Dawn Murphy. "U.S.-China Interactions in the Middle East, Africa, Europe, and Latin America" In *Tangled Titans: The New Context of U.S.-China Relations*, edited by David Shambaugh. Lanham, MD: Rowan and Littlefield, 2013.

Shambaugh, David, and Michael Yahuda, eds. *International Relations of Asia.* Lanham, MD: Rowman & Littlefield, 2008.

Shelton, Garth. "Trading with the Dragon: Prospects for a China–South Africa FTA." *South African Journal of International Affairs* 11, no. 2 (2004): 59–71.

Shelton, Garth, April Yazini, April Funeka, and Li Anshan, eds. *FOCAC 2015: A New Beginning of China-Africa Relations.* Pretoria, South Africa: African Institute of South Africa, 2015.

Shichor, Yitzhak. *The Middle East in China's Foreign Policy.* Cambridge: Cambridge University Press, 1979.

———. "China's Upsurge: Implications for the Middle East." *Israel Affairs* 12, no. 4 (2006): 665–683.

Shinn, David H. "An Opportunistic Ally." *Harvard International Review* 29, no. 2 (2007): 52–56.

Shinn, David, and Joshua Eisenman. *China and Africa.* Philadelphia: University of Pennsylvania Press, 2012.

Shirk, Susan L. *China: Fragile Superpower.* New York: Oxford University Press, 2007.

Shu, Xianlin. "Analysis of Sino-US Relations in the Middle East Oil." *Arab World Studies* 5 (2009): 27–33.

Simelane, Thokozani, and Lavhelesani Managa, eds. *Belt and Road Initiative: Alternative Development Path for Africa.* Pretoria, South Africa: Africa Institute of South Africa, 2018.

Simpfendorfer, Ben. *The New Silk Road: How a Rising Arab World Is Turning Away from the West and Rediscovering China.* Basingstoke: Palgrave Macmillan, 2011.

Singh, Michael. "Chinese Policy in the Middle East in the Wake of the Arab Uprisings." In *Toward Well-Oiled Relations?* edited by N. Horesh. London: Palgrave Macmillan, 2016.

Snow, Philip. *The Star Raft: China's Encounter with Africa.* Ithaca, NY: Cornell University Press, 1988.

Sohn, Injoo. "After Renaissance: China's Multilateral Offensive in the Developing World." *European Journal of International Relations* 17, no. 1 (2012): 77–101.

Sorensen, Georg. 2011. *Liberal World Order in Crisis: Choosing between Imposition and Constraint.* Ithaca, NY: Cornell University Press, 2011.

Stivachtis, Yannis A., ed. *International Order in a Globalizing World.* Burlington, VT: Ashgate, 2007.

Stuenkel, Oliver. *Post-Western World: How Emerging Powers Are Remaking Global Order.* Cambridge: Polity Press, 2016.

Suh, J. J., Peter J. Katzenstein, and Allen Carlson, eds. *Rethinking Security in East Asia: Identity, Power, and Efficiency.* Stanford, CA: Stanford University Press, 2004.

Sun, Bigan. "Obama's New Middle East Policy and China's Energy Security." *Asia and Africa Review* 5 (2009): 17–20.

Sun, Degang. "International System Transformation and the Big Powers Quasi Alliance Diplomacy in the Middle East." *Arab World Studies* 6 (2009): 18–25.

Sun, Degang, and Yahia H. Zoubir. "China's Economic Diplomacy toward Arab Countries: Challenges Ahead?" *Journal of Contemporary China* 24, no. 95 (2015): 903–921.

Sun, Xia, and Guang Pan. "Energy Politics in the Middle East and China's Energy Security Strategy." *Arab World Studies* 4 (2009): 38–45.

Sun, Yun. "March West: China's Response to the U.S. Rebalancing." *Brookings* (blog), January 31, 2013.

Sutherland, Dylan, and John Anderson. "The Pitfalls of Using Foreign Direct Investment Data to Measure Chinese Multinational Enterprise Activity." *China Quarterly* 221 (2014), 21–48.

Sutter, Robert G. "Strategic and Economic Imperitives and China's Third World Policy." In *China and the Third World: Champion or Challenger?* edited by Lillian Craig Harris and Robert L. Worden, 14–33. Dover, MA: Auburn House, 1986.

———. *Chinese Foreign Relations: Power and Policy since the Cold War.* Lanham, MD: Rowman & Littlefield, 2010.

Swaine, Michael D. "Chinese Views and Commentary on Peripheral Diplomacy." *China Leadership Monitor* 44 (2014).

———. "Chinese Views and Commentary on the 'One Belt, One Road' Initiative," *China Leadership Monitor* 47 (2015).

Swaine, Michael D., and Ashley J. Tellis. *Interpreting China's Grand Strategy: Past, Present, and Future.* Santa Monica, CA: Rand, 2000.

Szamosszegi, Andrew, and Cole Kyle. *An Analysis of State-Owned Enterprises and State Capitalism in China.* Washington, DC: U.S.-China Economic and Security Review Commission, 2011.

Tan, See Seng, and Amitav Acharya, eds. *Bandung Revisited: The Legacy of the 1955 Asian-*

African Conference for World Order. Singapore: National University of Singapore Press, 2008.

Tang, Jiaxuan. *Heavy Storm and Gentle Breeze: A Memoir of China's Diplomacy.* New York: HarperCollins, 2011.

Tanner, Murray Scot, with James Bellacqua. "China's Response to Terrorism." CNA, June 2016. hwww.uscc.gov/Research/china percentE2 percent80 percent99s-response-terrorism

Taylor, Ian. "China's Oil Diplomacy in Africa." *International Affairs* 82, no. 5 (2006): 937–959.

Tiezzi, Shannon. "China at Geneva II: Beijing's Interests in Syria." *Diplomat*, January 22, 2014.

———. Shannon. "ISIS: Chinese Hostage 'Executed.'" *Diplomat*, November 19, 2015.

———. Shannon. "US General: China Has 10 Year Contract for First Overseas Military Base." *Diplomat*, November 26, 2015.

Tull, Denis M. "China's Engagement in Africa: Scope, Significance and Consequences." *Journal of Modern African Studies* 44 (2006): 459–479.

Tunsjo, Oystein. *The Return of Bipolarity in World Politics: China, the United States, and Geostructural Realism.* New York: Columbia University Press, 2018.

Vakil, Sanam. "Iran: Balancing East against West." *Washington Quarterly* 29, no. 4 (2006): 51–65.

Van Ness, Peter. *Revolution and Chinese Foreign Policy: Peking's Support for Wars of National Liberation.* Berkeley: University of California Press, 1970.

———. *China as a Third World State: Foreign Policy and Official National Identity.* Working Paper 1991/5, Canberra: Research School of Pacific Studies, Australian National University, 1991.

Wakefield, Bryce, and Susan Levenstein, eds. *China and the Persian Gulf: Implications for the United States.* Washington, DC: Woodrow Wilson Center for International Scholars, 2011.

Waldron, Arthur, ed. *China in Africa.* Washington, DC: Jamestown Foundation, 2008.

Walt, Stephen M. "Alliance Formation and the Balance of World Power." *International Security* 9, no. 4 (1985): 208–248.

Waltz, Kenneth N. *Theory of International Politics.* New York: Random House, 1979.

———. "Structural Realism after the Cold War." *International Security* 25, no. 1 (2000): 5–41.

———. *Man, the State and War.* New York: Columbia University Press, 2001.

Wang, Fei-Ling. "Self Image and Strategic Intentions: National Confidence and Political Insecurity." In *In the Eyes of the Dragon: China Views the World*, edited by Yong Deng and Fei-Ling Wang, 21–45. Lanham, MD: Rowman & Littlefield, 1999.

Wang, Jianwei. "Managing Conflict: Chinese Perspectives on Multilateral Diplomacy and Collective Security." In *In the Eyes of the Dragon: China Views the World*, edited by Yong Deng and Fei-Ling Wang, 73–96. Lanham, MD: Rowman & Littlefield, 1999.

Wang, Jinglie. "Review and Thoughts over the Relationship between China and the Middle East." *Journal of Middle Eastern and Islamic Studies (in Asia)* 4, no. 1 (2010): 16–39.

Wang, Jisi. "China's Search for a Grand Strategy." *Foreign Affairs,* 90. no. 2 (2011): 68–79.

———. "March West: China Geostrategic Rebalancing." *Global Times,* October 2012.

———. "China in the Middle." *American Interest* 10, no. 4) (2015).

Wang, Lian. "Economic and Trade Relations between China and Middle Eastern Countries." *International Studies* 4 (2008).

Weber, Steven, Naazneen Barma, Matthew Kroenig, and Ely Ratner. 2007. "How Globalization Went Bad." *Foreign Policy* 158 (2007): 48–54.

Wei, Liang-tsai. *Peking versus Taipei in Africa.* Taipei: Asia and World Institute, 1982.

Wendt, Alexander. "Anarchy Is What States Make of It: The Social Construction of Power Politics." *International Organization* 46, no. 2 (1992): 391–425.

Wolf, Charles Jr., Wang Xiao, and Eric Warner. "China's Foreign Aid and Government-Sponsored Investment Activities: Scale, Content, Destinations, and Implications." Santa Monica, CA: Rand, 2013.

Wong, Monina. "Chinese Workers in the Garment Industry in Africa: Implications of the Contract Labour Dispatch System on the International Labour Movement." *Labour, Capital and Society* 39, no. 1 (2006): 68–110.

Wood, Peter, and Kerry Brown. "China ODI: Buying into the Global Economy." Hong Kong: Exceptional Resources Group, October 2009.

Wu, Fang. "Analysis of the Opportunities of Economic Development and Energy Cooperation between China and the Gulf Cooperation Council." *International Economic Cooperation,* no. 5 (2009): 11–14.

Wu, Frederich. "Corporate China Goes Global." In *Handbook of Research on Asian Business,* edited by Henry Wai-Chung Yeung, 445–465. Cheltenham: Edward Elgar, 2007

Wu, Lei, and Xuejun Liu. "China or the United States: Which Threatens Energy Security?" *OPEC Review* 31, no. 3 (2007): 215–234.

Wu Xinbo. "China in Search of a Liberal Partnership International Order." *International Affairs* 94, no. 5 (2018): 995–1018. Wuthnow, Joel. *Chinese Diplomacy and the UN Security Council.* New York: Routledge, 2013.

Xu, Xiaojie. "Chinese NOCs Overseas Strategies: Background, Comparison and Remarks." Prepared in conjunction with an Energy Study sponsored by Japan Petroleum Energy Center and the James A. Baker III Institute for Public Policy, Rice University, 2007.

Xu, Xiaolu, Li Xiaoyun, Qi Gubu, Tang Lixia, and Langton Mukwereza. "Science, Technology, and the Politics of Knowledge: The Case of China's Agricultural Demonstration Centers in Africa." *World Development* 81 (2016): 82–91.

Xu, Yixiang. "Evolving Sino-Russian Cooperation in Syria." United States Institute of Peace Brief, 2017.

Xue, Li. "Xi Jinping's Foreign Policy Takes Shape." *China Net,* January 9, 2015.

Yan, Xuetong. "A Bipolar World Is More Likely Than a Unipolar or Multipolar One." *China-US Focus*, April 20, 2015.

———. "Diplomacy Should Focus on Neighbors." *China Daily*, January 27, 2015.

———. "China Needs to Purchase Friendships." *Nikkei Asian Review*, March 2, 2015.

———. "Inside the China-U.S. Competition for Strategic Partners." *Huffington Post*, November 2, 2015.

———. "Urging China to Adopt a More Assertive Policy." *New York Times*, February 9, 2016.

———. "Strategic Challenges for China's Rise." *International Security Research*, February 23, 2017.

———. "China Must Not Overplay Its Strategic Hand." *Global Times*, August 9, 2017.

Yang, Dexin. *China's Offshore Investments: A Network Approach*. Cheltenham: Edward Elgar, 2005.

Yang, Hongxi. "The Big Power Factors Influencing the Middle East Situation." *Peace and Development* 4 (2008): 23–26.

———. "Analysis of the Middle East Transformation of the International System." *Arab World Studies* 6 (2009): 11–17.

———. "The Big Power Factors Influencing the Middle East Situation." *Peace and Development* 4 (2008): 23–26.

Yang, Xiaohua, and Clyde Stoltenberg. "Growth of Made in China Multinationals: An Institutional and Historical Perspective." In *Globalization of Chinese Enterprises*, edited by Ilan Alon and John R McIntyre. New York: Palgrave Macmillan, 2008.

Yao, Kuangyi. "China-Arab State Cooperation Forums in the Last Decade." *Journal of Middle Eastern and Islamic Studies (in Asia)* 8, no. 4 (2014): 26–42.

Yetiv, Steve A. and Katerina Oskarsson. *Challenged Hegemony: The United States, China, and Russia in the Persian Gulf*. Stanford: Stanford University Press, 2018.

Yeung, Henry Wai-chung, and Liu, Wedong. "Globalizing China: The Rise of Mainland Firms in a Global Economy." *Eurasian Geography and Economics* 49, no. 1 (2008): 57–86.

Youde, Jeremy. "Why Look East? Zimbabwean Foreign Policy and China." *Africa Today* 53, no. 3 (2007): 3–19.

Yu, George T. "China and the Third World." *Asian Survey* 17, no. 11 (1977): 1036–1048.

Yuan, Jing-dong. "China and the Iranian Nuclear Crisis." *China Brief* 6, no. 3 (2006): 1–3.

Zambelis, Chris, and Brandon Gentry. "China through Arab Eyes: American Influence in the Middle East." *Parameters*, 38, no. 1 (2008): 60–72.

Zanotti, Jim, Carol Migdalovitz, Jeremy M. Sharp, Casey L. Addis, Christopher M. Blanchard, and Rhoda Margesson. "Israel and Hamas: Conflict in Gaza (2008–2009)." Congressional Research Service Report for Congress, February 19, 2009.

Zeng, Ka. "China's Free Trade Diplomacy," *Chinese Journal of International Politics* (2016): 277–305.

Zha, Daojiong. "China's Energy Security and Its International Relations." *China and Eurasia Forum Quarterly* 3, no. 3 (2005): 39–54.

Zhang, Denghua. "Why Cooperate with Others? Demystifying China's Trilateral Aid Cooperation." *Pacific Review* 30, no. 5 (2017): 750–768.

———. "A Tango by Two Superpowers: China-US Cooperation in Trilateral Aid and Implications for Their Bilateral Relations." *Asian Journal of Political Science* 26, no. 2 (2018): 181–200.

Zhang, Denghua, and Graeme Smith. "China's Foreign Aid System: Structure, Agencies, and Identities." *Third World Quarterly* 38, no. 10 (2017), 2330–2346.

Zhang, Yongjin. "China and the Struggle for Legitmacy of a Rising Power." *Chinese Journal of International Politics* (2015) 301–322.

———. "China and Liberal Hierarchies in Global International Society: Power and Negotiation for Normative Change." *International Affairs* 92, no. 4 (2016): 795–816.

Zhao, Hong. "China-US Oil Rivalry in Africa." Edited by Michael Jacobsen. Copenhagen Discussion Papers 2007–24. Frederiksberg: Asian Research Center, CBS, 2007.

Ziegler, Charles E. "The Energy Factor in China's Foreign Policy." *Journal of Chinese Political Science* 11, no. 1 (2006): 1–23.

Zweig, David, and Jianhi Bi, "China's Global Hunt for Energy." *Foreign Affairs* 84, no. 5 (2005): 25–38.

INDEX

Printed in the USA
CPSIA information can be obtained
at www.ICGtesting.com
JSHW022004051123
51491JS00001B/1